K Mary Reid
Deepak Dinesan
Rayman Khan

T0173190

Heinemann
Information
Technology
for CSEC®

Contents

Introduction

This book was written to meet all the requirements of the new syllabus for the Caribbean Secondary Education Certificate (CSEC) examinations in Information Technology. It is designed for you and your teacher. To make it easy to follow, the book is divided into sections to match the eight sections in the syllabus.

As you flick though, you will see that Sections 3, 6A, 6B, 6C, 7 and 8 are printed on a blue background. These sections introduce you to practical activities, and you should have access to a computer and the relevant software to get the most out of them. At the end of each practical (blue) section you will find End-of-Section questions. Both multiple choice and structured questions are given, to give you a chance to practice the styles of questions that you will be given in the examinations.

Sections 1, 2, 4A, 4B and 5 are printed on a white background and provide you with the theory that you need to know. A section is divided into a number of topics, each of which should occupy you for one or two lessons. At the end of each topic you will find a summary of the key points you have learned in that topic, and a short set of questions to check whether you have understood it. You will once again find End-of-Section questions at the end of each theory section.

School Based Assessment

The School Based Assessment (SBA) accounts for 30% of the final grade in the examination. Section 9 gives advice to students and teachers on how to present your material.

Section 9 also includes one complete sample SBA project. This can either be used for practice, or it can be adapted by the teacher for use as the official SBA project for the class. For that reason, no solutions are provided for this sample SBA.

However, there are also Practice SBA questions at the end of Sections 2, 3, 6A, 7 and 8. None of these should be used as part of a SBA submitted by a school.

The Fundamentals of Hardware and Software

Objectives

By the end of this section, you will be able to:

- Describe the four basic operations of a computer system.
- Identify and describe the functions of the major hardware components.
- Outline the functions of primary storage devices and indicate their uses.
- Classify units of storage and convert among them.
- List the functions of secondary storage devices and indicate their uses.
- State and explain terms associated with storage devices.
- Explain the uses of the various input and output devices, and media.
- Differentiate among number systems used with computers and use them to perform computation.
- List and describe computer specifications.
- Distinguish between systems programs and application programs.
- Explain the roles of an operating system.
- Define the concepts of multitasking, multiprocessing and multiprogramming.
- Explain the different types of processing modes.
- Differentiate between the types of user interfaces.

Computers are complex machines, made of many different components. In this section, you will learn about the hardware components of a computer system, and the systems and application software used with computers. You will also learn about the different number systems used with computers and how data is stored and manipulated in a computer system.

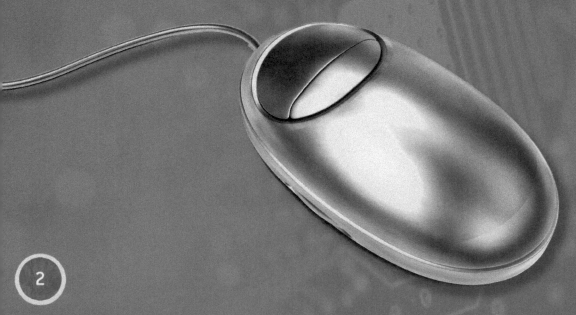

1.1 Why do we use computers?

In our society today, we use **computers** to do a variety of tasks. Supermarkets use computers to track purchases, calculate the amount of money to be paid, print bills and update the supermarket's inventory. Government organisations use computers to assist with law enforcement, manage financial data, and to record and update statistics. At home, many of us use computers to access information from the Internet, complete our homework and communicate with friends and family around the world. Some of us also use computers to access our online bank accounts, subscribe to online lessons and apply for jobs.

Computers are used widely in our society because of their ability to store and process large amounts of data with speed, accuracy and reliability. In addition, computers have the ability to communicate with other computers.

The term **computer system** refers to all the hardware equipment together with all the software programs that make it work.

THINK ABOUT IT

Identify THREE uses of computers in your school.

WHAT DOES IT MEAN?

computer
A computer is an electronic machine that manipulates data according to a set of instructions called a program.

computer system
A computer system includes hardware devices and software to make the computer function.

Fig 1.1: A typical computer system.

What can a computer system do?

Computer systems were designed to perform four basic operations, as shown in Table 1.1.

Operation	Activity
Input	Accept data
Processing	Process data according to instructions stored in computer's memory
Output	Produce results
Storage	Store data and results for future use

Table 1.1: The basic operations of a computer system

Let us consider a checkout station at a supermarket and see how the computer system will carry out the four basic operations.

1 The clerk at the checkout station scans the product(s) you want to purchase. If you are buying more than one of the same item, the clerk scans one of the items and enters the quantity you are purchasing. This is called INPUT.

2 After the clerk has scanned all the items you are buying, the sales program computes the amount of money you have to pay for the items according to the instructions contained in the sales program. For example, after calculating the total value of the items, the sales program may apply a sales tax of 16% based on the instructions it contains. This is called PROCESSING.

3 After you have paid for the items by cash, credit card or some other form of payment, the sales clerk prints out your sales receipt. This is called OUTPUT.

4 After your transaction is completed, the program remembers your transaction so that it can be retrieved later if needed. This is called STORAGE.

CHECK YOUR PROGRESS

The Power and Light Company processes and sends out monthly bills to consumers of electricity. Identify the input, processing, output and storage.

Summary of key points

In this topic you have learned:

- that input, processing, output and storage are the four basic operations of a computer system.
- that computers can store and process large amount of data with speed, accuracy and reliability.

QUESTIONS

1 You are attending secondary school and your parents have bought a computer system for you. List THREE tasks you would use your computer to do.

2 A computer is calculating the monthly salary for an employee by multiplying the number of days worked for the month by the daily rate of pay. What is the name given to this operation?

3 A computer system was used to print out a list of employees in an organisation and their marital status. What is the name of this operation?

4 It is required to keep an electronic copy of a company's timesheets for each month for future use. How can this be done?

5 You have developed a small program to calculate a person's age. What data would your program ask the user to input?

1.2 The hardware components of a computer system

Computer systems consist of a variety of **hardware** components that work together with **software** and **peripheral devices** to achieve specific tasks.

Hardware components include:

* Central Processing Unit (CPU) or processor, is found inside the system unit of the computer system. The processor has two main parts called the Arithmetic and Logic Unit (ALU) and the Control Unit (CU). The ALU performs arithmetic and logical operations while the CU controls the flow and execution of data and instructions.

WHAT DOES IT MEAN?

peripheral devices
Peripheral devices are pieces of computer hardware that are connected to the computer either internally or externally.
For example, some computer hardware devices such as keyboard, mouse, monitor and printer are regarded as peripheral devices.

software
Software is a set of instructions (called a program) that governs the operation of a computer system and makes the hardware run.

hardware
Hardware is the set of physical components in a computer system.

Fig 1.2: The front and back of a processor

- **Main memory** is commonly referred to as primary storage or immediate access storage. Main memory holds the data that is currently being executed by the computer. We will learn more about the main memory in the topic *Primary storage devices* on page 7.
- **Secondary storage** or permanent storage retains programs and data for future use. Hard disks, CD-ROMs and USB flash drives are common secondary **storage media**. We will learn more about them in the topic *Secondary storage devices and media* and media on page 11.
- **Input devices** allow data and instructions to be entered into the computer system. Common system input devices include keyboard, mouse and scanner. We shall discuss the various types of input devices in depth in the topic *Input devices* on page 16.
- **Output devices** allow data processed by the computer to be available to users. Common output devices are the monitor, printer and speakers. We shall discuss the various types of output devices in depth in the topic, *Types and functions of output devices* on page 22.

WHAT DOES IT MEAN?

main memory (primary storage or immediate access storage)
The main memory temporarily holds the data that is currently being executed by the computer.

secondary storage
Secondary storage stores programs and data for future use.

storage medium (plural: media)
A storage medium is the physical material on which a computer stores data, such as a CD-ROM.

input device
An input device allows commands, programs, data or responses to be entered into a computer.

output device
An output device is any hardware component that communicates processed data to the user.

CHECK YOUR PROGRESS

Name the hardware components of a computer system that perform each of the following functions:

1 Perform mathematical operations.
2 Store programs and data that are currently being used by the processor.
3 Allow the user to enter data based on a prompt on the screen.
4 Store programs and data to be used in the future.
5 Allow the user to see the results after processing.

Summary of key points

In this topic you have learned:

- that the hardware components of a computer system are categorised as Central Processing Unit (CPU), main memory, secondary storage, input devices and output devices.
- that the CPU controls the flow and execution of data and instructions and performs arithmetic and logic operations.

- that main memory temporarily stores the program and the data that is currently being executed by the computer.
- that secondary storage retains programs and data for future use.
- that input devices allow data and instructions to be entered into the computer.
- that output devices allow the results of processing to be made available to the users.

QUESTIONS

1 The processor is often referred to as the 'brain' of the computer. Why?
2 List ONE hardware component that stores data on a temporary basis and ONE hardware component that retains data permanently.
3 You are using your computer with a special program that allows you to design a birthday card for your friend. Which hardware component of the computer currently holds the program and the birthday card you are designing?
4 What are the differences between input and output devices?

1.3 Primary storage devices

Primary storage devices are used by the computer for its own use. Some of these devices hold data temporarily while the computer is working on it, while other devices store data that does not change frequently. Primary storage devices are built from millions of bi-stable devices. A bi-stable device can be set to one of two possible states usually referred to as 1 or 0.

There are two types of primary storage devices: volatile and **non-volatile storage** devices. **Volatile storage** can only hold data when the power is switched on, while non-volatile storage does not require power.

WHAT DOES IT MEAN?

non-volatile storage
Non-volatile storage devices retain their content when the power is turned off.

volatile storage
Volatile storage devices lose their content when the power is turned off.

Non-volatile primary storage devices

ROM (Read-Only Memory)

The ROM is a permanent storage device that contains data that cannot be changed. This data, usually called firmware, is a set of instructions that tells the computer what to do when it starts up. For example, instructions to load the operating system into memory are placed in the ROM. The data, instructions or information is usually added to the chips when they are manufactured and then cannot be altered.

Programmable ROM (PROM)

PROM is a type of ROM that can be programmed only *once* after manufacturing. Once programmed, the content cannot be changed. This type of ROM can be used in speed control devices. For example, a device could be placed in a car to automatically slow the car down to a specific speed limit.

Erasable-and-Programmable ROM (EPROM)

EPROM is a type of ROM that can be programmed like PROM. However, the content in the EPROM can be erased and re-programmed repeatedly. An ultraviolet light is used to reset the chip to the initial state. EPROM is useful for testing and developing new applications.

Volatile primary storage devices

Random Access Memory (RAM)

RAM holds program and data that is currently being processed by the computer. You will learn more about RAM in the topic *Interpreting the hardware specifications of a computer system* on page 26.

CHECK YOUR PROGRESS

1 Consider the following tasks and indicate which primary storage device is being used:
   a Opening a word processing program.
   b Indicating the manufacturer's properties of a CD-ROM.
   c Indicating the computer's system time.
   d Acting as a holding place for data to be processed.
   e Recording new instructions for the computer to use when it is starting up.
2 State ONE difference between a ROM and an EPROM.
3 You are using your computer and suddenly the power went off. What would happen to the data in the RAM?

Summary of key points

In this topic you have learned:

- that ROM, PROM, EPROM and RAM are primary storage devices.
- that primary storage devices are used by the computer during its operations.
- that primary devices are either volatile or non-volatile storage devices.
- that primary storage devices are built with millions of bi-stable devices.
- that bi-stable devices can be set to either one of two states, referred to as 0 and 1.

QUESTIONS

1 List TWO types of ROMs and explain how they are different.

2 List the name of the primary storage device that stores information:
  a permanently
  b temporarily

3 Give an example of an instruction contained in the ROM.

4 State ONE difference between a RAM and a ROM.

5 Explain briefly the term 'firmware'.

1.4 Units of storage

We all know that computers can store large amounts of data. How much data they can store is dependent on the capacity of the storage media being used. But how do we measure the capacity of storage media? We have to use some units of measurement. For example, when we talk about how much gasoline a car tank can hold we say a specific amount of litres. In the same way, when we talk about how much data can be stored on storage media we usually use the term **Byte**. We will now discuss the various units of measurement and how each one relates to a Byte.

Types of storage unit

* **Bit**
  A computer stores data in combinations of 1 and 0. On page 7, we learned that storage devices are built from bi-stable devices that can be set to 0 or 1. Each state is a binary digit that is usually referred to as a **bit**.

* **Byte**
  A group of eight bits is called a Byte. For example, 01000110 is a Byte. Every character you type (letter, digit, symbol) takes one Byte of storage.

* **Word**
  A word is the basic unit for accessing computer storage. For example, a 32-bit computer can access 32 bits of data from the computer storage in one operation. The word size is measured by the amount of bits in the word. Computers currently have a word size of 32 bits and 64 bits. This means that the computer can process four characters (32 bits) or eight characters (64 bits) at a time.

* **KiloByte, MegaByte, GigaByte and TeraByte**
  Commonly a KiloByte (KB) is referred to as a thousand Bytes, a MegaByte (MB) as a million Bytes, a GigaByte (GB) as a billion (a thousand million) Bytes and a TeraByte (TB) as a trillion (a million million) Bytes. As such, a Megabyte is referred to as one thousand Kilobytes; a Gigabyte as one thousand Megabytes and a Terabyte as one thousand Gigabytes. Table 1.2 shows the actual values and the conversions. We use the approximate values because they are easier to remember.

Unit	Abbreviation	Approximate value	Actual value
Bit	b		0 or 1
Byte	B		8 bits
KiloByte	KB	1 thousand Bytes	1024 Bytes
MegaByte	MB	1 million Bytes	1024 KB = 1,048,576 Bytes
GigaByte	GB	1 billion Bytes	1024 MB = 1,073,741,824 Bytes
TeraByte	TB	1 trillion Bytes	1024 GB = 1,099,511,627,776 Bytes

Table 1.2: Units of storage

We may see these units when we talk about transfer of data. The rate at which data is transferred is measured in bits per second (b/sec). For example, when we download a file from the Internet, we may see that the file is transferring to our computer at the rate of 30 Kb/sec (note the small b, representing bits). This means that we are downloading 30 Kilobits every second from the Internet to our computer.

Manipulating units of storage

Using Table 1.2, you should be able to convert from one unit of storage to another unit of storage. Let us consider the following examples:

Example 1: Convert 1.2 MB to KB

Solution:
1 MB = 1024 KB
1.2 MB = 1.2 X 1024 KB
 = 1228.8 KB
So, 1.2 MB = 1,228.8 KB.

Example 2: Express 2 TB as MB

Solution:
1 TB = 1024 GB and 1 GB = 1024 MB
2 TB = 2 x 1024 GB = 2048 GB
2048 GB = 2048 x 1024 MB = 2097152 MB
So, 2 TB = 2,097,152 MB.

Summary of key points

In this topic you have learned:

- that Bit, Byte, Word, Kilobyte, Megabyte, Gigabyte and Terabyte are units of storage.
- that we can manipulate and convert the units of storage.

QUESTIONS

1 Your friend bought a 64-bit computer. How many characters of data can your friend's computer process at a time?

2 You bought an external storage device that is capable of storing 1.2 TB of data. What is the size of your device in GB?

3 Arrange the following units of storage from the largest to the smallest: Megabyte, Terabyte, Kilobyte, Gigabyte.

4 Convert 16 Mb to Kilobyte (KB).

5 A file is transferred from one computer to another at the rate of 320 Kb/sec. How long would it take to complete the transfer if the file was 12.4 MB?

1.5 – 1.6 Secondary storage devices and media

We mentioned on page 6 that secondary storage such as USB drives and hard disks provide secondary storage for data and programs. This topic will give examples of the different types of secondary **storage devices** and media, and compare them in terms of their capacity, the speed at which they access data and their portability.

There are a number of different types of storage media used to store data on a computer system. Here, we will discuss the following types:

* Magnetic media such as floppy disk (diskette), hard disk and magnetic tape cassette.
* Optical media such as CD-ROM disk and DVD-ROM disk.
* Miniature mobile storage media such as USB flash drives and Flash memory cards.

When a storage device places new data on to the medium it performs a **write operation**. When it finds data already stored on the medium it performs a **read operation**.

Magnetic storage media

Floppy disk (diskette)

Up to the year 2000, the diskette was the most popular form of portable media. However, the diskette has lost its popularity due the availability of higher capacity portable storage media.

Diskettes have a limited storage capacity of 1.44 MB of data but are portable because of their size (3.5") and light weight. However, diskettes are unreliable, as dust, moisture and magnetic interference can damage the data stored.

Fig 1.3: The front and back of a disk

WHAT DOES IT MEAN?

storage device
A storage device is the computer hardware that records data to and retrieves data from the storage medium. For example, a CD-ROM drive is used to retrieve data stored on a CD-ROM.

read operation
A read operation retrieves data from a storage medium by a storage device.

write operation
A write operation records data onto a storage medium by a storage device.

Before a storage medium can be used to store data it must be prepared by the storage device to accept data. The floppy disk is divided into **tracks** and **sectors**. Data is then stored in one or more sectors, as shown in Fig 1.4.

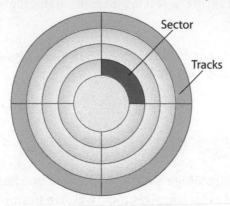

Fig 1.4: Tracks and sectors

The data on the diskette is accessed by a **direct access** method. With direct access, the computer can go directly to a specific location on the storage medium without having to access any other data. This is possible because each sector is numbered so that every location can be identified and found quickly. But, a diskette's **access time** (84 milliseconds or ms) is still relatively slow when compared with other storage media.

WHAT DOES IT MEAN?

track
Tracks are concentric rings on the storage medium. Each track is numbered for identification.

sector
A sector is a segment of a track on which data is stored. Each sector is identified by a unique number.

direct access
Direct access allows the computer to go directly to a specific piece of data on the storage media without having to access any other data.

access time
The time taken to locate and retrieve data from a storage medium.

Hard disk

The most common medium used to store data in a computer system is the hard disk. The hard disk is found inside of the system unit of a computer system and it is the central storage for programs and data.

Hard disk capacity ranges from GigaBytes to TeraBytes (120 GB – 2 TB). The time to access data from hard drive is as low as 8 ms as compared with 84 ms for a floppy disk. External hard drives are used to make the data stored on the hard drive portable.

The structure of the hard disk

A hard drive consists of a set of metal disks called platters, mounted on a spindle. Each platter has its own **read/write heads**, one for each surface of the platter.

To access data, the read/write head moves to the track that contains the data while the disk is spinning. All the read/write heads are joined, as shown in Fig 1.5, so they all move together.

A **cylinder** is a set of matched tracks on all platters. For example, a cylinder consists of track 3 of platter 1, track 3 of platter 2 and track 3 of platter 3, and so on. When a large file of data is stored it is usual for it to be spread over several platters. By storing all the data on one cylinder, that is, on the same track on each platter, the read/write head will not need to move. This speeds up the reading and writing of data.

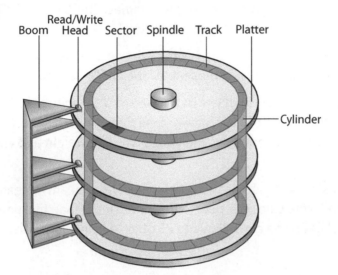

Fig 1.5: The structure of a hard drive

WHAT DOES IT MEAN?

read/write head
A read/write head is a mechanism that reads from or writes data to a disk storage medium.

cylinder
A cylinder is a set of matched tracks on all platters.

Fig 1.6: Hard drive showing one platter with read/write head

Magnetic tape

Magnetic tape, also known as data tape, is commonly used for data archival purposes. It is used for off-site storage so that in the case of a disaster, such as a fire, the data could be retrieved from the tape. Data tapes are popular because they store a large amount of data at a relatively low cost when compared with other storage media, such as hard drives, and because they are portable due to their size and light weight. Magnetic tapes use **sequential access**, so it takes longer to find and retrieve an individual item of data from data tape than from storage media that use direct access.

WHAT DOES IT MEAN?

sequential access
With sequential access data is retrieved in the order in which it was stored. Magnetic tape drives use this type of method to retrieve data stored on data tapes.

Fig 1.7: A data tape

Optical storage media

Most of us are familiar with CD-ROM (Compact Disk) or DVD-ROM (Digital Versatile Disk) containing songs, computer programs, movies and games. CD-ROM and DVD-ROM drives come with the ability to read and/or write data to the disk.

Optical drives use laser beam or blu-ray to read or write data to disk. Drives that are labelled as ROM can only read data and those that labeled RW can read and write data.

A CD-ROM has a capacity of 700 MB while a DVD-ROM has a capacity of 4.7 GB. The time to retrieve data from CD-ROM or DVD-ROM is slower than that of a hard drive. However, optical storage media are very popular as they are small, lightweight and very portable with a large capacity.

Blu-ray is a new optical disk format that uses blue-violet laser beam instead of the red laser beam to read and write data. This new format offers more than five times the storage capacity of traditional DVDs and can hold up to 25 GB on a single-layer disk.

Miniature storage media

Flash drives

USB flash drives, also referred to as thumb drives, jump drives, pen drives, key drives, tokens, or simply USB drives have become popular for storing data due to their size and portability. USB drives come in various shapes, styles and are faster than a floppy disk. A USB flash drive using the USB 2.0 standard has a transfer rate of 480 millions of bits per second or megabits per second (Mbps).

Fig 1.8: A USB flash drive

Flash memory cards

This type of miniature storage media is commonly used on digital cameras, music players, photo printers and cell phones. They come in different sizes and are very small and portable. They also come in different types to enable them to be used on different devices, such as compact flash memory cards (CF) cards, Secure Digital (SD) cards, mini SD cards, micro SD cards, memory sticks, multimedia cards and xD picture cards.

Fig 1.9: A flash memory card

Items used with storage devices

Device interfaces

A **device interface** determines how the storage devices are physically connected to the computer. For example, internal hard drives are connected to the computer by the IDE (Integrated Drive Electronic), SATA (Serial Advanced Technology Attachment), SCSI (Small Computer System Interface) or SAS (Serial attached SCSI) interface.

Buffers

A **buffer** is a temporary storage area for data that has to be transferred from one device to another. Buffering is used to match different speeds of the various storage devices and peripherals. For example, when the CPU is sending information to be printed, because the speed of the CPU is very fast when compared with the speed of the printer, the information is sent to a buffer (temporarily held in the computer's memory) and then from the buffer to the printer.

WHAT DOES IT MEAN?

device interface
The device interface connects the storage device to the computer.

buffer
A buffer is a location in the computer's memory where information can be held while being sent between devices of differing speeds.

Summary of key points

In this topic, you have learned:

- that magnetic, optical and miniature mass storage media are used to store data.
- which storage media are preferred with respect to their capacity, speed and portability.

QUESTIONS

1 For each of the following storage media, indicate the access method used to retrieve data:
   a Hard disk
   b DVD-ROM
   c Magnetic tape
2 Name TWO devices that are:
   a portable
   b fast
   c large in capacity
3 Give an example of:
   a magnetic media
   b optical media
4 State THREE factors you would consider in deciding which storage media to use for archiving data.
5 Give TWO reasons for using USB flash drives over floppy diskettes.

1.7 Input devices

We know from previous topics that one of the basic operations of a computer system is to accept instructions and data. To enter data and instructions into the computer we need to use input devices.

Types and functions of input devices

A variety of input devices are currently used with computers.

Keyboard

A keyboard is the most common device used to input data into a computer. Some keyboards are attached to the computer via cables while others are wireless. Keyboards come in different designs to make them easy to use. Special keyboards are also available for specific use, such as the Braille keyboard for persons who are visually impaired.

Fig 1.10: A keyboard

Fig 1.11: A mouse

Mouse

Another common input device used with computers is the mouse. The mouse is a **pointing device** that is used to control the movement of a pointer on the screen (the mouse pointer) to select a task. A mouse can either be connected to the computer via cables, or it can be wireless.

WHAT DOES IT MEAN?

pointing device
A pointing device is an input device that allows the user to control a pointer on the screen. Pointing devices include the mouse, joystick, trackball, light-pen and touchpad.

Joystick

People playing games on the computer or using flight or driving simulation programs often use a joystick. A joystick, as shown in Fig 1.12, is a vertical lever mounted on a base. The vertical lever can move in different directions to control the action of the games or simulation. The joystick usually comes with buttons called triggers which can be pressed to activate certain events.

Fig 1.12: A joystick

Trackball

A trackball is like an upside-down mouse. Rather than moving the whole mouse to move the pointer on the screen, the user rotates the ball with their thumb, finger or palm.

Fig 1.13: A trackball

Touchpad

A touchpad is found on notebook computers and is sometimes called a trackpad. It is a small, flat, rectangular device that is sensitive to pressure and motion. To move the pointer on the screen, you slide your finger across the surface of the pad. You make a selection by pressing the left button or tap the pad's surface to imitate mouse action, such as clicking.

Fig 1.14: A touchpad

Light-pen

A light-pen looks like a pen, but can detect light. To make a selection with the light-pen, you touch it against the surface of the monitor screen or point it at the screen and then press a button on the pen. Some light-pens work with standard monitors while others require a specially designed monitor.

Light-pens are useful with healthcare professionals who need to keep their hands free from contamination. In this case, a protective sleeve can be placed over the pen. Light-pens are also used in areas where employees' hands can get contaminated with food, grease, oil and other materials that could damage the computer on contact.

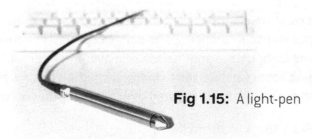

Fig 1.15: A light-pen

Touch screen/terminal

A touch screen or terminal is a touch-sensitive display with which you interact by touching areas of the screen with your finger. Touch screens are used with ATM machines and booking screens at hotels and airports.

Fig 1.16: A touch screen

Graphic tablet

Architects, designers and artists can use graphic tablets, or graphic pads, to create drawings and sketches. An electronic pen called the stylus is used to draw on a graphic tablet called a digitiser. Every location on the graphic tablet corresponds to a specific location on the computer screen. Graphic tablets are used with specialised computer-aided design software.

Fig 1.17: A graphic tablet

Voice response unit

Using specialised voice recognition software, the computer can accept spoken words as data or instructions. With a microphone the user speaks the data or commands, which are recognised by the voice response unit and acted on. The voice recognition software may require the user to train the software to recognise his or her voice pattern.

A voice response unit is useful for people who are physically challenged, as they can input data and commands into the computer without the need for typing.

Sound capture devices

Sound capture devices, such as sound cards, record and digitise sound so that it can be understood by the computer. Sound capture devices can be used for monitoring and for communicating with others. For example, a computer can be used to facilitate voice communication over the Internet.

Webcam

A webcam is a video capturing device. It is used in video chat and videoconferencing. The image captured is transmitted from one computer to another, usually over the Internet. For example, a webcam can be used to monitor children at a nursery school where live pictures are sent over the computer network.

Fig 1.18: A webcam

Sensors

Sensors are used to capture data automatically and to pass the data to a computer, where it is analysed, stored and manipulated. Sensors are used widely in weather forecasting and in security systems, where they monitor heat, light, pressure, wind speed and motion.

Remote control

A remote control is a wireless device that emits a beam of infra-red light to operate another device. For example, in a computer with a TV card, a remote control device is used to turn on peripheral devices such as speakers, change the TV channels, and to increase or decrease the volume.

Biometric systems

Biometric systems use body characteristics such as finger prints and iris or retina scans to identify the user and allow or deny access to the computer system. Many notebook computers come with fingerprint scanners for security.

Fig 1.19: A biometric fingerprint reader

Digital cameras

Digital cameras are used to take and store pictures digitally. Images are generally stored on a compact flash memory card, which is removable. In addition, pictures can be downloaded to a computer and then edited. Most digital cameras also have a screen to allow the user to review the pictures and to delete if necessary. Digital pictures can be printed, inserted in a document and sent digitally to another person via the Internet.

Fig 1.20: A digital camera

CHECK YOUR PROGRESS

1 The National Weather Office uses remote sensors to monitor the weather and to provide feedback to a computer, which is used to produce the daily weather forecast. List THREE types of data provided by the remote sensors.
2 List FOUR pointing devices that can be used with a computer system.

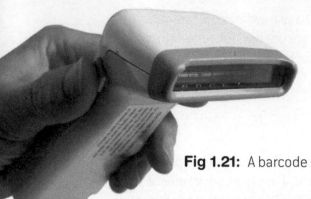

Barcode reader/scanner

A barcode is an identification code that provides data on the item, including item name, item number, manufacturer and country of manufacture. A barcode reader, or a barcode scanner, uses laser beams to read the set of vertical lines spaced at different widths on a product's barcode. In supermarkets barcode readers are used to check out items at the point of sale. In a library, a barcode reader is used to facilitate the borrowing and returning of books.

Fig 1.21: A barcode scanner

Point of sale (POS)

Point of sale systems are common at supermarkets and retail stores. They consist of the main computer system located in a back room and terminals at checkout stations. When an item is scanned using a barcode reader/scanner at the terminal, it sends all the information regarding the product to the main computer so that it can adjust its stock reading. The main computer also contains information regarding the price of the item so the checkout station can keep a tally of the cost of the transaction.

Optical mark recognition devices (OMR)

OMR devices use lights to read hand drawn marks such as small circles, crosses or rectangles on special forms. OMR devices are often used by institutions. For example: by examination boards and universities to process responses on multiple-choice tests or data on registration forms; by research institutions to process responses to surveys and questionnaires; by lottery organisations to read the ticket selection made by lottery players.

Optical character recognition devices (OCR)

OCR devices read handwritten and printed characters and convert them into an electronic form where they can be edited by a specific application. Most OCR devices include an optical scanner for reading the characters and special software for analysing what is read. OCR devices are often used in post offices to read typed or handwritten addresses for mail sorting.

Document scanners are used to scan pages of text and store it in electronic form so that it can be edited with a word processing or some other program.

Fig 1.22: A document scanner

Magnetic ink character recognition (MICR) reader

A MICR reader reads text printed with magnetic ink. MICR is used mainly for the processing of cheques at the bank. The MICR characters at the lower-left corner of a cheque represent the cheque number, bank number and the account number. After the cheque is processed, a MICR inscriber prints the amount of the cheque in MICR characters in the lower-right corner of the cheque.

Fig 1.23: MICR characters on a cheque

MEMO _____

⑆376⑆ ⑈03322⑈004⑆

Summary of key points

In this topic you have learned:

- the various devices used to input data into a computer.
- how each input device captures data.
- the uses of input devices.

QUESTIONS

1 You need to secure your computer system from being used by other persons. List TWO biometric devices you could use to ensure you alone have access to your computer system.
2 An engineering company uses a computer system to design its building plans. In addition to a computer system with keyboard and mouse, and a specialised software program, state ONE device the company could use with the computer system to input data when designing the plans.
3 The Ministry of Education would like to read students' responses in an exam paper of multiple-choice questions. What input device would you recommend? Why?
4 List TWO advantages of using a digital camera over a regular camera.
5 A retail store is interested in setting up a point of sale system. In addition to the computer system with keyboard and mouse, name ONE input device that is common in point of sale systems.

1.8 Output devices

When a computer processes data, an output device needs to be connected to the computer so that the user can see the results of processing, either in **hard copy** or **soft copy**. Many types of output devices can be used with a computer system. The most common output devices used are the monitor and the printer.

Types and functions of output devices

Visual display unit

Computers display output on a screen or monitor called the visual display unit (VDU). Cathode ray tube (CRT) monitors were used widely in the past but are now being replaced by liquid crystal display (LCD) monitors. LCD monitors take up less space, consume less electricity, produce less heat, produce better quality images, and are lighter and more portable.

Monitors come in different sizes ranging from nine inches to over 20 inches (measured diagonally across the screen). In addition to the size of a monitor it is important to consider the resolution of the monitor, which determines the clarity and sharpness of an image displayed. Pictures on a screen are made up of tiny dots called pixels, which is short for "picture element". The higher the number of pixels per inch used to display images, the greater the clarity and detail of the picture.

Fig 1.24: CRT and LCD monitors

WHAT DOES IT MEAN?

hard copy
Hard copy is output in printed form. These outputs exist physically and are generally permanent, but can be destroyed.

soft copy
Soft copy is output displayed in electronic form. For example output displayed on a computer monitor or sound output from speakers. Soft copy output exists for a temporary period.

Printers

Printers are output devices that produce hard copy output on a physical medium such as paper or transparency film.

Printers can be classified as impact or non-impact. Impact printers form characters and graphics on paper by striking a mechanism against an ink ribbon that physically contacts the paper. Examples of impact printers include dot-matrix and line printers. Non-impact printers form characters and graphics on paper by spraying ink or by using heat and pressure. Some commonly used non-impact printers include inkjet printers and laser printers.

Printers also differ in the selection of text that they print at a time. It can vary between a character, a line or page.

Types of printer

Dot-matrix printers

Dot-matrix printers are impact printers that produce characters and images as a series of dots. These dots are formed when the print head containing wire pins strikes an inked ribbon. When the print head presses against the paper, it creates dots that form characters and graphics. Dot-matrix printers can print on continuous paper, which could be single, duplicate or many sheets.

The speed of a dot-matrix printer is measured by the number of characters it can print in a second. This ranges from 50 to 700 characters per second (cps). The printing quality of the dot-matrix printer is determined by the number of pins in the print head, which ranges from nine to 24 pins. The greater the number of pins in the print head, the higher the quality of print.

Fig 1.25: A dot-matrix printer

Inkjet printer

Inkjet printers are non-impact printers. They use both black cartridges and colour cartridges that contain quick-drying ink. The print head located on the cartridge has nozzles that release ink through the appropriate nozzle.

The speed of the inkjet printer is measured by the number of pages it can print in a minute, which can be as high as over 20 pages per minute (ppm). The quality of an inkjet printer is determined by its resolution. Printer resolution is measured by the number of dots per inch (dpi) a printer can output. The higher the dpi, the better the print quality. Most inkjet printers have over 300 dpi.

Inkjet printers are common for home use but are also used in many organisations where colour and good quality output are required.

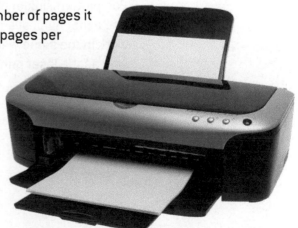

Fig 1.26: An inkjet printer

Laser printer

Laser printers are high speed and high quality non-impact printers. A laser beam creates an image of the page on a light sensitive drum, treated with a magnetically charged powder called toner. The paper is then pressed against the drum, and heat and pressure are applied to transfer the image to the paper.

Laser printers are available in both colour and black, and can print over 40 ppm with quality over 600 dpi. Laser printers are used in many large organisations that require high volume printing with a high quality.

Fig 1.27: A laser printer

Factors to consider when selecting a printer

When choosing a printer, in addition to the speed and resolution, you also need to consider the noise level of the printer, paper handling features (number of trays, capacity of trays, type of paper), the printer interface (USB, parallel, wireless) and the memory capacity of the printer.

Plotters

A plotter is a type of printer used for printing accurate and precise high-quality charts, graphs or maps on large sheets of paper. Plotters are used by engineering organisations to produce maps and building plans, and to draw machine parts with precision.

Pen plotters, inkjet plotters and electrostatic plotters are currently in use. Pen plotters use a mechanical arm or rail that holds a pen that moves across the paper. Inkjet plotters work in the same way as an inkjet printer, while the electrostatic plotters work the same way as the laser printer.

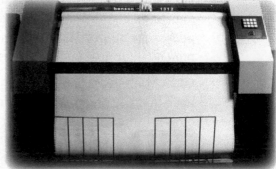

Fig 1.28: A plotter

Microfilm/microfiche output

The output of a computer can also be on a roll of film called a microfilm, or a rectangular sheet of film called a microfiche. Data is printed very small on the microfiche or microfilm, so a special magnifying machine called a microfiche reader is required to read the data. This type of output is often referred to as Computer Output Microfiche (COM) output. COM outputs are used to store a large volume of data for archival purposes and are found in libraries, archives and newspaper offices.

Fig 1.29: A microfiche reader and microfiche

Sound output

Output from a computer can also be in the form of sound. Devices such as speakers and headphones enable the sounds to be heard. A computer sound card is used to play sounds. Combined with the correct kind of software, computers can read text and convert them to words, making them appropriate for a visually impaired person to use.

Fig 1.30: Computer speakers and headphones

Summary of key points

In this topic you have learned:

- the various output devices used with computers.
- the terms associated with output devices.
- the uses of the various output devices.
- the operations of the output devices.

QUESTIONS

1 Classify dot-matrix, inkjet and laser printers as impact or non-impact printers.
2 One of your friends is interested in buying a printer to use at home. What printer would you recommend and why?
3 List THREE organisations that would make use of microfiche.
4 What output device would you use to print a large size plan of a building?
5 State TWO advantages of using a laser printer.

● *1.10* # Interpreting the hardware specifications of a computer system

It is important to understand the hardware **specifications** of a computer so that you know what it is capable of in terms of memory, speed, etc. It is also useful in case you ever want to buy a computer – you need to know what you're buying and what it can do. This topic will help you recognise and understand the specifications of various pieces of computer hardware.

The CPU or processor

You learned about processors (or CPU) in the topic *The hardware components of a computer system*. The two main features of CPUs that you need to be aware of are its speed and type. The two most popular companies that currently produce CPUs are Intel and AMD (Advanced Micro Devices). CPUs are also manufactured by Centaur Technology, Elbrus and Transmeta corporation.

Fig 1.31: An Intel CPU

Speed of computer

As the 'brain' of the computer, the CPU determines how fast instructions can be carried out. The CPU contains a clock. Each time the clock 'ticks', one instruction is carried out. So the faster the clock ticks, the more instructions can be carried out. The processor speeds of most of today's personal computers (**PC**) are measured in MHz (Mega **Hertz**) or GHz (Giga Hertz). MHz means that it can execute approximately 1 million instructions per second and GHz means that it can execute approximately 1 billion instructions per second. Based on what you would use the computer system for, the speed will vary. In recent times, most of the PCs are distributed with a speed of 2 GHz or more.

Type of computer

The CPU type determines the type of application for which a particular type of processor is used. For example, the CPUs used for **mainframe computers** are not the same as the CPUs used for PCs. There are many types of processors that are developed by Intel and AMD. Three main types of Intel processors are Pentium, Core and Celeron and four main types of AMD processors are Athlon, Sempron, Turion and Phenom. Intel processors are little more expensive than AMD's due to the small difference in performance. Based on the performance requirements for a specific task you have to decide which processor you need to buy.

CHECK YOUR PROGRESS

1 State the difference between MHz and GHz as it relates to the processor speed.
2 Why is it important that you need to know the processor speed?
3 What are the TWO main features of a CPU that you should consider when you are planning to purchase a computer system?

Main memory

You learned in the topic *Primary storage devices* that main memory is used to store programs and data that are being used or are about to be used. In terms of a computer's memory, it is important to know its capacity, type, word size and speed.

Memory capacity

The capacity of a computer's memory determines the number of programs that it can hold at a time, which affects the performance of a computer system. More memory capacity indicates that it can hold more programs at a time. In modern PCs, memory capacity is measured in Gigabytes (GB) and is distributed with 2 GB or more.

Memory type

There are two main types of RAM – SDRAM (Synchronous Dynamic RAM) and RDRAM (Rambus Dynamic RAM). RDRAMs are faster and more expensive than SDRAM, and are used mainly for high-performance computers. SDRAMs (also called PC100 or PC133) are more common and can be Double Data Rate (DDR) RAM, which offers double data transfer rates.

Fig 1.32: RAM chips

Word size

As you learned in the topic *Units of storage*, word size determines the number of bits that can be stored and processed at a time by the CPU. Most of today's PCs have word sizes of 32-bit or 64-bit.

Speed

RAM speed indicates how fast the chip updates the data that it contains. In modern PCs, RAM speed is measured in Mega Hertz (MHz) and is usually above 400 MHz.

CHECK YOUR PROGRESS

1   List FOUR features of RAM that you should consider when you are about to purchase a RAM chip.
2   What is the advantage of having more memory in a computer system?
3   State TWO differences between SDRAM and RDRAM.
4   State the purpose of word size.

Hard disk

You learned in the topic *Secondary storage devices and media* that the main secondary storage medium used by a computer system is the hard disk. The two main specifications to note for a hard disk are its storage capacity and its speed.

Storage capacity

The storage capacity of a hard disk determines the amount of information that it can store for later use. More hard disk space means you can store more programs and data. In modern computers, the hard disk capacities are measured in Gigabytes ranging from 120 GB – 2 TB.

Speed

Hard disk speeds are normally expressed as **data transfer rates** or **revolutions per minute**. The data transfer rate measures the speed by which data can be transferred from the hard disk to the CPU. In modern PCs, the hard disks have data transfer rates around 1–3 Gigabits per second (Gb/sec).

WHAT DOES IT MEAN?

data transfer rate
The data transfer rate is the rate at which data can be transferred from the hard disk to the CPU.

revolutions per minute (rpm)
Revolutions per minute indicate how fast the hard disk spins.

The rate at which data can be transferred partly depends on how fast the disk is spinning. If the drive spins faster, it can position the read/write head faster over a particular piece of data. The spin speed is measured in revolutions per minute (rpm). Hard disks vary in speed from 5400 rpm to 15000 rpm.

Looking at hardware specifications

Now let's look at a portion of hardware specification and interpret it.

Intel Pentium IV 64-bit 3.6 GHz

2 GB 533 MHz SDRAM (Max – 4 GB)

160 GB SATA HDD 7200 rpm

Fig 1.33

In the above specification, the first line indicates the processor manufacturer, type, word size and processor speed.

Processor manufacturer: Intel
> **Type:** Pentium IV
> **Word size:** 64-bits
> **Processor speed:** 3.6 GHz

The second line indicates the memory capacity with its maximum capacity, speed and type.

> **Memory capacity:** 2 GB and can allow up to a chip with 4 GB.
> **Speed:** 533 MHz
> **RAM type:** SDRAM

The third line indicates the hard disk capacity, speed and type of hard disk controller.

> **Storage capacity:** 160 GB
> **Speed:** 7200 rpm
> **Hard disk controller:** SATA

CHECK YOUR PROGRESS

1. List TWO specifications of hard disk you should take into consideration when you are about to purchase it.
2. What are the TWO common measurements of hard disk speed?
3. Why is it important to know the hard disk capacity when you are about to purchase a computer system?

Other specifications

In addition to memory capacity, speed, type, word size, etc, it is important that you take note of some other specifications such as ports and expansion slots.

Ports

A computer system needs to send and receive information from peripheral devices. A port is a piece of technology that is used to connect external devices to a computer system. There are different kinds of ports such as:

- Parallel: Used mainly to connect printers but can also be used to connect certain scanners and external hard disks.

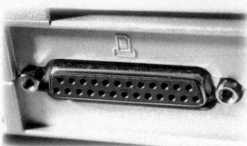

Fig 1.34: A parallel port

- Serial: Used to connect certain types of mouse, modem and printer.

Fig 1.35: A serial port

- USB: Used to connect around 127 devices including keyboards, mouse, printers, scanners, flash drives and digital cameras. This is the most common port used in modern computers. There are USB-1 and USB-2. USB-2 is faster.

Fig 1.36: A USB port

- Firewire/ IEEE 1394: used to transfer video images from digital devices.

Fig 1.37: A firewire port

Expansion slots

Expansion slots are sockets found on the main circuit board (motherboard) that are used to insert additional circuit boards. They can be used for adding more memory, graphics facilities and other special devices. Three types of expansion slots are:

1 PCI (Peripheral Component Interconnect), used for attaching sound cards, network cards and video cards.

2 AGP (Accelerated Graphics Card), mainly used for connecting Graphics cards.

3 ISA (Industry Standard Architecture), used for attaching modems and not commonly seen on most modern computers.

PCI slots

AGP slot

Fig 1.38: AGP and PCI slots

Summary of key points

In this topic you have learned:

- how to read and understand the specification for a computer system.
- how to describe the speed and capacity of various hardware devices.
- that expansion slots and ports make it possible to add further devices.

QUESTIONS

1 What is the use of ports in a computer system?
2 Give the purpose of a firewire port in a computer system.
3 List THREE main types of expansion slots used in modern PCs.
4 List TWO common uses of PCI slots.

● *1.11 – 1.13* # Systems and application software

So far in this section, you have learned about hardware. However, a computer system consists of hardware *and* software. We use software or programs to complete any activity in a computer. Software can be used for running the hardware or for performing various tasks. There are TWO major categories of software. They are:

1 Application software
2 Systems software

Application software

Application software is designed to solve a specific problem or perform a particular task. It is used to enable a computer to perform a specific task such as processing text, controlling inventory, accounting or billing.

The two main types of application software are:

1 General purpose software
2 Special purpose software

You will learn more about application software in Section 4B.

General purpose software

General purpose software is designed to help the user perform general tasks such as word processing, database management or manipulating spreadsheets. This type of software is readily available an computer stores. Microsoft Word, Corel Quattropro and Lot general purpose software.

General purpose software can be obtained as a **software suite** or as **integrated software**. A software suite is a combination of application programs sold as a package that can run as separate applications, if needed, e.g. Microsoft Office.

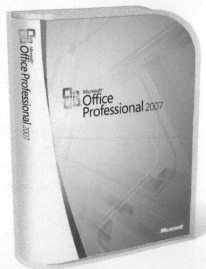

Fig 1.39: Microsoft Office - a software suite

Integrated software is also a combination of application programs, but it can run only as a *single program*, e.g. Microsoft Works.

Fig 1.40: Microsoft Works – integrated software

Both software suites and integrated software typically contain word processors, spreadsheets, database management systems, graphics and communications software.

There are some advantages and disadvantages associated with both integrated software and software suites.

Advantages

1 They cost less than buying individual programs.
2 Learning will be easier, since similar screen displays are used.
3 Transfer from one program to another is hassle-free as there are no compatibility issues.
4 Installation will be less time-consuming.

Disadvantages

1 Programs that may not be used have to be installed as they come as a single package, especially in integrated software.
2 Some features that are available individually may not be available in these packages.

> **WHAT DOES IT MEAN?**
>
> **software suite**
> A software suite is a combination of application programs sold as a package that can run as separate applications.
>
> **integrated software**
> Integrated software is a combination of application programs that can run only as a single program.

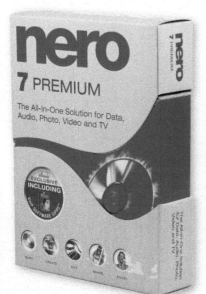

Special purpose software

Special purpose software is designed to perform specific or special tasks such as accounting, engineering design, playing games, etc. It may be readily available, like integrated software and software suites, or it may be custom-written for the organisation. Peach Tree Accounting and Nero are examples of special purpose software.

Fig 1.41: Special purpose software

> **WHAT DOES IT MEAN?**
>
> **special purpose software**
> Special purpose software is application software which is used to carry out specialist tasks, such as designing products.

Custom-written software

Both general purpose and special purpose application software can be purchased through software retailers. As an alternative, an organisation may decide to have software specially written for them.

Custom-written software is designed for an organisation to handle its specific operations. For example, if a company wants to computerise its Accounts department it can commission a software firm or the company's technical team to create the exact software they require, customised to meet the specific needs of the user. Customisation is the modification of a program to meet the specific needs of a user, for example a billing program for the Electricity department and a stock control program for a supermarket.

You will learn more about custom-written software in Section 4B.

CHECK YOUR PROGRESS

1 List TWO advantages of software that can be bought from a retailer over custom-written software.
2 What is the difference between a software suite and integrated software?
3 List TWO advantages and TWO disadvantages of integrated software.
4 Define the term customisation.
5 List TWO advantages for an organisation of having software custom-written for them.

Systems software

Systems software is designed to control the performance of the hardware and facilitate the running of application software. There are three types of systems software:

1 Operating Systems
2 Utilities
3 Translators

Operating systems (OS)

Operating systems are a set of programs that monitor and co-ordinate software and hardware within a computer system. Operating systems are the most important programs and must be present in all computer systems for other programs to run. Examples of operating systems are Windows, UNIX, Linux, Mac OS and DOS. When a computer system is switched on the OS will be loaded into memory in order for the computer to start up. This process is called booting.

The OS is needed in a computer system to perform the following main functions:

- Process management
- File management
- Memory management
- Input/output device management
- Provide security
- Provide a friendly user interface

Fig 1.42: An operating system

Process management

A program that is running can be considered as a process and a program can have many sub-programs. Therefore, many processes would occur in a computer system when a program is being executed. The process management function of the operating system involves allocating adequate time and resources of the CPU to each process.

File management

All the files created in secondary storage media, such as the hard disk, are stored within its various files. The OS is responsible for creating, deleting, renaming of files and folders and also making back-up copies of files.

Memory management

Main memory or RAM stores programs and data that are presently being used by the CPU. The OS allocates areas of memory to different programs so that each program can function effectively.

Input/output device management

There are many peripheral devices such as keyboards, mouse and monitors that can be connected to the system unit. The OS makes the communication possible between the peripheral devices and the system unit.

Provide security

Modern computer systems require the entry of a password in order to access the system. The operating system provides the user with password protection to prevent unauthorised access. It also provides back up and recovery routines in case of system failure.

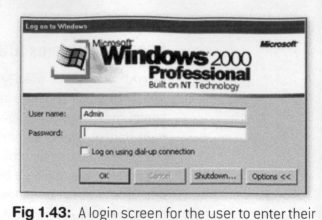

Fig 1.43: A login screen for the user to enter their password to access the system

Provide a friendly user interface

The method by which a user interacts with a computer system is called its **user interface**.

The operating system provides the user with a friendly interface that will help the user to interact with the computer system. For example, if your computer has a Windows operating system you will see a **desktop** from which you can interact with the computer system.

Both systems software and application software have user interfaces. You will learn more about them later in this section.

WHAT DOES IT MEAN?

user interface
A user interface is the method by which the user interacts with the computer system.

desktop
The desktop is the name given to the main screen that acts as the interface to the operating system.

Fig 1.44: The Windows desktop is an interface that helps the user to interact with the computer

CHECK YOUR PROGRESS

1 The operating system is the most important software in a computer system. List FIVE functions of operating systems.
2 What does the process management function of an operating system involve?
3 List THREE examples of commonly used operating systems.
4 How does the operating system provide security?

Multitasking, multiprogramming and multiprocessing

Based on the type of operating system, it can also perform the following:

- Multitasking: When the operating system allows the user to perform several tasks at the same time, switch between them and share information. For example, in the Windows operating system a document can be edited while another document is being printed.

- Multiprogramming: When users can run two or more programs at the same time using a single processor.
- Multiprocessing: When users can run two or more programs using multiple processors.
- Time-sharing: When each user is given a 'time slice' so that each user feels that they get the full attention of the CPU.

Utilities

Utilities are systems software that support the operating system in its housekeeping tasks to increase the efficiency of the computer system. Examples include text editors, anti-virus software, back-up software, anti-spam software and compression utility.

Fig 1.45: Norton AntiSpam Utility Software

Translators or language processors

Computers understand only binary language. All other programming instructions have to be converted into binary language or machine language. **Translators** are systems software that convert other programming language instructions to machine language. Three main types of translators are assemblers, interpreters and compilers. You will learn about these in detail in Section 3.

WHAT DOES IT MEAN?

utilities
Utilities are system programs that can be added to the main operating system to carry out extra tasks.

translator
Translators are systems software that convert other programming language instructions to machine language.

Summary of key points

In this topic you have learned:

- that systems software consists of operating systems, utilities and translators.
- that operating systems control the processes running on a computer.
- that operating systems manage the use of the CPU and all the devices connected to it.
- that utilities and translators add extra functions to the operating system.

QUESTIONS

1 State the difference between:
   a multitasking and multiprocessing
   b multiprocessing and time-sharing
   c multiprogramming and multitasking
2 What is a utility software? Give THREE examples.
3 What is the purpose of a translator?
4 List THREE types of translators used by computers.

● 1.14 Processing modes

Types of processing

You learned on page 4 that processing involves accepting data and converting it into output, or information. The data will be collected and processed in different ways, depending on what you want to do. Some data needs to be processed immediately; some can be processed on weekly basis or some on monthly basis. In most organisations, processing is completed using any of the following methods.

Batch processing

Batch processing is when the data collected is grouped together and processed at a certain point of time such as *weekly* or *monthly*. Batch processing is often used in utility bill preparation and salary preparation (payroll). In billing applications, bills are sent to the users at the end of the month or week; the daily data of their usage of the utility is collected and run as a batch. Similarly, salaries are calculated and paid to employees at the end of the day, week or month. Batch processing is also known as offline processing.

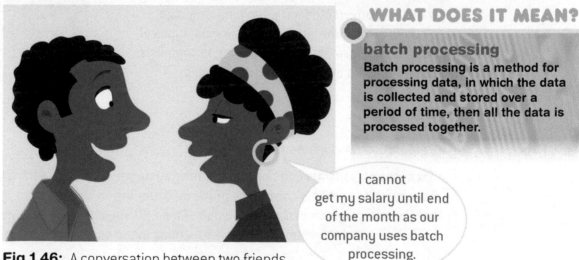

WHAT DOES IT MEAN?

batch processing
Batch processing is a method for processing data, in which the data is collected and stored over a period of time, then all the data is processed together.

I cannot get my salary until end of the month as our company uses batch processing.

Fig 1.46: A conversation between two friends

Online processing

Online processing is when the data collected is processed *right away* and is updated immediately. Here, the user can interact directly with the computer at any time through the input/output devices, which are under the direct control of the processor. Examples include ATM machines, online games and flight reservation systems. ATM machines allow you to interact directly with the system and your money withdrawal or deposit is processed almost instantaneously (as soon as you receive and deposit cash, the system will update your account balance).

WHAT DOES IT MEAN?

online processing
Online processing is a method for processing data in which the data is collected and processed immediately.

Sir, please check your details on your flight ticket carefully as mistakes cannot be changed once the information is processed.

Fig 1.47: A conversation between a travel agent and a client

Real-time processing

In **real-time processing**, there is a continual input, processing and output of data. Data has to be processed in a small, stipulated time period (real time), otherwise it will create problems for the system. For example, in flight simulation, it is important that the data reaches the end-user as quickly as possible so that they know what is happening in the air and can react accordingly. In online processing there is still a slight delay for processing but in real-time processing, the updating of data will take place in *real time*.

WHAT DOES IT MEAN?

real-time processing
Real-time processing is a method for inputting, processing and outputting data continuously, and is used to control activities as they happen.

Using our latest system with real-time processing, we are able to predict that a tropical depression is close to Barbados.

Fig 1.48: A meteorologist

Time-sharing

Time-sharing is a processing mode where the computer's time is allocated to multiple tasks of multiple users. Each user gets the feeling that their task is being carried out continuously. Time-sharing was commonly used in earlier mainframe computers.

Hey I thought you accessed the file first. But I got it at the same time.

Yes, with the time-sharing option both of us get the feeling that both of our requests were carried out together.

Fig 1.49: A conversation between two mainframe users

Summary of key points

In this topic you have learned:

- the differences between and uses of several computer processing modes:
  - Batch processing
  - Online processing
  - Real-time processing
  - Time-sharing

QUESTIONS

1 State the difference between batch processing and online processing.
2 List TWO advantages of online processing over batch processing.
3 Give ONE disadvantage of online processing compared to batch processing.
4 State the difference between online and real-time processing systems.
5 For each of the following tasks, suggest an appropriate processing mode:
   a controlling a robotic arm
   b monthly stock processing
   c checking criminal records
   d ATM transactions
   e reserving a movie

1.15 Types of user interface

As you learned in the topic *Systems software*, a user interface is the way in which a user interacts with a computer system. It can be a **software interface**, such as command-driven interfaces, menu-driven interfaces and graphical user interfaces (GUI), or a **hardware interface**, such as touch screens, special keyboards, non-visual interfaces and sensors. The quality of the user interface determines how efficiently you can use the computer system.

Software interfaces

Software interfaces help you to interact with different programs that are available on the computer system. The three common software interfaces are:

1 command-driven

2 menu-driven

3 graphical user interface

Command-driven interfaces

In early computers, the only way for a user to interact with a computer program was by using a display screen with a command line and a set of commands. Computer responses were exchanged, as shown in Fig 1.49. The users were supposed to give the instructions to the computer using words and symbols in a specific format called syntax. (You will learn about syntax in Section 3).

In modern computers, the operating system MS DOS still uses a **command-driven interface**. The major disadvantage of this interface is that it requires you to remember the commands and their correct syntax. But experienced users like programmers prefer using the command-driven interface because many tasks can be done with a single command. The major interfacing device in command-driven interface is the keyboard.

Fig 1.50: A screen showing a command-driven interface

Menu-driven interfaces

Because people without the knowledge of commands and syntax found the command-driven interface difficult, the **menu-driven interface** was developed. This interface gives the users a list of command options called a menu. Just like a menu from a restaurant where you make a choice of food, this interface allows the user to choose an option.

A menu can be drop-down or pop-up. In a drop-down menu, users get options displayed in a vertical list that may have horizontal dividers and links to submenus. For example, in certain programs such as MS Word, you get the file menu by pulling down the file option from the menu bar, as shown in Fig 1.51.

In a pop-up menu, the menu is displayed when the user positions the mouse over an object and clicks or activates the menu. For example, when you right click on the mouse button, you get the menu in the form of a pop-up, as shown in Fig 1.52.

The advantage of a menu-driven interface is that the user does not have to remember the commands and its correct syntax. The disadvantage is that sometimes users cannot see all options that are available in the menu straight away.

WHAT DOES IT MEAN?

menu-driven interface
A menu-driven user interface is one where the user can select commands from one or more menus.

Fig 1.51: Example of a menu-driven interface

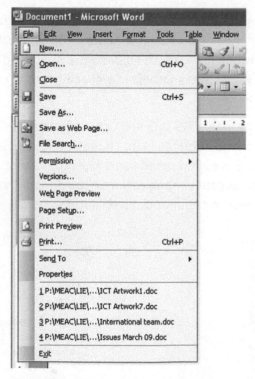

Fig 1.52 A drop-down menu

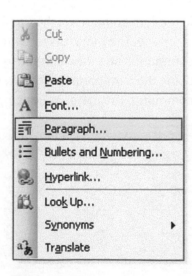

Fig 1.53: A pop-up menu displayed when a mouse is right clicked

Graphical user interface or GUI

Since the menu-driven interface also had its disadvantages, a new interface called GUI or graphical user interface was developed. This interface provided the user with Windows, Icons, Menus and Pointers in earlier computers and was also know as WIMP interface. In modern computers, the graphical user interface provides the user with the options of toolbars, drag and drop, labels, onscreen assistants, slide bars, buttons, selection boxes and dialogue boxes.

The main interfacing device for a GUI is the mouse. This interface can be very helpful for a novice user as the user does not have to remember the commands and syntax, and is provided with small icons to choose from. But it is slower than command-driven interface as you might have to click and choose many icons to complete a task that could be done in a single command.

Fig 1.54: A GUI

Hardware interfaces

Hardware interfaces are special devices with additional features that will make the interaction much easier. Keyboards, mice, screens and speakers are part of the standard user interface, but many additional hardware devices can be used as part of the user interface to suit the needs of particular users.

Special keyboards

A keyboard is the most popular device used to enter information to the computer system. There are various types of modified keyboard that are much easier to use.

- An ergonomic keyboard is shaped so that it is more comfortable to use. Someone who uses a keyboard for long periods can avoid injury, such as repetitive strain injury, by using one of these. See Fig 1.54.

Fig 1.55: An ergonomic keyboard

- An overlay (or Concept) keyboard replaces the keys with a flat touch-sensitive panel. An overlay placed on the panel marks out areas that can act as buttons. The program will identify the relevant sensors used by each overlay. These keyboards can provide a very simple keyboard for children and other people who cannot manage a normal keyboard. They are also used in environments such as fast food restaurants, where grease and dust may become lodged in a normal keyboard.

Fig 1.56: An overlay keyboard

- Braille keyboards are available for blind users. The simplest type has Braille symbols on each key on a normal keyboard. Alternatively, an overlay style keyboard can be used, in which the surface is embossed with Braille symbols. A third type, shown in fig. 1.57, provides a small number of keys, and the user hits a combination of these keys to produce each character.

Fig 1.57: A Braille keyboard

Touch screens

Touch screens are special devices that make it easier to input data using a stylus or fingers. You have probably seen touch screens on PDAs, cell phones and ATMs. Touch screens make the input much faster than a keyboard and mouse. See Fig 1.16.

Fig 1.58: Scientist Stephen Hawking is well-known for communicating through the portable computer and speech synthesiser fitted to his wheelchair.

Sensors

On page 19 you learned that a sensor captures data automatically and passes it to a computer. Sensors can be used within hardware devices; for example, an overlay keyboard has sensors located under the surface of the panel.

Sensors are particularly useful in providing interfaces for people who cannot use standard devices such as keyboards. A user with very limited movement can use a device with a sensor which they can press with a finger or a foot, or by moving their head. This makes it possible for people with severe physical disabilities to communicate with a computer and hence with everyone else.

Non-visual interfaces

Many GUIs provide sounds as well as graphics. Sounds can be used to represent actions (for example, when opening a file) or to alert the user (for example, to warn if a virus is detected). More complex sounds can also be used to support users.

- Speech synthesis is the production of human speech with the help of special software. This can be useful for users with visual impairment to read back documents that they created, or to read text scanned or viewed on the Internet.
- Voice recognition is the use of computers with special software that will accept the voice from the user and convert it to it text.

Speech synthesis along with voice recognition can allow a completely hands-free two-way interaction between the user and a computer.

Summary of key points

In this topic you have learned:

- that a user interface enables a user to interact with a computer system.
- that user interfaces can be command-driven, menu-driven or graphical.
- that standard hardware devices, such as keyboards, are also part of the user interface.
- that specialist hardware interfaces can be provided to match the needs of users.

QUESTIONS

1 List TWO types of menus that are available in a menu-driven interface and suggest how these menus help in carrying out different operations.
2 Give ONE main interfacing device for:
   a command driven interfaces
   b graphical user interfaces
3 State TWO advantages and ONE disadvantage of using a GUI.
4 List THREE hardware interfaces that are available for physically challenged persons.
5 'Command-driven interfaces are more suitable for expert users.' Do you agree? Support your answer.

• 1.9 Manipulating, storing and representing data

Computers store and represent data in a coded form that is not easily read or understood by humans. In this topic you will learn about the number systems that computers use.

Representing numbers as bases

Although you are probably only familiar with the decimal number system, there are actually quite a few. In a number system, the **base** determines the number of digits that are available in it. For example, base 10 uses ten digits. Bases are normally placed as a subscript such as 35_{10}, 1010_2, 72_8, 37_{16}.

The following are four main types of number systems used in computers:

1 The decimal number system or base 10 number system is a number system that involves ten digits (0, 1, 2, 3, 4, 5, 6, 7, 8 and 9). This is the number system that is used by us in our daily lives.

2 The binary number system or base 2 number system is a number system that involves two digits (0 and 1). This is the number system used by computers for processing.

3 The octal number system or base 8 number system is the number system that involves eight digits (0, 1, 2, 3, 4, 5, 6 and 7). The octal system was used extensively in early mainframe computer systems, but has become less popular today because of binary and hexadecimal systems.

4 The hexadecimal number system or base 16 number system is the number system that involves 16 digits (0, 1, 2, 3, 4, 5, 6, 7, 8, 9, A, B, C, D, E and F). When you have to deal with large values, binary numbers become difficult to manage and the hexadecimal numbering system can be used to make it compact.

WHAT DOES IT MEAN?

base
The base is the number of digits that are available in a number system, for example, base 10 uses ten digits.

CHECK YOUR PROGRESS

1 All data being inputted must be converted into binary. Suggest ONE reason for this.

2 List the digits that are available in
   a the octal number system.
   b hexadecimal number system
   c decimal number system

Converting decimal to binary

Because we generally use the decimal number system, and computers use the binary system, when you input data into the computer system it has to be converted into binary for the computer to understand. So let's look at how decimal numbers are represented in binary.

Suppose you want to convert $35_{\text{base }10}$ or 35_{10} to its binary, the following steps can be used.

Example: Convert $35_{\text{base }10}$ or 35_{10} to binary.

1 Divide the number by 2 and note the remainder. If the number is odd, there will be a remainder of 1. If the number is even there will be no remainder, so note the remainder as 0.

	Quotient	Remainder
35/2 =	17	1
17/2 =	8	1
8/2 =	4	0
4/2 =	2	0
2/2 =	1	0
1/2 =	0	1

2 Repeat step 1 until the quotient (the answer you get after each division) is 0.

3 List the remainders starting from the bottom (the last number you divided). In our example, this gives us 100011.

4 Add zeroes to the start of the number to make it eight bits long. (A group of eight bits or a Byte are normally used to represent binary codes and numbers.) In our example, this gives us 00100011.

Answer: $35_{10} = 00100011_2$ (Remember that the subscript 2 means the answer is in base 2.)

CHECK YOUR PROGRESS

Convert the following decimal numbers into eight-bit binary numbers:

a 99_{10}
b 64_{10}
c 127_{10}
d 17_{10}
e 39_{10}

WHAT DOES IT MEAN?

place value
In any number system, the place values of digits are the powers of the base. They are assigned by starting from power 0 on the right and increasing towards the left.

Converting binary to decimal

After a computer has processed the numbers in binary, the results are displayed in the form of decimal, so we also need to know how the binary number is converted back to decimal.

Before looking at the conversion of binary numbers to decimal numbers it is important to understand about the **place values** of numbers.

All numbers in our decimal number system have place values such as ones, tens, hundreds, thousands, etc. For example, the number 654 contains 4 ones, 5 tens, and 6 hundreds. Each of these digits multiplied by their place values would give you the number 654.

$(6 \times 100) + (5 \times 10) + (4 \times 1) = 600 + 50 + 4 = 654$.

In the above example, the places are the powers of 10 because we are working in the decimal system. So the breakdown can also be expressed as:

$(6 \times 10^2) + (5 \times 10^1) + (4 \times 10^0) = (6 \times 100) + (5 \times 10) + (4 \times 1) = 654$.

Similarly, when working in the binary system, place values are the powers of 2.

Suppose you want to convert the binary number $10011_{base\ 2}$ to its decimal, the following steps can be used:

Example: Convert binary 10011_2 to decimal.

1 Note the place values (2^0, 2^1, 2^2, 2^3, etc.) for each binary digit starting from the right.

Binary number	1	0	0	1	1
Place value	2^4	2^3	2^2	2^1	2^0

2 Multiply each digit with its place value.

$(1 \times 2^4) + (0 \times 2^3) + (0 \times 2^2) + (1 \times 2^1) + (1 \times 2^0)$

$(1 \times 16) + (0 \times 8) + (0 \times 4) + (1 \times 2) + (1 \times 1)$

3 Add them together.

$16 + 0 + 0 + 2 + 1$

Answer: $10011_2 = 19_{10}$ (the subscript 10 tells you that the answer is in decimal)

CHECK YOUR PROGRESS

Give the decimal values of the following binary numbers:

a 01001111　　b 00101010　　c 00011011　　d 01110111　　e 01011011

Binary addition

Because the binary number system only uses 0 and 1, binary numbers are added using the following rules:

Rule 1: $0 + 0 = 0$

Rule 2: $0 + 1 = 1$

Rule 3: $1 + 0 = 1$

Rule 4: $1 + 1 = 0$ carry 1 (This is because in decimal $1+1 = 2$, and when you convert it into binary you will get a remainder of 0 and carry 1. The table below shows what happens when you convert decimal 2 into binary.)

	Quotient	Remainder
2/2 =	1	0
1/2 =	0	1

Rule 5: $1+1+1 = 1$ carry 1 (This is because in decimal $1+1+1 = 3$, and when you convert it into binary you will get a remainder of 1 and carry 1. The table below shows what happens when you convert decimal 3 into binary.)

	Quotient	Remainder
3/2 =	1	1
1/2 =	0	1

Suppose you want to add two binary numbers 110111 and 1111, you can use the following steps.

Example: Add the binary numbers 110111 and 1111.

1 Put the numbers in a vertical sum and add them together, carrying where necessary.

	1(carry)	1(carry)	1(carry)	1(carry)	1(carry)	
	1	1	0	1	1	1
+			1	1	1	1
1	0	0	0	1	1	0

2 List your answer from left to right. The answer is in binary.

Answer: $110111 + 1111 = 1000110_2$

CHECK YOUR PROGRESS

Perform the following binary additions:

a $11111 + 11011$

b $11011 + 101111$

c $10111 + 1001$

d $111000 + 10000$

e $11111 + 111111$

Converting decimal to octal

In order to convert a decimal number to an octal number, the following steps are used.

Example: Convert 119_{10} to octal.

1 Divide the number by 8 and note the remainder. Keep dividing by 8 until the quotient is 0. Each time you divide, note the remainder in order.

	Quotient	Remainder
119/8 =	14	7
14/8 =	1	6
1/8=	0	1

2 List the remainders in reverse order. The answer is in octal, hence the subscript number 8.

Answer: $119_{10} = 167_8$

CHECK YOUR PROGRESS

Convert the following decimal numbers into octal:

a 84_{10} **b** 32_{10} **c** 96_{10} **d** 132_{10} **e** 176_{10}

Converting octal to decimal

The method of conversion from octal to decimal is similar to conversion from decimal to binary except that the place values would be the powers of 8 instead of 10. Suppose you want to convert the octal number 3206_8 to its decimal, you can use the following steps:

Example: Convert 3206_8 to decimal.

1 Note the place values for each digit starting from the right.

Octal number	3	2	0	6
Place value	8^3	8^2	8^1	8^0

2 Multiply each digit by its place value.

(3×8^3) + (2×8^2) + (0×8^1) + (6×8^0)

(3×512) + (2×64) + (0×8) + (6×1)

3 Add them together. The answer is in decimal.

$1536 + 128 + 0 + 6 = 1670$

Answer: $3206_8 = 1670_{10}$

Convert the following octal numbers to decimal:

a 33_8 **b** 57_8 **c** 64_8 **d** 173_8 **e** 100_8

Converting from binary to octal

Now let's look at how a number in binary is converted into octal form.

Example: Convert 1010110_{10} to octal.

1 Group the digits into three bits each, starting from the right.
Add zeroes in front of any remaining bits to make it three bits.

```
  1     010    110
  ↓      ↓      ↓
0 0 1  0 1 0  1 1 0
```

2 Note the place values for each group of three bits and convert them into decimal.

Binary digits	0	0	1
Place value	2^2	2^1	2^0

Binary digits	0	1	0
Place value	2^2	2^1	2^0

Binary digits	1	1	0
Place value	2^2	2^1	2^0

$(0 \times 4) + (0 \times 2) + (1 \times 1)$ $(0 \times 4) + (1 \times 2) + (0 \times 1)$ $(1 \times 4) + (1 \times 2) + (0 \times 1)$

$0 + 0 + 1$ $0 + 2 + 0$ $4 + 2 + 0$

1 2 6

3 Put them together. The answer is in octal.
Answer: $1010110_{10} = 126_8$

Convert the following binary numbers into octal:

a 110111001   **c** 110110011   **e** 10001000001
b 1110111   **d** 1100110011

Converting from octal to binary

Let's now look at how octal numbers are converted into binary.

Example: Convert 572_8 to binary.

1 Convert each octal digit to its 3-bit binary, just how you converted the decimal numbers into binary. (If the number of bits is less than three, add zeroes in front to make it three bits each as before.)

5	7	2.
↓	↓	↓
1 0 1	1 1 1	0 1 0

2 Put them together to form a single binary number. The answer is in binary.

Answer: $572_8 = 100111010_2$

CHECK YOUR PROGRESS

Convert the following octal numbers into binary:

a 73_8 **b** 21_8 **c** 653_8 **d** 460_8 **e** 732_8

Converting from decimal to hexadecimal

This conversion method is very similar to the one you learned to convert decimal to octal. Let's look at how a decimal number is converted into hexadecimal using the following example:

Example: Convert 428_{10} to hexadecimal.

1 Divide the number by 16 and note the remainder. Keep dividing the quotient by 16 until the quotient is 0. Each time you divide, note the remainder in order. (If the remainder is more than 9 use the corresponding letters: 10 = A, 11 = B, 12 = C, 13 = D, 14 = E and 15 = F).

	Quotient	Remainder
428/16 =	26	12 (C)
26/16 =	1	10 (A)
1/16 =	0	1

2 List the remainders in reverse order. The answer is in hexadecimal.

Answer: $428_{10} = 1AC_{16}$

Converting from hexadecimal to decimal

Let's look at how hexadecimal numbers are represented in decimal. Suppose you want to convert a hexadecimal number to its decimal form, you can use the following steps.

Example: Convert $1AC_{16}$ to decimal.

1 List the place values $(16^0, 16^1, 16^2, 16^3,$ etc$)$ for each digit starting from the right.

Hexadecimal digits	1	A (10)	C (12)
Place value	16^2	16^1	16^0

2 Multiply each digit by its place value.

$(1 \times 16^2) + (A \times 16^1) + (C \times 16^0)$

$(1 \times 256) + (10 \times 16) + (12 \times 1)$

3 Add them together. The answer is in decimal.

$256 + 160 + 12 = 428$

Answer: $1AC_{16} = 428_{10}$

Converting from binary to hexadecimal

When you want to convert a binary number to hexadecimal, the following steps can be used.

Example: Convert 111110111_2 to hexadecimal.

1 Group the digits into four bits each, starting from the right. Add zero or zeroes in front of the last bit or bits to make it four bits.

$$1 \qquad 1111 \qquad 0111$$
$$\downarrow \qquad \downarrow \qquad \downarrow$$
$$0\,0\,0\,1 \qquad 1\,1\,1\,1 \qquad 0\,1\,1\,1$$

2 List the place values for each group of four bits and convert them into their decimal form. (Note that in hexadecimal the values 10 to 15 take the letters A to F.)

Binary number	0	0	0	1
Place value	2^3	2^2	2^1	2^0

Binary number	1	1	1	1
Place value	2^3	2^2	2^1	2^0

Binary number	0	1	1	1
Place value	2^3	2^2	2^1	2^0

$(0 \times 8) + (0 \times 4) + (0 \times 2) + (1 \times 1)$
$\downarrow$
$0 + 0 + 0 + 1$
$\downarrow$
1

$(1 \times 8) + (1 \times 4) + (1 \times 2) + (1 \times 1)$
$\downarrow$
$8 + 4 + 2 + 1$
$\downarrow$
$15 (F)$

$(0 \times 8) + (1 \times 4) + (1 \times 2) + (1 \times 1)$
$\downarrow$
$0 + 4 + 2 + 1$
$\downarrow$
7

3 Put them together. The answer is in hexadecimal.

Answer: $111110111_2 = 1F7_{16}$

CHECK YOUR PROGRESS

Convert the following binary numbers to hexadecimal:

a 10110111

c 0101101100

e 11001001000110

b 110010001011

d 10110110001

Converting from hexadecimal to binary

Let's now look at how a hexadecimal number is converted into binary using the example $3BA_{16}$.

Example: Convert $3BA_{16}$ to binary.

1 Convert each hexadecimal digit to its decimal equivalent and then to its four-bit binary. If the number of bits is less than four, add zeroes in front to make it four bits each. (Note that in hexadecimal the letters A to F have the values 10 to 15.)

Hexadecimal	3	B	A
Decimal values	3	11	10
4-bit binary values	0011	1011	1010

2 Put them together to form a single binary number.

Answer: $3BA_{16} = 001110101011_2$

CHECK YOUR PROGRESS

Convert the following hexadecimal numbers to binary:

a AC_{16} c $7D5_{16}$ e 364_{16}

b $82B_{16}$ d $EF3_{16}$

Summary of key points

In this topic you have learned:

- that a numbers can be written in binary, octal and hexadecimal number bases.
- how to convert numbers written in one number base to another.
- how to add binary numbers.

QUESTIONS

1 Convert the following decimal numbers into eight-bit binary numbers:
   a 25_{10} b 201_{10} c 96_{10}

2 Give the decimal values of the following binary numbers:
   a 00100011   b 10111010   c 01011001

3 Perform the following binary additions:
   a $11101 + 1010$ b $11010 + 101011$ c $111011 + 1111$

4 Convert the following decimal numbers into octal:
   a 66_{10} b 157_{10} c 23_{10}

5 Convert the following octal numbers to decimal:
   a 75_{8} b 406_{8} c 2310_{8}

6 Convert the following binary numbers into octal:
   a 111011   b 1000110   c 1001011001

7 Convert the following octal numbers into binary:
   a 62_{8} b 300_{8} c 25_{8}

8 Convert the following decimal numbers to hexadecimal:
   a 83_{10} b 617_{10} c 14_{10}

9 Convert the following hexadecimal numbers to decimal:
   a $E5_{16}$ b 816_{16} c $C00_{16}$

10 Convert the following binary numbers to hexadecimal:
   a 10010101   b 110110   c 10011011011

11 Convert the following hexadecimal numbers to binary:
   a 38_{16} b $1C9_{16}$ c $C7B_{16}$

1.9 Storing and representing numbers

In this topic you will learn to recognise how computers store and represent numbers. This builds on what you have just learnt about number bases.

Representation of positive and negative integers

As you know, whole numbers are called integers. They can be either positive, represented by a plus sign, e.g. +5, or negative, represented by a minus sign, e.g. -5. In order to represent integers, computers use two main methods – sign and magnitude, and two's complement.

Sign and magnitude representation

In this representation, the sign (positive or negative) is being represented by using the most significant bit (MSB). The most significant bit is the very first bit in a binary number, which has the highest place value. A '0' in the MSB represents the number as positive and a '1' in the MSB represents the number as negative.

Example: Represent +30 and -30 in sign and magnitude form.

1 Convert the number into its binary, ignoring its sign.

	Quotient	Remainder
30/2 =	15	1
15/2=	7	1
7/2=	3	1
3/2=	1	1
1/2=	0	1

2 List the remainders and add zeroes to the start to make it eight bits long: 00011111. The answer is sign and magnitude positive representation.

3 Changing the first bit (the Most Significant Bit) to 1 will change the number to its negative form.

```
                 MSB
+30 = 00011111      -30 = 1001111
```

Answer: +30 = 00011110   -30 = 1011110

Two's complement representation

In computers, binary subtraction is carried out by the complementary method. In the complementary method, the number to be subtracted will be represented in negative form and will be added. For example, if you want to perform the calculation 30 - 15 you use the method 30 + (-15) to get the answer.

In two's complementary method, first you need to get the one's complement of a binary number by changing all zeroes (0) to ones (1) and ones (1) to zeroes (0). You then add 1 to the one's complement to obtain the two's complement.

In two's complement system, a positive integer is represented in standard eight-bit binary, and the negative integer is represented by the two's complement of the positive integer.

For example, the standard binary representation of 50 is 00110010, so the two's complement representation of +50 would also be 00110010. You then have to carry out a calculation on this value to find the two's complement representation of -50.

In order to represent a negative integer in two's complement, the following steps may be used:

Example: Represent -50 in two's complement.

1 If it is not already in binary, convert the number into its eight-bit binary. The answer is then in its two's complement positive representation.

	Quotient	Remainder
50/2=	25	0
25/2=	12	1
12/2=	6	0
6/2=	3	0
3/2=	1	1
1/2 =	0	1

Eight-bit binary = 00110010

2 Change all zeroes to ones and ones to zeroes. Now the number is in its one's complement.

0 0 1 1 0 0 1 0

↓ ↓ ↓ ↓ ↓ ↓ ↓ ↓

1 1 0 0 1 1 0 1

One's complement = 11001101

3 Add 1 to the one's complement value. The answer is in its two's complement negative representation.

```
  11001101
+        1
  11001110
```

Answer: -50 = 11001110

CHECK YOUR PROGRESS

1 Give the one's complement representation of the following integers:
  a -79 **b** -80 **c** -47
2 Give the two's complement representation of the following integers:
  a -91 **b** -57 **c** -38

Converting a two's complement integer to decimal

Suppose you want to represent the two's complement value of an integer as a decimal, the following steps may be used.

Example: Represent two's complement value 11001110 of a negative integer as a decimal.

1 List the place values $(2^0, 2^1, 2^2, 2^3$, etc) for each binary digit starting from the right. Since the MSB would be 1 as the number is negative, the place value of its most significant bit (leftmost bit) should be written also as negative.

MSB →	1	1	0	0	1	1	1	0
Negative representation of the place value →	-2^7	2^6	2^5	2^4	2^3	2^2	2^1	2^0
	-128	64	32	16	8	4	2	1

2 Multiply each digit by its place value.

$(1 \times -2^7) + (1 \times 2^6) + (0 \times 2^5) + (0 \times 2^4) + (1 \times 2^3) + (1 \times 2^2) + (1 \times 2^1) + (0 \times 2^0)$
-128 + 64 + 0 + 0 + 8 + 4 + 2 + 0

3 Add them together. The answer is in decimal.

-128 + 78 = -50

Answer: $11001110 = -50_{10}$

CHECK YOUR PROGRESS

What is the decimal value of the following two's complement representations:

a 11001101   **b** 10110111   **c** 11100011   **d** 11001100   **e** 11011111

Binary subtraction

Earlier, you learned how to add binary numbers. Now that you understand how to use two's complement, you can learn how to subtract binary numbers. The following steps can be used to perform binary subtraction in the complementary method.

Example: Perform the calculation 75_{10} - 30_{10} , using the two's complement method.

1 Convert both numbers into their eight-bit binary, ignoring their sign.

	Quotient	Remainder
75/2=	37	1
37/2=	18	1
18/2=	9	0
9/2=	4	1
4/2=	2	0
2/2	1	0
1/2 =	0	1

$75_{10} = 01001011_2$

	Quotient	Remainder
30/2=	15	0
15/2=	7	1
7/2=	3	1
3/2=	1	1
1/2 =	0	1

$30_{10} = 00011110_2$

2 Represent the number to be subtracted in its two's complement negative.

30 = 00011110

```
  11100001      (one's complement)
+        1
  11100010
```

Answer: -30 = 11100010

3 Add the positive two's complement of 70 and the negative two's complement of 30 together.

```
     01001011    (75)
    +11100011    (-30)
{1}  00101101
```

You will notice that there are now nine bits. You can ignore the extra bit as eight bits are commonly used to represent numbers.

Answer: $75 + -30 = 00101101_2$

(You should check for yourself that 00101101_2 is the binary representation of the correct answer, 45.)

CHECK YOUR PROGRESS

Using two's complement ONLY, perform the following calculations:

a 90 - 30   **b** 52 - 27   **c** 88 - 49

Summary of key points

In this topic you have learned:

- that positive and negative integers can be represented by the sign and magnitude method or by the two's complement method.
- that binary subtraction can be carried out using two's complement.

QUESTIONS

1 Give the sign and magnitude values of the following integers:
 a +24   **b** -24   **c** -119

2 Give the two's complement representation of the following integers:
 a -37   **b** -95   **c** -1

3 What is the decimal value of the following two's complement representations?
 a 10001011   **b** 01001111   **c** 11100010

4 Using two's complement ONLY, perform the following calculations:
 a 121 - 7   **b** 75 - 37

1.9 Storing and representing digits and characters

Computer systems use the number systems you have been studying in order to carry out calculations. Once a calculation is completed, the result has to be displayed in decimal format on a screen, for example on electronic scoreboards at sports events, calculators, microwave ovens and digital clocks.

For this purpose, each individual digit is given its own binary code.

Binary coded decimal (BCD) representation

Binary coded decimal (BCD) is an encoding system where each decimal digit is represented by 4 bits, before it is transmitted to the display. The display device then interprets the code and generates the digit. BCD representation is not usually used for calculations.

Converting from decimal to BCD

The following steps are used to convert decimal digits to BCD.

Example: Represent the digits 4901 in BCD form.

1 Convert each decimal digit into its four-bit binary value.

4	9	0	1
↓	↓	↓	↓
0100	1001	0000	0001

Answer: 4901 = 0100100100000001

Fig 1.59: A digital display in a calculator using BCD

CHECK YOUR PROGRESS

Give the BCD representations of the following numbers:

a 91 b 430 c 256 d 781 e 2852

In order to convert the BCD representation to decimal you can use the following steps.

Example: Convert BCD representation 010101111001 to decimal.

1 Group the binary code into sections of four bits.

2 Convert each group of four bits into decimal. Put them together.

0	1	0	1	0	1	1	1	1	0	0	1
2^3	2^2	2^1	2^0	2^3	2^2	2^1	2^0	2^3	2^2	2^1	2^0

$$5 \qquad\qquad 7 \qquad\qquad 9$$

Answer: $010100001001 = 579$

CHECK YOUR PROGRESS

1 If the binary representation 100000000101 is a BCD representation of an integer, what is its decimal value?

2 Convert the following BCD values into decimal:

   a 00101001   **d** 10010111

   b 00110000   **e** 10000001

   c 01110101

Converting from binary to BCD

The digits used on display screens, such as calculators, will often be the result of a calculation. That calculation will have been carried out by the system in binary, which means that the system will have to convert a binary integer into its BCD display values.

The following steps are used to convert binary integers to BCD.

Example: Represent 10011011_2 in BCD form.

1 Convert the binary integer to decimal.

Binary number	1	0	0	1	1	0	1	1
Place value	27	26	25	24	23	22	21	20

$(1 \times 2^7) + (0 \times 2^6) + (0 \times 2^5) + (1 \times 2^4) + (1 \times 2^3) + (0 \times 2^2) + (1 \times 2^1) + (1 \times 2^0)$

$128 + 0 + 0 + 16 + 8 + 0 + 2 + 1 = 155$

2 Convert the decimal to BCD

1	5	5
↓	↓	↓
0001	0101	0101

Answer: $10011011_2 = 000101010101$ in BCD

CHECK YOUR PROGRESS

Convert the following binary integers to BCD:

a 1101_2 **b** 110100_2 **c** 01010101_2 **d** 01110011_2 **e** 10000000_2

Converting from BCD to binary

Example: Convert the BCD value 01111001 to binary.

1 Convert the BCD value to decimal.

0	1	1	1		1	0	0	1
2^3	2^2	2^1	2^0		2^3	2^2	2^1	2^0

          7   9

2 Convert the decimal to binary.

	Quotient	Remainder
79/2=	39	1
39/2=	19	1
19/2=	9	1
9/2=	4	1
4/2=	2	0
2/2 =	1	0
1/2 =	0	1

Answer: 01111001 in BCD = 1001111_2

CHECK YOUR PROGRESS

Convert the following BCD values to binary integers:

a 0101 **b** 00110100 **c** 01010101 **d** 01110011 **e** 10000000

Character	ASCII (7-bit code)	Decimal value
0	0100000	48
1	0100001	49
2	0100010	50
3	0100011	51
4	0100100	52
5	0100101	53
6	0100110	54
7	0100111	55
8	0101000	56
9	0101001	57
A	1000001	65
B	1000010	66
C	1000011	67
D	1000100	68
E	1000101	69
F	1000110	70
G	1000111	71
H	1001000	72
I	1001001	73
J	1001010	74
K	1001011	75
L	1001100	76
M	1001101	77
N	1001110	78
O	1001111	79
P	1010000	80
Q	1010001	81
R	1010010	82
S	1010011	83
T	1010100	84
U	1010101	85
V	1010110	86
W	1010111	87
X	1011000	88
Y	1011001	89
Z	1011010	90

ASCII representation

A character is considered to be anything that you can key in from a keyboard. It can be a digit, a letter, a space or a special character. Characters are represented using binary patterns called **character codes**. The most common character code used by modern computers is ASCII (American Standard Code for Information Interchange).

ASCII uses seven-bit binary patterns to represent characters. An extra bit is added to the front as the eighth bit to form the byte. Table 1.3 shows some characters, their ASCII representations and their decimal values.

WHAT DOES IT MEAN?

character code
Character codes are binary patterns used to represent characters.

Table 1.3: The ASCII character codes

Let's look at how to give the ASCII representation of a character.

Example: In a computer system using the seven-bit ASCII representation, the letter J would be represented by 1001010 or 74_{10}. Give the ASCII representations of letters E and P.

1 If the ASCII representation is in binary form convert it into decimal. If it is in decimal calculate the decimal value for the letters you want to find the ASCII representation.

Since J is 74, E will be 69 (E = 74-5, because E is 5 letters behind J) and P will be 80 (P = 74+6, because P is 6 letters away from J).

2 Convert the decimal value for each letter into its binary and the answer will be the ASCII representation of the letter.

	Quotient	Remainder
69/2 =	34	1
34/2=	17	0
17/2=	8	1
8/2 =	4	0
4/2 =	2	0
2/2 =	1	0
1/2 =	0	1

	Quotient	Remainder
80/2 =	40	0
40/2 =	20	0
20/2 =	10	0
10/2 =	5	0
5/2 =	2	1
2/2 =	1	0
1/2 =	0	1

E = 69

P = 80

Answer: E = 1000101, P = 1010000

CHECK YOUR PROGRESS

1 The ASCII representation of letter F has a decimal value of 70. What is the ASCII representation of letter K? Try not to use Table 1.3.
2 Suppose the ASCII representation of letter J is 1001010, what is the representation of letters F, M, Q and Y?

Summary of key points

In this topic you have learned:

- that digits used in a display can be represented by binary coded decimal (BCD).
- that characters are represented by ASCII.

QUESTIONS

1 Give the BCD representations of the following numbers:
   a 79   **b** 856   **c** 5901

2 Convert the following BCD values into decimal:
   a 10010011   **b** 011100100001   **c** 100010010000

3 Convert the following binary integers to BCD:
   a 1110102   **b** 110100112   **c** 111111112

4 Convert the following BCD values to binary integers:
   a 01110001   **b** 10000001   **c** 01000101

5 The ASCII representation of letter P has a decimal value of 80. What is the ASCII representation of letter S? Try not to use Table 1.3.

End-of-section questions

Multiple-choice questions

1 Which of the following is a major function of the Control Unit?
   A To store information that is currently being used.
   B To read and interpret instructions.
   C To store information that is not currently being used.
   D To perform logical operations

2 Which of the following statements best describes word size?
   A The number of seconds a computer takes to complete an operation.
   B The number of times the process needs to be executed to complete an operation.
   C The number of bits that computer can handle in one operation.
   D The number of bytes or kilobytes in a sector of a secondary storage medium.

3 John got an email with a size of 100b. The total number of characters that the email would contain would be:
   A 1024   C 1000
   B 100   D 102400

4 The secondary storage medium commonly used in archiving is:
   A flash memory   C movable head hard disk
   B fixed head hard disk   D magnetic tape

5 Which of the following is a direct access secondary storage medium?
   A reel to reel tape   C magnetic disk
   B cartridge tape   D magnetic tape

6 An input device commonly used in marking multiple-choice examination questions is:
   A OCR   C MICR
   B OMR   D POS

7 The following are all non-impact printers except:
   A Laser   C Plotter
   B Inkjet   D Dot matrix

8 Which of the following is the most suitable output device to print an architectural drawing on a very large paper?
   A laser printer   C dot-matrix printer
   B inkjet printer   D plotter

9 The decimal value of BCD representation 010101110001 is:
   A 560   C 561
   B 570   D 571

10 Which of the following are functions of an operating system?
   I process management
   II memory management
   III user interface
   IV security
   A I and II only   C I, II and IV only
   B I, II and III only   D I, II, III and IV

Structured questions

1 A computer system completes a task by using four stages of operations: input, processing, output and storage.
   a State the difference between input and output.
   b What is processing?
   c Why is storage needed in a computer system?

2 Two types of ROM are PROM and EPROM.
   a What do the abbreviations PROM and EPROM stand for?
   b State the difference between PROM and EPROM.
   c Give one application in which PROM can be used.
   d Give one application in which EPROM can be used.

3 In terms of storage size, state the difference between:
   a Megabyte and Terabyte
   b Gigabyte and Kilobyte
   c Word and Byte

4 The following descriptions refer to secondary storage media and devices. Give the correct terms they describe.
   a A device that reads/writes information on disks.
   b The concentric circles or rings into which a disk is divided.
   c The pie-shaped sections found on the concentric circles.
   d The same track numbers joined together in a hard disk.
   e A device that makes electronic marks on a disk in preparation for storage.

5 Two popular character readers are OCR and MICR.
   a What do the abbreviations OCR and MICR stand for?
   b Give one application in which MICR is commonly used.
   c Give one application in which OCR is commonly used.
   d List two advantages of using OCR/MICR for data entry over using manual methods.

6 Suggest suitable input devices for the following tasks:
   a to video chat
   b to make a soft copy text from hard copy text
   c to accept voice instructions and give answers
   d to indicate temperature differences
   e to input text data

7 a If a system uses Binary Coded Decimal for representing integers, what will be the representation of the following:
   i -390110 and +390110
   ii -278510 and +287510
   b What will be the decimal value of the following BCD representations?
   i 1010100100000011
   ii 1011000101100111

8 a Convert the following:
   i   3510 to hexadecimal
   ii 3510 to octal.
   iii 10010010012 to octal
   iv 10010010012 to hexadecimal

b Suppose the two's complement representation of an integer is 10010011, what is its decimal equivalent?

c ASCII is one of the most popular character representations.

   i What does the abbreviation ASCII stand for?

   ii Suppose the ASCII representation of letter H is 1001000, what is the representation of M & D?

9 Harry went to a computer shop to get the specification for the computer system he intended to purchase. The sales man gave him the following specifications:

Intel Pentium IV 2.6 GHz

2 GB DDR RAM (Max 4 GB) 256 MHz

1.5 TB SATA HDD 10000 rpm

6 USB ports

1 Firewire port

1 wireless keyboard

1 wireless mouse

a List TWO reasons why it is important to know the specifications of a computer system before you purchase it.

b From the specifications given above, list:

   i the speed of the processor

   ii the storage capacity of the hard disk

   iii the memory size

   iv the memory type

   v the memory speed

   vi the speed of hard the disk

c What is the purpose of a firewire port in a computer system?

d In the second line of specification (2 GB DDR RAM (Max 4 GB) 256 MHz) what does Max 4 GB represent?

10 Access time and storage capacity are two factors that you should consider when you are purchasing storage media.

a State why it is important to know the access time of a storage media.

b List the following in order of their access time, fastest first:

Floppy disk, fixed head hard disk, CD, movable head hard disk, pen drive

c What is meant by 'storage capacity'?

d List the following in order of their storage capacity, largest first.

Floppy disk, hard disk, CD, pen drive

Objectives

By the end of this section, you will be able to:

- Outline the steps in problem-solving and break down a problem into its parts.
- Understand the variables, constants and data types used when solving problems on a computer.
- Explain and develop algorithms.
- Represent algorithms in pseudocode or flowcharts.

Sections 2 and 3 introduce you to a number of techniques for solving problems on a computer. In this section you will learn about the methods you use when you first start thinking about a problem. In the next section you will learn how to convert your solutions into computer programs.

Computers can only do exactly what they are instructed to do. That means that we have to be very precise when planning the solution to a problem that will be programmed into a computer system.

So it is important that you analyse a problem and develop its solution on paper before you start programming. That is why you need to spend some time really getting to grips with the methods introduced in Section 2 before you start on Section 3.

● *2.1–2.4* # Problem-solving using computers

General problem-solving

In our life we are faced with many problems. Every problem requires a solution to resolve it. For any problem, you might have more than one solution. Finding the correct solution to a problem can be considered as *problem-solving*. Problem-solving involves identifying, analysing and resolving problems using logic, reasoning skills and analytical skills.

You can go to school every day using various means of transportation. We can consider this as a problem. You have options like:

a Go with your parents in their vehicle.

b Go with your friend or neighbour in their vehicle.

c Catch a bus.

d Go by bicycle.

e Walk.

Maybe the school is far and you or your parents are not comfortable that you travel with others on a daily basis, then you would choose the first option. Sometimes your parent's vehicle is not available then you have to use the other options. From this you get the clear idea that a problem can have many solutions, but you should use whichever solution is most suitable to solve the problem.

Generally problems can be solved by following stages:

Stage 1: Definition of the problem

In this first stage, you have to look at the problem carefully and identify what is the actual problem, and then write it down. This is known as the *problem statement*. By doing this you will be able to ensure that you have the right problem to solve. In the above example your definition of problem would be *how to reach school on time*.

Stage 2: Analyse the problem

In this stage, you need to look at the problem and identify the inputs, outputs and processing that is required to complete the task. In order to reach school your input will be getting the transportation, output will be reaching school on time, and processing would be travelling in the chosen transportation.

Stage 3: Propose and evaluate possible solutions

As realised above, problems may have more than one solution. In this stage you are to identify the solutions that are available, see which ones are suitable for solving the task and the strength and weakness of each solution. In the above problem statement you

THINK ABOUT IT

Think about problems you may have solved recently, for example, choosing some new shoes, or deciding what career you would like to pursue. Did you use these five stages of problem-solving? Could you have solved the problem better if you had used the five stages?

had many options so you would need to decide which one of them is most suitable for you.

Stage 4: Select and justify the optimal solutions

By looking at the solutions and their strengths and weaknesses, choose the most efficient or suitable (optimal) solution that will solve the problem. If your parent's vehicle is broken, you might catch a bus.

Stage 5: Implementation and review

In this stage, the optimal solution is put into practice and checked to see if it works. Observe the solution and review it to see everything is fine with it. For example, after choosing the option of catching the bus, you may find that the bus stopped many times and made you late for school. So when you choose an option next time you will be able factor that into your decision as to whether you should go by bus or implement another option.

Computer-based problem-solving

Breaking down the problem into its significant parts

When computers are used for solving problems, the stages or steps used for general problem-solving have to be modified as we have to give the instructions to the computer to make it solve the problem for you. So the revised steps for computer-based problem-solving will be:

Stage 1: Definition of the problem

As mentioned earlier in the stages of general problem-solving, this is where the actual problem is clearly defined. The problem must be looked at carefully and if it is not phrased properly, you should modify that to make sure that it is clearly stated. We know that once a problem is well understood, we can solve it easily.

Stage 2: Analyse the problem

In this stage, you need to identify the inputs to be used, outputs required, values to be stored (if any), and the processing that needs to be done to get the correct outputs. Inputs will be the instructions that are needed to solve the problem, processing will be working with the given instructions, output will be the expected results and storage will be the values that need to be stored in order to display the results. It is a good practise to break down the problem into its four pieces as input, processing, output and storage.

Now let's look a simple problem that needs to be solved using a computer:

Example: *Get two numbers, add them together and display their sum.*

First of all, you might wonder if this is a problem statement, as you can solve it easily once you have a calculator to add the numbers or if you can get a piece of paper to add them manually. But it is not easy for the computer to solve this problem as it can't work on its own. You need to give all the instructions for it to perform. This is the reason why it is good to break down the problem into its parts to make the computer easily solve it for you.

An IPO (Input-Processing-Output) diagram can be used to breakdown the problem. An IPO diagram is a table with three columns showing the input, output and processing parts of the problem. Storage is a form of processing because the computer stores data by using its processing capabilities.

Table 2.1 is an IPO diagram showing the breakdown of problem into its parts.

Input	Processing	Output
Two numbers	Accept two numbers Add the numbers Store results Display the result	Sum

Table 2.1

As you can see, input will be two numbers, processing involves accepting these two numbers, adding them and storing the results, and output is the sum, the result of adding these two numbers together.

Stage 3: Propose and evaluate possible solutions

In the problem of how to get to school, we noted that there are many solutions. Generally, all problem statements have more than one option. So, you evaluate each option to see which is most appropriate for you and choose the best option.

Stage 4: Develop and represent an algorithm

In this stage, break down the problem into simple manageable steps, so that you can handle them easily. These simple steps of a problem are known as an **algorithm**. You will learn about the algorithms in detail later in the section on page 76.

Stage 5: Test and validate the algorithm

Check the algorithm you wrote using some values to ensure that it produces the required results. This process of **desk checking** allows you to solve some errors before you convert it into computer instructions.

Stage 6: Implement the algorithm

In this stage, the steps of algorithm are written using a programming language so that a computer can operate on it. When the instructions are in a programming language, the instructions are called a **program**.

Stage 7: Run the program

In this stage, run your program using a programming language to see if the program is producing the correct results.

Stage 8: Document and maintain the program

This involves preparing documentation that will help the user to operate the program and maintain the program by making changes to the program from time to time, if needed.

Constants, variables and literals

Computers use memory to store data and information. Each of the data items being inputted has to be stored in a location in the computer's memory. You could consider memory as a collection of boxes. Each of these boxes can hold values, that is, data items. To represent a box to store a value, it is represented with a label called an **identifier**.

There are two kinds of identifiers: **variables** and **constants**.

An identifier that can store any value is called a variable. An identifier that always holds the same value is called a constant.

Num1

Num2

| 10 | 15 |

Fig. 2.1: Storing values in a memory location

In Fig 2.1 above, Num1 and Num2 are identifiers for two memory locations and they store the values 10 and 15. Num1 and Num2 are variables as they are identifiers of storage locations that can store any values.

Please note that when a new value is placed in a variable, the old value is *overwritten* by the new value because, as you can see, only one place is there to store the value for each variable. The value stored in a constant cannot be changed.

Literals are constants that are written *literally* as itself rather than as a value. Examples of literals include 'the sum is', 'largest=' and 'enter number'. They are normally used with the input/output instructions that appear as a message for the user.

Data types

The problem statements that we looked at earlier required data or inputs to be given to the computer to solve the problem. To do this, data must be given to the computer in a way it recognises. **Data type** determines the type of data that a variable can store. A data type that treats a variable as a single unit is called an elementary data type.

A variable can store any of the following data types:

- Integers: These are whole numbers, positive or negative without decimal places, e.g. 5, -45, 39, and +126.
- Floating point or real numbers: These are positive or negative numbers with decimal values, e.g. 0.55, 39.2, -5.6 and +6.7.
- Characters: A character is anything that you can key in from a keyboard. This includes letters, numbers and special characters, e.g. k, L, # and *.

Summary of key points

In this topic you have learned:

- that a problem can be solved in stages.
- how a problem can be broken down in parts.
- that data is stored as variables, constants and literals.
- that the data stored in variables belongs to a data type.

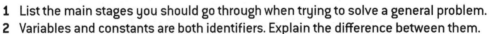

QUESTIONS

1 List the main stages you should go through when trying to solve a general problem.
2 Variables and constants are both identifiers. Explain the difference between them.
3 What is the difference between an integer and a floating point number?

2.5 Problem-solving using algorithms

As you are aware, computers are problem-solving devices. But computers cannot solve problems by themselves; you have to give them very clear instructions.

When we want instructions to be very clear, we often break them down into smaller parts, or steps. For example, if your mom wanted you to bake a chicken, she would give you the instructions in several steps that you could easily follow, like

1 Preheat your oven to 350 degrees.

2 Wash the chicken thoroughly with water.

3 Sprinkle salt and seasoning over each piece.

4 Put the chicken in the baking dish and place it in the oven without covering.

5 Bake at 350 degrees for about one and a half hours or until the skin becomes a golden brown colour.

6 Take it out from the oven and your baked chicken is ready to serve.

We do the same when writing instructions for computers. These steps or instructions that can be used to complete a task are called an algorithm. The word algorithm comes from the word 'algorism', meaning the process of doing calculations with Arabic numerals. Later, 'algorism' combined with the word arithmetic to form 'algorithm'.

Bear in mind that these sets of steps or instructions will help us to create instructions that are understandable to computers. When algorithms are converted into a language that is understandable to a computer, it becomes a program. Also remember that, you should create an algorithm before writing a program, not the reverse.

THINK ABOUT IT

A recipe is a kind of algorithm. Have you come across any other algorithms in real life? They are not usually referred to as algorithms, but perhaps as instructions.

Characteristics of algorithms

A good algorithm should have the following characteristics:

1 **The number of steps must be *finite***

This means that the computer has a definite number of instructions to follow, and when it comes to the end of those steps, it has completed the task. For example, when telling you how to bake the chicken, your mom wouldn't leave out any steps, or forget to tell you to take it out of the oven once it was baked. Some algorithms might have steps or instructions that need to repeated, but there should still be a clear end to the process.

2 **The steps must be *precise***

The instructions or steps must be accurate; a computer cannot think for itself, so if you make a mistake in the instructions, it will have an incorrect outcome. For example, if your mom told you to bake the chicken for six hours instead of one and a half, your chicken would be burned!

3 **The steps must be *unambiguous***

The steps must be very clear so that they can be carried out easily – it wouldn't work if your mom just told you to put the chicken in the oven without saying for how long or at what temperature. An instruction that can be carried out is called an **efficient instruction**.

4 **The steps must have flow of control from one process to another.**

There may be many processes involved in a problem, but each process must be related and should have a clear flow from one to the other. For example, you mom would tell you to get the ingredients together for seasoning, then to mix the seasoning, and then apply it to the chicken.

5 **The steps must *terminate***

There must be a clear end to the instructions. The final step in the process of baking a chicken would be to take the chicken out of the oven. The steps for solving the problem must have a start and end.

6 **The steps must lead to an *output***

An algorithm must have at least one output. In the example of baking a chicken, the output would be to have a baked chicken!

WHAT DOES IT MEAN?

efficient Instruction
An efficient instruction is one that is clear and can be carried out.

flow of control
A logical flow from one process to the next is known as a flow of control.

Steps for developing an algorithm

Any algorithm that is used to solve a problem or task can be divided into three main steps:

1 **The input step** – This is where the instructions from the user are being gathered.

2 **The processing step** – This is where the instructions are worked through. It can involve all or some of the following steps:

   a Assignment – In this step the values are assigned to variables.

   b Decision – This step will be included when you have to check for any conditions to be followed.

   c Repetition – When you have to repeat a task a specified number of times then you would include this step.

3 **The output step** – This step is used to display the results.

Let's look at the three steps for the following problem statement:

Example: *Get the length and width of a rectangle and calculate and display its area.*

In this problem statement, you would notice that inputs are the length and width of the rectangle, and output is its area. Processing involves accepting the length and width, calculating the area and storing it. This problem requires you to use the formula for calculating the area (multiply length by width).

So when a statement of a problem is given, you need to identify these three main steps, as we did in the previous problem statement. Look at the statement carefully and identify the input, output and processing that are required. Normally, the input and output will be expressed in the form of nouns and adjectives. The processing required will be in the form of verbs or adverbs.

Summary of key points

In this topic you have learned:

- that a solution can be found by breaking the problem down into steps in an algorithm.
- that an algorithm should be finite, precise, unambiguous.
- that an algorithm should have a logical flow of control, should terminate and should produce an output.

QUESTIONS

1 What is an algorithm?
2 List four characteristics of a good algorithm.
3 What are the three main steps involved in creating an algorithm?
4 What is meant by assignment?

Control structures

● *2.5–2.6*

The steps that are identified for preparing algorithms can be written using three basic **control structures** or program constructs to indicate how instructions will be carried out or how the flow of control from one statement would take place. They are:

1 Sequence
2 Selection
3 Iteration (Repetition)

Sequence

The **sequence** control structure is used when you have instructions to be carried out in a *particular* order. In an algorithm these instructions can be written in the order you want it to happen, as follows:

Instruction 1 or step 1
Instruction 2 or step 2
Instruction 3 or step 3
Instruction 4 or step 4

Here, the instructions will be completed in the order given. This control structure can be used for problems involving accepting inputs, performing calculations and storing them, and displaying the outputs. The following is a typical example of an algorithm that uses the sequence control structure where Steps 1 to 5 will be completed in the order given.

> **Step 1:** Start
> **Step 2:** Get two numbers
> **Step 3:** Add the numbers and store it in Answer
> **Step 4:** Display Answer
> **Step 5:** Stop

WHAT DOES IT MEAN?

control structure
Control structures are instructions or statements that determine the flow of control of steps in an algorithm.

sequence
Sequence is a control structure where instructions are written in the order they should take place.

selection
Selection is a control structure where a choice has to be made between two or more options.

Selection

The **selection** control structure is used in problems with instructions to be carried out *if a certain condition is met*. The choice of options will be dependent on whether the condition is true or false. Selection control structure statements commonly used in algorithms are normally written as:

If <condition> then <instructions to be performed if the condition is true> else <instructions to be performed if the condition is false>

The following is an example of an algorithm with a selection control structure.

> **Step 1:** Start
> **Step 2:** Accept score

Step 3: If score more than 59 then display 'the student has passed' else display 'student has failed'

Step 4: Stop

In the above example, if the score of a student is more than 59 it will display 'the student has passed' and if it is less than 60 it will display 'the student has failed', which means only one of the two messages can be displayed. If the condition is true (the score is more than 59), the part after 'then' will be carried out, otherwise the part after 'else' will be carried out.

Iteration or repetition or loop

Iteration forms the repetitive stage of the processing step. There are times where we have to repeat a process. Suppose you want to accept 100 numbers from the user and find their sum, it would be wise to *repeat the process* of getting the numbers 100 times rather than writing instructions 100 times to accept the numbers. Repetition of a set of instructions a fixed number of times is called **bounded iteration**. Commonly used iteration statements in algorithms include *for-endfor*.

There are also situations where the process has to be repeated until a specific condition becomes false. For example, find the sum of a set of numbers terminated by 0. Here, getting numbers and finding their sum will be repeated until the user supplies 0 as the value for the number. Repeating a set of steps a number of times until a particular condition becomes false is called unbounded iteration. Common **unbounded iteration** statements are *while-endwhile*, and *repeat-until*.

WHAT DOES IT MEAN?

repetition or iteration
Repetition or iteration control structures are used to repeat a certain process a number of times.

bounded iteration
Bounded iteration is the process of repeating a set of steps or instructions a fixed number of times.

unbounded iteration
Unbounded iteration is the process of repeating a set of steps or instructions until a particular condition becomes false.

Summary of key points

In this topic you have learned:

- that algorithms use the control structures of sequence, selection and iteration.

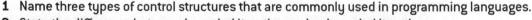

QUESTIONS

1 Name three types of control structures that are commonly used in programming languages.
2 State the difference between bounded iteration and unbounded iteration.
3 Give one example of statement used in following control structures:
   a Selection
   b Bounded iteration
   c Unbounded iteration

How to create algorithms for problem statements

Now that you understand how algorithms are created and their components, let's look at some problem statements and write algorithms for them.

Problem statement 1

Write an algorithm that will accept three numbers, add them together and print their sum.

1 First we gather the user values. In the problem statement, 'three numbers' is the input and 'sum' is the output required. 'Accept', 'add' and 'print' represent the processing that needs to be done. Storage will take place when the calculated values of the three numbers are assigned to sum.

   You should also check the problem statement to see if any control structures are needed. Since there is no need for decision making, the selection control structure is not required. Also there is no need for repeating processes, so the repetition stage is not required.

2 Now let's break down the problem into steps and write it in the form of single specific tasks to form the algorithm:

   Step 1: Start.
   Step 2: Accept three numbers.
   Step 3: Add the numbers entered.
   Step 4: Display the sum.
   Step 5: Stop.

Problem statement 2

In the above problem statement, the processing step only required you to carry out assignment of the values, so now let's look at one that involves decision.

Prepare an algorithm that will read the price of an item and display its new price after a discount of 10% if the price is more than $100.

1 In this problem statement, the input is 'price' and output is 'new price'. The processing involves checking the price, and finding the discount, if required. As the potential discount depends on what the price is, the decision step will be required. However, this statement does not involve repeating a process, so there is no need for the repetition step.

2 The algorithm can be written as:

   Step 1: Start.
   Step 2: Get the price.

Step 3: Check to see if price is more than $100.

Step 4: If price is more than $100, calculate the discount using the formula discount = price * 10/100.

Step 5: Calculate the new price by using the formula new price = price − discount.

Step 6: Display the new price.

Step 7: Stop.

Problem statement 3

Create an algorithm that will read three numbers and find the largest among them.

1 For this problem statement you need to understand that the processing involves checking and comparing three numbers to find the largest. You could approach this problem in many ways, but let's concentrate on two popular methods. The two versions of the algorithm are as follows:

2 **Method 1**

In the first method you could compare the first number with the other two numbers to see which is larger, and then compare the second and third numbers the same way.

Step 1: Start.

Step 2: Get three numbers.

Step 3: Check if the first number is bigger than the second and third number, if it is bigger then display first number as the largest.

Step 4: Check if the second number is bigger than the first and third number, if it is bigger then display second number as the largest.

Step 5: Check if the third number is bigger than the first and second number, if it is bigger then display third number as the largest.

Step 6: Stop.

3 **Method 2**

In the second method, comparison is made of the first and second numbers to find the largest and then the largest of the two is compared with the third number.

Step 1: Start.

Step 2: Get three numbers.

Step 3: Check if the first number is bigger than the second number, then store the value of first number as the largest. Otherwise store the value of second number as the largest.

Step 4: Check if the largest of the first two numbers is bigger than the third number. If it is, then store the value of third number as the largest.

Step 5: Display the largest number.

Step 6: Stop.

From this process, you can see that you can have several solutions for a problem-solving statement based on the approach of the programmer.

Summary of key points

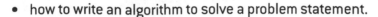

In this topic you have learned:

- how to write an algorithm to solve a problem statement.

1 For each of the following problem statements
   a identify the input, output and processing steps.
   b write the algorithm.
   - Write an algorithm to read three numbers and find their product.
   - Write an algorithm that displays the area of a rectangle by accepting length and width from the user.
   - Write an algorithm that will read the radius of a circle and calculate and display its perimeter.

● 2.6–2.7 # Representing an algorithm using narrative and pseudocode

In the previous topics, you learned that algorithms are step-by-step definitions of a task or a problem. In this topic you will learn about how they are represented. Algorithms can be represented in three different ways, they are:

1 Narrative
2 Pseudocode
3 Flowchart

Narrative

Narrative, also called general algorithm, is where each step in the algorithm is written in clear, simple language. It does not use any computer language or coding. This is similar to how you have been writing algorithms so far.

For example, if you wanted to write an algorithm to read in three numbers then find and display their sum, the narrative could be:

Step 1: Start.
Step 2: Get the three numbers.
Step 3: Add the numbers.
Step 4: Store the results in Sum.
Step 5: Display Sum.
Step 6: Stop.

WHAT DOES IT MEAN?

narrative
Narrative is a representation of an algorithm where each instruction is written in everyday language.

As you can see, each instruction would be clearly understood by any person who speaks English.

Now let's look at some other examples of narrative.

Narrative algorithm 1

Write an algorithm in narrative form to read in three numbers from the keyboard and calculate and display their product.

Remember that, when given a problem statement, you first need to identify the words that describe input, output and processing. So, in the above problem statement, the inputs are the three numbers and their product is the output. The processing involves accepting three numbers and calculating the product, which is multiplying the numbers. So the narrative would be:

Step 1: Start.
Step 2: Get the three numbers.
Step 3: Calculate the product by multiplying the numbers.
Step 4: Store the results in Product.
Step 5: Display Product.
Step 6: Stop.

Narrative algorithm 2

Prepare an algorithm in narrative that will accept the length and width of a rectangle and calculate and display its area.

In the problem statement above, the inputs are the length and the width of the rectangle and output needed is its area. The processing involves accepting the values for length and width and calculating the area by multiplying the length and width. So the narrative can be:

Step 1: Start.
Step 2: Get the length and the width.
Step 3: Calculate the area by multiplying the length and width.
Step 4: Store the results Area.
Step 5: Display the area.
Step 6: Stop.

Narrative algorithm 3

Create an algorithm in narrative that will prompt the user to enter the salary of an employee and calculate the income tax at 15% if the salary is more than $5000. Display the salary and tax.

Now, in this algorithm, the input is the salary and the processing involves prompting the user to enter the salary, checking to see if the salary is more than 5000 and calculating the income tax. The output is displaying the salary and the income tax. So the narrative can be written as:

Step 1: Start.
Step 2: Prompt the user to enter the salary.
Step 3: Get the salary.
Step 4: Check if the salary is more than 5000, if it is calculate the tax by multiplying the salary by 15%.
Step 5: Display the salary and tax.
Step 6: Stop.

Pseudocode

As you know, we create algorithms in preparation for giving instructions to the computer. The instructions have to be in a form that is understandable to computers, so are written using a programming language.

Narrative steps are very simple and useful for when you start learning about programming, but when you are comfortable with programming you can create algorithms using instructions with words and symbols that closely resemble computer **programming language** instructions. This form of representation is called **pseudocode**. The name 'pseudocode' comes from 'pseudo', meaning 'fake' and 'code' meaning program. In pseudocode even though the terms used closely resemble programming language terms, they are used without following the rigid rules of the language.

Pseudocode language

The pseudocode can contain variables, constants, operators, and terminology used in programming languages.

Variables

As you know, variables are used to store values that can change. These values can be a user input or result of a calculation and are stored in a location in the memory with a name chosen by the programmer called a variable name. Examples of variable names that can be used in pseudocode are num1, num2, sum, average, etc.

Constants

Constants are fixed values used when you need to keep a value fixed. For example, when you have to calculate the area of a triangle using the formula 1/2* base* height, the value 1/2 will be a constant.

Operators

Operators are symbols used for performing calculations or making comparisons. Commonly used operators in pseudocode are:

1 Arithmetic operators – operators used to perform mathematical operations. Table 2.2 represents the main arithmetic operators and their operations.

Arithmetic operator	Operation
+	Addition
-	Subtraction
*	Multiplication
/	Division

Table 2.2

2 Relational operators – operators used to check for comparisons. The table below shows commonly used relational operators and their operations.

Relational operator	Operation
>	greater than
<	less than
> =	greater than or equal to
< =	less than or equal to
< >	not equal to
=	equal to

Table 2.3

3 Logical operators – operators used to make comparisons with multiple criteria.

Logical operator	Operation
AND	And
OR	Or
NOT	Not

Table 2.4

Just as in mathematics, in computing all the operations are carried out in a hierarchical order. The computer follows the **BODMAS** rule. So anything in Brackets will be done first, followed by Orders (such as powers and square roots), then Division and Multiplication. Addition and Subtraction will be done last. So when you are writing instructions you must ensure that you write them in the order in which you want the computer to carry them out.

Pseudocode terminology

The general programming language terms used in pseudocode are:

- Terms used for the input step: input, read
- Terms used for the output step: output, write, display
- Terms used for the assignment step: set, store
- Terms used for selection: if-else-endif
- Terms used for iteration (bounded): for-endfor
- Terms used for iteration (unbounded): while-endwhile, repeat-until

Some programmers use terms in their pseudocode from other programming languages that they are comfortable with. However, this can create problems for somebody who is not familiar with that particular programming language. Generally it is wise to use terms like the ones given above so that any person can follow the logic of the program.

Pseudocode algorithm 1

Write a pseudocode algorithm to find the average of three numbers.

For this example, let's look at the narrative first and then write the corresponding pseudocode for it.

1 Narrative

Step 1: Start.
Step 2: Get the three numbers.
Step 3: Add the three numbers, divide by 3 and store the results.
Step 4: Display the results.
Step 5: Stop.

2 Pseudocode

Step 1: start
Step 2: read a (Accept the value for the first number and store it in a.)
Step 3: read b (Accept the value for the second number and store it in b.)
Step 4: read c (Accept the values for the third number and store it in c.)
Step 5: set average ← (a+b+c)/3 (Add the three numbers and divide it by 3 and store the results in average. The left arrow represents the assignment and it takes place from right to left meaning after the calculations the results will be stored in variable average. Also note that the brackets allow the addition of three numbers to take place before the division.)
Step 6: write average (Display the results stored in the variable average.)
Step 7: stop

Notice that in pseudocode, instructions are transformed into general programming language terms with variables, constants and statements.

Pseudocode algorithm 2

Prepare a pseudocode algorithm that will accept the length and width of a rectangle and calculate and display its area.

Step 1: start
Step 2: input length (Accept length and store it in variable length.)
Step 3: input width (Accept width and store it in variable width.)
Step 4: set area = length * width (Calculate the area by multiplying the values of length and width and store the results in area.)
Step 5: output area (display the results stored in variable area.)
Step 6: stop

As you can see, the two examples above used the control structure sequence, so each instruction will be carried out in the order it has been written. Now let's look at examples of pseudocode where the control structure selection is used.

Pseudocode algorithm 3

Create a pseudocode algorithm that will prompt the user to input two unequal numbers and find which is the larger.

Step 1: start
Step 2: write "Enter first number." (Prompt the user to input the value for the first number.)
Step 3: read a (Accept the value for the first number and store it in variable a.)
Step 4: write "Enter second number." (Prompt the user to input the value for the second number.)
Step 5: read b (Accept the value for the first number and store it in variable b.)
Step 6: if a>b then
        set large ← a
        else
        set large ← b
    endif (Check to see if a is bigger than b. If it is, then store the value of a in variable large otherwise store the value of b in variable large.)
Step 7: write large (Display the value of the variable large.)

In the example above, the selection construct if-then-else was used. When writing instructions over several lines, it is a good practise to write them in an indented format as in Step 6, because it increases the readability of the program and also helps to easily identify any errors.

Now, let's look at another example that involves multiple selection statements.

Pseudocode algorithm 4

Write a pseudocode that will accept three unequal numbers and find the smallest among them.

Step 1: start
Step 2: read num1,num2,num3 (Accept three numbers and store them in variables num1, num2 and num3.)
Step 3: if num1<num2 then
　　　　　　　　　　set sml ← num1
　　　　　　　　　　else
　　　　　　　　　　set sml ← num2
　　　　　endif　(Find the smaller of the first two numbers and store it in the variable sml.)
Step 4: if num3<sml then
　　　　　　　　　　sml = num3　(Check if the third number is smaller than the smaller value of the first two numbers, stored in variable sml. If it is, store the value of the third number in variable sml.)
　　　　　endif
Step 5: write sml (Display the value stored in sml.)
Step 6: stop

You will probably have noticed that in Step 2, the three variables are used in the same line instead of breaking them into three separate steps.

Now let's look at examples where iteration constructs are used. First, we will write some pseudocode that involves bounded iteration.

Pseudocode algorithm 5

Write a pseudocode algorithm that will accept 20 numbers and find their product.

Step 1: start
Step 2: set product ← 1 (Start product off with a value of 1.)
Step 3: for i ← 1 to 20 (This step repeats as the counter counts from 1 to 20.)
　　　　　　　　　　write "Enter next number"
　　　　　　　　　　read num
　　　　　　　　　　set product ← product * num　(Multiply the current value of product by the latest number entered.)
　　　　　endfor
Step 4: write "The product is" product
Step 5: stop

The variable i acts as a counter for the iteration that begins at Step 3. A counter must be an integer. When the algorithm reaches endfor it loops back to the 'for' line and adds 1 to the value of i. This continues until the last time, in this case, when i has a value of 20.

Now let's look another example with the unbounded iteration construct, using a while-endwhile loop.

Pseudocode algorithm 6

Write a pseudocode algorithm that will accept a group of numbers and calculate its sum. The program stops when the user enter 0 as the number.

Step 1: start
Step 2: set sum = 0 (Start sum off with a value of 0.)
Step 3: write "Enter first number."
Step 4: read num
Step 5: while num<>0 do

set sum ← sum + num (Add the current value of sum to the latest number entered.)
write "Enter next number. Enter 0 to finish"
read num

endwhile

Step 6: write "The sum is" sum
Step 7: stop

Summary of key points

In this topic you have learned:

• how to write an algorithm in narrative and pseudocode formats.

QUESTIONS

1 Write a narrative algorithm that will accept the radius of a circle and calculate and display its area.
2 Write a pseudocode algorithm that will accept three numbers and calculate and display the largest of the three.
3 Write a pseudocode algorithm that will accept the marks in a test for a group of 25 students then calculate and display the average mark.
4 Add steps to the previous algorithm so it also displays the highest mark.

2.6–2.7 Representing an algorithm using a flowchart

Flowcharts

WHAT DOES IT MEAN?

flowchart
A diagrammatic representation of an algorithm is called a flowchart.

Many of us find it easier to follow steps when they are represented diagrammatically or graphically. You may have come across **flowcharts** in your maths or design classes. They give a graphical representation of a process. Flowcharts for algorithms use the variables, constants and operators that are used in pseudocode language, but linked together by different shapes that represent each type of step. They are shown in Fig 2.2.

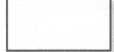

Terminator symbol (oval) – used to indicate the beginning/ending or start/stop of a problem.

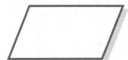

Process symbol (rectangle) – used to indicate the processing (assignment, calculations, etc).

Input/output symbol (parallelogram) – used to indicate the input and output of the problem.

Decision symbol (rhombus or diamond) – used in making a decision between two options – yes or no.

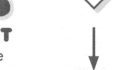

Flow control (arrow) – used to show the flow of control of steps.

Connector symbol (small circle) – used to connect sections of a flowchart when a flowchart is long and cannot fit on a page. A letter or digit can be placed in the small circle to indicate the link on the first page. Another identically labelled connector is placed on the next page to indicate the continuation of flow. So, two connectors with identical labels will serve the purpose of a long line of flow.

Fig 2.2

THINK ABOUT IT
Why do some people prefer seeing an algorithm as a diagram and others prefer seeing it in pseudocode?

Drawing flowcharts

The following steps will guide you in drawing a flowchart.

1 Go through the problem carefully and ensure that all the information needed to solve the problem is available, such as the inputs, processing that needs to be done and the outputs required.

2 Prepare a pseudocode algorithm so that you can get the steps.

3 Arrange the steps in a logical order – the order in which the instructions should take place.

4 Draw the flowchart for each step using the correct symbols or shapes and arrows to indicate the direction of flow.

Now let's draw some flowchart for examples of algorithms which were done earlier.

Flowchart algorithm 1

Write a pseudocode algorithm and draw a flowchart to find and display the sum of 10 and 20.

Pseudocode

Step 1: start
Step 2: set a ← 10
Step 3: set b ← 20
Step 4: set sum ← a+b
Step 5: write sum
Step 6: stop

Flowchart

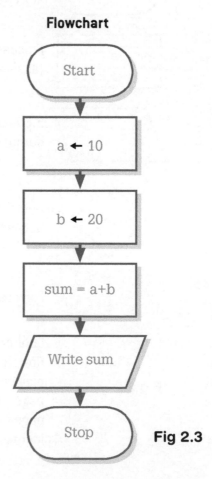

Fig 2.3

Flowchart algorithm 2

Draw a flowchart that will read three numbers and find the product of three numbers.

Pseudocode

Step 1: start
Step 2: read n1,n2,n3
Step 3: set product ← n1*n2*n3
Step 4: write product
Step 5: stop

Flowchart

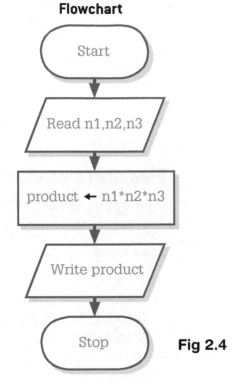

Fig 2.4

Flowchart algorithm 3

Draw a flowchart that will accept three numbers from the user and find and display their average.

Pseudocode

Step 1: start
Step 2: read n1,n2,n3
Step 3: set average ← (n1+n2+n3)/3
Step 4: write average
Step 5: stop

Flowchart

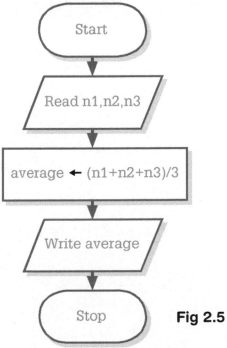

Fig 2.5

Let's now look at flowcharts that use the selection construct.

Flowchart algorithm 4

Draw a flowchart that will prompt the user to enter two unequal numbers and find the largest between them.

Pseudocode

Step 1: start
Step 2: write "Enter two unequal numbers."
Step 3: read n1,n2
Step 4: if n1>n2 then
           set large ← n1
           else
           set large ← n2
       endif
Step 5: write large
Step 6: stop

Flowchart

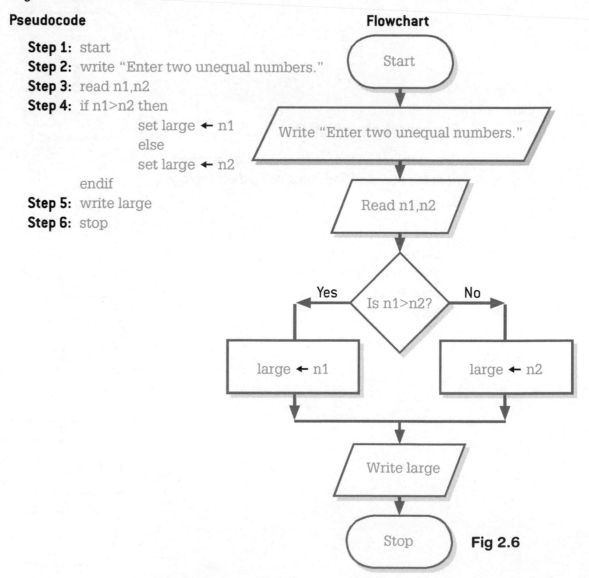

Fig 2.6

Flowchart algorithm 5

Draw a flowchart that will prompt the user to enter three unequal numbers and find the smallest among them.

Pseudocode

Step 1: start
Step 2: write "Enter three unequal numbers."
Step 3: read n1,n2,n3
Step 4: if n1<n2 then
        set sml ← n1
        else
        set sml ← n2
    endif
Step 5: if n3<sml then
        set sml ← n3
    endif
Step 6: write sml
Step 7: stop

Flowchart

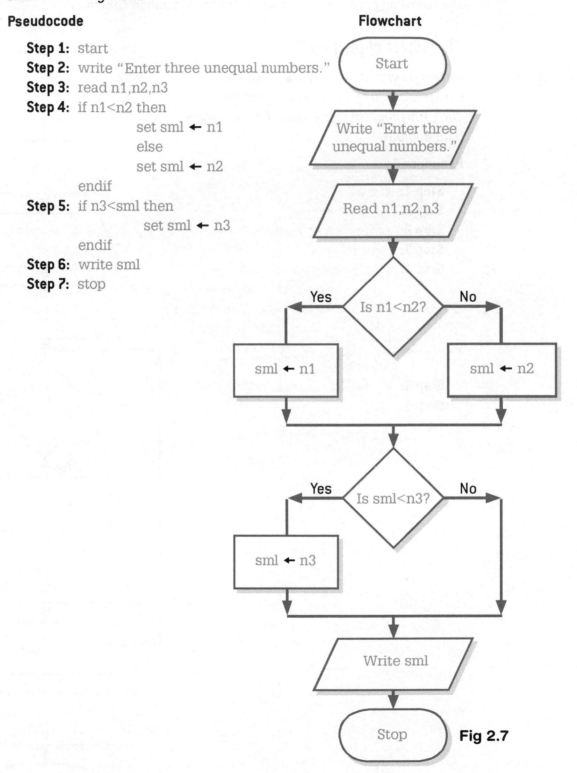

Fig 2.7

Flowcharts with unbounded iteration

The flowcharts that we have looked at so far were based on sequencing and selection. The following are flowcharts with repetition or iteration construct.

Flowchart algorithm 6

Draw a flowchart for a program that will accept a group of numbers and find their sum. The program stops when the user enters 0 for number.

Pseudocode

Step 1: start
Step 2: set sum ← 0
Step 2: write "Enter number."
Step 3: read num
Step 4: while num<>0 do

set sum ← sum + num
write "Enter number.
Enter 0 to finish"
read num

endwhile
Step 5: write "The sum is" sum
Step 6: stop

Flowchart

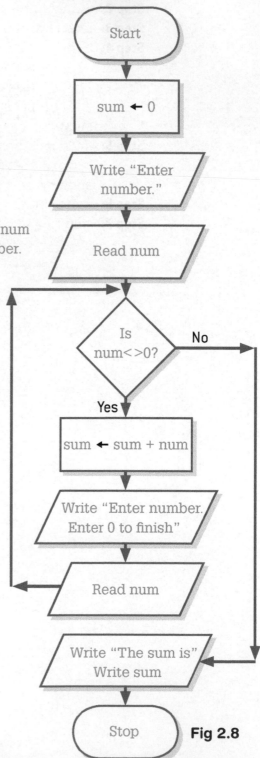

Fig 2.8

Flowchart algorithm 7

Draw a flowchart for a program that will accept a group of numbers and find the largest among them. The program stops when the user enters the value 999 for number.

Pseudocode

Step 1: start
Step 2: lgst ← -1 (A value has been set as we are going to compare the rest of the numbers with it.)
Step 3: read num
Step 4: while num<>999
      if num>lgst then
        set lgst ← num
      endif
      read num
      endwhile
Step 5: write lgst
Step 6: stop

Flowchart

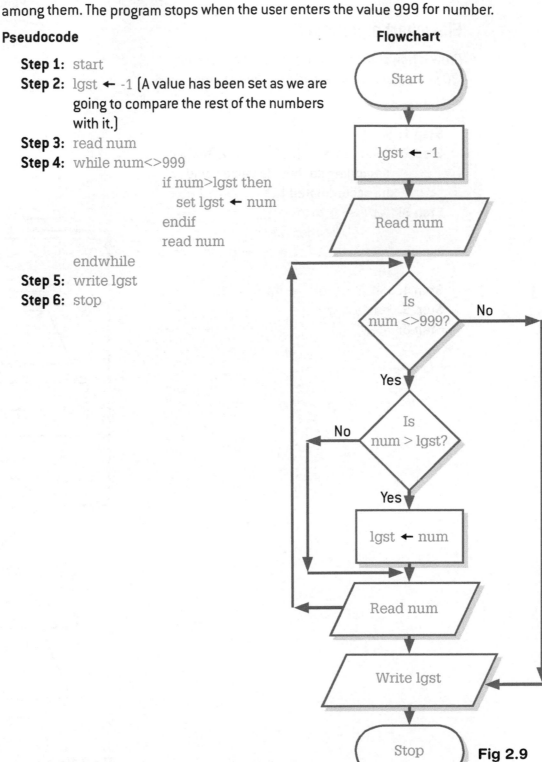

Fig 2.9

Flowcharts with bounded iteration

Flowchart algorithm 8

Draw a flowchart for a program that will accept 20 scores of students and find their average mark.

Pseudocode

    Step 1: start
    Step 2: totscore ← 0 (Set a value at the beginning so that the value could be accumulated.)
    Step 3: for x ← 1 to 20
                read score
                set totscore ← totscore + score
           endfor
    Step 4: set avgscore ← totscore/20
    Step 5: write avgscore
    Step 6: stop

Flowchart

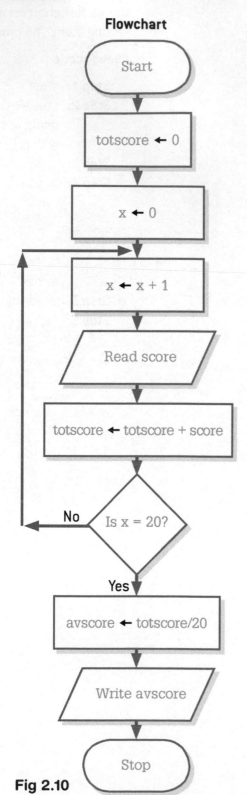

Fig 2.10

Flowchart algorithm 9

Draw a flowchart for a program that will accept 30 integers and print the number of positive and negative numbers.

Pseudocode

Step 1: start
Step 2: set poscount ← 0
Step 3: set negcount ← 0
Step 4: for n ← 1 to 30
      read num
      if num>0 then
         set poscount ←
           poscount+1
      else
         negcount ←
           negcount+1
      endif
    endfor
Step 5: write poscount, negcount
Step 6: stop

Flowchart

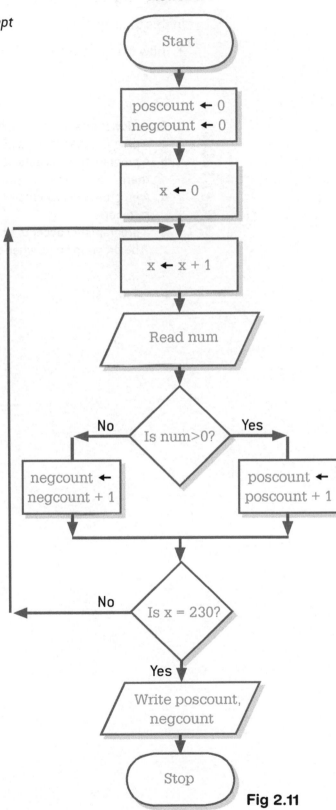

Fig 2.11

Summary of key points

In this topic you have learned:

- how to represent an algorithm in a flowchart.

1 Draw flowcharts for the following:
   a A program that accepts 20 numbers and finds their product.
   b A program that accepts 45 numbers and finds the number of zeroes and non-zeroes in them.
   c A program that accepts a set of integers and finds the number of positive and negative numbers.
   d A program that accepts a set of numbers and finds the largest among them.
   "The program stops when the user enters 99 as the number"

● *2.8–2.9* **Testing algorithms**

Once the algorithm for a problem is determined, it is important that you test it to see if it works properly and it can be implemented using a programming language.

Trace tables

One good way of testing an algorithm is to use a **trace table**. A trace table is a table into which you write the values of the variables in your algorithm, one statement at a time, using appropriate values, just as a computer would, to see if it is producing the correct results.

This prevents going back to the analysis stage of problem-solving as the trace will help to identify and solve the logical errors. If an error is detected after the trace, you know the problem lies in the way the program is written, not the logic of the algorithm

Trace tables contain a column for each of the variables and a row for each pass (line) of the algorithm.

Now let's look at some trace tables for the algorithms that involve sequencing, selection and iteration (repetition) constructs.

Trace table with sequence construct

Complete the trace table below for the following algorithm, if x = 5, y = 10, z =15. What will be printed by the algorithm?

Step 1: read x
Step 2: read y
Step 3: read z
Step 4: set k ← x
Step 5: set y ← z
Step 6: set z ← k
Step 7: set y ← z
Step 8: write x,y,z,k

Step	x	y	z	k
Step 1	5	-	-	-
Step 2	-	10	-	-
Step 3	-	-	15	-
Step 4	-	-	-	5
Step 5	-	15	-	-
Step 6	-	-	5	-
Step 7	-	5	-	-

Table 2.5

- In Step 1, the value 5 is read and assigned to x, so the value 5 is placed in the first row of the column with variable x.
- In Steps 2 and 3, the values of y and z are read, so the value 10 is placed in the second row of the column with variable y and the value 15 is placed in the third row of the second row of the column with variable z.
- In Step 4, the value of x is assigned to k, so k has the value of x which is 5. So the value 5 is placed in the fourth row of column k.
- In Step 5, value of z is assigned to y. The current value of z is 15, so the new value of y is 15.
- In Step 6, value of k is assigned to z, since k is 5 the new value of z will be 5.
- In Step 7, the value of z is assigned to y which is 5, so the new value of y will be 5. (When a new value comes, the old value is replaced with the new value.)

Therefore, the final values of x, y, z and k are 5, 5, 5 and 5 respectively, so the output of the algorithm will be **5 5 5 5**.

CHECK YOUR PROGRESS

1 Create a trace table to determine the output of the following algorithm:

Step 1: set x ← 5
Step 2: set y ← 10
Step 3: set z ← 3
Step 4: set x ← x+y
Step 5: set y ← x +z
Step 6: set z ← x+y+z
Step 7: display x, y,z

Trace table with selection construct

1 What is printed by the following algorithm?

Step 1: set m ← 5
Step 2: set n ← 4
Step 3: set p ← m+n
Step 4: set q ← m*n
Step 5: if p > q then
            q ← 0
          else
            p ← 0
          endif
Step 6: display p, q

Step	m	n	p	q
Step 1	5	-	-	-
Step 2	-	4	-	-
Step 3	-	-	9	-
Step 4	-	-	-	20
Step 5	-	-	0	-

Table 2.6

- In Steps 1 and 2 of the algorithm, the values 5 and 4 are assigned to m and n.
- In Step 3, the value of m+n (5+4) is assigned to p,
- In Step 4, the value of m*n (5 * 4) is assigned to q,
- In Step 5, the values of p and q are compared to see if p is bigger than q. Since 9 is smaller than 20 the condition is false and so the else statement is implemented, and p is changed to 0.
- Step 6 is the output and the algorithm's output will be **0, 20.**

CHECK YOUR PROGRESS

Create a trace table to determine the output of the following algorithm:

Step 1: set a ← 10
Step 2: set b ← 12
Step 3: set c ← 23
Step 4: set a ← a+b+c
Step 5: set b ← a-b
Step 6: set c ← b-c
Step 7: if a>b then
        set m ← a
        set n ← b
        set p ← c
        else
        set m ← c
        set n ← a
        set p ← b
        endif
Step 8: display m,n,p

Trace table with unbounded iteration construct

Consider the following algorithm and create a trace table. What will be the output?

Step 1: set c ← 1
Step 2: set m ← 5
Step 3: **i** while c<=5
     ii set m ← m +5
     iii write c, m
     iv set c ← c+1
     v endwhile
Step 4: write m

Let's look at this algorithm step-by-step, like before.

1 In Steps 1 and 2, the value 1 is assigned to c and the value 5 to m.

2 Step 3 is broken down into i-iv as it will be repeated until the variable c is less than or equal to 5.

3 In Step 3i, a check is made to ensure that c is less than or equal to 5. Since c= 1 and it is less than 5 the condition is evaluated to be true so it will continue with the loop and carry out the statements in Step 3ii and 3iii inside the loop.

4 In Step 3ii, m is assigned to m+5, so the new value of m would be 5+5 which is 10.

5 In Step 3iii, the values of c and m will be outputted.

6 In Step 3iv, the value of c will be incremented by 1.

7 In Step 3v, the control will be passed back to Step 3i and the process will be repeated until the condition becomes false. So Steps 3ii to 3iv will be carried out five times. Each time the value of m will be increased by 5 and c will be increased by 1.

Therefore, the trace table for the algorithm will look like this:

Step	c	m	Calculation
Step 1	1	-	
Step 2	-	5	
Step 3i	-	-	c<5 so repeat 3(ii)−(v)
Step 3ii	-	10	m ← m+5 = 5+5 = 10
Step 3iii	-	-	Display c,m
Step 3iv	2	-	c ← c+1 = 1+1 = 2
Step 3v	-	-	
Step 3i	-	-	c<5 so repeat 3(ii)−(v)
Step 3ii	-	15	m ← m+5 = 10+5 = 15
Step 3iii	-	-	Display c,m
Step 3iv	3	-	c ← c+1 = 2+1 = 3
Step 3v	-	-	
Step 3i	-	-	c<5 so repeat 3(ii)−(v)
Step 3ii	-	20	m ← m+5 = 15+5 = 20
Step 3iii	-	-	Display c,m
Step 3iv	4	-	c ← c+1 = 3+1 = 4
Step 3v	-	-	
Step 3i	-	-	c<5 so repeat 3(ii)−(v)
Step 3ii	-	25	m ← m+5 = 20+5 = 25
Step 3iii	-	-	Display c,m
Step 3iv	5	-	c = c+1 = 4+1 = 5
Step 3v	-	-	
Step 3i	-	-	c=5 so repeat 3(ii)−(v)
Step 3ii	-	30	m ← m+5 = 25+5 = 30
Step 3iii	-	-	Display c,m
Step 3iv	6	-	c ← c+1 = 6
Step 3v	-	-	c>5 so stop loop
Step 4			Display m

The blank lines where no calculations take place are included here just for your reference, but you can omit them when you create your own trace tables.

Table 2.7

The output of the algorithm will be:

1	10
2	15
3	20
4	25
5	30
30	

CHECK YOUR PROGRESS

1 Create a trace table to determine the output of the following algorithm:

Step 1: set a ← 7
Step 2: set x ← 1
Step 3: while a<>0
    set x ← x+a
    set a ← a-1
    endwhile
Step 4: write x

Trace table with bounded iteration construct

What will be the output of the following algorithm?

Step 1: set x ← 5
Step 2: set j ← 3
Step 3: **i.** for m ← 1 to 5
    ii. set j ← j+x
    iii. display j
    iv. endfor

Step	x	m	j	Calculation
Step 1	5	-	-	
Step 2	-	-	3	
Step 3i	-	1	-	m ←1 so repeat 3(i)-(iv)
Step 3ii	-	-	8	j ← j+x = 3+5 = 8
Step 3iii	-	-	-	Display j
Step 3 iv	-	-	-	
Step 3i	-	2	-	m = 2 so repeat 3(i)-(iv)
Step 3ii	-	-	13	j ← j+x = 8+5 = 13
Step 3iii	-	-	-	Display j
Step 3iv	-	-	-	
Step 3i	-	3	-	m = 3 so repeat 3(i)-(iv)
Step 3ii	-	-	18	j = j+x = 13+5 = 18
Step 3iii	-	-	-	Display j
Step 3iv	-	-	-	

Step 3i	-	4	-	
Step 3ii	-	-	23	$j = j+x = 18+5 = 23$
Step 3iii	-	-	-	Display j
Step 3iv	-	-	-	
Step 3i	-	5	-	
Step 3ii	-	-	28	$j = j+x = 23+5 = 28$
Step 3iii	-	-	-	Display j
Step 3iv	-	-	-	

Table 2.8

In the algorithm above, you should have noted that Steps 2 to 5 will be repeated five times as the variable m changes its value from 1 through to 5. The column with variable x has a fixed value and is not involved in any calculation inside the loop. In Step 3, j is assigned to j+x.

The output of the algorithm would be:

8
3
18
23
28

QUESTIONS

1 Create a trace table to determine the output of the following algorithms:

Step 1: x ← 5
Step 2: for I ← 1 to 10
           set x ← x+5
        endfor
Step 3: write x

Summary of key points

In this topic you have learned:

• how to test an algorithm using a trace table.

2.9 Using algorithms to solve complex problems

Most of the problems for which we created algorithms so far have been relatively simple. They have generally included only one task, such as calculate the average, find the largest, or find the area of a square. But complex problems can involve more than one task.

To tackle complex problems, we apply what is known as a **top-down design approach** or stepwise refinement to problem-solving. This involves breaking down a problem into smaller, manageable parts.

In top-down design a generalised solution to the problem is created at the beginning. This is broken down further and further into smaller manageable tasks or steps until all the details have been completed. The algorithms are developed for major tasks first and the rest of the tasks are considered only after major tasks are finished.

For example, if you were carrying out the registration of students at school, you might have to break down this problem into smaller simpler tasks like:

1 Entering student information (data entry).

2 Modification of student information.

3 Searching student information.

Fig 2.12 shows an example of a top-down design for the registration of students at a school.

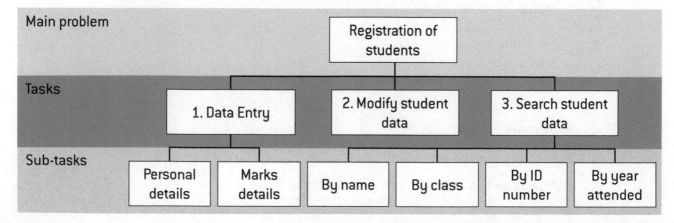

Fig 2.12 As you can see in the example above, the idea is to identify the main problem that is involved and then divide it into simpler tasks. You then look at these individual tasks and see if there are any further sub-tasks. Some tasks may have more sub-tasks than others.

By doing this, the problem will become more manageable, simpler and organised and the algorithm produced will have fewer errors.

Using a top-down design approach to find the solution to a problem has the following advantages:

1 Reusability – sections of algorithm can be used again in other algorithms that require a similar solution, which saves time in future development of algorithms.

2 Easy to follow – as each task or sub-task performs only one function.

3 Easy to maintain – as each task is by itself, if there is a need for change in one task you need to concentrate on that task only.

CHECK YOUR PROGRESS

1 What is meant by stepwise refinement or top-down design?
2 List three advantages of using top-down design to solve a problem.

Summary of key points

In this topic you have learned:

- that complex problems can be solved by breaking them down into smaller tasks.
- that a top-down design approach can be used to draw a diagram to show the tasks that make up a complex problem.

QUESTIONS

1 Explain why a top-down design approach is sometimes used to solve problems.
2 A hotel wants to have a room booking system. When a guest arrives the receptionist would be able to see which rooms are free and allocate one to the guest. When the guest leaves, the room would be marked as free again. Each day the cleaners would be given a list of the rooms that are in use. At any time the receptionist would be able to use the room number to find the name and home address of a guest, or could search the room system for a named guest. Draw a top-down design diagram to show how the room booking system could be developed.

End-of-section questions

Multiple-choice questions

1 The following are problem-solving stages
   I   analyse the problem
   II   suggest possible solutions
   III implement and review
   IV   define the problem
   V   select the best solution

   The correct order of stages is:
   A I, IV, II, III, V   **B** IV, I, II, V, III
   C IV, II, I, V, III   **D** I, II, IV, III, V

2 Which one of the following is a variable?
   A x   **B** "x"
   C 5   **D** "5"

3 To store fractional values, use the data type:
   A integer   **B** floating point
   C character   **D** string

4 Which of the following is not a characteristic of a good algorithm?
   A precise   **B** finite number of steps
   C ambiguous   **D** logical flow of control

5 Diagrammatic representation of an algorithm is a:
   A flowchart   **B** data flow diagram
   C algorithm design   **D** pseudocode

6 Which of the following are control structures?
   A selection   **B** sequencing
   C repetition   **D** all of the above

7 An example of a bounded iteration statement used in algorithm is:
   A while-endwhile   **B** while-wend
   C for-endfor   **D** repeat-until

8 Which one of the following is a selection construct used in algorithms?
   A while-endwhile   **B** if-then-else
   C for-endfor   **D** repeat-until

9 Which one of the following involves a logical operation?
   A x>y   **B** x>=y
   C x>y and x=y   **D** x<>y

10 Consider the following algorithm segment:

   x ← x+y

   y ← x-y

   write y,x

   Suppose x = 10 and y = 15, after the completion of the above statements, the values of x and y will be:
   A 25 and 10   **B** 10 and 25
   C 10 and -5   **D** -5 and 10

Structured questions

1 a List the main stages of the problem-solving process for computer-based problem-solving.
   b For each of the stages identified in 1a above, briefly describe the activities that are involved in it.

2 IPO diagrams can be used to break down a problem into its components.
   a State what is meant by 'IPO diagrams'?
   b Create an IPO chart for the following problem statement: 'Accept the values of length and width of a rectangle and calculate its area'.

3 a State the difference between:
      i   constants and variables
      ii integer data type and floating point data type
      iii character data type and string data type
   b Define the following terms:
      i   identifier
      ii literal

4 Create a narrative algorithm that will prompt the user to enter two numbers and find their difference.

5 Write a pseudocode algorithm that prompts the user to enter a value and display its square and cube values.

6 Draw a flowchart and write a pseudocode algorithm that will prompt the user to enter two numbers and display their product.

7 You need to calculate the area of rectangle using its length and width. Draw a flowchart and write a pseudocode algorithm that will accept the length and width and calculate and print the area of the rectangle. (area = length * width)

8 Write a pseudocode algorithm that will accept 25 integers and display the number of positive and negative numbers.

9 a Draw a trace table for the following algorithm.
      x ← 10
      y ← 20
      z ← 5
      x ← x+y
      y ← x-y
      z ← z+x
      x ← y
      y ← z
      z ← x
      print x,y,z
   b What is printed by the algorithm?

10 a Draw a trace table for the following algorithm.

x ← 10
y ← 15
z ← 20
x ← x+y
y ← x+z
z ← x+y+z
if x>y then
x ← x+5
else
x ← x-3
endif
if y<z then
y ← y+10
else
y ← y-10
endif

b What is the output of this algorithm?

Practice SBA

Due to a donation of some computers, the Caribbean Sports Club (CSC) is in the process of automating their club activities.

There are 25 members in the club and they belong to different categories. Each category attracts a different rate of membership fee. Based on the category of membership the members have different responsibilities and privileges. The categories of membership with current rates are given in the table below. The membership rates have remained the same for the last five years.

Category	Code	Rate per month
Regular	R	$50
Special	S	$100
Golden	G	$150
Platinum	P	$200

Tasks

1 Make a problem statement and create an IPO chart for the problem.

2 Using your IPO chart, develop an algorithm that will accept the names and the total amount collected in fees over the last five years (2005–2009) for each member. The algorithm must calculate the outstanding amount and the amount in fines due for each member, which is 25% of the outstanding amount. The algorithm should also display the name, outstanding amount, and fines of each club member. It should also display the maximum fines and the

number of persons with outstanding fees. The algorithm must be created as follows:

a narrative algorithm

b pseudocode or flowchart

3 Design and execute a trace table with the column headings Name, Total amount, Outstanding amount and Fines. Using a trace table, display the maximum outstanding amount and the number of persons with outstanding fees.

Program implementation

Objectives

By the end of this section, you will be able to:

- Distinguish between low-level and high-level programming languages and understand the five generations of languages.
- Understand the steps in creating a program, and be able to write, compile, execute and maintain a program.
- Understand the different types of errors that can occur in a program and carry out testing and debugging techniques.
- Write and test programs in Pascal using the following techniques:
  - elementary data types
  - variables and constants
  - reading and writing data to and from variables
  - arithmetic operations
  - control structures
  - one-dimensional arrays
- Write documentation for your programs.

You should study Section 2 before you start on Section 3.

In this section you will be learning the programming language Pascal. This is a high-level language which is looks very similar to the algorithms you were developing in Section 2.

When you implement an algorithm in a programming language you are able to run the program and see what it does. You can then make any corrections to the program until it is working as intended.

You will be developing your programs in a programming environment, which is a software package that enables you to edit and test your programs. You can choose between several Pascal programming environments, and it does not really matter which one you use; the step-by step instructions given in this section ask you to enter some program code, and this code would be exactly the same whichever software you are using.

Programming languages

As you are aware, we use language to communicate with each other. In the same way, in order to communicate with a computer we have to use programming languages. Programming languages are broadly classified as low-level or high-level. **Low-level languages** are programming languages that use words and symbols that are similar to binary or are in binary. **High-level languages** use words and symbols like those we use in daily life.

Based on their order of development, there are *five* levels or generations of programming languages, with each generation improving on its previous level.

1 First generation or Machine-level language
2 Second generation or Assembly-level language
3 Third generation or High-level languages
4 Fourth generation languages
5 Fifth generation languages

First generation or Machine-level languages

Machine-level languages were the first languages that were developed for computers, and so are also called first generation languages. In these languages, instructions are written using binary (0s and 1s), for example 10110011110011011. These are the only languages understood by computers. A machine language program written for one type of computer may not run on another type of computer as machine language instructions are **machine dependent**.

Advantages of Machine-level languages include being:

1 able to be executed very fast by the computer, as there is no need for translation.

Disadvantages of Machine-level languages include being:

1 difficult to read, write and understand by humans as the programs involve only 0s and 1s.

2 machine dependent, so unable to be used on another machine.

3 difficult to modify or correct mistakes.

Second generation or Assembly-level languages (ALL)

Since the writing of programs using Machine-level language was cumbersome, second generation languages were developed – Assembly-level languages. In assembly language, instructions are written using mnemonics or abbreviated forms of words. For example, it uses words like ADD for addition and SUB for subtraction. As Machine-level language is the only language understood by the computer, Assembly-level language instructions have to be converted into Machine-level language. A translator program called an **assembler** is used to convert Assembly-level language instructions to Machine-level language.

Advantages of Assembly-level language include being:

1 easier to read, write and understand than Machine-level language.

2 easier to modify or correct mistakes than Machine-level language.

Disadvantages of Assembly-level language include being:

1 slower in execution than Machine-level language.

2 still machine dependent.

Machine-level languages and Assembly-level languages are considered as low-level languages as they are closer to the language that the computer can understand.

> **WHAT DOES IT MEAN?**
>
> **assembler**
> An assembler is a translator that converts Assembly-level language to Machine-level language.

Third generation or high-level languages

The third generation of computer languages, or high-level languages, such as BASIC, Pascal, FORTRAN, C, were developed in order to make the programming easier than ALL. In these languages, instructions are given using basic English words such as INPUT, PRINT, etc. High-level language instructions also need to be converted into Machine-level language using translators.

There are two types of translators that are available for high-level language translation – **compilers** and **interpreters**. Interpreters are used by some high-level languages while compilers are used by others. High-level languages are machine independent, therefore they are portable.

> **WHAT DOES IT MEAN?**
>
> **compiler**
> Compilers are translators that convert high-level language instructions to machine language by taking all instructions together to form a single file that can run on its own.
>
> **interpreter**
> Interpreters are translators that convert high-level language instructions to machine language by taking one instruction at a time. They do not produce files that can run independently.

Advantages of high-level languages include being:

1 easier to read, write and understand than Machine-level language and ALL.

2 easier to modify or correct mistakes than Machine-level language and ALL.

3 machine independent.

Disadvantages of high-level languages include being:

1 slower in execution than Machine-level language and ALL.

Fourth generation languages (4GL)

Fourth generation languages, such as Power builder, SQL, Oracle and Coldfusion, can be considered as advanced high-level languages. These languages also consist of English-like instructions and are much more user friendly than high-level languages. A 4GL program would contain fewer instructions than a high-level language program as it has instructions that are in the form of modules. Unlike high-level language, in 4GLs the programmer just has to specify *what* is to be attained instead of giving steps for *how* to attain it.

The following are some examples of 4GL instructions:

SORT STUDENT BY LASTNAME

TOTAL PRICE BY STATE

Fifth generation languages (5GL)

In fifth generation languages, instructions are used in a conversational way, so it is also called 'natural language programming'. For example, 5GL instructions can be written like GIVE ME THE TOTAL NUMBER OF ITEMS PURCHASED BY CUSTOMERS FROM BARBADOS. 5GLs were developed to make the computer solve the problem (using artificial intelligence) instead of programmers writing programs for various tasks. 5GLs, such as PROLOG and Mercury, are used mainly in the research of artificial intelligence.

WHAT DOES IT MEAN?

artificial intelligence
Computers that can behave like humans with qualities of a human being are said to have artificial intelligence.

CHECK YOUR PROGRESS

1 List TWO advantages and ONE disadvantage of high-level languages over Machine-level languages.

2 Match the following program instructions with their corresponding language:

Instruction		Programming Language	
a	SORT STOCK BY ITEMNAME	**i**	High-level
b	SUB A, B	**ii**	Machine-level
c	PRINT SUM	**iii**	4GL
d	101001101	**iv**	5GL
e	GET ME THE LARGEST NUMBER	**v**	Assembly-level

3 A Machine-level language program runs on one type of computer, but not on another type of computer. Why?

4 Define the following terms:
   a program
   b assembler
   c 4GL

5 High-level languages also need translators to convert to machine level. Give TWO types of translators.

The stages of implementing a program

In Section 2 you learned that when you have to create a program that solves a problem, you can create an algorithm to give a clear logic of the program, using the following steps.

1 Understand the problem thoroughly and look for the terms that describe the inputs.

2 Look for terms that identify the outputs from the program that are needed and the format in which they are required.

3 Identify what processing is needed in order to produce the outputs from the input given. This is the formal logic of the program.

4 Using narrative, flowchart or pseudocode, write an algorithm to show the breakdown of the logic.

Once you've developed your algorithm, you need to implement the program. This can be done in stages.

Stage 1: Create the source code

You need to translate the steps of your algorithm into programming language instructions to form a program that solves your problem. These instructions are known as source code. As people generally work in high-level language these days, source code is usually in a form understandable to humans. Before you translate these instructions in to a language understandable to computers it would be a good practise to go through each program instruction manually, to see if the program has any errors. This process is called a dry run.

Stage 2: Translating source code - compiling

Computers only understand machine language instructions, i.e. binary, so other programming language instructions have to be converted into machine language. You can use translators like assemblers, interpreters or compilers to translate programming language instructions.

Each language has its rules and regulations – in English language it is called grammar. The rules and regulations of a programming language are called syntax. When you do not follow the rules of the programming language the translators report these errors. They are called syntax errors.

High-level programming languages like Pascal use compilers such as the translator. If the program does not contain any syntax errors, a compiler will translate your program into machine language form. This process is called compiling. After compilation you will get object code, which is in machine language form.

Stage 3: Linking

Source code is usually stored in more than one file and the compiler converts each source code file into separate object code files. These individual object code files need to be combined to create a single **executable program**, that is, one that will run. This process of combining object code files to form a single executable program is called **linking**.

Stage 4: Run or execute the program to test that it is working correctly

Sometimes when you run or **execute** the program it does not produce the required results. This is often the result of a **logic error**, one that is due to an error in the logic of the programming. For example, the following algorithm is written by a programmer to output the sum of three numbers.

Step 1: read A,B,C

Step 2: sum ← A+B+C

Step 3: write sum

Suppose the values of A, B and C are 5, 10 and 15 respectively. The program's output would be 15 as the value of C is not added to calculate the sum. So the program would not produce the correct results because the programmer forgot to add the value of C or did not go through the solution properly. This type of error is called a logic error. The values 5, 10 and 15 that are used in the program to see if it is producing correct results are called **test data**.

It is important that you correct the syntax errors and logic errors to get the correct results out of the program. For that, you need to test to detect if there is any error, locate where the error is and correct the error. This process of identifying and correcting errors is called **debugging**.

Sometimes even though the program does not have any syntax or logic errors, it might have to stop before its completion due to problems like division by zero (for example when you try to divide a number with a 0 the program would stop as you cannot divide by 0) or repeating a process an unlimited number of times (endless or infinite loop). This type of error is known as **run time error**.

Stage 5: Maintaining the program

If you are not happy with the results or want to make further changes, you modify the logic of the program and continue to modify it until it is satisfactory to you. This is called **program maintenance**.

Below is a simple diagram that shows the sequence of different stages involved in implementation of an algorithm into a program.

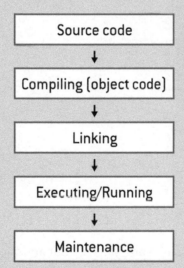

```
┌──────────────────────┐
│     Source code      │
└──────────────────────┘
           ↓
┌──────────────────────┐
│ Compiling (object code)│
└──────────────────────┘
           ↓
┌──────────────────────┐
│       Linking        │
└──────────────────────┘
           ↓
┌──────────────────────┐
│  Executing/Running   │
└──────────────────────┘
           ↓
┌──────────────────────┐
│     Maintenance      │
└──────────────────────┘
```

CHECK YOUR PROGRESS

1 List the five stages involved in program implementation.
2 State the difference between source code and object code.
3 Define the terms:
   a testing
   b dry run
   c test data
4 List three tasks involved in debugging a program.
5 What are the three different types of program errors?
6 Distinguish between syntax errors and logic errors.

Getting started with Pascal

You are now ready to write a program yourself. You will use a Pascal programming environment, which is a software package that includes an editor (rather like a word processor for programs), a compiler and a linker. The compiler will carry out syntax analysis on your program and tell you any syntax errors you have made. You will then be able to run your program, test it and identify any further errors.

In this section we have used the program Free Pascal for the screen shots. If you are using a different programming environment then the screen may look slightly different, and the menus and buttons may be arranged differently. However, you should be able to find everything you need.

When you launch Free Pascal, the window looks like this:

Fig 3.1: A Free Pascal window

Writing and compiling a program

A typical Pascal program consists of a program header and the block. The program header consists of the word program followed by a program name given by the user. Any other lines of programming after the program header are called the block. The block section consists of two main parts – declarations and program statements. Items of data used in the program such as variables and constants are declared in the declarations part and program instructions that need to be performed are placed in the program statements section between begin and end statements.

The following shows the typical structure of a Pascal program:

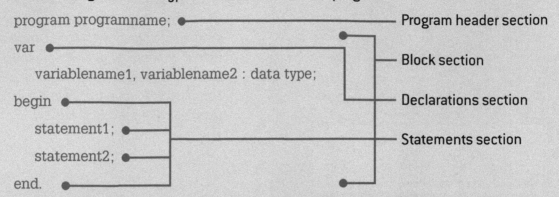

program programname; ●━━━━━━━━━━━━━━━━━━━━━ Program header section

var ●━━━━━━━━━━━━━━━━━━━━━━━━

━━ Block section

    variablename1, variablename2 : data type;

begin ●━━━━━━━━━━━ ━━ Declarations section

    statement1; ●

━━ Statements section

    statement2; ●

end. ●

Starting a Pascal program

1 Double click on the Free Pascal's icon on your desktop. You will see a screen similar to the one in Fig 3.1 Click on *File* ➜ *New* from the menu bar. You will get a screen that looks like Fig 3.2.

2 Type in the program instructions. For example, if you want your program to display a message 'Hello World', you should have instructions in the format shown in Fig 3.3.

All Pascal programs should have a program header. Here it is given the name helloworld. The declaration part of the block section is omitted as this program does not require any variables or constants. The program statements are placed between Begin and End statements. (Note that the End statement must have a full stop at its end.)

Fig 3.2

Fig 3.3

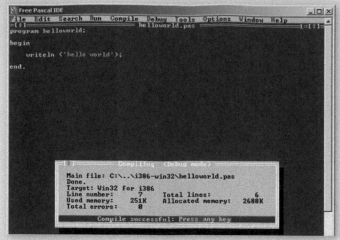

Fig 3.4

3 Once the program is entered following the correct rules of the language, you can compile the program. To compile choose *Compile* → *Compile* from the menu bar or press Alt and F9 simultaneously on your keyboard. If the program compiles without errors, it will display the message like the one in Fig 3.4.

If there are errors in the program, it will display the message 'Compiled failed' as shown in Fig 3.5 and you will have to fix the errors before you can get to see the results of the program.

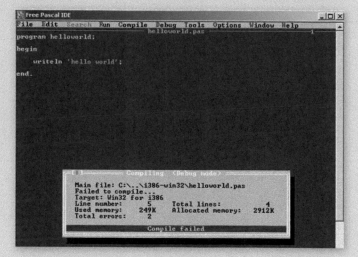

Fig 3.5

4 In order to see if the program is working correctly, choose the *Run* → *Run* from the menu bar or press Ctrl and F9 simultaneously on your keyboard. The results will be displayed on another screen and in order to view this output choose *Debug* → *Output* from the menu bar and you will see the following screen as in Fig 3.6.

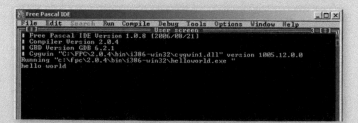

Fig 3.6

5 As you can see in Fig 3.6 the message 'hello world' appears with lots of other text. If you want to display the message without the rest of the text information you can use Pascal's clrscr statement.

In order to use this statement you need to declare either monitor or CRT as the media for output. So your program has to be modified as in Fig 3.7.

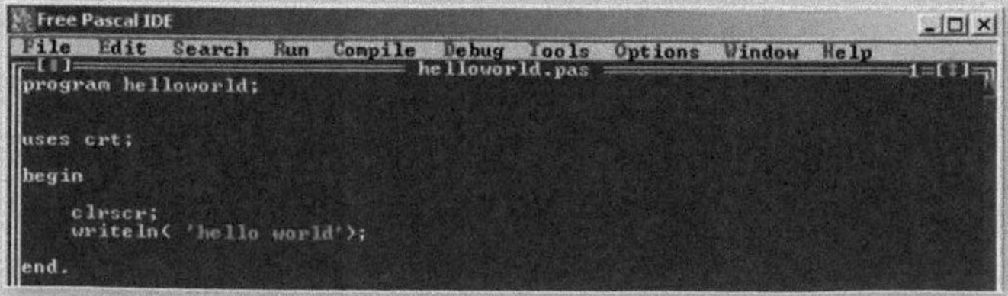

Fig 3.7

6 When you run this new modified program, the output will be as in Fig 3.8.

In order to switch back to your program from the output screen, choose *Window* → *Close* and you will be back to your program screen.

Fig 3.8

7 In order to save this file choose *File* → *Save*, it will give you a screen like Fig 3.9.

Give it a name and choose OK to save the file. It will automatically add a file extension (.pas).

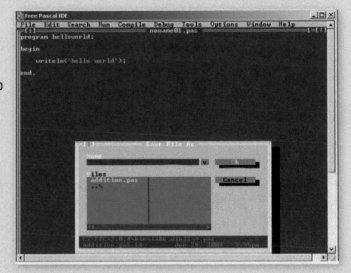

Fig 3.9

Data types, constants and variables in Pascal

Elementary data types

Most computer programs are written to operate on data of various types to solve a problem. For example, a program to find the sum of two numbers will accept two numbers as input and process them according to an operation to produce the sum of the two numbers. The type of data the program will accept as input and the operations that can be performed on the data will depend on the data type declared.

In Section 2 you read about data types in relation to algorithms. Each programming language, including Pascal, offers a range of data types. For this section, we will focus on the following data types in Pascal: integers, real numbers, characters and strings. To remind you

1 Integers: Whole numbers such as 10, -3, 2010
2 Real numbers: Numbers that include decimals such as 2.78, -3.25, 7.33. These are also called floating point numbers.
3 Characters: The items that you type, such as:
   - digits (0 to 9)
   - letters of the alphabet (a to z or A to Z)
   - special symbols ($, ?, etc)
4 Strings: A sequence of one or more characters, such as a single word, a code or a sentence.

Declaring the data type

When you write a Pascal program to solve a problem, you have to declare the type of data you are going to use in the solution of the problem.

For example, if you write a program to find the sum of two numbers, then you have to indicate whether the two numbers the user will enter can be real or integer, and what type of data the sum will be given in. This is called declaring the data types.

Taking the example of finding the sum of two numbers, we can use n1 and n2 as the identifiers for the data the user will enter, and sum as the identifier for the result of the sum of the two numbers. We can then declare the data type using the following format:

    <identifier> : <data type>;

As you can see, the identifier is given, followed by a colon (:), then the data type you want to specify for those identifiers is given, followed by a semicolon (;).

In our example, we would declare the data types like this:

    n1: integer;
    n2: integer;
    sum: integer;

We could also combine all three declarations into one, as follows:

    n1, n2, sum: integer;

Suppose a program was asking the user to enter the first character of his/her last name. If we decide to use ln (for Last Name) as the identifier, then we could declare the data type as follows:

    ln: char;

If the program had wanted the user to enter his/her last name in full, and we decide to use surname as the identifier, then we can declare the data type as follows:

    surname: string;

Note that the 'char' data type only accepts a single character while the string data type accepts up to 255 characters.

When data type is declared, as in the examples above, the program sets aside space in the computer's main memory where the data can be stored. The amount of memory space allocated will depend on the data type used.

For example:

- ln: char; will set aside one byte to store a single character.
- sum: integer; will usually set aside four bytes to store the number (although this may be different for different compilers).
- surname: string; will set aside 255 bytes of storage.

WHAT DOES IT MEAN?

string
A string is a set of characters, such as, *abc67xy* or *Mrs Joy Redmond* or *West Indies Cricket Board.*

Variables

In the examples above, n1, n2, sum, ln, and surname are all **variables**. In a Pascal program, a variable is used to hold values that can change. Variables can be of any data type.

In programming, variable identifiers are usually referred to as **variable names**.

Variables are typically used to store data that the user enters to allow the program to perform some calculations and to store the results of the calculations.

In our program, when the program is run, the first number is stored in a memory location that is given the name n1. The second number is stored in n2. The program then carries out the simple calculation and stores the result in sum.

n1 and n2 could have any values you like, which is why n1 and n2 are variables.

WHAT DOES IT MEAN?

variable
A variable identifies a memory location in which an item of data can be stored. The value of the data can be changed. In Pascal a variable can be of any data type, e.g. integer or string.

variable name
A variable name is the identifier of a variable.

Declaring variables

All variables we are going to use in a program must be declared before we can use them. In declaring the variable, we must assign a meaningful name to it and indicate its data type. For example, in a program to find the sum of three numbers, we could use n1, n2, n3 and sum as the variables with data type integer.

To declare a variable in Pascal, we use the VAR statement. For the above program, we could declare the variable as follows:

```
var
    n1, n2, n3, sum: integer;
```

You should note that in the above instructions, four memory locations with the names n1, n2, n3 and sum are used to store the values of the variables.

In Pascal most programmers follow a convention that indents some lines, that is, starts some lines further along, as with n1, n2, n3, sum: integer;.

var is a kind of heading that tells the program what is to follow.

Giving names to variables

We have used the identifiers n1, n2 and sum for our variables. A variable can be given almost any name. However, there are a few rules that will make your life easier, which are listed below:

1 Choose a meaningful variable name so that the name can suggest what value will be stored in the variable.

2 The Pascal language is case-insensitive, which means that an uppercase letter is same as a lowercase letter. For example, *B* is the same as *b*.

3 Pascal-reserved words, that is, words that already have a meaning in the Pascal language, such as begin, end, var, integer, real, char and const cannot be used as variable names.

4 Spaces cannot be used in a variable name. For example, date of birth is not allowed but date_of_birth is allowed.

5 A variable name must start with a letter or with an underscore _. After the first character it may consist of any combination of letters, digits or underscores.

6 A variable name cannot exceed 31 characters.

Assigning an initial value to a variable

It may be necessary to initialise a variable at the start of a program, that is, give it an initial value. For example, if you have a variable called sum, you may want to ensure that the value in sum at the start of the program is zero.

In pseudocode we write an assignment like this:
```
sum ← 0
```

In Pascal we use the assignment statement.
```
sum:= 0;
```

You should note that the variable sum must be declared previously and the symbol for assignment is ':='.

Writing a program using variables and data types

Let's look at the basic structure of a Pascal program:

```
program<name>;
const
    ................;
var
    ..................;
begin
    <statement>;
    <statement>;
    ...........
    ..........;
end.
```

This is an example of a syntax statement. The triangular brackets < and > are not part of Pascal. We have used <name> to show that the programmer needs to insert the name of the program here. Similarly, real statements in Pascal should be inserted instead of <statement>.

Note the semicolons at the end of each statement, and the full stop after the final end.

Here is a pseudocode algorithm to find the sum of two numbers.

Step 1: start
Step 2: set sum ← 0
Step 3: set num1 ← 20
Step 4: set num2 ← 33
Step 5: set sum ← num1 + num2
Step 6: stop

Here is the program in Pascal.

```
program add;
var
    num1, num2, sum: integer;
begin
    sum := 0;
    num1 := 20;
    num2 := 33;
    sum := num1 + num2; {calculating the sum}
end.
```

Let's look at this program line by line.

- {calculating the sum}   This is a comment.
- sum:= 0;   This initialises sum to 0
- num1:= 20;   20 is assigned to num1
- num2:= 33;   33 is assigned to num2
- sum:= num1 + num2;   The values in num1 and num2 are added and stored in sum

It is good practice to include comments in your programs. They help you and other programmers to remember what a program does. The compiler ignores them when the program is compiled.

Creating a simple Pascal program

1 Enter the program exactly as it is written in Pascal above.

2 Compile and run this program. It does not appear to do anything! That is because it does not ask the user to enter any numbers, and the result of the calculation is not displayed on the screen.

You will learn how to ask the user to input data, and how to display results in the following pages.

CHECK YOUR PROGRESS

1 You are writing a program to find the average of three integers. The average is stored in a variable named avg. What is the data type for the variable avg? Give a reason for your answer.

2 Write a statement to declare the variable avg.

3 You need to initialise the variable avg to zero at the beginning of the program. Write the Pascal statement to do this.

4 Which of the following are valid variable names?
   a 4you
   b _all
   c date of birth

5 Consider the following program and identify all the errors.
   ```
   program calc;
   no: = 2
   a, b, c: integer;
   begin
   c = 0
   a:= 5;
   b:= 10.75:
   c:= no + b +c;
   end.
   ```

Manipulating data

Over the next few pages, you will learn how to manipulate data in a Pascal program.

Reading data entered by the user

On page 130, we discussed a program where the values are assigned to the variables in the program and the user is not given an opportunity to enter any data. In most programs, the user will be required to enter data when prompted to do so.

In Pascal, the statement read is used to read data that is input by the user. Read statements will be part of the input, processing and output statements, which are placed between begin and end, after you have declared your constants and variables.

The statement, read(mark) takes a value entered by the user and stores it in the variable mark.

The value entered must be valid for the data type declared for the variable. For example, if the variable mark is declared as an integer, then the value entered for mark must be an integer.

Writing data to the screen

We have just learned how a program reads the data entered by the user using the read statement. But how does the user know when to enter the data or how does the user see the result of the processing done by the program? Pascal uses the write and writeln statements to display information on the computer screen. This information could be a prompt to input some data or it could be used to show the result of processing onscreen.

The write and writeln statements are useful if we wish to prompt the user for some data. Notice that quotation marks must be used with text in a write or writeln statement.

We use write if we want the data to be shown on the same line as the prompt. For example, the statements:

```
write('Enter your marks: ');
read(mark);
```

would display the message Enter your marks and the marks would be entered by the user on the same line. If the user had entered 76, then the following will be displayed:

Enter your marks: 76

If we had used the statement:

writeln('Enter your marks: ');
read(mark);

Then the following will be displayed:

Enter your marks:

76

You can use write or writeln depending on how you would like the information to be laid out on the screen.

The text 'Enter your marks:' is an example of a literal, as mentioned on page 132. Note that in Pascal single (not double) quote marks are placed around a literal.

The instruction writeln by itself will create a blank line.

Reading and writing data

Now consider the following narrative algorithm:

Step 1: Prompt for the first number.
Step 2: Read the number.
Step 3: Prompt for the second number.
Step 4: Read the second number.
Step 5: Print the two numbers.

The program to implement the algorithm is given as follows:

```
program show;
var
    number1, number2: integer;
begin
    write('Enter the first number:');
    read(number1);
    write('Enter the second number:');
    read(number2);
    writeln('The numbers are: ', number1, 'and ', number2);
end.
```

If the two numbers entered were 10 and 12, then the program will display the following:

Enter the first number: 10

Enter the second number: 12

The numbers are 10 and 12

If we wanted a blank line after each message displayed, then we can use the writeln command.

Creating a Pascal program 2

1 Enter the program exactly as shown above.

2 Compile and run the program, correcting any errors.

Performing arithmetic operations

The arithmetic operators are:

Operator	Purpose	Example
+	addition	2 + 3 = 5
-	subtraction	10 - 8 = 2
*	multiplication	2 * 3 = 6
/	real division	5.94 / 3.6 = 1.65
div	integer division	10 div 3 = 3 (the remainder is discarded)
mod	finding the remainder in a div operation	10 mod 3 = 1

Table 3.1

You met arithmetic operators in Section 2 when learning about algorithms. In the Pascal programming language, arithmetic operators are used to perform arithmetic calculations. You will see that there are two different operators in Pascal for division.

- The / operator can be used with integers or real numbers but always produces a result that is a real number. The result must be stored in a variable that has been declared with the real data type.

- The div operator can only be used with integers and the result is always an integer. It is usually used with the mod operator, which gives the remainder after a div operation.

Execution of operators

Just as in pseudocode, Pascal evaluates arithmetic expressions based on the precedence of the operators. Pascal will evaluate an arithmetic expression in the following order of precedence:

- Brackets
- Multiplication and division, which includes integer division and remainder (mod)
- Addition and subtraction

When two operators have the same precedence, such as multiplication and division, Pascal evaluates them from left to right. For example:

5 * 10 + 3 = 53   the multiplication is done first followed by the addition

(7 + 3) * 5 = 50   the bracket is done first followed by the multiplication

11 div 3 * 5 = 15   the division is done first followed by the multiplication

Using operators

Let us consider the following program to find the remainder, r, when one integer, a, is divided by another integer, b.

```
program remainder;
var
    a, b, r: integer
begin
    write('Enter the first number: ');
    read(a);
    writeln;
    write('Enter the second number: ');
    read(b);
    writeln:
    r:= a mod b;
    writeln('When ', a, ' is divided by ', b, ' the remainder is ', r);
end.
```

Suppose the user had entered 25 as the first number and 7 as the second number, then the following will be displayed:

```
Enter the first number: 25
Enter the second number: 7
When 25 is divided by 7 the remainder is 4
```

Creating a program using operators

1 Enter the program exactly as shown above

2 Compile and run the program, correcting any errors.

Constants

When we write a program, it is sometimes necessary to use a value that does not change during the execution of the program. We call this a constant, as it remains

WHAT DOES IT MEAN?

constant
A constant is a value that is given a name. The constant can be used anywhere in a program and will always have the same value.

constant. For example, if we were writing a program to compute hours to seconds the value *hr = 3600* would be a constant as there are always 3600 seconds in an hour.

Declaring constants

In Pascal we declare a constant by using the statement const, and then indicating the name of the constant and its fixed value.

For example, if we continue with our conversion of hours to seconds, we would declare the constant *hr = 3600* as follows:

```
const
    hr = 3600;
```

You should note that name of the constant (*hr*) is followed by an equal sign, then the value of the constant (*3600*) and then the semi-colon (;).

In programs dealing with the area or circumference of a circle, we can use the constant pi with the value *3.142* and declare it as follows:

```
const
    pi = 3.142;
```

Here is a program that uses constants as well as operators.

A store is offering 20% discount on all items. The original price is listed on the item. To find the new price of the item, the store has placed a computer that is running a program where the customer can input the price of the item and get the new price. The following program was created to compute the new price of the item, where dr is the 20% discount:

The pseudocode algorithm would be:

```
Step 1: start
Step 2: set newprice ← 0
Step 3: write 'Enter price of item: '
Step 4: read price
Step 5: set newprice ← price – (price * dr)
Step 6: write 'The new price of the item is $', newprice
Step 7: stop
```

In Pascal that becomes:
```
program newprice;
const
    dr = 0.20;
var
    price, newprice: real;
begin
    newprice: =0;
    write('Enter price of item: ');
    read(price);
    writeln;
    newprice:= price - (price * dr);
    writeln('The new price of the item is $', newprice);
end.
```

Suppose the user enters 50 as the price, then the following will be displayed:

Enter price of item: 50
The new price of the item is $40

At the beginning of the program newprice is assigned the value 0. This makes sure that newprice is reset back to zero every time the program is run.

Creating a program using constants and operators

1 Enter the program exactly as shown above

2 Compile and run the program, correcting any errors.

CHECK YOUR PROGRESS

1 What is displayed by the following statements if the user enters 10?
```
write('Enter your years of service: ')
read(yrs);
```

2 What is printed by the following two statements?
```
write('Hello');
writeln('Everyone');
```

3 What is the value of (36 div 5) * (35 mod 4)?

4 Write an algorithm and a program to compute the VAT payable on an item. The program should ask the user to enter the price of an item and compute the VAT payable on the item using a fixed rate of 16% of the price.

Using control structures

Programs become really useful when they can take decisions based on data provided, or when they can perform actions repeatedly. The Pascal programming language provides us with control structures to handle these things. You met control structures on Page 79 of Section 2, when learning about algorithms. You may want to re-read the relevant topic before commencing this work.

Here, you will learn how to use two types of control structures in Pascal:

1 Selection control structures (conditional branching), such as if-then and if-then-else.
2 Repetition control structures (loops), such as the while loop (while-do), the repeat loop (repeat-until) and the for loop (for-do).

Selection control structures (conditional branching)

As you learned in Section 2, selection control structures are used to test a condition and take action based on whether the condition is true or false. This is also called conditional branching, because the program branches out in a new direction to the next statement based on whether the condition is true or false.

To test a condition in a control structure, the following relational operators are used:

Operator	Description
=	Equal to
<>	Not equal to
>	Greater than
>=	Greater than or equal to
<	Less than
<=	Less than or equal to

Table 3.2: The operators used in conditions

The if-then control structure

The syntax of the if-then control structure is:

```
if <condition> then
    <statement>;
```

For example:

```
If t=100 then
    write ('Perfect score!');
```

where 't=100' is the condition. If the condition is met then the message will be displayed; if it is not met then nothing will happen.

Let's look at an example to demonstrate the use of the if-then structure. The following program asks the user to enter his/her mark in a course, checks if the mark is 50 or more and then displays a message indicating that the student has passed the course.

The pseudocode would be:

Step 1: start
Step 2: write 'Enter your mark: '
Step 3: read m
Step 4: if m>= 50 then
            write 'You have passed the course'
        endif
Step 5: stop

```
program marks;
var
    m: integer;
begin
    writeln('Enter your mark: ');
    read(m);
    if m>=50 then
            writeln('You have passed the course');
end.
```

Creating a program using the if-then structure

1 Enter the program exactly as shown above.

2 Compile and run the program, correcting any errors.

3 You should test your program to see what happens when you enter a value greater than 50, a value less than 50, or exactly 50.

Suppose we want to execute two or more statements if the test is true, then you have to use a new pair of begin and end statements to group the statements to be executed. The new begin and end statements act like brackets around the statements that follow then.

The following program shows the if-then structure in use:

```
program marks;
var
   m: integer;
begin
   writeln('Enter your mark ');
   readln(m);
   if m>=50 then
      begin
         writeln('The mark you entered is ', m);
         writeln('You have passed the course');
      end;
end.
```

Executing more than one statement in an if-then statement

1 Alter your previous program as above.

2 Compile and run the program, correcting any errors. Note the semi-colon after the first end statement.

3 Test the program as before.

The if-then-else control structure

In the last program, if the user entered a mark less than 50, nothing happened. To tell the program what to do when the mark is less than 50 we have to use the if-then-else control structure as follows:

```
if <condition> then
   <statement1>
else
   <statement2>
else <statement2>;
```

For example:

```
if t=100 then
   write ('Perfect score!')
else
   write ('Oh Dear!');
```

Note that there is no semi-colon after <statement1> but there is one after <statement2>. No semi-colon should be placed before an else statement.

Here is a pseudocode algorithm using the if-then-else structure:

Step 1: start
Step 2: write 'Enter your mark: '
Step 3: read m

Step 4: if m>=50 then
write 'You have passed the course'
else
write 'You have failed the course'
endif
Step 5: stop

The following program shows the if-then-else structure in use:

```
program marks;
var
  m: integer;
begin
  writeln('Enter your mark: ');
  read(m);
  if m>=50 then
     writeln('You have passed the course')
  else
     writeln('You have failed the course');
end.
```

Using an if-then-else statement

1 Alter your previous program as above.

2 Compile and run the program, correcting any errors.

3 Test the program as before.

Multiple selection control structures

It may be necessary to test more than one condition at the same time. In this case, we put the conditions in brackets and join them using the AND or OR operators.

AND and OR operators

<condition1> AND <condition2> is only true if condition1 *and* condition2 are *both* true.

For example, the sentence 'I am tired AND I am hungry' is only true if I'm both tired *and* hungry.

<condition1> OR <condition2> is true if *either* condition1 *or* condition2 (or both) are true.

For example, the sentence 'I will either go to the beach or I will go shopping' is true if I do *either* of those activities. It is also true if I managed to go to shopping on the way back from the beach.

The following program is testing if you are eligible for a scholarship, using the AND operator. You are eligible for the scholarship if your age is between 20 and 40 inclusively:

```pascal
program scholarship;
var
    a: integer;
begin
    writeln('Enter your age: ');
    read(a);
    if (a>=20) and (a<=40) then
            writeln('You are eligible for the scholarship');
end.
```

Using more than one selection condition

1 Enter the program exactly as shown above.

2 Compile and run the program, correcting any errors.

3 Test it with the following ages: 17, 20, 34, 40, 56

Repetition control structures (loops)

Repetition control structures, also called loops, are used when a program performs one or more actions repeatedly while a certain condition is met. Loops are useful for repeating parts of a program until some condition is satisfied. We will consider the following two types of loops here:

1 Unbounded loops, such as the while-do and repeat-until loops, where we do not know in advance how many times to repeat the loop.

2 Bounded loops, such as the for-endfor loop, where we know in advance how many times to repeat the loop.

The while-do loop

The while-do loop repeatedly executes a statement or block of statements as long as the condition is true. The condition in the while loop is tested at the beginning of the loop, using this syntax:

```pascal
while <condition> do
    <statement>;
```

The following program tests a set of numbers to see if they are less than 5, using the while-do loop in Pascal:

```
program test;
var
    a: integer;
begin
    a:= 0;
    while a < 5 do
        begin
            a:= a+1;
            writeln(a, ' is less than 5');
            end;
        writeln('I am out of the loop');
end.
```

Note that when the condition is false, in this case when a gets the value 5, the loop terminates since 5 < 5 is a false statement. When the loop terminates, control is returned to the first statement after the block of statements within the loop, writeln('I am out of the loop');.

Creating a program using the while-do loop

1 Enter the program exactly as shown above.

2 Compile and run the program, correcting any errors.

The repeat-until loop

The repeat-until loop executes a statement or block of statements as long as the specific condition in the until statement is false. The condition is tested at the bottom of the loop, using this syntax.

```
repeat
    <statement>
until <condition>;
```

If you have a block of statements to be executed between the repeat and until statements, then you do not need to place the statements inside a begin and end block.

The following algorithm and program use the repeat-until loop to allow someone to enter their password on a door entry system until they get it right.

Step 1: start
Step 2: password ← 3798
Step 3: repeat
          write 'Enter the 4 digit password'
          read p
      until p = password
Step 4: write 'You may enter'
Step 5: stop

```
program rloop;
const
    password=3798;
var
    p: integer;
begin
    repeat
        writeln('Enter the 4 digit password ');
        read(p);
    until p=password;
    writeln('You may enter');
end.
```

Note that the statements between the repeat and until statements are executed repeatedly until the user enters the right password.

Creating a program using the repeat-until loop

1 Enter the program exactly as shown above.

2 Compile and run the program, correcting any errors.

The for-do loop

The for-do loop is used when the start and end values are known. An integer variable is used as a loop counter, and controls how many times the loop is executed. For example, if the loop counter counts from 1 to 5 then the loop would be executed 5 times. If the loop counter counts from 0 to 6 then it will executed the loop seven times (0, 1, 2, 3, 4, 5, 6).

The syntax is like this:

```
for <loop counter> := <range> do
    <statement>;
```

The following program demonstrates the use of the for-do loop in Pascal.

```
program loops;
var
    a: integer;
begin
    for a:= 1 to 5 do
        writeln('This is loop: ', a);
end.
```

If we want to execute more than one statement inside a for loop, then we must put them between another pair of begin and end statements. This can be seen in the following program:

```
program loops;
var
    a: integer;
begin
    for a:= 1 to 5 do
        begin
            writeln('This is loop ', a);
            writeln('+++++++++');
            writeln;
        end;
end.
```

You can also use the for-do loop to print out all the multiples of a number provided by the user.

```
program multiples;
var
    a, multiple, answer: integer;
begin
    write('Enter a number ');
    read(multiple);
    for a:= 1 to 10 do
            begin
                    answer:=a * multiple;
                    writeln(a,' times ',multiple, ' = ', answer);
            end;
end.
```

Creating a program using the for-do loop

1 Enter the program above

2 Compile and run the program, correcting any errors.

CHECK YOUR PROGRESS

1 A store uses the following policy to award discounts. If the customer purchases products costing more than $500 she is given a discount of 10%, otherwise she is given a discount of 2%. Write a program to compute the discount a customer will receive based on the purchase she makes.

2 Write a program to print the message 'Your tuition is wavered' if the student scores over 85 marks in the entrance examination.

3 Consider the following while loop:

```
begin
    a:= 0;
    while a<5 do
        begin
            a:= a+3;
            writeln(a, 'is less than 5');
        end;
end.
```

How many times would the program go through the loop?

4 Consider the following segment of code:

```
begin
for a:= 1 to 5 do
writeln('Help');
writeln('me');
end.
```

Is the above statement correct? Give reason for your answer.

5 Consider the following segment of code:

```
begin
    a:= 0;
    repeat
        a:= a+1;
        writeln('The number is ', a);
    until a>5;
```

In the third repetition of the repeat-until segment, what is printed out?

Arrays

You have learned in previous topics that a variable can store one value. But there are times you might have to store a *list* of items for one variable. For example, a shopping list may contain a few items such as milk, eggs, butter, juice, potatoes and bread. In order to store these values, you can use many variables such as item1, item2, item3, item4, item5 and item6 and it would be stored in various locations in memory as the following:

item1	item2	item3	item4	item5	item6
milk	eggs	butter	juice	potatoes	bread

Suppose you want to store 100 items instead of these six items, it would be difficult for you to create variables for that many items in a list. Also it would be hard to manipulate this list with so many variables. For storing so many values to one variable you can use an array.

An array is made up of elements, each of which acts like a separate variable. Every element in the array has the same name, but they are distinguished from each other by a subscript, which is a number placed in brackets, All the elements in an array must be of the same data type.

WHAT DOES IT MEAN?

array
An array is a variable that can store a number of elements of the same data type.

The structure of an array

The simplest form of an array is a one-dimensional array. In a one-dimensional array you can store a finite number of items with same data type. The number of items for which you create the array is called the size of the array. As you can see below, the array variable called 'items' with an array of size 100 can store 100 items of same data type in successive memory locations.

items

items[1]	Milk
items[2]	Eggs
items[3]	Butter
.....	.....
.....	.....
.....	.....
items[99]	Rice
items[100]	Flour

WHAT DOES IT MEAN?

array size
The size of an array determines the number of elements it can hold.

Similar to variables you have been using so far, an array variable also needs to be declared before using it.

The array variable 'items' would be declared like this:

items = 'Array name'

1..100 = 'Range'

var

integer = 'Data type (all elements are of same data type)'

items: array[1..100] of integer;

The syntax for declaring array statement in Pascal is:

var <array name>: array[<range>] of <data type>;

In the syntax above,

- <array name > is the name of the array variable
- [<range>] with a beginning value and ending value separated by two dots e.g. [1..100] indicates the number of elements that can be held in the array
- <data type> indicates the data type of the elements that will be stored

Writing to an array and reading from an array

Suppose you want to store seven marks of students in an array called scores, you can declare it as:

var
    scores: array[1..7] of integer;

Suppose the scores achieved by the students are 78, 76, 74, 82, 83, 81 and 80, you can assign these values in array locations by using simple assignment statements like

scores[1]: = 78;
scores[2]: = 76;
scores[3]: = 74;
scores[4]: = 82;
scores[5]: = 83;
scores[6]: = 81;
scores[7]: = 80;

and they would be stored in array as the following:

scores[1]	78
scores[2]	76
scores[3]	74
scores[4]	82
scores[5]	83
scores[6]	81
scores[7]	80

If you want to know the scores of the fourth student, you can use the statement
writeln(scores[4]);

and it would display 82 as it is the fourth element in the array.

Suppose you want to store the marks of 100 students, this method for assigning values would not suitable as you might end up writing 100 statements to store these values. So it would be wise to use a variable as the range value and also a loop that can help you to read the values a number of times.

So, let's look at how scores of 100 students can be stored in an array using a loop:

```
program arraystorage;
var
    i: integer;
    scores: array[1..100] of integer;
begin
    write ('Storing values in an array');
    for i:= 1 to 100 do
        begin
            write('Enter student mark ');
            readln(scores[i]);
        end;
end.
```

In the above example, you can see that the loop will execute 100 times with the value of the subscript for 'scores' changing from 1 up to 100. The marks of each student will be stored in successive locations of the array variable 'scores' as the value of i changes each time.

When you want to display these values stored in the array, you can use another loop that will read the marks from the locations of the scores and display them. The following statements illustrate the display of data stored in scores earlier.

```
begin
    write('Reading values from an array');
    for i:= 1 to 100 do
        begin
            write('The values are ');
            writeln(scores[i]);
        end;
end.
```

To avoid having to enter 100 values, for the exercise we will reduce the number of elements in the array back to seven.

```
program arraystorage;
var
    i: integer;
    scores: array[1..7] of integer;
begin
    write ('Storing values in an array');
    for i:= 1 to 7 do
        begin
            write('Enter student mark ');
            readln(scores[i]);
        end;
    write ('Reading values from an array');
    for i: = 1 to 7 do
        begin
            write('The values are ');
            writeln(scores[i]);
        end;
end.
```

Using an array

1 Enter the program above.

2 Compile and run the program, correcting any errors.

Traversing and searching an array

In addition to reading from and writing into arrays, you can also do other operations on them such as:

a traverse

b search

Traversing an array

Traversal in a one-dimensional array involves processing all the elements from first to last, one by one. For example, in the program above, the array was traversed twice, once when reading in the data, and once when writing the data to the screen.

WHAT DOES IT MEAN?

traversal
You traverse an array when you process each element in turn.

Suppose there are seven elements in the array that are 5, 10, 15, 20, 30, 40 and 50. If you want to double the values of the elements in an array, you can traverse the array as follows:

```
program traversal;
var
    i:integer;
    scores: array[1..7] of integer;
begin
    writeln('Linear traversal');
    writeln('Enter the scores');
    for i:= 1 to 7 do
        begin
            write('Enter score');
            readln(scores[i]);
        end;
    writeln('New scores are ')
    for i = 1 to 7 do
        begin
            scores[i]:= scores[i] * 2;
            write(scores[i]);
        end;
end.
```

Traversing an array

1 Enter the program above.

2 Compile and run the program, correcting any errors.

Searching an array

If you want to search the array for a particular element, then you traverse the array until you find the location of an element in the array and retrieve it.

Suppose you want to conduct a search in your array to see if there is a score of 85 as an element. You can search arrays in many ways. The most common search is a linear search. In linear search, *each* element of the array is compared with the given item to be searched for, one by one.

The following program will show how a linear search can be conducted to find the array element where a particular value is stored.

```
program linear_search;
var
    searchitem, i:integer;
    found: char;
    scores: array[1..7] of integers;
begin
    writeln('Linear search');
    writeln('Enter the scores');
    for i: =1 to 7 do
        begin
            readln(scores[i]);
        end;
    i:= 0;
    found:= 'n';
    writeln('Enter the score that you want to search for');
    readln(searchitem);
    repeat
        i: =i+1;
        if scores[i]=searchitem then
            found: = 'y';
    until ((i=7) or (found='y'));
    if found = 'y' then
        writeln('Element found at position ', i)
    else
        writeln('Element not found');
end.
```

In the above program, if the search item is found in the array, it will display the message 'Element found' and if it is not found 'Element not found'.

Searching an array

1 Enter the program above.

2 Enter the scores one at a time when prompted. Make sure that at least one of them is 85.

3 When prompted for the search element, enter 85.

4 Run the program again and this time search for a score that is not stored in the array.

Testing and debugging the program

You can either test a program manually and using the computer. After a program is developed, it is important to perform checks and tests to verify its correctness before it is put into live operation. This is called debugging. Once a program is placed into live operation, many users will rely on the program to carry out their daily activities and to make decisions. As such, the goal of program testing is to find all remaining errors.

As you learned earlier in this section, two types of errors can be found when testing a program:

1　Syntax error – when the program code does not follow the rules of the programming language. For example, the omission of a semi-colon at the end of a statement will result in a syntax error.

2　Logic error – when the reasoning used in the program is incorrect, so that the program does not do what it is supposed to do. For example, placing instructions in the wrong order will often result in a logic error.

Manual testing

Also called dry running or desk checking, manual testing involves working through the program on paper by using test data as input values for variables and recording what takes place after each instruction is executed. This technique is called tracing the program, and you came across it in Section 2, when you learned about trace tables on page 101. As you know, a trace table is created with the variables written as the column headings. With each execution of the program, the changes in the value of the variables are recorded in the trace table. The trace table is used to detect any logic error in the program.

Consider this extract from the program you wrote earlier. We have added line numbers to make it easier to follow the trace table.

```
Line 1:  i:=0;
Line 2:  found: = 'n';
Line 3:  writeln('Enter the score that you want to search for ');
Line 4:  readln(searchitem);
Line 5:  repeat
Line 6:     i: =i+1;
Line 7:     if scores[i]=searchitem then
                found: = 'y';
Line 8:  until ((i=7) or (found='y'));
```

Let's create a trace table to record the changes in the variables i, found and scores as each statement in the program is executed.

The test data for this test is:
scores: 25, 37, 45, 12, 78, 95, 62
searchitem: 45
expected output: i=3

Trace table

Line	i	found	searchitem	scores [1]	scores [2]	scores [3]	scores [4]	scores [5]	scores [6]	scores [7]
				25	37	45	12	78	95	62
1	0									
2		n								
4			45							
6	1									
7		n								
6	2									
7		n								
6	3									
7		y								

Computer testing

Testing can also be done using the computer to run the program with suitable test data to deal with all possible kinds of conditions. The results generated by the computer are then compared with the expected solutions.

Both valid (correct) and invalid (incorrect) test data sets should be constructed and used to test the program. When valid test data is entered, the program should produce the correct result. If the expected and the actual results do not match, then the program has a logic error.

Debugging the program

When syntax and logic errors are identified these must be debugged and fixed. Some programming language includes a debug utility or a debugger to identify syntax errors and to find logic errors.

Even if the program has been tested and debugged, errors can still occur when the program is run. These types of errors are called run time errors. An example of a run time error is when the program is stuck in an infinite loop.

CHECK YOUR PROGRESS

1 Construct a trace table for the following segment of code:
```
begin
    a: =1;
    b: = 2;
    c: = 1;
    while a<20 do
        begin
            b: = a * 2;
            c: = b + 1;
            a: = c + 2;
        end;
end.
```
2 Consider the following lines of code:
```
a: = 1;
b: = a - 1;
c: = a div b;
```
What type of error would be generated when the three statements above are executed? Give a reason for your answer.

3 A program has been tested and all errors are corrected. What type of errors could still occur when the program is executed?

Program documentation

Once the program is completed and is running error-free, it is important that you have clear documentation of the program so that other users can follow it easily, whether they are other programmers like you, or operators of the program.

The following are some reasons why we need to have very good documentation:

- Clear documentation makes it easier for users to comprehend and use the program.
- If there is a problem with a section of the program, users can refer to the documentation to solve it.
- Users, like programmers, can easily make a modification to the program.

Documentation can be internal or external.

Internal documentation appears inside the program.

External documentation is created separately and supplied with the program, e.g. in the form of a user manual.

Internal documentation

A well internally documented program makes the reading and understanding of the program easier. Internal documentation involves the use of meaningful variable names in the program, descriptive comments, indentation and effective use of white spaces.

When you create programs, variable names used must be meaningful as it would indicate what type of data will be stored in it. For example, if you need to have two variables to store two numbers it would be wise to use num1 and num2 instead of A, B.

Descriptive comments for each section of the program to document the logic of it will also enhance the understanding of the program. The comments help in determining the ease with which a program can be modified, not only by other programmers, but by the original programmer. For example, when programs are created you can place comments to indicate the date, author and the aim of the program.

In Pascal you can add a comment to a program like this:

```
total: = total+1 {This adds 1 to the total each time round the loop}
```

You can use (* and *) as alternative brackets for comments.

Comments are ignored by the compiler, but they are a useful way of adding notes to the source code.

Your program also should efficiently use indentation for sections of the code to increase readability. Using indentation lets you use your eyes to quickly pick out the flow of control or mistakes in that flow of control. For example, when a loop is used in the program, the statements inside the loops are normally indented so that you can easily identify the flow of control,

Efficient use of white (blank) spaces such as tabs, spaces and blank lines in between also will enhance the program readability, and will also reduce eye strain.

External documentation

External documentation is documentation that is created separately and supplied with the program for reference by the user, if there is a need. It normally includes how to install the program, the required hardware specifications, how to solve the errors that may occur, and how to use the program.

External documentation can be technical documentation or user documentation. Technical documentation contains the technical aspects of the program such as its version, the operating system that it can work with, the amount of memory and hard disk space required, and the installation procedure.

User documentation (the user manual, user guide or instruction manual) suggests how the users should use the program and how to solve some simple program error situations. It contains instructions like how to start or stop the program, move around different parts of the program and solve simple program errors. User documentation can be in the form of a written booklet or online tutorial with FAQs (Frequently Asked Questions) and screen shots, to make it easier for the users to follow.

CHECK YOUR PROGRESS

1 List three advantages of proper documentation in a program.
2 State the difference between internal and external documentation.
3 For each of the following, classify them as internal documentation or external documentation.
   a Meaningful variable names
   b Frequently Asked Questions
   c Tutorial
   d Indentation
   e Tabs
4 What is technical documentation?
5 Most programs come with user documentation. What are the typical contents of user documentation?

End-of-section questions

Multiple-choice

1 Which one of the following is a low-level language:
   - A HLL
   - B ALL
   - C 4GL
   - D 5GL

2 Which one of the following is not a feature of third generation languages?
   - A they need to get translated
   - B they are faster than MLLs
   - C they are easier to use than MLLs
   - D they use compilers and interpreters

3 The translator used by second generation languages is:
   - A compiler
   - B linker
   - C assembler
   - D interpreter

4 The following are steps associated with implementing the program
   - I compiling
   - II create source code
   - III linking
   - IV maintain program
   - V executing

   The correct order is:
   - A I, II, III, IV, V
   - B II, I, III, V, IV
   - C II, I, V, III, IV
   - D II, V, I, III, IV

5 The error that occurs when the program has to stop before its completion due to a bad condition such as division by 0 is a:
   - A debug error
   - B syntax error
   - C logic error
   - D run time error

6 Which of the following is not a data type found in Pascal?
   - A integers
   - B real
   - C text
   - D string

7 An example of a conditional branching statement in Pascal is:
   - A goto
   - B if-then
   - C for
   - D while

8 The following are loop statements used in Pascal except:
   - A while
   - B if-then
   - C for
   - D repeat

9 The major advantage of Machine-level languages over other programming languages is:
   - A they are slower in execution
   - B they are slower in correcting mistakes
   - C they are faster in execution
   - D they are faster in correcting mistakes

10 Programming languages that use mnemonics are called:
   - A Machine-level languages
   - B high-level languages
   - C Assembly-level languages
   - D fourth generation languages

Structured questions

1 a State the difference between first generation and second generation languages.
  b List one advantage and two disadvantages of first generation languages compared to second generation languages.
  c List three examples of third generation languages.

2 a List the sequence of steps associated with implementing a program.
   b State the difference between:
      i testing and debugging
      ii syntax error and logic error
      iii logic error and run time error
      iv testing and dry running
   c Define the term 'test data'.

3 a State one conditional branching statement in Pascal.
   b State one example of a bounded iteration statement in Pascal.
   c State one example of an unbounded iteration statement in Pascal.

4 A well documented program makes it easy for the user to use.
   a List two types of program documentation.
   b State the difference between the types of documentation you identified in your answer to 4a

5 Using the algorithm you created for 15 in Section 2's End-of-section Questions, write a program in Pascal that prompts the user to enter a value and display its square and cube values.

6 Using the flowchart you created for 16 in Section 2's End-of-section Questions, write a program in Pascal that will prompt the user to enter two numbers and display their product.

7 Using the flowchart you created for 18 in Section 2's End-of-section Questions, write a program in Pascal that will accept 25 integers and display the number of positive and negative numbers.

8 a Write pseudocode that will accept a set of marks of students and display the highest marks. The pseudocode stops when the user inputs -1 for marks.
   b Using the pseudocode you created in your answer to 8a as a guide, implement the program in Pascal.

9 a Write a pseudocode that will accept scores of 33 batsmen in a cricket tournament and display the number of batsmen who scored 0 and the number who scored more than 0.
   b Using the algorithm you created in your answer to 9a as a guide, implement the program in Pascal.

10 Write a program in Pascal that will read the sales of 50 sales men into an array and display the sales of all sales men who have total sales more than $10,000.

Practice SBA

Task

Using the programming language Pascal, write a program to implement the algorithm you created for SBA practice question 2 in Section 2. Make sure that you use appropriate variable names, data types and control structures.

Test your program using values suggested by your teacher. It should produce correct outputs for all the values entered.

Your program listing must have your name, date created and comments indicating what you intend the program to do.

Objectives

By the end of this section, you will be able to:

- Explain the main concepts of computer networks.
- Describe the types of data transmission media used in computer networks, including wired and wireless media.
- State the key concepts of wireless networks.
- State the main data communication modes.
- Distinguish between the Internet, intranets and extranets.
- Explain the communication facilities offered by the Internet, such as email and voice transmission.
- State the functions and uses of the World Wide Web.
- Describe how data can be kept secure using software and physical methods.
- Describe how data can be recovered if things go wrong.

The Internet is one of the most significant developments in Information Technology since computers were first invented. But it only became widely known through the invention of the World Wide Web in the early 1990s. Since then, the Internet has transformed communications in almost every country in the world.

The Internet is a vast computer network, so we begin this section by looking at much smaller networks, in order to understand the basic principles. All networks connect together separate computers and other devices, so it is important to understand the data communications methods by which the data is transferred from one machine to another.

• 4.1 Data communications and networks

Many home computers are stand-alone systems. They cannot communicate directly with other computers. If you want to share a file that is saved on a stand-alone system with another computer then you will have to copy it onto a USB flash drive, CD or DVD.

Computer systems can be connected together in a **network**. The network will also include devices such as printers and plotters. The computers in a network can:

- access the same files held on a central hard disk.
- send files to a shared printer.
- send files to each other.

The Internet is a very special type of network and you will be looking at it later.

In many networks one or more powerful computers act as the **servers**, which manage the activity on the whole network. All the computers in a network can access files that are held on the file server's hard disk. A print server allows any of the computers in the network to use a printer.

The computers and other devices in a network communicate with each other by sending data either directly to each other or through a server. Data can be sent between the devices in a network either through cables or wirelessly, that is, without cables. This is called **data communications**.

WHAT DOES IT MEAN?

network
A network is a set of computers that are linked together so they can share facilities such as printers and hard drives.

server
A server is a powerful computer that helps to manage a network of computers. A file server handles all the shared files and data. A print server handles access to a printer.

data communications
Data communications refers to all the methods by which computers and other devices in a network send data to each other.

Area networks

Area networks link together a limited number of computer systems. There are three types of area network:

1 Local area network (LAN)
2 Metropolitan area network (MAN)
3 Wide area network (WAN)

Later in the section you will see that the Internet is a network of networks.

Local area network (LAN)

A **local area network (LAN)** is a network of computers that are connected by cables over a fairly small area, usually within one building, such as an office or a school. There are several types of LAN, but most of them look like Fig 4.1

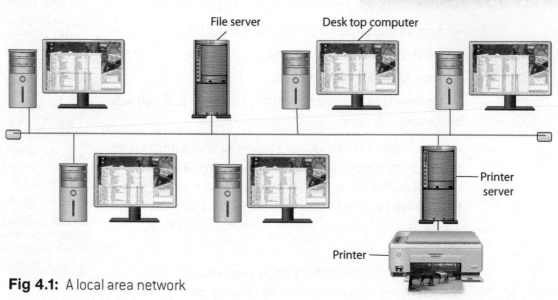

Fig 4.1: A local area network

One advantage of using a LAN is that you do not have to store all the application software on the hard disk of the computer you are using. When you want to use some software, like a word processing package, you can **download** it from the file server's hard disk into the internal memory of your computer.

You can also share a file with someone else. If you are working on a report with a group of other people, you can **upload** it to the file server's hard disk. Another user can then download it and make any changes they want to it.

You can also use a file at the same time as other people. This often happens when a large database is used in, for example, a shop.

Metropolitan area network (MAN)

Sometimes a network is needed that serves a limited area but is bigger than a LAN. The first **metropolitan area networks (MAN)** were built across a whole town or city, hence the name. A MAN is run by a single organisation and connects together the LANs within it.

Wide area network (WAN)

In many circumstances it is useful to link computers together even when they are too far apart to be connected by a cable. A **wide area network (WAN)** is a network that connects computers over a wide area or even across the world.

Instead of normal computer cables, a WAN uses a number of different methods to connect the workstations, including telephone lines, satellite links and broadband connections.

Most WANs are private networks that are run by organisations so that they can share business information.

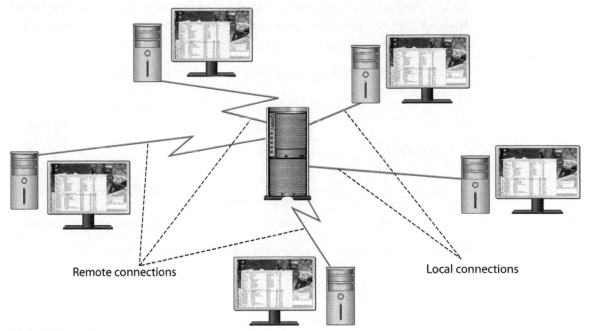

Remote connections   Local connections

Fig 4.2: A wide area network

A WAN lets the members of an organisation share information between all their branches. They can also work on the same files, such as a database, from anywhere in the country or even the world.

However, it may be possible for a criminal to get into a WAN. They do not have to get into the organisation's building, but they may find out how to access the system from any computer.

CHECK YOUR PROGRESS

What are the differences between a LAN, a MAN and a WAN?

Modem

You can connect a computer to a server that is a long distance away by using the normal telephone lines. This means that a stand-alone computer can become a part of a WAN during the time that it is connected by telephone. In order to make the connection the computer has to dial the number of a telephone that is connected to the server. This is usually known as a dial-up connection.

Computers and telephone lines use different types of signals for sending data. Computers use digital signals, while many telephone systems use the older analogue system. Although many telephone systems have been upgraded to take digital signals, many still handle analogue only.

The digital signals sent by the computer have to be converted into analogue signals before they can be sent down an analogue telephone line. When they reach the other end they have to be converted back to the digital format. A modem is a device that converts the signals between analogue and digital.

The connection between a computer and a server through modems is very slow by today's standards.

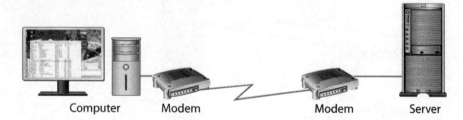

Computer   Modem   Modem   Server

Fig 4.3: A computer connected to a server using modems

Summary of key points

In this topic you have learned:

- how computer networks link together computers and other devices.
- the differences between LANs, WANs and MANs.
- the uses of servers and modems.

1 Why does a network need a file server?
2 What is the function of a printer server?
3 Distinguish between uploading and downloading a file in a network.
4 What is a modem?

4.1 Data transmission

Networks use a number of different methods to send data from one computer or device to another. For example, if you send an email to someone living on the other side of the world, your message may be transmitted by computer cables, telephone cables and microwave signals before reaching its destination.

Those cables and signals are together known as **transmission media**.

Transmission media

Transmission media all fall into two groups: those that use wires and those that do not.

Wired transmission media

There are many types of cables and wires used for transmission.

- **Coaxial cables** carry electric current at radio frequencies. It is used for cable television and broadband Internet connections.
- **Fibre-optic cables** contain a bundle of glass fibres that each transmit light. This is a very fast and reliable form of data transmission. Although light travels in straight lines, a light beam bounces off the sides of the fibre along its length so the cable can be quite flexible. Fibre-optic cables are now widely used in telephone systems.
- **Twisted pair cables** have been used for telephone networks for over a century, although they are gradually being replaced by fibre-optic cables.

All of these transmission media can be used in LANs.

Wireless transmission media

Computer data is more and more frequently transmitted using technologies that do not use cables or wires. Generally, wireless connections are not as fast or as reliable as cables, but they can be very convenient.

All wireless connections use electromagnetic waves. Different wavelengths are used for different purposes. Starting from the longest wavelength, electromagnetic waves include radio, microwave, infrared, light and X-rays. Wavelengths vary from kilometres (for long-wave radio) to less than a millimetre (for infrared).

The frequency of a signal is the number of waves that can be completed in a second. So long wavelengths, like radio, have low frequencies and short wavelengths like infrared have very high frequencies.

- **Radio signals** are the most common form of wireless transmission. They are used as the main means of communication for cell phones and also in many small LANs. Satellites enable radio signals to be sent around the world. Data is transmitted by radio up to a satellite in stationary orbit then directed back down to a receiving station in another country.

- **Microwave transmission** uses a signal with a shorter wavelength than radio. It can be used over distances of up to 50 km, but it cannot get round or through objects in its way.

- **Infrared transmission** is used in remote controls for televisions and other domestic devices. The signal has a very much shorter wavelength than radio. It is occasionally used in computer systems, for example, when controlling robots. However, the signal cannot travel very far and also needs clear space for the signal to travel.

Fig 4.4: Radio transmission

Wireless networks

Wireless networks use no cables. They are an increasingly popular technology for small networks, because the computers, especially laptops, can be moved around but still remain connected to the network. Wireless networks normally use radio transmissions.

- Wi-Fi is a wireless radio technology that can be used to send data between devices and computers. Small LANs can be built using only Wi-Fi, and the signal is good enough to be used with a shared Internet access. Some cell phones can use Wi-Fi technology to access the Internet.

WHAT DOES IT MEAN?

Wi-Fi
Wi-Fi is a wireless method of data transmission that is used in LANs and for Internet access.

- **Bluetooth** is a radio technology that is similar to Wi-Fi but only works over short distances, and is slower. It is mainly used to send data between two devices such as a cell phone and headset, or between a digital camera and a laptop.

If you have a laptop you can sometimes link into a Wi-Fi network whilst you are out and about. Many Wi-Fi networks are private and the owner should make sure that no-one else can log in, by using security measures such as passwords. But there are also public Wi-Fi networks that you are encouraged to use. These may be provided by a commercial organisation like a hotel or coffee shop, or they may be provided by government. Some charge a fee for Wi-Fi access, while others offer a free service to anyone who wants to use it. A public area where you can use Wi-Fi is known as a **hotspot**.

> **WHAT DOES IT MEAN?**
>
> **Bluetooth**
> Bluetooth is a wireless method of data transmission that uses radio signals to send data between devices over short distances.

> **WHAT DOES IT MEAN?**
>
> **hotspot**
> A hotspot is a public place where you can access Wi-Fi.

Fig 4.5: Using a Wi-Fi hotspot

Bandwidth

Bandwidth measures the capacity of a communications channel. The larger the bandwidth, the more signals can be sent. The channel with the biggest capacity is usually referred to as broadband.

We are interested in bandwidth of two different types of communication, radio transmissions (analogue) and Internet connections (digital).

Radio bandwidth

The **bandwidth** of a radio transmission measures the frequencies that it can handle.

Radio transmissions can be classified into three bandwidths:

1 Narrowband covers frequencies up to 300 Hz and can be used for simple signalling such as Morse code.
2 Voiceband covers frequencies from 300 Hz to 3000 Hz, and can carry voice well.
3 Broadband (also known as wideband) is the term used for frequencies over 3000 Hz, and can be used for high quality music broadcasts.

Digital bandwidth

The **bandwidth** of a digital connection measures the speed at which data can be transmitted. It is often stated in bits per second. Earlier we looked at dial-up modems. Typically, connections to the Internet through a dial-up modem have a maximum rate of 56 Kilobits per second.

You might find this confusing because most sizes in computing are measured in bytes, and most speeds in bytes per second, but here we are talking about a speed of 56 Kilobits per second. Now you have to divide that figure by 8 to see how many bytes are being transmitted each second, and the answer is 7 Kilobytes (7KB) per second.

WHAT DOES IT MEAN?

bandwidth
In a digital connection (such as a connection to the Internet) the bandwidth is the speed, measured in bits per second, at which data can be transmitted. In radio transmissions, bandwidth refers to the range of frequencies that the medium can handle.

Normally a single character uses up one byte, so this means that the fastest dial-up modem can handle over 7000 characters per second. That kind of speed was fine in the days when web pages were mainly text and did not have many pictures. Today a single photo on screen may be 100 KB in size. At 7 KB per second it would take 14 seconds for the picture to appear on screen. And the picture would only be a small part of all the data that makes up a web page.

The result is that at 56 K bits per second it can take a very long time for a web page to download from the Internet. That is why faster transmission rates are desirable.

Broadband Internet connections generally use speeds of over 1 M bits per second, which is over 1000 K bits per second.

Communication modes

You may have used a walkie-talkie device with a friend. You speak into your walkie-talkie and then press a button when you have finished. Your friend then gets a chance to speak on their walkie-talkie. Only one person can speak at a time. This is just one of three communication modes.

1 In simplex mode the transmission is in one direction only. A baby monitor that allows the parent to hear when a baby is crying in another room is a simplex device.

2 In duplex mode both devices can transmit at the same time. Telephones use duplex mode.

3 In half-duplex mode both devices can transmit, but only one at a time. This is the mode used with walkie-talkies.

Point-to-point and broadcast communications

The computers and devices in a network have to send data to each other. Sometimes that data is sent to the whole network, and sometimes data is sent very specifically from one device to another. When data is sent from one device to exactly one other, this is called **point-to-point communication**. For example, when a file is sent from a print server to the printer, there will be one cable (or other communication link) between the printer server and the printer so the data can only go to the one device.

In Fig 4.1 you can see that the computers in the network share a common cable. That means that data being sent between the computers and the servers all pass along the same communication link. It also means that it is possible for the same data to be sent to all the computers in the network. This is known as **broadcast communication**. You will be more familiar with the term 'broadcast' in relation to radio or television, where the programs are sent to every radio or television set in the network.

WHAT DOES IT MEAN?

point-to-point communication
Point-to-point communication occurs when data is sent directly from one device to another along a connecting channel.

broadcast communication
Broadcast communication occurs when data is sent from one device to all the others in the network.

Summary of key points

In this topic you have learned:

- how wired and wireless transmission media can be used for data communications.
- the uses of wireless networks.
- the meanings of bandwidth and various communication modes.

QUESTIONS

1 List two wired transmission media and two wireless transmission media.
2 How could you measure the bandwidth of an Internet connection?
3 What is a wireless network? What are the advantages of having a wireless network over a network that uses cables?
4 Explain the terms simplex, duplex and half-duplex when applied to data communications.

4.2–4.3 The Internet

The **Internet** connects networks with each other. It is a vast public wide area network that creates connections between individual LANs and WANs.

The Internet is available in every country of the world, so is sometimes referred to as a global network. Data can be transferred across the world in seconds using the Internet.

The Internet has existed since the 1970s and was originally used by universities, research institutions and the military. It was mainly used to transfer files from one computer to another over long distances. Most of these files could be downloaded and read by anyone. But files which were sent from one person directly to another person became known as electronic mail, or email.

WHAT DOES IT MEAN?

Internet
The Internet is a public network that connects millions of computers across the world. It is sometimes referred to as the Net.

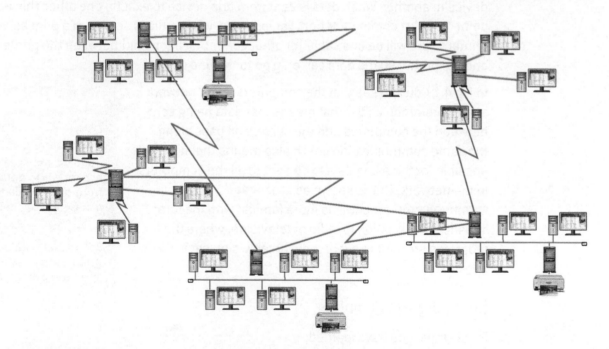

Fig 4.6: The Internet connects many different LANs and WANs across the world

The Internet only became widely used by the general public in the 1990s. The reason for the sudden growth in the use of the Internet was the launch of the **World Wide Web** in 1991. Before then, you could transfer files across the world, but you had to know where files were stored, and they were not always easy to find.

Web pages can be laid out attractively on the screen and can contain graphics, sound and video clips. Before the Web was invented most files available on

WHAT DOES IT MEAN?

World Wide Web (also known as WWW or the Web)
The World Wide Web is a method for displaying public pages of information through the Internet.

the Internet were simple text files. Today all the pages that you visit when you go on the Internet are part of the Web.

Intranets and extranets

An organisation, such as a large company or a university, will often provide many of the services you can find on the Internet, but restrict them to its employees or students. For example, people will be able to send emails to anyone else in the organisation. They will also be able to view pages of onscreen information.

The pages will be developed using the same techniques as those used on the Web. However, they will be only be available through the organisation's LAN or WAN and members of the public will not be able to view them on the Internet. Members of the organisation will have to log on to the organisation's network before they can see any pages or use the internal email system. This internal system is known as an **intranet**. (Notice the lower case 'i' in comparison with the upper case 'I' in the Internet.)

Sometimes an organisation wants to make some of the pages on an intranet available to people who do not use the organisation's LAN or WAN. For example, an employee may be working from home, or the organisation may want to provide some information for customers. This can be done by making certain pages and files available through the Internet. Users will have to log on with a password in order to see these pages. In that way, only people with permission to read the files will be able to see them, but the general public will not. This extension to an intranet is known as an **extranet**.

WHAT DOES IT MEAN?

intranet
An intranet offers email, pages and files through an organisation's LAN, which cannot be accessed from the Internet.

extranet
An extranet is an extension to an intranet that is made available through the Internet to people with permission to view it.

Remote log-in

It is possible to connect to a MAN or a WAN using the Internet.

Internet connections are public, and anyone can use them. So if someone wants to log in to a private MAN or WAN they will have to prove who they are before being given access. The network will ask the user for their username and password. Once the user has logged in successfully they can then use the network in exactly the same way as if they were working in the offices of the organisation.

It has been possible to use remote log-in through the Internet since the 1970s. The method that was used at first was known as Telnet. Telnet is still used occasionally by engineers in order to sort out data communications problems, but is not in general use any more.

Data communications via the Internet

The Internet includes the Web, but offers several communication services as well:

- email
- newsgroups
- instant messaging (chat)
- file transfer
- VoIP (online voice conversations)

email

Electronic mail, or email, is very widely used by Internet users. You can:

- send an email.
- receive an email.
- store copies of all the emails you have sent or received
- send an attachment, which is any kind of computer file, along with an email

There are two main ways of handling your emails.

1 An email client is a specialist software package, such as Outlook. This is installed on your own computer, and all the emails that you receive are downloaded and stored on your own computer. You must be connected to the Internet in order to send or receive emails.

2 Webmail is a system, such as Hotmail, for managing your emails entirely on the Web. You can log on to your webmail account from any computer that is connected to the Internet.

When you receive an email it appears in a folder called the Inbox. When you finish writing an email it is placed in another folder called the Outbox until you are ready to send it. Once an email has been sent it is placed in the Sent folder.

You can usually create additional folders so you can organise the copies of the emails that you have sent and received.

When you send an email you have to enter the email address of the recipient (the person you are sending an email to). You can copy an email to several people. An email address usually looks like myname@example.com.

The main recipient

This email is also copied to these people

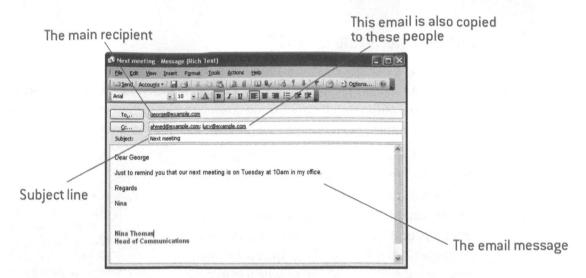

Subject line

The email message

Fig 4.7: Creating an email in Outlook

Newsgroups

You may have joined a group of people who share an interest online. After signing up with your email address, you will be able to send an email that will then be copied to the whole group. In this way you can discuss ideas and share information.

This is known as a newsgroup. The term newsgroup was originally only applied to groups set up on a system called Usenet on the Internet. Today it is used for any online discussion group.

When you send an email to the group it is usually referred to as posting a message or sending a post. Most newsgroups also have a website where you can view online all the posts. The messages are often organised into threads. A thread is a series of posts that all refer to the same subject.

Instant messaging (chat)

You may have used the Internet to chat with your friends. You key in messages to one another and both your message and the replies can be seen on screen. You can choose between many messaging services, including Windows Live Messenger, Yahoo Messenger and the chat facilities on social networking sites like Facebook.

Instant messaging services can also be used in business for on-line meetings. Most of the more serious services are based on Internet Relay Chat (IRC) software. There are several IRC programs available, such as mIRC which runs on Microsoft Windows.

Some instant messaging networks allow you to use webcams (web-based cameras) so you can see the person you are chatting with.

File Transfer Protocol (FTP)

When a file is transferred from one computer to another across a network, the file has to be structured according to rules, known as protocols. The **File Transfer Protocol (FTP)** is widely used for this purpose. It breaks the file down into several blocks, which are sent one at a time. The computer that receives the blocks combines them again into a single file.

FTP is particularly important on the Internet. Long before the World Wide Web was invented, it was the standard method for transferring files between servers on the Internet, and it is still used today. For example, you may design a web page on your own computer. You then use FTP to upload a copy of the web page file to the webserver, which is a computer that could be located anywhere in the world. The web page can then be seen on the World Wide Web.

WHAT DOES IT MEAN?

FTP

File Transfer Protocol (FTP) is a method for transferring all types of files between computers on a network. It is used on the Internet for a number of purposes, including uploading web pages to a webserver.

VoIP

VoIP is short for Voice over Internet Protocol. Services such as Skype allow you to use the Internet to have voice conversations. These calls are usually free, so this is an excellent way to chat with people internationally. You can use VoIP on any computer that has an Internet connection, a microphone and speakers. You can even add webcams and see the person you are talking to.

VoIP technology has also been used in organisations by combining the phone system with a LAN. This means that all internal phone calls are sent through the LAN system, so they use digital formats instead of analogue. In these cases the phones look like normal phones, although they often have additional features, such as the ability to search telephone directories to contact other people in the organisation.

Summary of key points

In this topic you have learned:

- the differences between the Internet, intranets and extranets.
- how the Internet can be used for various types of communication, such as email and VoIP that do not depend on the World Wide Web.

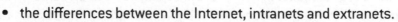

1 What is the difference between an intranet and extranet?
2 Name three services that you can use on the Internet without using the World Wide Web.

● 4.3 The World Wide Web

We have seen that the World Wide Web displays pages of information through the Internet. The most important feature of the Web is the use of hyperlinks – the text or images that allow the user to jump to another page. All the pages on the Web are ultimately linked together through hyperlinks, giving a vast network of information.

A **web page** is a single document that can be viewed on the Web. A collection of web pages stored together, with the same title, are known as a **website**. The home page in a website is the main page that you normally see first of all. You should be able to find all the other pages on the website by following links from the home page.

WHAT DOES IT MEAN?

web page
A web page is a file that can be displayed on the World Wide Web.

website
A website is a collection of web pages that belong together.

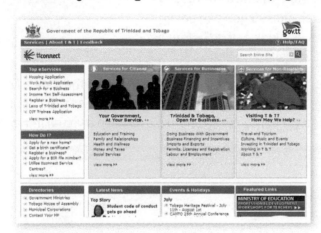

Fig 4.8: The home page for a website

HTML and XHTML

Most pages on the web are created by web developers using **Hypertext Markup Language** (HTML). This is rather like a simple programming language that lays out the information on the screen. HTML contains the code for the hyperlinks, and allows you to place images and sounds on a web page. Web pages created in HTML are stored as files with filenames ending with .htm or .html.

WHAT DOES IT MEAN?

HTML and XHTML
HyperText Markup Language (HTML) is a simple programming language that is used to create web pages. EXtensible HTML (XHTML) is a more recent development of HTML that is stricter and has more features.

Although HTML is still widely used by web developers, a more advanced system called XHTML (Extensible HTML) was introduced in 2000. XHTML is much stricter than HTML. One advantage of creating a page in XHTML is that every browser will be able to handle the code. In the past some browsers could not handle some HTML code.

Web browsers

A **web browser** is a piece of software that is used to view pages on the Web. Internet Explorer is a well known example of a browser. It is installed on your computer and it is able to interpret the HTML/XHTML code of a web page. The code is really a set of instructions for displaying the text and images on the screen as a web page.

When you visit a web page the HTML or XHTML code is downloaded to your computer and the browser interprets the code to create the web page itself. A browser also makes hyperlinks work, so that when you click on a link the browser will find the correct page and download it.

A browser usually lets you store the web addresses (URLs) of your favourite websites so you can easily find them again. It also lets you look at the History list, that is, all the sites you have visited recently.

Many browsers have other useful features to meet the needs of the users. For example, you can zoom in on a page so it is displayed much larger on the screen, or you can enlarge the text only. These are particularly useful if you have a visual impairment.

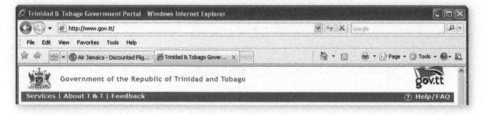

Fig 4.9: The Internet Explorer web browser

Webservers

All websites are stored on **webservers**. A webserver is a computer that has special webserver software and is also connected to the Internet.

Web developers have to transfer pages and other files from their own computers to the webserver. This is known as uploading a file. When you want to look at a website, your browser finds the correct webserver and then copies the file or files to your own computer. This is known as downloading a file.

Two different methods are usually used for uploading and downloading files.

- FTP is used to upload files to a webserver.
- HTTP is used to download files from a webserver.

URLs

Every single page on the Web has a special web filename, known as a **Uniform Resource Locator (URL)**. For example, http://www.example.com/contact.htm is the URL for the contact page on a website. Sometimes you download other files from the Internet, such as documents or music files. Each of these also has its own URL, such as http://www. example.com/song.mp3. URLs are sometimes referred to as web addresses.

A URL consists of several parts:

- http – this part tells the browser to download the file using the Hypertext Transfer Protocol
- www.example.com – this part is the domain name for the website. Domain names are purchased from a domain name registrar
- contact.htm – this part is the name of the file. In this case, the filename ends in .htm so must be a web page.

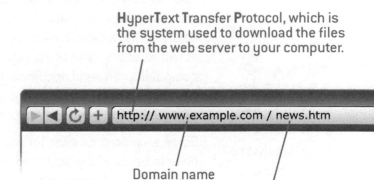

HyperText Transfer Protocol, which is the system used to download the files from the web server to your computer.

http:// www.example.com / news.htm

Domain name

File name

Fig 4.10: The parts of a URL

Uses of websites

The Internet offers some excellent opportunities to individual users, businesses and all kinds of organisations.

- You can find vast amounts of information from all over the world. The Web contains many millions of pages, provided by public bodies, universities, commercial companies, societies and individuals. It could take you many days to find some of this information in libraries and archives.
- You can find other people and organisations that share your interests.
- You can communicate easily with people wherever they live, using email, newsgroups, VoIP, instant messaging, blogs, social networking and chat rooms.
- You can transfer documents and other computer files to another person instantly.
- You can shop on-line and save lengthy trips to shopping centres or specialist shops.

e-commerce

Businesses can sell either goods or services. Goods are actual objects that you can buy, such as a washing machine, breakfast cereal, soap or a car. Services are all the other things that you pay for such as entertainment, insurance, holidays and travel. Some services, such as banking, appear to be free but are paid for by the interest that the banks charge on loans.

An **e-commerce** website lets you buy something via the Internet. There are e-commerce websites that sell goods and others that sell services, while others sell a mixture of goods and services.

Goods have to be sent to the customer either by post or using a distribution company, and successful on-line businesses usually guarantee delivery within 24 hours or a few days.

Some Internet businesses offer services that avoid the need to deliver goods. For example, on-line banking has grown very rapidly, and customers can view their balance, make payments and generally manage their accounts at any time of the day. Similarly, travel companies can send documents, such as ticket confirmations, by email and may not need to use the post at all.

Some e-commerce sites let you book a seat at a show or sports event. These services have to be carefully designed, to make sure that only one person is booked for each seat. They are linked to powerful databases that can check whether a seat has already been booked.

THINK ABOUT IT

Can you find any e-commerce websites that sell any of these items: books, music, food, household goods, furniture, computer equipment?

WHAT DOES IT MEAN?

e-commerce
e-commerce is the use of the Internet for selling goods and services to customers.

Fig 4.11: An e-commerce site

e-learning

It is possible to take courses on-line. You could log on to an **e-learning** site, choose the topic you want to learn, and then work through a series of web pages that would teach you step by step. You would be asked questions at several points to check that you have understood the material.

Some e-learning courses have been developed to support standard school or college programs, and you would use these alongside normal classes. In other cases, you can take a complete course on-line, and even obtain a qualification, without actually meeting a teacher.

Bulletin boards

Bulletin boards were used on the Internet before the World Wide Web made it easy to find information. Bulletin boards provided text-based information and also allowed users to leave messages for everyone else to see. A user had to log on to the bulletin board before they could view the information or take part in discussions.

Since the Web was invented, bulletin boards have been replaced by Internet forums, although forums are still sometimes referred to as bulletin boards. An Internet forum is a website where users can discuss issues together. On most forums you need to register before you can join in, and you can be barred from taking part if you post offensive comments.

Blogging

Blog is short for web log, and it is a kind of personal website. The blogger will post (that is, publish) entries at frequent intervals, giving their own thoughts on the issues and topics that concern them. Readers may also leave comments on any of the postings, so lively discussions can develop.

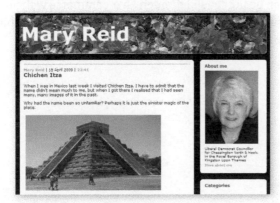

Fig 4.12: The blog of one of the authors of this book

Pod-casting

Pod-casting is a method for distributing audio files, known as pod-casts, using web feeds. The word pod-casting is a combination of i-Pod and broadcasting, and was first developed to support the Apple i-Pod audio players. However, pod-casts can now be received by any system that is connected to the Internet.

The audio pod-cast files are stored on a website. A web feed is created for each pod-cast, or for a collection of pod-cast files. Users can subscribe to a web feed by clicking on an icon, and the pod-cast will be downloaded. If the pod-cast is part of series then the new pod-casts will be downloaded automatically when they become available.

Fig 4.13: RSS is the most common type of web feed

The web feed technology (also known as syndication) is now used for other types of file. You can subscribe to web feeds for news and for blogs, so that the latest entries can be downloaded and displayed on your screen automatically.

Summary of key points

In this topic you have learned:

- about the services offered by the World Wide Web.
- how web pages can be created and viewed.
- how websites can be used for a number of purposes.

QUESTIONS

1 Explain how FTP and HTTP are used on the Internet.
2 List three types of goods that can be purchased through an e-commerce website.
3 List three different services that can be purchased through an e-commerce website.
4 What are the advantages for the learner in using an e-learning course?

• 4.4 Data security

Computers and computer networks hold vast amounts of information, all of which have to be kept safe and accurate.

Data that is not accurate is not useful at all. For example, a school needs to have accurate information about each of the pupils. It is essential that the name is spelled correctly, and that the date of birth and home address of each pupil is accurate. Pupils leaving the school have to be noted, and new pupils have to be added.

Data can be inaccurate for a number of reasons:

- The data may have been entered wrongly in the first place.
- Some of the information may have been altered by mistake.
- Data may not have been updated when it should have been, for example, if a pupil moves to a new address.
- Someone may have changed the data deliberately when they were not supposed to – this is, of course, a criminal activity.

If data is accurate then we say that is has **integrity**. Data integrity must be an aim for everyone who holds information that is important for them.

Data can also be missing for a number of reasons:

- The computer system may have developed a software fault and some data may have been erased.
- The computer system may have been damaged, for example, by a lightning strike or heavy rain.
- Someone may have deleted data deliberately when they were not supposed to.
- Parts or all of the computer system may have been stolen.

So data can be inaccurate or missing because people have made mistakes, because the computer systems have been accidentally damaged, or as a result of criminal activity.

Data security is a general term for all the things that can be done to keep data safe and accurate.

WHAT DOES IT MEAN?

data integrity
Data integrity is achieved when all the data is accurate and up to date.

data security
Data security covers all the methods that can be used to keep data safe and accurate.

Fig 4.14: Keeping data safe

Using software to protect data

Passwords

A computer in a network can access files that are stored on the hard disk of the file server. But that does not mean that you can access just any file you like when you use the network.

If you have a network system at your school, you probably have to key in two pieces of information when you log in:

1 Your username (sometimes called your User ID)

2 Your password

The person who looks after a network is called a network administrator. The job includes sorting out the permissions for users. The network administrator will have given you your own username, which may be a number or a version of your name. Your username is not confidential.

You will also have been given a password, and you should keep it secret. You will probably be allowed to change your password whenever you like, and you should remember it without writing it down anywhere.

If another person tries to log on pretending to be you, they would need to know both your username and your secret password to do so. Never allow anyone else to do this, as they could alter your files or even delete them. Even if they mean no harm they could change your work by accident.

When someone logs on to the network with their username and password, the network software makes sure that they can only use the files for which they have permission.

Usernames and passwords are also used on some websites. This is done for two reasons:

1 To identify people who are using the website, especially if they want to buy something, receive information or join an on-line community.

2 To restrict access to private websites.

Encryption

Usernames and access control can prevent most data from falling into the wrong hands. But a determined criminal may still find ways of getting at data. The data can be protected further if it is stored in some kind of secret code. This technique is known as **encryption**.

WHAT DOES IT MEAN?

encryption

Data is encrypted when it is converted into a secret code. Encrypted data is decrypted when it is converted back to ordinary text.

When confidential information is stored on a database, it is sometimes encrypted first. This means that someone who does not know how to decrypt (decode) the data will not be able to make any sense of it.

To encrypt a file the system needs an algorithm (a set of rules) and a key (a special number). Encryption uses the algorithm and key to convert each character of the original file into another character, and the encrypted file is saved. Spaces and punctuation marks are also encrypted.

The algorithms used are quite complicated. It is not a simple case of replacing a letter by the same letter each time it appears. Another key is usually needed to decrypt the file back to its original state. It is virtually impossible for anyone to decrypt the file unless they know the algorithm and key to use.

Mrs Jones, of 12 Station Street, has filed a complaint against one of our sales staff.

ajhp r4us rqst xdft 7pkl oO4d eety drgh 1ws4 anmk dery qscx einh 5tgh sdft rtyl dvnk sedk y6io plas rdh4 y8

Fig 4.15: Plain text and encrypted text

When someone orders or books anything on the Internet they usually pay for it by credit card. Many people are anxious about giving their credit card details over the Internet. They are afraid that someone else will be able to access their information from the database and then use it to buy goods fraudulently.

The solution is to store all the credit card information in an encrypted form. This is done by using a separate secure webserver that stores the personal and financial data and handles the encryption and decryption.

Fig 4.16: A site on a secure server

When a website is on a secure server you may see a small padlock icon in the window. This means that the data is being transferred using HTTP Secure, which combines HTTP with encryption.

Virus protection

A virus is a computer program that has been created in order to cause damage to computer systems. A virus may be installed on to your computer without you being aware of it.

Viruses can be transferred to your computer when you visit a website, but are most commonly spread from one computer to another through email. The virus is usually contained in an attachment. You should be very careful about opening any attachments that come with an email and should certainly never open one if you don't know who the sender is.

Other ways in which viruses can reach your computer are through CDs, DVDs or USB drives, or across a network system.

The only safe way to protect a computer from viruses is to install virus protection software. If you are using a computer on a network then this will have been done for you. Virus protection software checks a list of viruses to identify any that are on emails or have found their way into your system.

Virus protection system can:

THINK ABOUT IT

What virus protection has been installed on the computers that you use?

- Check every email that you receive, including its attachments.
- Check every email that you send.
- Check every document you open.
- Carry out a full scan of everything stored on your computer – this should be done regularly, and at least once a week.

If the software finds a virus it will then delete the virus or tell you how to get rid of it.

New viruses are being produced every day, so it is important that the lists used by virus protection software are completely up to date. Many offer a service that will update the virus list on a daily, or even hourly, basis. The updating process can take place in the background whenever the computer is connected to the Internet.

Firewalls

Someone could try to get into a network system from outside when they do not have permission to do so. On the other hand, a user on the network might be trying to visit a website that is banned by the organisation.

Firewalls are devices controlled by software programs that check all the data communications that come into and go out of the network. A firewall will block any communications that do not match its rules. The rules can be set to give the level of protection that is needed for the network.

Using physical means to protect data

Computer hardware is quite valuable so thieves will try to steal it if it is not properly protected. But there is also a risk that someone may break into a building and then use the computer system to find the data without actually removing anything from the room.

Preventing people from getting into buildings

It goes without saying that buildings and rooms that hold computer systems should be locked when no-one is around. Keys can be stolen or mislaid, so sometimes electronic locks are used instead. There are several types of electronic door entry systems.

- Keypad: This requires you to key in a code on a keypad. This method relies on people remembering the code. After a while a lot of people may know the code, so it is wise to change it from time to time.

- ID card: You swipe an ID card through a card swipe. This will read the data held on the magnetic strip and identify you as a person with permission to enter. One advantage of this method is that if someone is barred from the site, the door entry system can be programmed to refuse them entry. However, ID cards can be lost or stolen, or even lent to other people to allow them to gain access without permission.

- Smart card: Smart cards are sometimes used as ID cards instead of swipe cards. A smart card has a chip embedded in it, and this can carry a considerable amount of information about you. Some smart cards do not even have to be inserted but can communicate with the door system by radio. Again, smart cards can be lost, stolen or borrowed, so are not foolproof.

- Biometric: A **biometric system** 'reads' your fingerprint or palm print and checks it against the images already stored in the system. Some systems can match faces and inspect you through a video camera. Other systems can even check the patterns on the iris of your eye.

> **WHAT DOES IT MEAN?**
>
> **biometric system**
> A biometric system measures one or more of your physical attributes, such as fingerprints, face and iris patterns, in order to check your identity.

Fig 4.17: A biometric system

Many organisations use night security guards to patrol the buildings and deter criminals. Intruder alarm systems should be installed. If anyone does try to break in a siren will sound and the police will be informed automatically.

In some buildings the security is arranged in layers, rather like the skins of an onion. It may be relatively easy to get into the outer layer of the building such as the reception area, but extra security measures are introduced as you move into more secure areas. In order to get into the room that houses the servers an employee may have to go through five or six different security checks.

Keeping important data away from harm

Computer data can be stored on magnetic storage media such as hard disks, tapes and floppy disks, or on optical media such as CDs and DVDs. These can all be damaged, either deliberately or by accident.

Storage media must be protected from:

- heat and fire
- oil and dust
- magnetic fields
- water and humidity

In general, storage media kept in a clean environment at room temperature will last longer than media expose to heat, dirt and humidity.

Storage media that contain important data should be stored in a safe. A safe is not only lockable, but it can also protect the media from fire and water. Some special fireproof and waterproof safes are sold precisely for this purpose.

Recovery when things go wrong

We all know that things go can go wrong with computers. Even though there are many ways of protecting data, there is always the possibility that disaster will strike. The worst disaster could mean that all the data and all the hardware is damaged or destroyed.

For example:

- The hardware can malfunction and this can damage the data held on disks.
- Errors in the software can mean that data is not saved properly.
- Viruses can attack the system and change data.
- Someone can delete a file or change data by mistake.
- The hardware can be destroyed by fire, flood, hurricane or lightning strike.
- Criminals can delete files, or they can steal or destroy hardware.

The data stored on computers is extremely valuable. If a large organisation like a bank loses all its data it would probably go out of business.

Fortunately, there are some ways of ensuring you are able to recover your data if something should go wrong.

Backups

The idea of a **backup** is very simple. It is a copy of a file that you can use if the original file is damaged or not available. But having a copy alone is not enough, because the backup copy must be stored somewhere safe. It must not be stored on the same hard disk as the original, because if the hard disk is damaged both files may be lost.

You can create a backup of a single file, but it is often easier to back up everything on the hard disks at the same time. A backup system can be set up for a single computer or for a whole network.

The two main types of backup are:

1 Full backup: The computer or network can be set up so that it automatically makes a backup of everything on a regular basis. Most organisations backup the data on their networks every night, when users will not be trying to access it.

2 Incremental backup: An incremental backup copies only the files that have been changed since the last backup. Several of these may be done between one full backup and the next. Although incremental backups will be done during the working day, they will be much quicker than full backups so should not interrupt normal work.

Backup files should be stored in on a medium that:

- makes fast copies.
- can be stored in a secure place away from the original.

Any storage medium, such as hard disks, CDs, USB drives or tapes can be used to make a backup. Digital tape is a popular choice to store full backups, as data can be copied to tape very rapidly. All backup tapes and disks need to be labelled very carefully with the date and time. Backups are very important so should be stored in a lockable fireproof and waterproof safe.

Organisations should always have a **disaster recovery** strategy that covers:

- replacing hardware as soon as possible.
- recovering data from backups.

This will help even if only a single computer file is lost. If disaster strikes, the last full backup will be used as a replacement for the files that are lost. If incremental backups have been used as well, then they will be combined with the last full backup to give the most up to date version of the lost files.

WHAT DOES IT MEAN?

backup
A backup is a copy of a file that is kept in a safe place in case the first one is damaged.

disaster recovery
Disaster recovery strategy is a means of getting back to normal as soon as possible if disaster does strike.

Archives

It is really important that the information that is held by an organisation is up to date. But information that is out of date may still be useful to an organisation. For example, data about pupils who have left a school should not be destroyed because other schools may need to check what the pupil has achieved, or an employer may ask for a reference.

Old information is normally copied to a new storage medium and stored safely. The old files are known as archives. The archived information may then be removed from the main computer system. If anyone needs to read the archived information, the files can be copied back into the computer system and made available.

Proprietary software

In Section 4B you will learn about proprietary software, which is software that is owned by a commercial company and available for anyone to buy and use under license.

If an organisation is working with highly sensitive information they may decide to have software written for them, instead of using off-the-shelf proprietary software. This will give them the opportunity to build additional security into the program. For example, it may use more complicated methods of encryption than might otherwise be used, and it might use biometric systems whenever a user logs on.

Summary of key points

In this topic you have learned:

- the importance of keeping data secure.
- that data security methods depend on software, such as virus protection and encryption.
- that data security methods depend on physical barriers.
- how data can be rescued when things go wrong.

QUESTIONS

1 What is data integrity?
2 Explain how a password is used with a log in procedure.
3 Why is it important to install virus protection on a computer system?
4 What kind of data should be encrypted? How does encryption increase data security?
5 Distinguish between a full backup and an incremental backup.

End-of-section questions

Multiple-choice questions

1 Which of the following types of network is commonly used for a small building?
   A LAN
   B MAN
   C WAN
   D VAN

2 All of the following are wireless transmission media except:
   A Fibre-optic
   B Satellite
   C Infra red
   D Microwave

3 The technology that allows you to make international phone calls using the Internet is called:
   A Bluetooth
   B VoIP
   C Wi-Fi
   D Wireless

4 Which of the following is the fastest bandwidth?
   A Voiceband
   B Narrowband
   C Broadband
   D Thinband

5 The data transmission mode that allows the transmission of data between devices in both directions but not at the same time is called:
   A Simplex
   B Duplex
   C Half duplex
   D Full duplex

6 The transfer of data from a user's computer to another computer is called:
   A Uploading
   B Downloading
   C Installing
   D Transferring

7 A device that converts digital signals to analogue at the sending end and analogue to digital at the receiving end is called:
   A Converter
   B Multiplexor
   C Modem
   D Router

8 A language commonly used in creating web pages and websites is:
   A HTTP
   B HTML
   C FTP
   D Telnet

9 Scrambling of a message while it is transmitted over the communication channels is called:
   A Coding
   B Encryption
   C Password
   D Encoding

10 All of the following are physical restrictions used in securing data except:
   A Firewall
   B Fire-proof cabinets
   C Padlocks
   D Guards

Structured questions

1. a Define the term 'data communication'.
   b Networks can be LAN, MAN or WAN.
      i What do the abbreviations LAN, MAN and WAN stand for?
      ii State the difference between LAN and MAN.
      iii State the difference between LAN and WAN.

2. Transmission media makes data communication possible and can be in wired/wireless form.
   a List three commonly used wired/cable transmission media.
   b List three commonly used wireless transmission media.

3. Bandwidth has an important role in digital transmission.
   a Define the term 'bandwidth'.
   b List three types of bandwidth.
   c Briefly describe each of the bandwidths you identified in your answer to 3b.

4. Transmission of data can take place in three modes.
   a List the three modes of data communication.
   b Briefly describe each of the data communication modes you identified in your answer to 4a.

5. State the difference between:
   a Email and bulletin board
   b Newsgroup and IRC
   c Uploading and downloading
   d HTTP and HTML

6. You can access (a) World Wide Web (WWW) using an appropriate (b) web browser that will use appropriate (c) protocols to display the (d) websites and (e) web pages. A web page can be viewed on the WWW by typing the (f) URL of the page into the browser.
   Give the meanings of the terms (a)-(f), underlined above.

7. a State the difference between data integrity and data security.
   b Data can be secured using software restrictions or hardware restrictions.
      i List three forms of software restrictions.
      ii List three forms of hardware restrictions.

8. a 'Software restrictions are better than physical restrictions.' Do you agree? Support your answer.
   b What is meant by 'data encryption'?

9. a One form of physical access restriction is the use of biometric systems. Give two examples of biometric systems.
   b What is meant by 'archiving'?

10. Give the correct computing terms for the following:
    a A place where the Internet is available with the help of wireless LAN.
    b Transmission of data in both directions at the same time.
    c The rules that control the format and transmission of data.

Objectives

By the end of this section, you will be able to:

- Describe how information can be used to violate the privacy of individuals.
- Explain how ICT systems can be misused by criminals.
- State which hardware and software is most appropriate for different types of user.
- Describe how technology is changing.
- Assess the effect that ICT has on job skills and careers.
- Describe the tasks and roles taken on by people who work in the computer industry.

Good information is essential for any organisation, and computing technology has made it much easier for information to be stored, processed and communicated to others. In this section you will be looking at people in many walks of life and discovering why they need to have ICT skills in order to carry out their work. You will also learn that these skills can be used for good and bad, that information can be misused as well as used for the benefit of society.

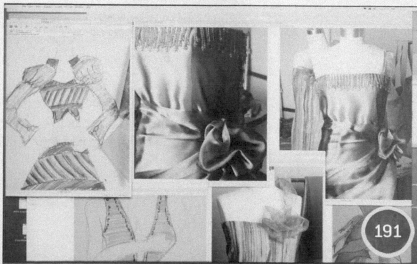

● 4.5　How information can be misused

This course is about Information Technology and Communications Technology. Today we can use the technology to produce and share information on anything and everything. Unfortunately, that also means that some people can misuse the technology for unpleasant purposes. Some of these misuses are actually illegal; others are not acceptable.

Privacy

Everybody is entitled to **privacy**. That means that no-one should take photos of you or try to find out private information about you without your knowledge. That would be a violation of your privacy.

When you visit a professional, such as a doctor, you do have to give that person some private information. But you do expect that any information will be kept confidential. That means that the professional may not pass it on to anyone else at all, unless you have given them permission.

WHAT DOES IT MEAN?

privacy
Privacy is the right of each of us to keep information about ourselves from other people.

Personal information

THINK ABOUT IT
Find out what laws exist in your country to protect personal data.

Personal information is data about living people and has to be treated with particular care to protect their right to privacy. Information about patients at a hospital, pupils in a school, customers of a shop and members of a club are all examples of personal information.

Many countries have laws that ensure that personal information can only be read by people who have been given permission to read it. In the same way, the information can only be changed or deleted by someone with permission to change it.

People expect doctors to keep medical information confidential, but they are not so sure about whether other organisations will respect their privacy. So an organisation should tell people how it is going to store their personal information and what it is going to be used for.

All this applies to personal information that is stored on paper as well as data that is stored in a computer database. However, computer data can be made available very easily to many people, so it is very important that data security measures are used.

Remember, data security has to protect the data from careless people as well as from criminals.

As we saw in Section 4A there are many ways of keeping data secure. Every person and every organisation that holds important or personal data must decide what types of security they need to have.

Surveillance

In the past, if anyone wanted to listen in on a conversation between two people they would have to be close enough to hear them speaking. In the same way, it was only possible to watch what someone was doing by standing nearby.

Today it is possible to listen to conversations and watch people without them knowing. ICT provides a lot of techniques that make surveillance possible, such as hidden microphones and cameras. Some microphones can pick up sounds through a wall and from some distance away. Some cameras are so small that no-one would normally spot them.

It is also possible to listen in on phone conversations. Old-fashioned phone tapping techniques can be used for landlines, but with cell phones the radio signals can simply be picked up between the phone and the mast. Cell phones can also be used to pinpoint where a person is.

Now you will probably agree that sometimes surveillance is necessary. For example, the police may want to track someone whom they suspect has committed a major crime. Surveillance techniques, such as closed circuit television cameras, are also used to provide extra security for buildings. Normally signs warn potential intruders that there are cameras present.

Fig 4.18: Types of surveillance

In other cases you may think that surveillance is probably wrong, such as when photographers try to catch pictures of celebrities in private.

There will be other cases where surveillance is used purely for criminal purposes and this will always be against the law. For example, criminals may decide to use hidden techniques to observe a wealthy victim so they can plan a theft.

CHECK YOUR PROGRESS

1 Describe how surveillance can be used by the police to solve crimes.

Electronic eavesdropping

When you send a letter by mail you do not expect anyone to open it before it reaches its destination. However, that does occasionally happen, and people have lost valuable items in the mail.

THINK ABOUT IT

Do you know what the law is in your country about who can have access to emails and text messages?

It is much easier for electronic messages to be intercepted. All the emails and text messages that you send pass through several computer systems before they reach the recipient. It is technically possible for all these messages to be stored and viewed.

In many countries police have the right to intercept emails and text messages, as well as mail, in order to solve or prevent a crime. But it may be possible for a criminal to get access to messages as well.

Millions of electronic messages are sent every day, so it is impossible for them all to be looked through by humans. Instead, computer programs can be used to search messages for key words, or for the names of specific people.

Propaganda

Propaganda is information that is designed to encourage you to think in a particular way and to hold a particular opinion. It may include false information, or it may give an unbalanced version of events.

The Internet holds a vast amount of information, some of which is correct and some of which is not. Information may be incorrect for a number of reasons: the person who wrote it may simply have misunderstood or made a mistake, or they may be deliberately trying to mislead you.

You should always ask whether any information you find really is true. That can sometimes be difficult because if you do not know the facts then you cannot judge its accuracy. However, you can ask some commonsense questions, such as:

- Who wrote this information?
- Is it a person or organisation that I can trust?
- Is other information on the same site accurate?
- What do other sources say about the same topic? You can compare it with printed material or other trusted websites.

Inaccurate information

As we saw in Section 4A, we say that data has integrity if it is accurate and up to date. One of the aims of data security is to maintain data integrity. In Section 5 you will be looking at techniques of verification and validation, which check data for accuracy at the point where it is input into a system.

Despite all these safeguards some information stored in computer systems is inaccurate. This can happen because:

- someone made a mistake when they collected the data.
- someone made a mistake when they entered the data into the computer system.
- someone deliberately altered the data after it was first entered.

Inaccurate data can have consequences that can be quite trivial or can be very serious indeed. For example, letters may be mailed to the wrong addresses, or the wrong person may be arrested for a crime.

THINK ABOUT IT

Give some examples of how the storage of inaccurate information could affect people's lives.

Summary of key points

In this topic you have learned:

- that information can be misused as well as used wisely.
- that some techniques can invade the privacy of individuals.
- that you should be aware that some information is inaccurate or designed to mislead.

QUESTIONS

1 Describe one way in which a computer system can be used to violate your privacy.
2 What is personal information?
3 Give one example of when surveillance could be used legally and one example of when it might be used illegally.
4 List two ways in which you can check whether information you have found on website is accurate.

● 4.5 Computer crime

ICT systems can make it easier for people and organisations to discover information that should be kept private. Most of this activity is against the law.

Industrial espionage

The term 'espionage' usually refers to spies who work for one country while trying to find the national secrets of another country. Industrial espionage is a similar concept but applied to businesses.

Businesses can be very competitive and often want to know about the plans of other companies. For example, a cosmetics company may be secretly developing a new product that they expect to become a bestseller. If a rival compnay discovers their plans then they might launch a similar product first and take away all their potential sales.

Businesses have been known to spy on each other. They usually need to have an insider who is willing to pass information on. All the surveillance and electronic eavesdropping techniques mentioned earlier, such as intercepting emails, hidden microphones and cameras, can be used to gain confidential information.

Software piracy

When someone writes a book, composes music, or creates a work of art they (or their employers) normally own the copyright to that work. This means that no-one else may print, copy, perform or film the work without their permission.

WHAT DOES IT MEAN?

software piracy
Software piracy refers to the illegal copying and selling of software.

If you worked on your own as a software developer and you created some software that people want to buy, you would expect to make some money from selling it. You would have the copyright to the software, and you would be very unhappy if someone else were to copy it and then sell it.

You should obtain permission from the copyright holder before photocopying books, copying music or videos, performing plays or reproducing photos etc. You may have to pay the copyright holder for a license to do so. Sometimes blanket permission is given, for example, a university may have a license to make limited copies of books for educational use. When you buy some software most of the price covers the cost of the copyright license for its use. This usually gives you permission to make one copy for your own use, plus any necessary back up copies.

Software piracy costs the ICT industry millions of pounds each year in lost sales. In some cases illegal copies of CDs are made and sold in markets or on-line. You should be aware of 'crack' websites that offer free or cheap downloads of proprietary software. The security codes on the software will have been altered illegally to avoid detection. These downloads are commonly used as a way of distributing viruses and spy software.

Software piracy means that software companies have to put up the price of their products and the customer has to pay more. You may be aware that a similar problem exists in the music industry.

Many countries now have laws that cover software piracy.

Fig 4.19: Illegal downloading

CHECK YOUR PROGRESS

1 What is copyright?
2 What is software piracy?

Computer fraud

Most computer fraud is carried out by employees. In Section 4A you learnt about many ways in which data can be kept secure. These usually prevent someone outside the organisation from gaining access to hardware, to software and, most importantly, to data.

However, employees often have access to the organisation's data as part of their work. They may be tempted to alter data, to transfer money, to create fictional accounts, or to use information to blackmail others.

WHAT DOES IT MEAN?

fraud
A fraud is a crime in which someone deliberately deceives someone else in order to gain money, goods or some other advantage.

Most organisations have a code of conduct for employees, which states the company rules. Generally, anyone who uses company data for any purpose other than work will be dismissed and may be referred to the law enforcement agencies.

Credit card fraud

In Section 4A you learned that e-commerce businesses sell goods and services on-line. The customer usually has to pay over the Internet, and the most common method is to use a credit card. People can be worried about security and fear that their credit card details may be used by criminals.

Credit cards have a magnetic strip that holds some data. This is usually the same data that appears embossed on the card, such as card number and name. Today, many credit cards also have a silicon chip embedded in them. These are known as smart cards. The chip can hold more data than a magnetic strip.

When a customer buys something using a credit card in a normal store, they usually have to provide additional data, such as a signature or a password known as a PIN (Personal Identification Number).

There are several ways in which credit cards can be used illegally. If a card is stolen then they may be used in a store with a forged signature. Even if a card is not stolen, an employee could fraudulently reuse the details they have obtained from a customer.

However, most of the concerns about credit card fraud relate to on-line shopping. In Section 4A you saw how secure websites can be used with HTTPS to encrypt credit card data.

Identity theft

Identity theft is a growing crime. The criminal gathers as much information as possible about another real person and then pretends to be that person.

Identity theft can be used for a number of purposes:

- To obtain money from an account.
- To buy goods and services.
- To get the benefits of medical and other insurances.
- To avoid being arrested for a crime.
- To obtain travel visas.

When identity theft is used on-line, on the phone, or by mail, the criminal does not even have to look like the person they are impersonating. They do need to obtain some significant items of personal information such as full name, address, date of birth, nationality, country of birth, names of spouse and children, plus details of credit cards, insurance accounts, passport number, driving license, and any state benefits.

WHAT DOES IT MEAN?

identity theft
Identity theft is a form of fraud in which the criminal pretends to be someone else.

Everyone needs to be careful about providing any of this information to another person or organisation. We should ask ourselves: Why do they want this information? Are they entitled to have it? Will they keep it safe?

It is thought that much of this information can be found by searching through people's refuse. You should always treat documents that contain private information with great care. They should be torn up, or shredded before being thrown away.

Summary of key points

In this topic you have learned:

- that criminals can use computer systems to commit crimes, such as espionage.
- that software piracy is illegal.
- that everyone should protect themselves from fraud and identity theft.

QUESTIONS

1 Which of the following is ALWAYS a crime?
   a electronic eavesdropping
   b credit card fraud
   c storing personal data
   d storing inaccurate data
2 List two reasons why software piracy is bad for the computer industry.
3 Explain how someone can protect themselves from identity theft.
4 State the main differences between credit card fraud and computer fraud.

4.6 Application software

We are now going to think about choosing the right software. Every organisation and every user has their own particular needs, so there is never one simple solution that will suit everyone. At the end of this section, you will be carrying out some projects where you will be recommending suitable hardware and software for a specific person or organisation.

In this topic we will consider the different types of application software that are available.

Application software can be thought of in two groups – general purpose software and special purpose software.

General purpose application software

You will already be familiar with a number of general purpose software applications such as:

- Office applications – word processing, spreadsheets, desktop publishing, presentation, database management, web page design
- Graphics software – painting and drawing packages, and photo manipulation
- Communications software – email, web browsers (see Section 4A for more about these)

CHECK YOUR PROGRESS

1 Make a list of all the application software that you can use at school. Are there other applications you would like to use?

Word processing

Word processing software is the most commonly used type of package in organisations. Many employees use word processors to prepare their own documents. They can create standard documents, such as letters, which they can use more than once, with only minor changes.

Word processing packages, such as Corel WordPerfect, Lotus Symphony Documents or Microsoft Word, can be used to produce letters, reports, memos, articles, orders and invoices, notices, leaflets, newsletters and books.

Word processing packages also offer additional features that can be used to create email messages, web pages, mailing labels and mail merge letters.

You will learn more about word processing in Section 6A.

Spreadsheets

After word processors, spreadsheet applications were the next business software packages to appear for desktop computers. A worksheet is laid out as a very large table consisting of many cells. Each cell can hold a value or a formula. A formula can carry out calculations based on values held in other cells. Each cell can also be formatted to hold data of a specific type, such as a number, a date or simple text. Spreadsheets also include graphing and charting functions, which will generate all kinds of charts using the data held in the cells.

Many users have also discovered that spreadsheets can also be used to print forms and other documents that need cells or tables.

A spreadsheet package, such as Lotus Symphony Spreadsheets, Microsoft Excel, or Corel Quattro Pro can be used for accounts, budgets, scientific calculations, statistical analysis, simple databases, interactive 'what if' calculations and form designs.

You will learn more about spreadsheets in Section 7.

Database management systems

Database management systems structure and organise the data used in a database.

A database management system, such as Filemaker, Corel Paradox or Microsoft Access, can be used in a business to store data about stock in a shop or factory, orders from customers, orders sent to suppliers, case notes (for doctors, social workers, etc), personnel (employees), mailing lists and logsheets.

You will learn more about database management systems in Section 8.

Presentation packages

Presentation packages, sometimes known as presentation graphics, are used to provide the illustrations for talks and lectures. They offer many useful templates that can be customised by the addition of your own text and images.

Presentation packages, such as Microsoft PowerPoint and Lotus Symphony Presentations, can be used to create slides that can be printed onto transparencies, create a slideshow that can be projected directly from the computer onto a screen, and print notes for the speaker and the audience.

You will learn more about presentations in Section 6B.

Web page design packages

Many websites are created by professional web developers, using programming languages and other specialist software. Other people also like to create their own web pages, and straightforward web page design software has been designed for them.

Web page design software, such as Microsoft FrontPage, can be used to design and upload small websites. They often provide useful graphics that can be used for buttons, as well as complete website colour schemes and templates.

You will learn more about web page design in Section 6C.

Desktop publishing packages

Desktop publishing software was originally developed for newspapers and magazines. Before the software was available, editors would assemble stories provided by journalists and literally cut and paste the stories onto a board. They would then add photographs, illustrations, headings and text.

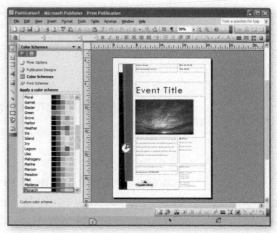

Fig 4.20: A desktop publishing package

Desktop publishing offers the same facilities, but in electronic format. Individual contributors can send their word processed stories to the editor's system, who can then import them into the page layout. Stories, headings and images can be easily edited and moved around to fit the space.

On a smaller scale, a desktop publishing package makes it easy to arrange text, and is often used in organisations to create newsletters, notices, leaflets, publicity materials and invitations.

Graphics software

The term graphics covers all kind of images stored in digital form. They include photos that have been scanned in or downloaded from a digital camera, or images 'painted' or 'drawn' using graphical software. 'Clip art' is used to describe pre-drawn images that you can use freely in your documents.

Fig 4.21: A graphics package

You can choose from a wide range of graphics software including photo editors and general image design packages. For many purposes, the simple Microsoft Paint program is very useful.

Graphics software can be used to create or edit images for use in standard stationery (as logos), publicity materials (leaflets, brochures, posters) and web pages.

Special purpose application software

General purpose software applications can be used for a wide variety of tasks. In contrast, special purpose software can do a more limited range of tasks, but can go into much more detail. Examples of special purpose software include:

- Engineering software – CADD, CAE, CAM (see page 209)
- Professional web design software
- Music production software
- Games
- Accounting packages

Fig 4.22: An accounting package

Selecting software

We are now going to consider how to find suitable application software for a user.

Application and systems software can be:

- Custom-written
- Proprietary
- Open source

Custom-written software

A large organisation may have software written specially for it. This is known as '**custom-written**' **software**. The software will be designed to do exactly what the organisation wants it to do. It will not be made available to anyone else. Because the software developers will not be able to sell it to other people as well, custom-written software is very expensive.

A large business like a bank will be able to afford to employ its own software developers. They will then spend all their time creating custom-written software that exactly matches the needs of the business. They might devote thousands of hours to produce software that is just right for handling cash machines, or customer accounts.

A smaller organisation may use consultants to develop custom-written software for them. A consultant is a self-employed person who works for a fixed time on a project for an organisation.

You can buy general application software just when you want it, but it does take time to develop custom-written software. Almost all custom-written software is special purpose software, because it is written to meet the very specific needs of the organisation.

WHAT DOES IT MEAN?

custom-written software
Custom-written software is software that has been written specifically to meets the needs of an organisation.

Proprietary software

Most software that is used in offices and at home is bought as a complete package. You can buy the CDs and instructions in a box either from a computer shop or through the Web. The term '**proprietary software**' refers to these commercial software packages.

Proprietary software has a proprietor, that is, an owner. The owner is usually the commercial company that holds the copyright. When you buy proprietary software you are really buying a license to use it. This usually restricts you to installing it on your own computer only and possibly making a backup copy.

WHAT DOES IT MEAN?

proprietary software
Proprietary software is software that is owned by an organisation who then sells licenses to use it.

The most commonly used application software, such as word processing and spreadsheet packages, are sold as proprietary software. You can also buy widely used systems software (i.e. operating systems) in this way. The best known proprietary software packages are general purpose applications, such as word processing and web browsers. But commercial companies also sell a number of special purpose packages such as those used by engineers. (See page 209 for more about this.)

If an organisation wants to use a proprietary application on a network that will be available to many users, they normally purchase a network license. This usually places a limit on the number of users. As we saw on page 196, it is a crime in most countries to copy and sell software that is sold under copyright. This is because it breaks the terms of the license.

Open source software

It is also possible to download good quality software from the Web that is both free and legal. Open source software is free because it has been developed by some of its users. In order for this to happen the programming code must be 'open', that is readable by another programmer.

Open source software will usually be divided into lots of smaller programs, called modules. Programmers will be able to add new modules to the application and will ask other users to test them in use and report any problems.

One advantage of using open source software is that you will be able to find plenty of help on the Web. Both developers and users will be able to post questions on a website and discuss the software with each other.

One disadvantage of using some open source software is that different applications are not always compatible with each other. When you buy proprietary software you will usually find other applications made by the same company, and the applications will work together. For example, you would be able to place a spreadsheet table without any difficulty in a word processed document. If you decide to use open source software you do need to check whether it is compatible with other applications that you own.

Open source software is usually general purpose software, but there are also some special purpose applications available, such as web development tools. In addition, Linux is a well-known example of systems software, mainly used on servers, that has been developed through the open source community.

Selecting hardware to support applications

Once the right software has been selected you can then consider what hardware is needed. In Section 1 you looked at a large range of hardware devices. You should now think about which hardware to choose by considering:

- Amount of storage needed, e.g. size of RAM and hard disks
- Types of secondary storage needed
- Speed, e.g. speed of printing, speed of broadband connection
- Quality, e.g. appearance of printed material
- Special devices, e.g. barcode readers
- Cost

Many hardware devices can be bought directly from computer suppliers.

In some special cases, hardware will be custom-made for the customer. This will often be the case if software has been custom-written for a large organisation. For example, if a bank decides it needs a new system for handling its cash machines, it will probably need to design new hardware for all the cash machines as well as new software.

Summary of key points

In this topic you have learned:

- about the many types of general purpose software that are available.
- that software can be custom-written, proprietary or open source.
- how to select software and hardware for a particular application.

QUESTIONS

1 What is the difference between custom-written and proprietary software?
2 What are the advantages of using open source software? What are the disadvantages?
3 For each of the following tasks state whether the user should use presentation, spreadsheet, word processing or desktop publishing software.
  a Writing a letter to a customer
  b Producing a fashion magazine
  c Creating a slideshow for a talk
  d Designing the menu for a restaurant
  e Writing up a project
  f Keeping track of personal expenditure

4.7 New technology

New computer applications are emerging all the time. You can find out about them from computer magazines, news stories and the Internet.

Expert systems

An **expert system** is a piece of software that helps people to make decisions. It is rather like having an expert in the room with you.

Some of the earliest expert systems were designed to help non-specialist doctors. Doctors often have to examine and diagnose patients who have a collection of fairly common symptoms, such as acute stomach pains. It is sometimes difficult for them to distinguish between two conditions that have similar symptoms, even though the treatment for each may be very different. The doctor is able to run an expert system program that asks a series of questions and suggests a number of tests that can be carried out on the patient. It then comes up with one or two likely diagnoses based on the data that has been input. At any point the doctor can ask the expert system why it is asking a question, and the system will explain the logic behind it.

Writing the program for an expert system is relatively straightforward. The difficult part is obtaining the knowledge held by an expert in the subject, but this has to be done carefully and accurately if the system is going to be of any use.

The knowledge is held in a database known as a knowledge base. The expert system then has a series of rules that help it to ask the right questions of the user and work towards a conclusion.

Some expert systems are embedded in other packages and work in the background. For example, you may have played a computer game in which you are competing against a computer opponent. In many cases, the actions taken by your virtual opponent will have been decided by an expert system.

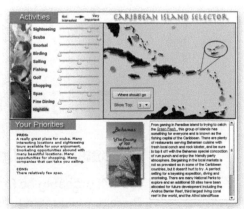

Fig 4.23: An expert system

Robots

We can use ICT to control machines automatically. That means that the machines can work on their own without humans. In Section 5 you will learn about control systems in more detail.

Robots are sophisticated computer-controlled machines that can move around and carry out physical tasks. They are extremely expensive, so are used in situations where it would be too dangerous to use a human, such as for bomb disposal. They are also used for manufacturing expensive products such as cars.

Fig 4.24: A robot arm at work in a factory

In science fiction films, robots are often portrayed as walking and talking human-like machines. In real life, most robots only vaguely resemble parts of the human body, such as an arm.

Many computer-controlled systems, such as robots, have sensors. Different sensors can check temperature, light levels or movement. The data gathered from a sensor is fed back into the computer so that it can adjust its actions. For example, a robot arm used in manufacturing will have sensors that detect when it touches something. This information will be assessed by the software to see whether it was expecting to touch anything at that position. If the object was unexpected then the robot arm will probably be stopped and possibly moved back to an earlier position.

Robots tend to move in a series of tiny movements one after another. After each movement, sensors check their position before the next tiny movement is made. This happens very fast so the overall movement appears smooth.

CADD, CAE, CAM

Computer Aided Design and Drafting (CADD)

You will probably be familiar with software that allows you to draw images on the screen. There are two main types:

- Painting software, like Microsoft Paint. You can use this to build up images made of thousands or millions of tiny dots of colour, known as pixels. Paint software can also be used to manipulate photographs.

- Drawing software, such as the Drawing tool that can be found in most Microsoft Office software. You can use this to draw lines and other shapes. Each shape is treated as a separate object, and you can move each one independently of the others.

A number of professionals use specialist drawing software to create their designs. For example:

- Architects draw up the plans for new buildings.
- Product engineers design products such as cars and domestic appliances.
- Civil engineers design roads and bridges.
- Mechanical engineers design machinery.
- Electronic engineers design electronic circuits.
- Interior designers draw up plans for rooms, bathrooms and kitchens.

All of these can use **Computer Aided Design and Drafting (CADD)** systems on their computers. They will be able to construct the design onscreen by moving standard components around. Some software lets them view a design in 3D from different angles.

Fig 4.25: A Drawing tool in Office

WHAT DOES IT MEAN?

CADD
Computer Aided Design and Drafting software (sometimes just known as Computer Aided Design) is used by professionals such as architects and engineers to design objects and structures.

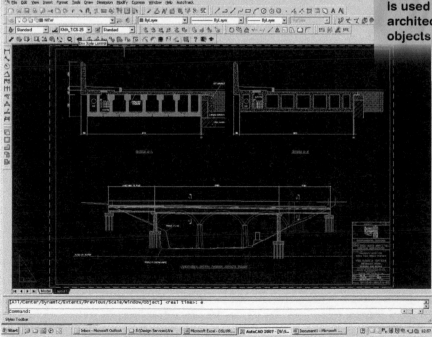

Fig 4.26: CADD software

Computer Aided Engineering (CAE)

Computer Aided Engineering takes CADD software one stage further. CAE systems can test a design almost as though it was a physical object. So, for example, it can check how a component designed for an aircraft is likely to behave under different pressures and temperatures.

Objects designed like this will eventually have to be rigorously tested in the real world. But by using a CAE system the engineer is able to try out ideas without going to the expense of manufacturing the object first. In that way, many problems can be solved at an early stage, and mistakes can be avoided.

Computer Aided Manufacturing (CAM)

Many products are constructed using computer-controlled systems, so it makes sense to link a CADD program to a manufacturing system. Computer Aided Manufacturing does just that.

When a designer has completed a design in a CADD package it can then be sent to a CAM program. The CAM program interprets the design and then controls the machine tools. The machine tools themselves shape the raw materials by cutting into them in various ways.

CAM systems can be extremely precise and can manufacture products that could never be put together by hand. They are often used to create a prototype object. This is then subjected to further testing, and adjustments may be made to the design as a result. Once the engineers are satisfied with a prototype, they will then use the final version to create a mould. This mould will then be used to manufacture the product. The CAM system itself is not usually used for mass manufacturing.

Telemarketing and teleconferencing

The suffix tele- means 'at a distance'. Both telemarketing and teleconferencing make use of the telephone and Internet to carry out tasks that in the past could only be done face to face.

Telemarketing

Have you ever received a phone call in which someone you don't know tries to sell you something? This is the basic form of telemarketing.

The business may have found your phone number from a public phone directory, and called you as well as everyone else. Alternatively, they may have purchased a list of names, addresses and phone numbers from a market research company, along with information about your interests and shopping habits. This will have been stored in a database so that the business can search for people whom they think will be interested in their product or service. If you are ever asked for your phone number you should always check what it is going to be used for, as it may find its way into one of these databases.

In some cases, telemarketing calls are made completely at random. A computer-based system rings every possible number in turn until one is answered. At that point a recorded message is played.

Teleconferencing

People do not always have to be in the same room in order to hold a meeting. You can use teleconferencing methods over the telephone or Internet instead.

For telephone conferencing all the people involved call the same number, enter a code and then can have a conversation together.

Fig 4.27: A teleconference call

To avoid everyone speaking at once, one person usually acts as the leader and controls who speaks next. People cannot see each other so it may be difficult to judge how others are reacting to ideas.

Internet conferencing can also take place using chat rooms and similar technologies. All the participants log into a chat room at the same time and then key in their messages to each other. Once again, it is a good idea to have a leader and also an agenda, to prevent messages from overlapping each other.

Also, video conferencing can take place over the Internet. The participants all need to have web cameras so they can view each other.

Summary of key points

In this topic you have learned:

- about new technologies such as expert systems and robots.
- the uses of CADD, CAE and CAM in industry.
- about the use of remote systems for communication such as telemarketing and teleconferencing.

QUESTIONS

1   Describe a situation in which an expert system might be used.
2   Explain the differences between CADD and CAE software.
3   Describe two contexts in which a robot might be used instead of a human to do a task. In each case explain why the robot is preferred.
4   What are the advantages of using teleconferencing facilities for a business meeting instead of meeting face to face?

4.8 ICT in the workplace

People who use ICT in their work fall into two broad groups:

1 People who use applications and data communications as tools within their normal work.
2 People who work in computer-related professions such as network administrators, or developers who create software.

In the next topic, we will be looking specifically at computer professionals, but in this topic we will think about the impact of ICT on other workers.

Working with standard applications

Many people use standard application software in order to carry out the business of their employer or for their personal use.

They could do any of these tasks:

- communicate with others through the Internet
- create documents, spreadsheets and presentations
- create and edit images
- interact with a database

Today, most employees have to have basic ICT skills, even if they do little more than read and reply to emails. Many office workers will have had some training in standard software applications, such as word processing, spreadsheets, presentation software, image editing and desktop publishing. They can become very proficient at using them. The same skills are often needed by professionals in other fields, such as teachers, medical staff and the police.

Computer users may also have to do some simple tasks with the operating system. For example, they may have to launch application software, set up new directories, move or delete files or configure the display.

Working with specialist software applications

Many employees have to use specialist software applications that have been designed specifically for their area of work. Here are some examples:

- Doctors may record the details of their patients on a medical records system. This means that they can easily look up the medical history of a patient, check their medication and store the results of any tests.
- Engineers may use CADD, CAE or CAM systems to design, test and create products.

- Police forces may use special databases to keep records of criminals. When they are trying to solve a crime they can refer to these databases to try to identify suspects. Criminal records may also hold biometric data such as fingerprints and DNA readings.

- Music producers use complex studio systems to record and mix musical tracks. Once they have captured live sound, they can create exactly the effects they want by using music production software on a normal computer system. Music is almost entirely distributed in digital formats these days.

- The movie industry uses ICT in every aspect of movie production. Cameras can be computer controlled, and the action can be recorded digitally rather than on traditional film. You will have seen examples of computer generated imagery (CGI), although in many cases you will not be aware that the image you are seeing is not live action but has been created with a graphics package. All movies are eventually transferred to a standard digital format, such as DVD, for home use.

- People working in the **mass media** use specialist software all the time. Books and newspapers are written and designed today on computers using desktop publishing software; editing software is used to produce the final versions of radio and television shows; people who are not professional web developers can use content management systems to update websites.

All these employees will normally need to be trained to use the specialist software in their industry.

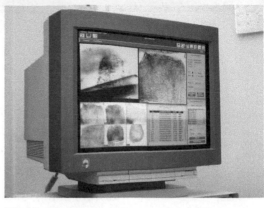

Fig 4.28: The police use specialist software to record criminals on a database

Fig 4.29: A producer using specialist music software

WHAT DOES IT MEAN?

mass media
The mass media (television, radio, newspapers and the Internet) all present constantly changing news and entertainment for the general public.

Fig 4.30: Computer generated imagery in a film

New skills

In the early days of computers many people were worried that they would lose their jobs because computers would be able to do things automatically. In fact, far more jobs have been created because of ICT. Think of all these careers, none of which existed before computers were invented:

- network administrator
- computer engineer
- database manager
- software developer
- computer sales person
- web designer
- technology journalist
- ICT teacher or trainer

THINK ABOUT IT

Can you think of any other areas of work that have changed as a result of ICT?

However, some jobs in some industries have disappeared and employees have had to learn new skills. For example, the way in which books and newspapers are printed has changed dramatically. For hundreds of years skilled craftspeople called typesetters arranged the individual letters by hand in a tray. The letters were then inked and pressed on to paper to create a printed page. Later, machines helped to speed up this process but people were still closely involved in the physical task of printing. Today, the typesetting is all done on a computer, using desktop publishing software. When a page is ready, the system automatically manufactures a printing plate.

Changes like this have happened in many areas of work. Some traditional jobs are no longer needed, but new ones are created. This can pose a problem for people who have worked in traditional industries for many years, and whose skills are no longer needed. They will often have to retrain in order to learn new skills.

Young people are entering the world of work today with good ICT skills. However, new technologies are appearing all the time, so all workers should expect to learn new skills throughout their working life.

Patterns of work

The use of ICT has changed the way in which people can do their work.

- **Telecommuting:** Many employees do not always have to be present in the office, for fixed hours from 9 am to 5 pm. You could work at home, using a laptop with communications links into your company's network. This is also known as home-working or teleworking.

- **Flexitime:** The use of email means that you can leave messages for colleagues who can deal with them when convenient. So you could work flexible hours (flexitime) to fit in with other commitments.
- **Time-displaced communications:** Communications around the world can be made simple through email. In the past if you were in Jamaica and wanted to speak to a colleague in Japan you would have to call in the middle of the night. Today an email can be sent one afternoon and the reply read the next morning.

Summary of key points

In this topic you have learned:

- that ICT skills are needed in many different jobs.
- how ICT affects the way people do their work.

QUESTIONS

1 List three jobs that have disappeared and three other jobs that have been created as a result of ICT.
2 Does telecommuting mean:
   a Travelling to work from a long distance.
   b Using a television as part of your work.
   c Working from home.
   d Working for a telemarketing business.
3 Describe three ways in which a doctor might use ICT in their work.
4 Explain why training in ICT is important in the workplace.

● 4.9

Computer-related professions

People in all kinds of jobs need ICT skills. They need access to software and hardware that meets their needs. In this topic we will look specifically at the computer professionals who create the systems that all those people use.

We can divide them into three groups:

- Software developers
- Computer systems staff
- Expert users

THINK ABOUT IT

Look through advertisements for jobs in the computer industry. You may find these in local newspapers and in local employment agencies. There are also some specialist papers and magazines that carry a large number of job advertisements. You can also find a number of employment agencies on the Internet that specialise in computer-related professions.

Note down the kinds of jobs you have found and what the post holders will be expected to do.

Software developers

The process of producing new software is very complex. In Sections 2 and 3 you will have looked in considerable detail at the tasks undertaken by programmers. Programming is only one aspect of software development, and many other people may be involved in creating a new application.

If the software project is a large one, then several people will be involved in the task. The software may have been designed by a systems analyst, who looks at the ways in which information is handled in an organisation and then designs a better system. The software developers will then create and test the software to match the design.

In a small project, the software developer will carry out all the tasks, from analysing the problem, to designing, creating and testing the software.

Systems analysts and designers

A systems analyst looks at how computers fit into a whole business. For example, a large shop may have point of sale terminals (cash tills) that are networked and linked to a fileserver. The fileserver will hold a database that has details of all the goods in stock. When an item is sold, this data will be amended. Also when new stock is delivered, the database will have to be updated. The shop manager will be able to print out sales reports, and it may also be possible to print the price tickets that are attached to goods or stuck on the shelves.

If a shop wants to install a new sales system then it may employ a systems analyst who will look at all the processes involved in the shop. Some of these processes will be done by people, such as attaching the price tickets to the goods, but other processes will be automatic, such as calculating the total when a shopper buys several items.

The systems analyst will investigate the systems that are already used and try to find where things may go wrong.

A systems designer plans a new system. This design will usually include descriptions of any new hardware and software needed, and also the tasks that people will have to do.

In many cases, the two jobs of systems analyst and systems designer are done by the same person.

Software engineers and programmers

A software engineer studies a new system design and looks specifically at the new software that is needed. Some software is very complex and many programmers will be employed to produce it. The software will consist of many separate programs or modules that will all be linked together. The software engineer plans and designs the whole software project, and then instructs the programmers on the parts they will be working on.

A programmer takes the design for a piece of software and then writes the computer program. Programmers can use a number of programming languages such as Pascal, Visual Basic, Java or C++.

Sometimes a new operating system has been designed, or some new utilities to add to an operating system. A programmer who writes operating systems programs is known as a systems programmer.

Once a program has been written it has to be tested. The systems designer will have listed all the tests that the new software should pass. The software tester carries out careful testing of all the parts of the new software. The aim of testing is not so much to prove that the software works, but to find and repair any errors.

On a very small software project, one person may carry out all the tasks of a software engineer, programmer and tester.

Fig 4.31: A team of people working on a software project

Software trainers

Once software has been thoroughly tested it may be installed. The employees who will be using the software will have to learn how to use it. A software trainer is a teacher who understands what the user has to do with the software, and is able to encourage and train the new users.

Fig 4.32: A software trainer teaching a group of people to use new software

Computer systems staff

People who have careers in computer systems look after all the hardware, software and communications needs of organisations.

Computer engineers

Computer engineers design computer systems, and will usually have been trained in electronic engineering. But they will also understand software engineering as well, because they will have to design some aspects of the software needed for networks.

IT managers

An IT manager will be employed in a medium-to-large organisation to manage all their ICT requirements. The job will include responsibility for deciding on new hardware and software, managing the system administrators, offering a help service to all the computer users, preparing for emergencies, and managing the IT finances including all the day-to-day costs.

Network administrators

A network administrator (or systems administrator) is a computer professional who works directly with the network operating system to ensure that the network functions as intended.

THINK ABOUT IT

Try to meet as many people working in computer-related professions as you can, and ask them about their work. Try to decide which of the jobs appeal to you as a possible future career.

Computer technicians

A technician carries out the day-to-day maintenance tasks with hardware and software. They may check and configure individual desktop computers, install new hardware and software, check the connections, and may provide help to users.

Fig 4.33: A computer technician fixing a printer

File librarians

In Section 4A you learned about backup procedures. It is very important that all the backup files are labelled properly and stored in the right place. That is part of the task of a file librarian. They also have to keep track of all the disks and tapes that are in use, and make sure that none of the files are deleted by mistake.

Expert users

As we have already seen, some computer users use specialist software, but only as a part of their everyday job. Here we will be concentrating on people who have highly developed skills in the use of specialist software, and spend their entire working hours on those tasks.

Database administrators

Many organisations are very dependent on their databases and could not run without them. Many people may have access to the database; some will only be able to read the data, others will be able to change the data or add new data. A database administrator makes sure that only the right people can either read or change the data.

Databases organise data, but they also provide many different ways of searching and viewing the data. A database administrator can set up searches and present the information in a format that is useful to the users.

Web developers and webmasters

Web pages are programmed by a web developer. They use Hypertext Mark-up Language (HTML) together with other specialist languages. Many websites are also linked directly to a database.

Web developers use similar techniques to system analysts and software engineers in order to work out what exactly is needed on website. They also have to consider the visual design of a site, which can have a very strong impact on the user.

The day-to-day running of a website is carried out by a webmaster, who will upload new information and check that the site functions correctly.

Multi-media artists

Images, video and sound are combined on many computer applications. Many of the exciting techniques were pioneered by the computer games industry, but they can now be seen on websites and in learning packages.

There are now many opportunities for music, video and graphic design professionals to use their skills together and these are referred to as multi-media artists.

Fig 4.34: Games developers

Summary of key points

In this topic you have learned:

- the tasks done by many people who work in the computer industry.

QUESTIONS

1. What are the differences between the tasks done by a systems analyst and a software engineer?
2. Describe the work done by a database administrator.
3. List four of the tasks undertaken by an IT manager.
4. What is the difference between a webmaster and a web developer?

4.6 Projects

In this section you have learned about different users of ICT, and the application software that is available to them. You are now ready to carry out some small projects in which you will recommend hardware and software for particular users.

In each of the case studies below the users want to buy completely new computer systems. You have been given the task of specifying software and hardware that will meet their needs.

In each case you should answer these questions:

1 What type of application software would best meet the user's needs? Note: they may need more than one type.
2 Should the user choose custom-written, proprietary or open source software?
3 Can you give the names of the specific application software packages and operating systems that they should install?
4 What hardware devices does the user need?
5 Are there specific makes of hardware that you could recommend?

You should be able to find all the background information you need in Sections 1, 4A and 4B of this book. You can also look in computer magazines and computer shops for details about hardware and software that are currently available. You can also check out the websites of computer suppliers.

There is more than one solution for each project. You might like to compare your recommendations with others.

Case Study 1

Veronique teaches in a secondary school. She wants to buy a home computer, for both work and personal use. To support her teaching she would like to write up her teaching notes, keep records of her pupils' exam marks, and prepare handouts and presentations. She would also like to keep in touch with her cousins who live in Canada and be able to exchange family photos with them. Her son enjoys playing fantasy computer games.

Case Study 2

Magic Island is a holiday hotel set by a beautiful beach. The hotel manager, Alex, is completely overhauling the administration of the hotel and is investing in a new network and software. He wants the new system to handle all these tasks:

- Hotel bookings – online, by phone and by mail
- Room allocations – which room each guest is given on arrival
- Staff rotas – which members of staff are on duty at any given time
- The hotel website
- Printing of menus and notices

THINK ABOUT IT

Can you suggest some other case studies that you could work on?

Case Study 3

Delice leads a team of research scientists. One of their projects is to observe the wildlife on an island in order to discover whether the populations have been affected by climate change. The scientists have been keeping records of the numbers of birds and insects of particular species over a period of several years, and they have been checking the data for trends. Delice would like each member of the team to be able to enter the data while out and about, and to be able to take photos of the animals they are studying.

End-of-section questions

Multiple-choice questions

1 The illegal copying and selling of software is called:
   A Copyright
   B Intellectual property
   C Piracy
   D Privacy

2 An example of open source software is
   A Windows
   B Linux
   C Microsoft Word
   D Microsoft Office

3 Which of the following statements is NOT true about robots?
   A They are faster than humans
   B They are easy to buy and maintain
   C They can do repetitive tasks
   D They can be used in places that are dangerous for humans

4 Which of the following devices is NOT a requirement in teleconferencing?
   A Microphone
   B Sensor
   C Speakers
   D Telephone

5 Even though telemarketing is possible, sometimes people prefer to go and buy from shops mainly because:
   A They can bargain the prices
   B They can assess the quality of items
   C They can shop at multiple shops and compare
   D All of the above

Structured questions

1 a List four types of computer crime.
   b Briefly describe any two of the crimes you identified in your answer to 1a.

2 a State the difference between telemarketing and teleconferencing.
   b State the difference between telecommuting and teleconferencing.
   c Expand the following abbreviations:
      i CADD   ii CAE   iii CAM

3 List two ways in which computers can be helpful for the following persons:
   i A medical doctor   ii A teacher   iii A movie director

4 List two main duties of the following computer professionals:
   i A database administrator   ii A system analyst   iii A computer technician

5 Robots are used by many industries due to their many advantages.
   a List two industries in which robots are commonly used.
   b State two advantages of using robots over manual methods in industries.

   Give one disadvantage of using robots rather than manual methods in industries.

5 Information Processing

Objectives

By the end of this section, you will be able to:

- Distinguish between data and information.
- Explain the importance of information processing in a wide range of contexts
- Identify the sources of data.
- Explain how data is verified and validated.
- Describe how files are organised.
- Select the best forms of file organisation for particular applications.

Information lies at the heart of Information Technology. Individuals and organisations buy computer technology because they want to store, handle and present information. The main purpose of computer software is to take data, then to process it so that it becomes useful. We call useful data 'information'. In this section you will be learning about the many ways in which data can be processed and useful information can be produced.

● 5.1–5.2 Data, information and information processing

As you learned in Section 1, **data** is input into a computer system and it is then processed.

Think about what is happening when you use word processing software. You press a key on the keyboard, and the character code is sent electronically to the Central Processing Unit. The CPU carries out the instructions contained in the software, and the character appears on the screen in the right place. Although this seems like a very basic operation it actually involves a large amount of processing.

The output on the screen is useful to us, which is why we refer to it as information. Put simply, a computer takes data as input, processes it and outputs **information**.

Here is another example. After you have word processed a long document you want to find the sentence where you wrote about someone. You use the 'Find' function to search for the person's name, and you input the name, as data. The search function in the software then carries out a process on the name and the document, and outputs the information you want.

Note that the term 'data' was originally a plural word, the singular being 'datum'. However, 'data' is now widely used for a set of items, so it is quite correct to say 'The data is processed by a computer system.'

> **Data → Process → Information**
>
> **Fig 5.1**

WHAT DOES IT MEAN?

data
Data is the raw material that is input into a computer system. It consists of characters, numbers and program code.

information
In Information Technology, information is data that has been processed by a computer system.

Information processing

There are many ways in which data can be processed to become information. Here are some of them:

- Carrying out calculations in a spreadsheet.
- Printing a document or image.
- Searching a document or database for a particular item of data.
- Updating data in a file.
- Displaying an image on the screen.
- Sorting data into alphabetical order.

You will be familiar with most of these processes

WHAT DOES IT MEAN?

data/information processing
Information (or data) processing refers to computer-based systems that take in data and generate information.

yourself, and will have carried them out on a personal computer.

In this topic we are concentrating on the large and complicated systems used in business and industry. These are often hidden away from members of the public, so you will not be so familiar with them. But the basic processes that are used are often very similar to the ones that you know.

Commercial data processing

Computer systems are used in many businesses to carry out some time-consuming administrative tasks. Here are some examples of business information processing activities:

- Payroll – calculating how much each employee should be paid every month.
- Orders – recording orders that customers place with the business and then keeping track of when the goods are sent.
- Sales – in a shop, dealing with purchases at the till.
- Invoices – sending requests for payment to customers and other businesses.
- Payments – paying other businesses who have supplied materials and services.
- Accounts – keeping track of all the payments made by the business and income.
- Budget – planning finances in the future.
- Correspondence – sending letters and emails to suppliers and customers.
- Marketing – designing packaging and advertising.
- Security – using door entry systems.

In some cases these activities run fairly automatically; in other cases employees use software to help them with their work.

For many of these tasks, general purpose software application packages can be used, such as those you looked at in Section 4B. For some tasks, specialist software packages are used, or software is custom-written.

Fig 5.2: Employees entering payroll data

Industrial data processing

Industrial and manufacturing businesses need to carry out all the business tasks listed in the last topic. In addition, they have further uses for data processing such as:

- Control systems – controlling the processes used when manufacturing products.
- Computer Aided Design – designing products.
- Computer Aided Engineering and Computer Aided Manufacture – using special software to develop and test products.

In Section 4B you looked at the CADD, CAE and CAM software that is used for design and manufacturing. We will now look in more detail at control systems.

Control systems

We can use information processing systems to control machines automatically. Here are some examples:

- Factories are often largely automated, e.g. manufacturing chemicals, packing goods.
- Some factories use robots to manufacture goods, such as automobiles.

Fig 5.3: Control systems are used in many types of electronic household equipment

- The signalling systems on many railways across the world are controlled by computers, to ensure that the trains pass safely.
- Most of the more advanced transport vehicles are controlled to some extent by computer systems, e.g. autopilots on aircraft, driverless trains, fuel injection systems for car engines.
- Most electronic equipment in the home has some element of computer control, e.g. video recorders, digital televisions, digital cameras, washing machines, microwave ovens, cell phones.

These are all referred to as **control systems**. In control systems the processor is often referred to as the controller.

There are two main types of control system:

1 **Automation systems** carry out straightforward tasks, such as running through a program on a washing machine. They do this without any human involvement at all. Once an automation system has been switched on it follows a set of predetermined actions to the end.

2 **Process control systems** are used for more complex operations. They constantly check the state of play and change the actions in response.

CHECK YOUR PROGRESS

In the examples given on   227 which are automation systems and which are process control systems?

Process control systems

In process control systems, data is captured automatically. This is done through input devices known as sensors. A sensor can measure things like temperature, humidity, light, sound, movement and pressure. It converts the measurement into an electronic signal that it sends to the controller (processor). A sensor can provide the data input in a steady stream, or it can take readings at intervals.

The software in the controller then processes the data from the sensors and determines what action, if any, to take. It then sends the instructions to other special devices such as motors and switches, which are part of the machine that is being controlled.

Imagine a food processing factory, where candy is being made. Paddles rotate in a large container to mix the ingredients as they are being heated. The control system takes input from a temperature sensor placed inside the container, which will be constantly sending back data to the controller. The controller can send signals to the paddles to switch them on and off, and to regulate their speed. When the temperature reaches a certain level the controller sends signals to the motors and switches to slow the paddles down and stop them, and to turn off the heater.

Fig 5.4: A process control system

Robots are very complex process control systems. In Section 4B you saw how a robot arm might be used in a factory.

Suppose a robot arm is being used to pick up and move a dangerous item like a radio-isotope. The controller instructs the motors in the arm to move the hand into position. It then slowly closes the hand around the object. A sensor in the hand sends data back continuously and as soon as it detects pressure the controller will instruct the motor to stop.

Scientific data processing

THINK ABOUT IT

Think about some of the scientific experiments that you have learned about in science classes. Do any of them need sensors that can feed data directly into a computer system? What sort of data processing needs to take place?

Scientists can gather a lot of data during an experiment. Sometimes they will use sensors to capture data over a period of time. In other experiments the scientists themselves may be recording readings on a source document.

Generally speaking, scientists will be looking for connections between the data. They will use statistical methods to analyse the figures they have collected. They will often want to display the results in a chart.

Fig 5.5: Scientists recording data

Summary of key points

In this topic you have learned:

- the differences between data and information.
- the many ways in which data can be processed to give information.
- how information processing is used in commerce, industry and science.

QUESTIONS

1 Explain the difference between data and information.
2 List three ways in which data can be processed.
3 What kind of proprietary software packages could be used for each of these tasks: correspondence, accounts, budgeting, marketing?
4 Explain the differences between automation and process control systems.
5 What kind of software could be used by a scientist to analyse and present their findings?

• 5.2–5.3 Information retrieval and management

Many businesses are not directly involved in manufacturing. Instead the employees are dealing all the time with information, often in written form. They will still be inputting data into the system, then using software to process that data and provide useful information.

For example, a customer has a car insurance policy. This means that if the car is damaged in an accident the insurance company will pay for the repairs. The customer will make a claim by filling in a claim form and posting it to the company. The words on the form have to be entered as data into the insurance company's computer system.

This is then processed in several steps. First the software checks that the name on the form matches the name of one of their customers. Then it checks the kind of policy that the customer has. It will then decide whether the claim is valid or not. In either case a letter will be printed automatically for the customer.

Data is input and information, usually in the form of a letter, is output. In addition, the information in the customer database will be updated.

Information processing like this always includes a stage of **information retrieval**. This is when the data is searched to find the right information.

This type of information processing will only work if the data that is held in the system, for example about customers and insurance policies, is stored in a sensible way. The data should be:

- accurate
- up to date
- structured in a way that makes it possible to search for specific data
- stored on a suitable storage medium

There are many ways of achieving this and you will be meeting some of them later in this section. The task of managing and storing data so it can be used is known as **information management**.

WHAT DOES IT MEAN?

information retrieval
When data stored on a computer system is searched and the relevant information is found, this is known as information retrieval.

WHAT DOES IT MEAN?

information management
Information management ensures that all data is input accurately, stored correctly, retrieved easily and output in a way that provides useful information.

Documents used for information processing

It is surprising how many paper documents are still used in computer-based information processing systems. As we saw in the insurance claim example, a claim form has to be filled in by hand, and letters are sent by mail. Some of these documents can be sent electronically, but only if the customer can receive and send email. However, for many important documents a signature is needed and this can only be done on paper.

Source documents

When an employee takes a document and enters the data into a computer system, the document is referred to as a **source document**. Once the data has been entered it should be filed away safely, and not thrown away. That is because the data may have to be checked again.

WHAT DOES IT MEAN?

source document
A source document is one that contains data that is going to be input into a computer system.

human-readable document
A human-readable document is any document that needs to be read by humans.

Human-readable documents

Many forms are filled in by hand and the employee has to read them before entering the data on a keyboard. These are called **human-readable documents**.

Handwriting can be very difficult to read, and sometimes the employee has problems working out what is written. This can be improved by asking the person writing the document to use capital letters. Sometimes a series of boxes are placed on a form to try to force the writer to separate out the letters to make them clearer.

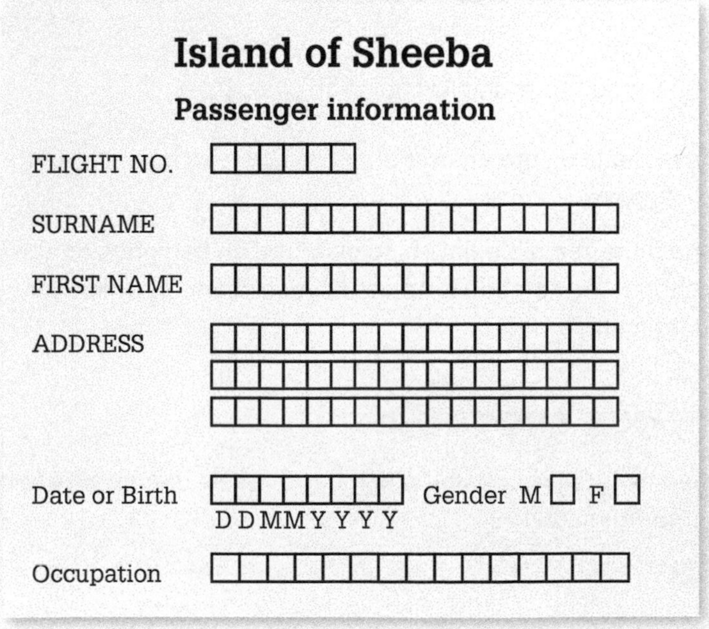

Island of Sheeba

Passenger information

FLIGHT NO.

SURNAME

FIRST NAME

ADDRESS

Date or Birth DDMMYYYY Gender M F

Occupation

Fig 5.6: A human-readable form

Machine-readable documents

Machine-readable documents are one solution to the problem of unclear handwriting. Instead of writing the data, the form is marked in some way. The document is then passed through a reader or scanner, which can identify where the marks are. This approach can be very successful but can only work for particular types of data.

You may have taken a multiple-choice test at some time. For each question you will be given three or four answers and you have to decide which one is correct. You may have been asked to record your results on a sheet like this:

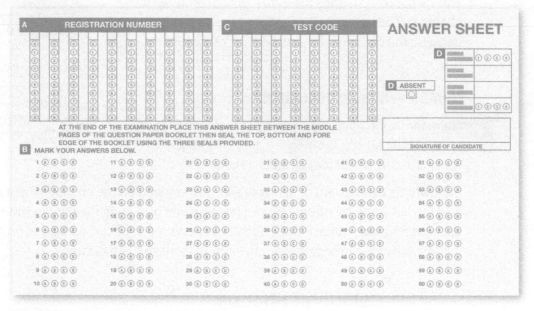

Fig 5.7: A machine-readable multiple-choice answer paper

The marks you have made on the answer sheet will be read by an input device directly into the computer system.

Another form of machine-readable data is to be found on barcodes on the labels of products sold in shops. The barcode is passed over a scanner, which converts the pattern of lines into a binary code.

CHECK YOUR PROGRESS

What are the advantages of using machine-readable documents for inputting data in a computer system?

Turnaround documents

A turnaround document is one that is printed by a computer system, but is later used to input new data into the same system.

THINK ABOUT IT

Can you think of other examples of turnaround documents that you have seen?

Suppose a customer phones up the insurance company and says that they want to make a claim. At that point the employee can ask the customer's name and address, and insurance account number. They can then search the stored data to find the customer's information. A claim form can then be produced with the customer's name, address and account number printed on it. This form is then sent to the customer.

The customer fills in the rest of the claim form and sends it back. The employee will know immediately which customer it is from, because the data will be clearly printed on the form.

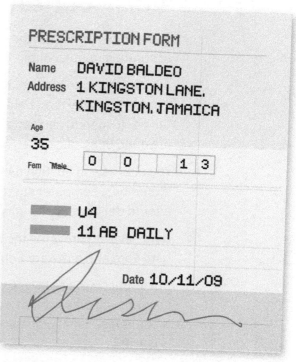

Fig 5.8: An example of a form with pre-printed customer details

Summary of key points

In this topic you have learned:

- that information management is the task of storing and retrieving information.
- that documents that hold input data can be human- or machine-readable.

QUESTIONS

1 What is a turnaround document?
2 What are the advantages of using machine-readable documents?
3 Why do forms sometimes make you write each character in a separate box?

● 5.4–5.5 # Verification and validation of data

In Section 4A you met the concept of data integrity. We say that data has integrity if it is accurate and up to date.

All organisations know that data is useless to them unless the data is kept up to date. For example, a hotel may hold the names and addresses of people who have stayed there in the past, so they can send them details about special offers. The names and addresses are of no use unless they are correct.

You also saw in Section 4A that the aim of data security is to keep data accurate. Data stored on a computer system may have been altered by mistake or it may have been altered deliberately by someone who should not have done so.

Data security prevents the wrong people from having access to data and protects the hardware and software from damage.

But suppose the data was entered incorrectly in the first place. No amount of data security will prevent that from happening. Data verification and data validation are two techniques that can be used when data is first entered, in order to check whether it is correct.

- Data verification is a process carried out by humans.
- Data validation is an automatic process carried out by software.

Data verification

There can be some problems when an employee keys in data that is written on a source document. Errors may occur because it is difficult to read the writing, or the person may simply make a typing mistake.

- Typographical errors are the typing errors that we all make when we hit the wrong key.
- Transposition errors happen when we enter numbers or characters in the wrong order. It is very easy to do this when entering long numbers, such as phone numbers, or when typing in an unfamiliar place name.

Typographical errors;

I sent down the stree tand saw my friends playing cricket.

Transpositional errors;

I wnet down the street and was my friends playing cricket.

Fig 5.9: Examples of typographical and transposition errors

One very simple way to reduce errors is for the employee to check the data a second time. Once the data has been input and displayed, the employee can read it back from the screen and check that it matches the data on the document. This process is known as **data verification**.

However, a simple visual check is not really appropriate for large amounts of data, so a more robust method, called double entry, is often used.

In double entry verification, a second person enters the data all over again. The computer system will have been set up so that it checks each data item that is entered the second time against the first data entry. It will display a warning if they do not match. The employee then has to check whether the error was made in the first entry or the second, and confirm which is correct. Data verification should identify many of the errors that humans make when keying in data.

WHAT DOES IT MEAN?

data verification
Data verification takes place when a person checks that data has been correctly keyed into a computer system.

double entry verification
Double entry is a common method of data verification in which the data is keyed in a second time, and the first entry is checked against the second.

Data validation

You may have entered your personal details into a web-based form on-line. If you leave out some data that ought to be included it will give you a message and ask you to enter it. Similarly, if you type in a password incorrectly it will tell you to try again.

These are examples of **data validation** checks. They are carried out automatically by the software.

Similar validation checks can be used when data is entered into any computer system from a source document, such as the insurance example on page 230. Data validation checks are carried out by the software as the data is being entered. If the data validation checks identify a possible error, a warning is displayed.

There are many kinds of data validation checks and suitable ones will be chosen depending on what data is being entered. Here are some of them.

WHAT DOES IT MEAN?

data validation
Data validation checks are carried out by a computer system when data is entered, to identify data that cannot be correct.

Range checks

These check whether numerical data is within expected limits. For example, if you are asked to enter someone's age, the number should be between 0 and 110. If the data required is the date when someone joined an organisation then clearly the date cannot be in the future. Similarly, figures entered for height, weight, shoe size, etc can all be checked against the range of numbers that could be reasonably expected.

Data type checks

These check whether the data is of the correct type, such as number, date or text. For example, phone numbers are numerical, so a data type check would notice if a letter was included.

Inconsistency checks (also known as consistency checks)

These check one piece of data against another. For example, the data may include both gender (M or F) and title (Mr, Mrs, Miss). If someone has entered M and Mrs, then the two data items are inconsistent.

The main purpose of data validation is to check that the data is reasonable. Data validation should identify some errors that will not be picked up by data verification. However, it will not spot other errors, such as the incorrect spelling of names. In these cases, the input data may be reasonable, but still wrong. Errors like these can only be checked by data verification.

To make sure that data entered is as accurate as it can be, both data verification and data validation checks should be used.

CHECK YOUR PROGRESS

An employee was keying in data written on an application form. Which of these errors could be identified by data verification, which by data validation, and which by neither?
- Year of birth is given on the form as 2003 but entered as 2103.
- Year of birth is given on the form as 1894.
- Surname is very indistinct on the form; it could be Davis or Davies.
- The Town of Birth is given on the form as 256.
- The address given on the form does not exist.

Summary of key points

In this topic you have learned:

- the importance of checking input data to make sure that it is accurate.
- the differences between data verification and data validation.
- what kind of data validation checks can be used.

QUESTIONS

1 What is the main difference between data verification and data validation?
2 Why is it better to use double entry for data verification rather than simply checking over what has been entered?
3 Describe three methods of data validation.

● 5.6 File organisation and file access

In Section 1 you read about sequential and direct access to storage media.

The data stored on magnetic tapes has to be read in sequence, from the start to the end. It is impossible to jump into the middle of a tape to find a particular data item. Tape is a sequential access medium.

Most other secondary storage media use a form of direct access, which allows the software to go directly to a specific piece of data on the storage medium without having to access any other data.

You may think that sequential access is no longer used as all the storage devices with which you are familiar use direct access. In fact, magnetic (digital) tape is still used in commercial information processing, for backups and archived data. Although it can take a long time to find a particular data item using sequential access, it is still a very fast and efficient way of copying large files in their entirety.

In this topic we are going to look at a number of different ways of organising data on storage media, depending on whether they use sequential or direct access.

Files of records

In any computer system data is stored in files. You will be familiar with a number of types of file:

- *Text files* contain just the characters that you include in them.
- *Word processing files* contain text, but they also contain instructions on how the document should be laid out, which fonts to use etc.
- *Files of records*.

A file of records is the simplest type of database. You will learn about more complex relational databases in Section 8, but for now we will concentrate on a single, simple file.

A record is a collection of all the data about a single item in a file. For example, the details of the members of a club may be held in a file. Each record would contain the data about just one club member. The file would hold a record for each member of the club.

The data about each member would fall under a series of headings, known as fields. The fields could include surname, forename and the date when they joined the club.

All the data in a file can be thought of as a table like Table 5.1 below.

Surname	Forename	Joining date
Huggins	Barrington	9 Nov 1996
Bellamy	Howard	23 Jun 1988
Periera	Bella	14 Mar 1993
Williams	Clarice	12 Oct 1975
Tang	Su	19 May 1990

This column is a field in the file. Forename is the fieldname.

This row is a record in the file.

Table 5.1

Each row is a record in the file. Each record will have data in one or more of the fields.

Files of records are used by many different software applications. For example, the phone directory on a cell phone is a file of records.

Of course, usually files will have many more records than those shown here.

File organisation

While some files are quite small, others are very large indeed. The challenge is how to store all these records so it is easy for the software application to find the data quickly.

There is more than one way of organising a file. The three main methods of file organisation are:

1 Sequential
2 Index-sequential
3 Random

Sequential files can be used with sequential access or direct access media. Index-sequential and random files can only be used with direct access media.

Sequential file organisation

In a sequential file all the records are stored in order. That means that the records have been sorted in some way.

One of the fields will be used for the ordering, that is, sorting the file. This field is known as the sort key. For example, it is very common to sort a file of personal

WHAT DOES IT MEAN?

sequential file organisation (sequential field ordering)
Sequential file organisation describes a file that is sorted using the data in one of the fields.

details using 'Surname' as the sort key. This is also known as sequential field ordering.

The records in the file on page 238 might look like Table 5.2 when ordered sequentially by Surname.

Surname	Forename	Joining date
Bellamy	Howard	23 Jun 1988
Huggins	Barrington	9 Nov 1996
Periera	Bella	14 Mar 1993
Tang	Su	19 May 1990
Williams	Clarice	12 Oct 1975

Table 5.2

Sequential files are searched using sequential access. That means that if you want to find a record in a sequential file you have to start at the beginning and work your way through until you find it.

Summary of key points

In this topic you learned:

- that the way in which a file is organised on storage media depends on whether the medium uses sequential or direct file access.
- how a file of records is structured.
- how files can be organised using sequential file organisation.

1 Explain the difference between sequential and direct file access.
2 When considering files of records, what is a record?
3 What is a sort key?
4 Give an example of a file that would be organised sequentially.

● 5.6–5.7

More about file organisation

Index-sequential file organisation

It is easy enough to find a record in a small sequential file. For example, if you needed to find the record with the surname Williams in the example on page 238, the system would only have to search through five records to find it. However, if the file had thousands of records you might have to wait a long time while the system searches through the records.

An **index-sequential file** is also a file that has been sorted into some order. But another file is also set up to act as an index, in much the same way as an index in a book.

Suppose the club file mentioned above has very many records. An index file could be set up and it might look like Table 5.3.

The letter field in the index file in Table 5.3 refers to the first letter of the surnames in the sequential file. The position field states where the first surname beginning with that letter is to be found.

Table 5.4 is an extract from the large sequential file that the index file refers to.

Letter	Position
A	1
B	20
C	49
D	72
...	
W	437
X	468
Y	469
Z	475

Table 5.3: The index file

Position	Surname	Forename	Joining date
437	Waldron	Pauline	14 Apr 1990
438	Walker	George	23 Aug 1985
439	Walsh	Joel	1 Sep 1989
440	Walters	Nadine	4 Mar 1972
441	Webb	Alonzo	17 Dec 1997
442	Williams	Clarice	12 Oct 1975

Table 5.4: The sequential file

So if you wanted to search for the surname Williams, the system would first search through the index file to find the letter W. It would jump to that position in the main sequential file. It would then search through all the surnames beginning with W until it found Williams.

The index-sequential file method makes it possible to search large sequential files very quickly.

Index-sequential file organisation cannot be used with sequential access media, such as tape. It can only be used with direct access media such as disks. The main sequential file containing all the records could be stored on a hard disk. Remember that it is possible to jump to any position on a disk. Each position is given a numerical address. The index file will also be stored on the hard disk alongside the main file of records. In the index file the position field will hold the address of a position on the disk.

Random file organisation

Like index-sequential files, random files can only be used on direct access media, such as disks. **Random file organisation** is the most efficient way of storing extremely large files, such as national databases.

Random files use a rather clever method of providing direct access to records. Each record will have its own specific position (or address) on the disk. But the records will not be sorted in any way at all. In fact, they will appear to be scattered randomly over the disk. In practice, the position of each record will not be as random as it appears. The position allocated to each record will be calculated by a special formula. This formula will use some of the data in the record then convert it into the address of a position on the disk.

When a new record is added to the file, the formula works out the address where it should be stored on the disk. When someone wants to search for a record, once again the formula will work out where it is.

This method means that no time is wasted when searching for a record, since the system can go directly to the right record.

> **WHAT DOES IT MEAN?**
>
> **random file organisation**
> Random file organisation uses a formula to find the position of a record on a direct access medium.

Choosing appropriate file organisation

When new application software is being developed the software engineers and programmers have to decide on the method of file organisation that they will use. There is rarely just one way of solving the problem, but here are some typical examples:

- A payroll is a list of all the employees in an organisation, together with their pay details. Every month a payroll application will calculate how much each person should be paid. It will print payslips and it may send the details of payments directly to the company's bank. The payroll file would normally be stored sequentially by surname. When the application is run each month it will access the record for each employee one at a time, so a simple sequential file is needed.

- A shop uses a computerised stock system. The stock records hold details of all the items for sale in the shop. Each item is identified by a stock code. The stock record for each item also holds the price of the item and the number in stock. When a customer wants to buy an item the sales assistant enters the stock code at a point of sale terminal. (A barcode reader can be used to scan in the stock code from a label on the item.) The stock system then finds the record for the item and sends the price to the point of sale terminal. It also updates the stock record to show that the number in stock has gone down. There will be a large number of records in the stock file, and each item has to be retrieved quickly, so the best way to organise the file would be as a random file.

- A library has a computer-based catalogue of all its books. The catalogue is sorted by the ISBN (International Standard Book Number) which you can find on the back of any book that has been published. There is usually a barcode that gives the ISBN as well. When someone borrows a book the librarian scans the ISBN barcode and this brings up the details of the book on screen. The catalogue file is large, but stored sequentially. Index-sequential file organisation will give fairly quick access to any record.

Summary of key points

In this topic you learned:

- how an index-sequential file is organised.
- how a random file is organised.
- how to choose a suitable method of file organisation for a specific application.

QUESTIONS

1 What is the role of an index file in index-sequential file organisation?
2 Of the three methods of file organisation (sequential, index-sequential and random) which, if any:
   a can only be used with direct access media?
   b can be used with both direct access and sequential media?
   c can only be used with sequential media?

End-of-section questions

Multiple-choice questions

1 The following are statements about data.
   I They are raw facts
   II They can be processed to form information
   III They are results of processing
   IV They can be numbers or characters

   Which statements are true?
   A I, II and III only   B I, III and IV only
   C I, II and IV only   D I, II, III and IV

2 All of the following are examples of business information activities except:
   A Payroll   B Accounts
   C Archiving   D Budget

3 Which of the following devices would most likely be present in a process control system?
   A Robots   B Sensors
   C Digital assistants   D Spreadsheets

4 Which of the following is a machine-readable document?
   A A handwritten letter   B Output from a speaker
   C A barcode   D All of the above

5 All of the following are validation checks except:
   A Consistency check   B Range check
   C Accuracy check   D Data type check

Structured questions

1 a State the difference between data and information.
   b Define the term 'information processing'.
   c List three forms of information processing.

2 a Briefly explain how a process control system works.
   b Give one example of a process control system.

3 a State the difference between a source document and a turnaround document.
   b Give one example of a machine-readable document.
   c Give one example of a human-readable document.

4 a Distinguish between data validation and data verification.
   b List three ways in which data can be validated.
   c Briefly describe any two of the types of data validation you identified in your answer 4b.

5 a List three methods of file organisation.
   b For each of the methods of file organisation you identified in your answer to 5a, give ONE example of an application where it is used.
   c State the difference between sequential access and direct access.

Word processing

Objective

By the end of this section, you will be able to:

- Edit characters, words, sentences, paragraphs and larger blocks of text, by deleting, inserting and moving text.
- Describe and use page layout features such as text alignment, margins, tab stops, page numbers and page breaks.
- Make sensible use of text formatting options such as bold, italics, underline, highlight, font types and sizes, superscript and subscript.
- Enhance a document with the use of headers, footers, footnotes, endnotes, columns and tables.
- Use mail-merge.
- Use helpful functions such as spell-check, search and replace.
- Add graphics to a page, and include material from other documents.
- Keep your documents secure by automatically saving and backing up files, and by using password protection.
- Track changes in a document.

You can use word processing software to create and save documents in electronic form. Sometimes you will want to print the documents, but often they can be shared with other people by email rather than by post. Here are some of the documents you can create using word processing software: letters, newsletters, invitations, posters, minutes and agendas of meetings, and reports.

You may have used word processing software many times before, but you should learn some new skills in these pages. In this section, you will be word processing some of your notes from this course. If you get into the habit of making notes like this, you will gradually build up a set of revision notes that will be useful at exam time.

All the step-by-step instructions in this section refer to Microsoft Word, and the diagrams were created in that package. However, you can gain the same skills by using any available word processing package. Check the buttons in the toolbars and the options in the menus to find the equivalent functions.

Word processing software

To get started, open a new document in Word. Depending on the version of Windows that you are using, the window will look something like this.

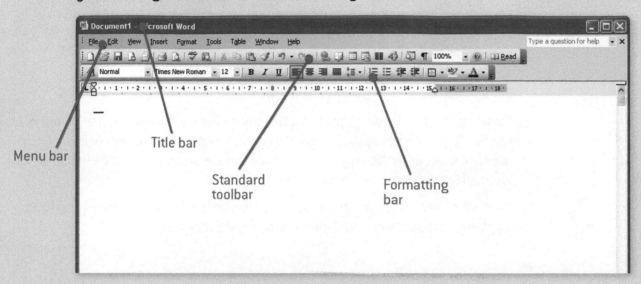

Fig 6.1: The Microsoft Word window

At the top of the window you can see the title bar. This shows the name of the document. The menu bar is immediately below the title bar. If you click on any one of the options a drop-down menu appears, with further options, as seen in Fig 6.2.

Below the menu bar you will see two or more toolbars with several buttons. Pass the mouse over each button in turn. If you wait a few seconds, a screentip will appear to describe each button.

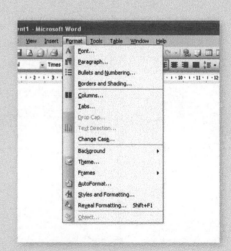

Fig 6.2: The Format drop-down menu

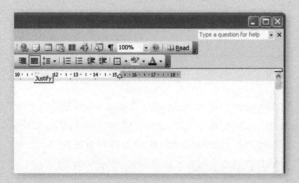

Fig 6.3: The screentip for the Justify button

Documents and text

Entering text

1 Click on the page and then start typing your notes. When you get to the end of a line, Word automatically moves onto the next line. This is known as 'word wrap'. To start a new paragraph, press the Enter key on the keyboard.

2 Save the document straightaway by clicking on the Save button in the Standard toolbar. If you are not sure which button to use, move the mouse over the toolbar and read the screentips. When you save a document in Word you give it a filename, and Word adds the filename extension '.doc'.

Don't wait until you have done a lot of work before saving it; save it frequently as you go along, perhaps every 5-10 minutes, to avoid losing anything.

WHAT DOES IT MEAN?

word wrap
Word wrap is when text is automatically carried forward to the next line when one line is full.

The status bar

In Fig 6.4 at the bottom of the window you can see the status bar. This gives some useful information.

Page number   Current page

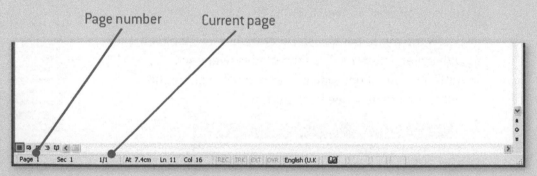

Fig 6.4: The status bar

On the left you can see Page 1; as your document gets longer will show the number of the page you are working on. The third piece of information from the left is shown as 1/1. The first number is the page number again. The second number is the total number of pages in a document. So if you were working on page 3 in a document with five pages it would display 3/5.

Editing text

When you finish typing out your notes, you may find that you want to go back and make some amendments, either adding or deleting text.

Adding text

1 Click in the spot where you want to add something. A **cursor** appears at the point where you want to edit the text, as shown in Fig 6.5.

2 Start typing. The extra text is fitted in between the existing words, as shown in Fig 6.6.

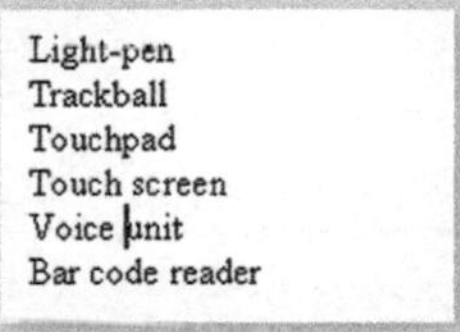

Light-pen
Trackball
Touchpad
Touch screen
Voice unit
Bar code reader

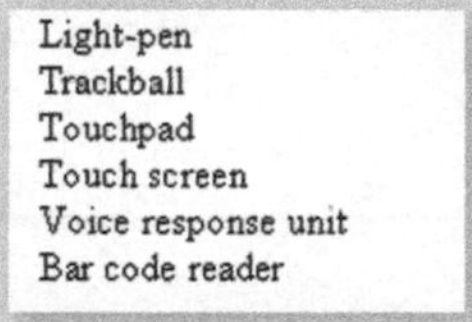

Light-pen
Trackball
Touchpad
Touch screen
Voice response unit
Bar code reader

Fig 6.5: The cursor at the insertion point   **Fig 6.6:** The extra text inserted

WHAT DOES IT MEAN?

cursor
A cursor is the name for the flashing vertical bar that shows your position in the text. When you type, the text appears at the cursor position.

Deleting text

You can delete text in several ways. Here are two methods.

Deleting: Method 1

1 Click immediately *before* the characters that you want to delete.

2 Press the key on the keyboard marked Delete. The **character** to the *right* of the cursor is deleted.

3 Carry on until all the text you want to delete has gone.

Deleting: Method 2

1 Click immediately *after* the characters that you want to delete.

2 Press the Backspace key on the keyboard. This key is usually marked with a back arrow ←. The character to the *left* of the cursor is deleted.

3 Carry on until all the text you want to delete has gone.

WHAT DOES IT MEAN?

character
A character is any letter, number or punctuation mark that you can use on a computer.

Type-over mode

Instead of inserting text between existing words, you could also write on top of some text that you don't want. To do this you need to change to type-over mode, also known as overwrite mode.

Changing to type-over mode

1 In the status bar, double click on the letters OVR (for OVeRwrite). The letters OVR will be faint when off, and bold when on, as in Fig 6.7

2 Now click where you want the new text to appear and start typing.

3 To change back to Insert mode, double click on OVR in the status bar once more.

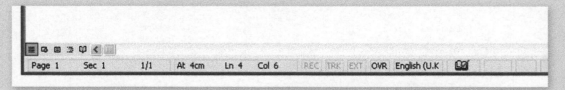

| Page 1 | Sec 1 | 1/1 | At 4cm | Ln 4 | Col 6 | REC | TRK | EXT | OVR | English (U.K | |

Fig 6.7: The status bar showing overwrite (type-over) mode

```
Light-pen
Trackball
Touchpad
Touch|screen
Voice response unit
Bar code reader
```

```
Light-pen
Trackball
Touchpad
Touch terminal
Voice response unit
Bar code reader
```

Fig 6.8: The cursor at the overwrite point   **Fig 6.9:** The overwritten text

Blocks of text

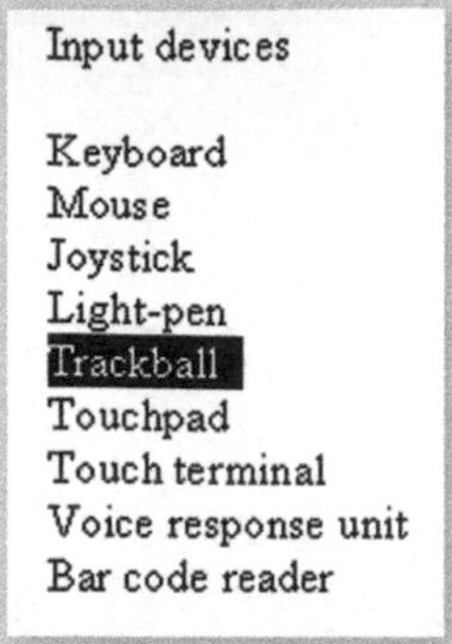

So far you have been changing characters one by one. There are some faster methods that you can use if you want to change larger sections of text.

First, you must select the text that you want to change. You can select an individual character, one or more words, a sentence, a paragraph or a large block of text.

```
Input devices

Keyboard
Mouse
Joystick
Light-pen
Trackball
Touchpad
Touch terminal
Voice response unit
Bar code reader
```

Fig 6.10: Selected text

Selecting text

1 Use the mouse to click at the beginning of the text.

2 Hold the mouse button down as you move the cursor across the text.

3 When you release the mouse button, the text will be selected. The selected text will appear in reversed colours, that is, it switches black to white and white to black, as shown in Fig 6.10.

You can use this method as another way of deleting text.

Deleting: Method 3

1 Select the text you want to delete.

2 Press either the Delete key or the Backspace key.

Cut, copy and paste text

Some of the buttons in the Standard toolbar are useful for editing text. Pass your mouse over the buttons to see what each one does.

Fig 6.11: The Standard toolbar

- Cut – deletes whatever is selected but stores it on the Clipboard.
- Copy – stores a copy of whatever is selected on the Clipboard.
- Paste – places onto the document a copy of the last item stored on the Clipboard.

The Clipboard is an area of internal memory where you can store text or images temporarily. If you want to see what is stored on the Clipboard, go to *Edit* → *Office Clipboard*.

Note: *Edit* → *Office Clipboard* means first click on *Edit* in the menu bar, then click on *Office Clipboard* in the drop-down Edit menu.

Copy and paste

Sometimes you may want to copy some of the text to another part of the document.

Copying and pasting text

1 Select the text that you want to copy.

2 Click on the Copy button in the Standard toolbar. This copies the selected text to the Clipboard.

3 Click on the page in the position where you want the copied text to appear.

4 Click on the Paste button.

The text will now be pasted to the new position as in Fig 6.13. Note that the words now appear twice.

In this example you could use the second set of words as headings for notes about each type of device.

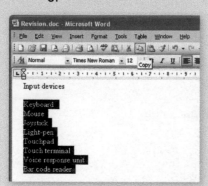

Fig 6.12: Using the Copy button

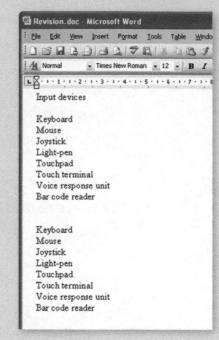

Fig 6.13: The selected text has been copied to the new position

Cut and paste

If you want to remove text from one position and place it elsewhere you have to cut it first – which places it safely on the Clipboard – then paste it to its new position.

Moving text by cutting and pasting

1 Once again, start by selecting the text you want to move. Click on the Cut button (or press CTRL + X).

2 This time the text disappears. But it is safely stored on the Clipboard, even if you can't see the Clipboard.

3 Now click on the page in the position where you want the cut text to appear.

4 Click on the Paste button.

Fig 6.14: Using the Cut button

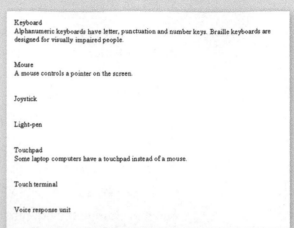

Fig 6.15: The cut text has been pasted into a new position

Drag and drop

You can also move a block of text by **dragging and dropping** it.

Moving text by dragging and dropping

1 Select the text you want to move. Then click again on the selected text, and hold the mouse button down. After a second or two, notice that the pointer changes to an arrow with a small box beneath it and that the cursor is displayed as a broken line instead of a solid one.

2 Keep holding the mouse button down and move the pointer to the position where you want to text to go.

3 When you release the mouse the text will appear in its new position.

WHAT DOES IT MEAN?

drag and drop
If you click on something that has been selected on the screen and hold the mouse button down, you can move it to a new position. When you release the mouse button it stays in its new position. This is known as 'drag and drop'.

CHECK YOUR PROGRESS

Can you explain the differences between copy and paste, cut and paste, and drag and drop as a way of moving text in a document?

Page formats

Most documents will eventually be sent to the printer so it is helpful to see what the pages will look like when printed.

Looking at the print layout

1 Go to *View* → *Print Layout*. That means, click on *View* in the Menu bar, then click on *Print Layout* in the drop-down View menu.

2 You can now see exactly where the margins lie, and if your document has more than one page, you can see the gaps between the pages.

You can change the orientation, size and margins of a page, and you can also decide where new pages should start and whether they should be numbered.

Orientation

Changing the **orientation** of a page

1 Go to *File* → *Page Setup*.

2 The Page Setup **dialogue window** will appear as in Fig 6.16. There are three **tabs** along the top of the dialogue window - Margins, Paper and Layout. Orientation is on the Margins tab, so click on *Margins* if it is not already open.

3 Under Orientation, select either *Portrait* or *Landscape*, then click on *OK*.

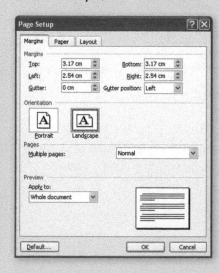

Fig 6.16: Changing the orientation of the page to Landscape

Margins

In the main Word window, there is a ruler just below the toolbars. It shows the width of the page and its **margins**, usually measured in centimetres.

Fig 6.17: The ruler at the top of the page

The white section on the ruler shows the area on the page where you can type. The grey areas on either side of the ruler show the widths of the left and right margins.

The page also has top and bottom margins, which can be seen in the ruler placed vertically on the left of the screen. The top and bottom margins sometimes hold text, such as page numbers, so you need to make sure they are large enough to hold whatever text you want there.

The page length is the amount of space available between the top and bottom margins. You can increase or decrease the page length by changing the top and bottom margins.

Changing the margins of the page

1 Go to *File* ➔ *Page Setup*.

2 Under the Margins tab change the size of the Top, Bottom, Left and Right margins.

3 Click *OK* to see the effect on the layout of the page and on the appearance of the rulers.

Paper size

You may want to change the size of paper you are working with. Most printers take standard Letter size paper, but some specialist printers work with larger or smaller sheets of paper.

If you change the paper size this will affect the page length of a document.

Changing the paper size

1 Go to *File* → *Page Setup*.

2 Under the Paper tab read what is shown under 'Paper Size'. It should display 'Letter' as its **default setting**, but you can click on the little arrow to see the alternative paper sizes that are available.

Page breaks

If you want text to start on a new page, you can insert a page break.

Inserting a page break

1 Click on the page at the point where you want a new page to begin.

2 Go to *Insert* → *Break*.

3 Click on *Page Break*.

A page break can be removed by clicking at the beginning of the next page, and then pressing the Backspace key.

THINK ABOUT IT
What size paper can be handled by the printer you use? Is the paper size set up correctly on Page Setup?

Default settings

When you install word processing software it will use standard settings, which are referred to as the default settings. For example, in Page Setup the paper size is initially set at 'Letter'. This is the default page size. You can change it to 'Legal' or to other international page sizes such as 'A4'. In the same way, the margins will have been set at a specific size.

You can reset everything back to the default settings by clicking on the Default button at the bottom of the relevant dialogue window.

Character formats

The Formatting toolbar contains lots of useful buttons. Pass your mouse over the buttons to see the screentips.

Fig 6.18: The Formatting toolbar

The bold, italic, underline and highlight formats

On the Formatting toolbar, you can use one or more of these buttons to change the format of any text:

- **Bold – You can use Bold to emphasise words or phrases. It is normally used for headings.**

- *Italics – You can use Italics for emphasis as well, and is sometimes used for quotes or for additional comments.*

- <u>Underline – You should be careful about using Underline in printed documents. It is mainly used in handwritten scripts as a substitute for Bold. Underlined text usually indicates a **hyperlink**., and you can use it in a web page or in a help file.</u>

- Highlight – You can also use highlight to draw attention to words or phrases. You can choose which colour to use for the highlight. Do not use a dark colour with black text as it will be difficult to read.

WHAT DOES IT MEAN?

hyperlink
A hyperlink is some text in a document that jumps to another document when you click on it. Hyperlinks are widely used on web pages, but can also be used on word processed documents, for example, in a Help file.

Using bold, italic and underline

1 Select the text that you want to put in bold, italics or underline. This can be a single character, a complete sentence or a whole block of text.

2 Click on the appropriate format button in the formatting toolbar.

Using highlight

1 Select the text that you want to highlight.

2 Click on the highlight button. The text will be highlighted in the colour the button displays.

3 To choose another colour click on the little arrow to the right of the highlight button.

4 To remove the highlight, select *None* in the highlight options.

CHECK YOUR PROGRESS

Give some examples to show how bold, italics, underline and highlight can be used effectively in a document.

Font size

The size of a character is measured in points, which is an old printing term. The **font size** of, say, 12 points, measures the length from the top of the highest character to the bottom of the lowest character. Generally speaking you should not use less than 12 points for normal text, although smaller sizes can be used for footnotes and picture captions.

Changing the font size

1 Select the text you want to change.

2 On the Formatting toolbar, find the Font Size box, which displays a number – probably 12. This is the point size of the characters you have selected. Click on the small arrow to the right of the number, then click on the size you want. You may need to try a few to find the size you want.

3 The characters will now be larger or smaller.

Fig 6.19: Selecting the size of the font

Fig 6.20: A larger font size

Font types

Different font types have been around since the invention of printing. Many more have been designed for use on computers, and there are now thousands to choose from.

Some font types are long and thin and others are short and fat, so even font types that have the same font size may look very different on the page. All the fonts shown in Fig 6.21 are the same font size.

There are three main kinds of font types – serif, sans serif and cursive.

- **Serif fonts** – Serif fonts have extra marks (serifs) at the ends of the strokes (see Fig 6.21). These imitate the chisel marks left when letters are carved into stone. The most widely used serif font is Times New Roman – so called because it was used by *The Times* newspaper and imitated the lettering used in ancient Rome. Serif fonts are generally very easy to read.

- **Sans serif fonts** – Sans serif fonts lack the extra marks and appear much plainer. However, you will find a greater variety of shapes amongst sans serif fonts.

- **Cursive fonts** – Cursive fonts imitate handwriting, although some of them are based on handwriting styles from over a century ago. Cursive fonts are often used for mock signatures. They can also be used to make headings look stylish and interesting, but they should be used with care, because they are not as easy to read as the other types of font.

Serif fonts	Sans serif fonts	Cursive fonts
This is Times New Roman	This is Arial	This is Bradley Hand
This is Goudy Old Style	This is Century Gothic	**This is Calligraphic**
This is Courier	**This is Comic Sans**	This is Felt
This is Bookman	This is Olive Oil	This is French Script

Fig 6.21: Font types

Changing the font type

1 Select the text that you want to change.

2 On the Formatting toolbar, find the Font box, which displays the name of the current font type – probably Times New Roman. Click on the small arrow beside the box, then click on the font you want to use.

THINK ABOUT IT

Look at some examples of printed materials, e.g. books, newspapers, leaflets, posters and catalogues. Check where serif, sans serif or cursive font types are used. Do you think they are used effectively? Would you have used different font types?

Choosing fonts

How are you going to choose which font types to use? It is a good idea to analyse printed materials and work out what looks professional. Here are some other guidelines:

1 Use a maximum of two font types in a simple document like a letter or a report – one font for the main text and another one for headings.

2 Only use a third font type for special emphasis, or for text in a separate section such as a footer.

3 For the main text use at least 12 point, and larger sizes for headings.

Upper and lower case

Sometimes you want to change a whole sentence into **uppercase**, for example, for a heading. There is an easy way to do this without retyping the text.

What does it mean?

uppercase and lowercase
Uppercase is an old printing term for CAPITAL LETTERS. Lowercase refers to small letters.

Changing case

1 Select the text you want to change.

2 Go to *Format* → *Change Case*.

3 Click on *UPPERCASE*, then *OK*.

Line spacing

In a normal paragraph the lines are fairly close together.

Some people find it useful to have a larger gap between lines. For example, someone with a visual impairment may like to have text written in large print and with bigger line spacing. Sometimes documents are printed out in double line spacing to leave room for handwritten comments. You can increase the line spacing, that is the gap between one line and another in the same paragraph.

Changing line spacing

1 Select one or more paragraphs where you want to change the line spacing.

2 Click on small arrow to the right of the Line Spacing button in the Formatting toolbar.

3 Select *2.0* to give double line spacing.

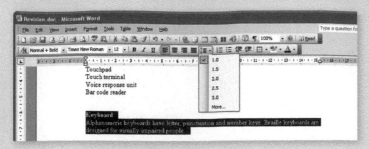

Fig 6.22: Setting the line spacing

Keyboard

Alphanumeric keyboards have letter, punctuation and number keys. Braille keyboards are designed for visually impaired people.

Fig 6.23: Double line spacing

Superscript and subscript

Sometimes you will need to put characters into superscript or subscript, which means having them raised or lowered slightly above or below the line of text. Subscript and superscript are often used in scientific and mathematical formulae, such as:

The raised characters are in superscript format. The lowered characters are in subscript format.

3^7　　$25m^2$　　H_2O　　157_{base8}

Using superscript and subscript

1 Select the character that is to be formatted.

2 Go to *Format* → *Font* to open the Font dialogue window.

3 Under *Effects*, click on *Superscript* or *Subscript*.

4 Click *OK*.

CHECK YOUR PROGRESS

Find some examples in printed documents of the use of superscript and subscript formats.

Text layout

Text alignment

You will find the four **text alignment** buttons in the Formatting toolbar, labelled Align Left, Center, Align Right and Justify.

Left-aligned text

Left-aligned text is lined up against the left margin of the page, like this. Left alignment is used for all kinds of documents, although it does mean that the text looks 'ragged' (uneven) along the right margin. This can be overcome by using fully justified text instead.

Right-aligned text

Right-aligned text is lined up against the right margin of the page, like this. Right alignment is normally only used for positioning addresses on letters. It is sometimes used to create special effects. But generally it looks rather odd and is difficult to read.

Centred text

Centred text is placed evenly between the left and right margins of the page, like this. Headings are often centre-aligned, but otherwise use it with care, as it can be difficult for eyes to dart from one starting point on a line to another.

Fully justified text

When text is fully justified, like this, the characters are spaced out so that they line up on both the left and the right margins. This looks neat in formal printed documents, although you may find that some words are stretched a little too much.

Aligning text

1 Select a paragraph or more of text that you want to align.

2 Click on the appropriate alignment button.

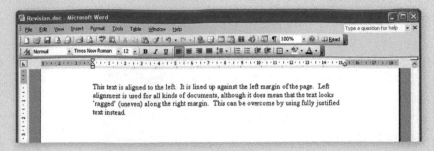

Fig 6.24: Left alignment

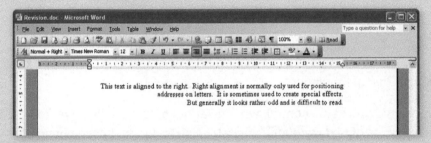

Fig 6.25: Right alignment

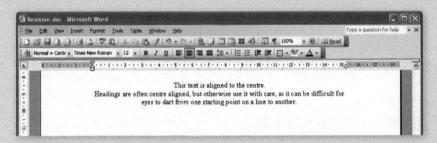

Fig 6.26: Centre alignment

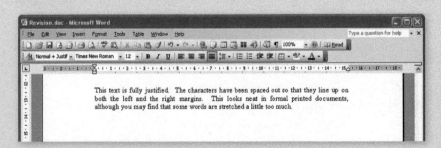

Fig 6.27: Fully justified

Tabs and tab stops

The key to the left of Q on the keyboard is known as the tabulation, or **tab**, key. When you press it, the text is shifted along the line by a fixed amount. The default positions of the tab stops are shown as tiny vertical lines just under the ruler.

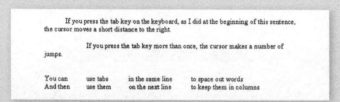

Fig 6.28: Use of tabulation

Tab stops give you some control over the layout of text on the page. You can use them to create columns of text, without using tables, or to simply space out words.

Creating your own tab stops

1. Go to *Format* ➜ *Tabs*

2. Under *Tab Stop Position* enter the distance of the new tab stop from the left margin.

3. Click OK, and you will see a small symbol on the ruler that represents the stop.

4. Go to *Format* ➜ *Tabs* again, and enter another tab stop position. This time, under *Alignment* select *Right*. Click *OK*.

5. Enter some text and see what happens when you press the Tab key.

Note that you can use the right alignment tab stop to arrange some text with right alignment anywhere on the page.

Fig 6.29: The ruler showing a left tab stop at 2 cm and a right tab stop at 8 cm

Headers and footers

A header is an area at the top of each page, and a footer is at the bottom, usually within the top and bottom margins. These areas are used to supply information relevant to the whole document, such as the title, author, date created, page number, etc, and so the content of the header or the footer is usually the same on each page.

To understand fully how headers and footers work you need to have a document with several pages.

Using headers and footers

1 Go to *View → Header and Footer*. The header and footer areas will be outlined at the top and bottom of the page.

2 The Header and Footer floating toolbar will appear. Check what each button does by moving your mouse over them.

3 Click in the header section on the document and type in some text. This text will appear on each page of the document.

4 You can format the characters using the buttons in the Formatting toolbar. The text in a header or footer is normally smaller than the main body of the text, to distinguish it from the rest of the document.

5 Click on the *Switch between Header and Footer* button to go to the footer section.

Fig 6.30: The header section with the Header and Footer floating toolbar

6 Click on *Close* to go back to the main page.

If your document has several pages you will probably want to place the page number of each page in the header or footer – the footer is most common.

Putting page numbers on your document

1 Go to *View → Header and Footer*.

2 Switch to the footer.

3 In the Header and Footer floating toolbar, click on the *Insert Page Number* button.

4 Use the text alignment buttons in the Formatting toolbar to place the page number to the left, centre or right of the footer.

You can also insert page numbers by going to *Insert → Page Numbers*.

CHECK YOUR PROGRESS

What kind of information might be found in a header or footer?

Footnotes and endnotes

You may have seen little numbers after text in a reference book. These are markers for the footnotes, which appear at the bottom of the page.

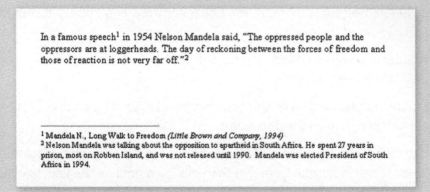

In a famous speech[1] in 1954 Nelson Mandela said, "The oppressed people and the oppressors are at loggerheads. The day of reckoning between the forces of freedom and those of reaction is not very far off."[2]

_____

[1] Mandela N., Long Walk to Freedom *(Little Brown and Company, 1994)*
[2] Nelson Mandela was talking about the opposition to apartheid in South Africa. He spent 27 years in prison, most on Robben Island, and was not released until 1990. Mandela was elected President of South Africa in 1994.

Fig 6.31: Footnotes

Sometimes all the notes are placed at the end of a chapter, in which case they are called endnotes. It is not good practice to have both footnotes and endnotes in the same document because the reader will be confused about where they need to look to find a note.

Footnotes and endnotes are not created by adding superscript numbers – you need to tell the computer where you want to add a footnote/endnote and it will create the numbers and keep count. This means that if you need to add in another note in the middle of a sequence, the computer will update the numbering automatically.

Fig 6.32: The Footnote and Endnote dialogue window

Adding footnotes

1 Click at the point in the text where you want to footnote marker to appear.

2 Go to *Insert → Reference → Footnotes*.

3 Click on *OK* in the dialogue window.

4 You will now find that you can type in the text of the footnote. When you have finished the footnote click in the main part of the page to carry on with your document.

5 To create an endnote click on *Endnotes* in the Footnote and Endnote dialogue window.

CHECK YOUR PROGRESS

Look at Fig 6.33 and identify all the formatting that has been done to achieve this output.

Fig 6.33: Formatted text

Columns and tables

Columns

Many documents arrange the text in columns, as they break large amounts of text into shorter rows, making it easier to read. Columns are common in newspapers and magazines, and can also be used for publicity leaflets and newsletters.

Adding columns

1 Click on the Columns button in the Standard toolbar.

2 Move the mouse over the columns until the required columns are selected. Click to apply.

3 As you enter your text it will flow from the bottom of one column to the next.

4 To remove the columns, click on the Columns button again and select only one column.

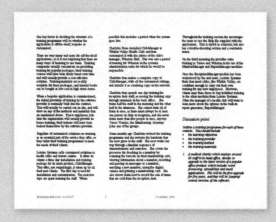

Fig 6.34: Three-column layout in a document

Tables

Tables allow you to arrange information in rows and columns. Each of the spaces in a table is known as a cell. A table can be used to display statistical data, but it can also be used to organise your text and images on a page. You can choose whether to have visible borders to a table or its cells.

Creating a table

1 Click on the Insert Table button in the Standard toolbar.

2 Highlight the number of cells you need. In Fig 6.35 the table will have three rows and four columns.

3 The table will then appear as in Fig 6.36. Click in one of the cells and start typing. The cells will expand so that your text can fit in.

4 You can select an individual cell or a group of cells by holding down the mouse button while passing over the cell or cells that you want to select. You can then apply text formatting, such as font size, type, colour, italics, etc.

5 If you need an extra row, click just to the right of the bottom right cell. You can see the cursor in the correct place in Fig 6.36. Then press Enter.

6 If you want to change the width of a column, click on the line between two columns and then drag it to the right or left.

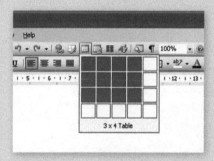

Fig 6.35: Creating a table

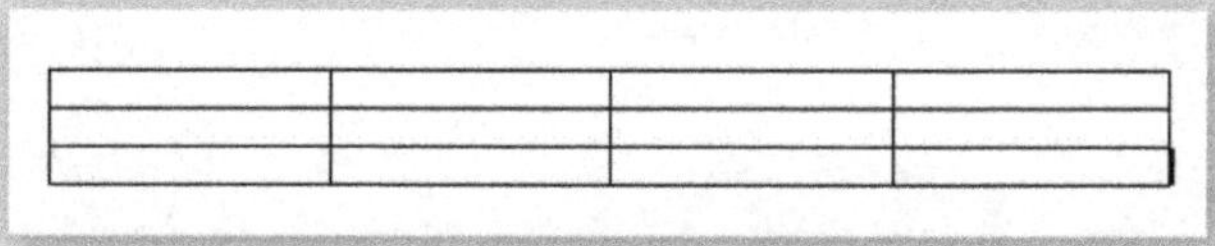

Fig 6.36: A new table showing the cursors when changing the column width and adding a row

Unit	Abbreviation	Approx value	Actual value
Kilobyte	KB	1 thousand byte	1024 bytes
Megabyte	MB	1 million bytes	1,048,576 bytes
Gigabyte	GB	1 billion bytes	1,073,741,824 bytes
Terabyte	TB	1 trillion bytes	1,099,511,627,776 bytes

Fig 6.37: A table used to lay out text

Removing gridlines from a table

You can remove the gridlines around a table, and this is sometimes useful for laying out a complete page.

1 Select all the cells in the table.

2 Click on the Tables and Borders button on the Standard toolbar. You will now see the Tables and Borders floating toolbar, as in Fig 6.38.

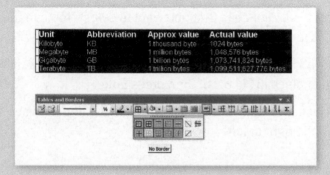

Fig 6.38: Choosing the No Border button

3 Find the All Borders button, and click on the small arrow beside it. You will then see a number of border buttons.

4 Click on the No Borders button.

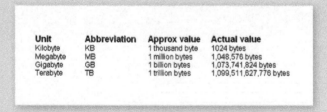

Fig 6.39: A table without borders

CHECK YOUR PROGRESS

Give three examples of documents that might use tables.

The spell-check, search and replace functions

Spell-check

Everyone makes mistakes from time to time when keying in text. Sometimes you simply hit the wrong keys. Sometimes you can't remember how to spell a word.

Checking the spelling in a document

1 Go to *Tools* ➜ *Spelling and Grammar*.

2 If there are any spelling errors in the document the Spelling and Grammar dialogue window will appear as in Fig 6.40. The incorrect spelling is shown in red. Suggested spellings are given below.

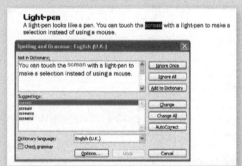

Fig 6.40: Spell-checking a document

3 Under *Suggestions* select the correct spelling then click on *Change*.

4 Sometimes the spell-check does not recognise a word, perhaps because it is in another language, but you want it to remain as you spelled it. In that case click on *Ignore Once*.

5 The spell-check will then find any remaining errors in the document.

The best way to check your spelling is to set up Word so that it checks all your words as you key them in. You may find that this is already set up on your system. If not, the following steps show you how.

Checking spelling as you type

1 Go to *Tools* ➜ *Options*. The Options dialogue window will appear as in Fig 6.41.

2 Click on the tab labelled Spelling and Grammar.

3 Make sure that there is a tick against the first option: *Check spelling as you type*. Click *OK*.

Fig 6.41: The Spelling and Grammar tab in the Options dialogue window

4 In your document, deliberately spell a word incorrectly and you will see a wavy red line appear beneath it as in Fig 6.42.

5 Now **right click** on the misspelled word and a menu will appear with some suggested corrections. If one of the words shown is the one you want, click on it.

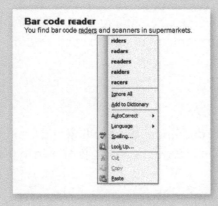

Fig 6.42: The misspelled word is underlined in red, and the menu gives some suggestions

THINK ABOUT IT

A student wrote this sentence, making some typing errors:
I herad about the holliday from my fiend.

After using the spellchecker, the sentence became: *I herald about the Holliday from my fiend.*

What has happened here?

WHAT DOES IT MEAN?

right click
If you click on the right button on your mouse a menu will pop up on the screen alongside.

Search and replace

If you write a long document you may forget where you have written particular information. To find it you can use the search function, which is called 'Find' in Word.

Using Find

1 Go to *Edit* → *Find*.

2 In the Find dialogue window type in the word or phrase that you want to find.

3 Click *Find Next*. It will then highlight the next occurrence of the word in the document.

4 Click on *Find Next* if you want to find another instance of the word or phrase. If you have found the words you wanted, click *Cancel*.

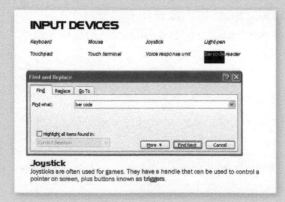

Fig 6.43: Finding a phrase in a document

Suppose you write a lengthy document, and when you get to the end you realise that you have spelt a name, or a word, wrongly several times. The easiest way to correct this is to use the Replace function.

Using Replace

1 Find one of the places where you have spelled the word incorrectly and select it.

2 Go to *Edit → Replace*. The *Find and Replace* dialogue window will appear.

3 The wrong spelling will appear in the *Find What* box.

4 Key in the correct spelling in the *Replace With* box.

5 Click on *Replace*.

6 Click on *Find Next*, and continue to replace the wrong spellings.

You will notice that there is a *Replace All* option, but you should only use it with great care. Suppose you had written St in some addresses and you wanted to replace it with Street. If you used Replace All it would not only replace St when used as a shortened form of Street, but it would also replace all the uses of St where it meant Saint.

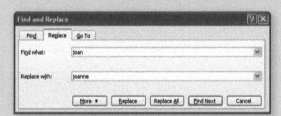

Fig 6.44: The Find and Replace dialogue window

Mail-merge

You will probably, at some time, have received a letter that was addressed to you personally, but you knew that very similar letters will have been sent to thousands of other people. These letters are generated by a process known as mail-merge.

Mail-merge takes name and address data and merges it with a standard letter document. The output is thousands of personally addressed letters. The name and address data can be stored in a database, in a spreadsheet or in another document.

You are going to set up a mail-merge letter to the customers of a small business telling them about a new product.

Using mail-merge

1 Create a new document in Word in the usual way.

2 Create a simple letter heading, with the name and address of the business. Add today's date to one side below the heading. This is your primary document for the mail-merge. Save it as 'Letter'.

3 Go to *Tools* ➔ *Letters and Mailings* ➔ *Mail Merge*.

4 You will be asked a series of questions in the task pane (see Fig 6.45). Answer as follows:

> *Step 1 Select document type: Letters*.
> Then click on *Next* at the bottom of the task pane.
> *Step 2 Select starting document: Use the current document*.
> Then click on *Next* at the bottom of the task pane.
> *Step 3 Select recipients: Type a new list*.
> Then click on *Create …*

The New Address List dialogue window will appear. You will use it to create the datafile for the mail-merge.

5 Key in the name and address of one customer. You do not have to fill in every box (see Fig 6.46).

6 Click on *New Entry* to add another customer. Add five or six customers. Click *Close*.

7 The next box displays all the addresses in a table and allows you to sort them if you wish.

8 Click *OK*. You will be prompted to save the address list in the My Data Sources folder. Call it 'Customers'.

9 In the task pane click on *Next* to go to *Step 4*. You will be placing the name and address of each customer on the left of the page and below the letter heading.

10 Click in the correct position on the letter, then in the task pane select *Address Block*. Click *OK* in the dialogue box. A placeholder for the address will appear on the letter like this: <<AddressBlock>>.

11 Click a little below the address block in the letter and then select *Greeting Line*. You can then choose what type of greeting to use. The default is 'Dear' followed by the person's title and name.

12 Now write the rest of the letter to customers (see Fig 6.47).

13 *Step 5* displays the merged letter using the name and address of the first person on the list. The arrows on the task pane allow you to browse through the remaining letters.

14 *Step 6* lets you print the letters, one for each customer. Instead of printing out copies of all the letters, when the *Merge to Printer* dialogue window appears choose *Current Record*. This will just print out the letter to the customer that you can see onscreen.

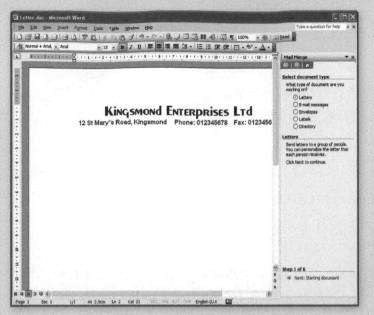

Fig 6.45: The Mail Merge task pane opens

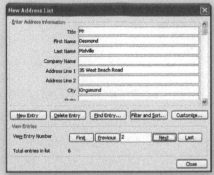

Fig 6.46: Entering data in the Address List

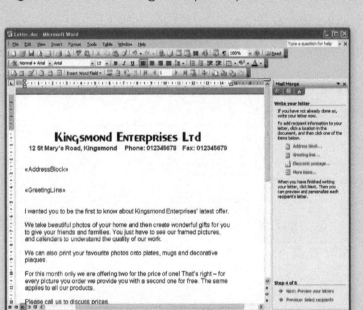

Fig 6.47: Adding the address and greetings blocks

Fig 6.48: A merged letter

When you created the address list you added data in a number of different boxes known as fields. The fieldnames, such as Title, First Name and City, told you what to put in each field. You then allowed Word to set up the address block by combining the data from several fields. The greeting line also consisted of a salutation (e.g. 'Dear') followed by one or more fields.

If you like you can add any fields anywhere in the letter. Suppose you wanted to write:
I am writing to all my customers in --- to tell you some exciting news.

You could then put the name of the customer's town in place of the blanks.

Adding extra fields

1 Open the mail-merge letter you created earlier.

2 Go to *Tools* → *Letters and Mailings* → *Mail Merge*.

3 In the task pane, answer as follows:

> *Step 3 Select recipients: Use an existing list*.
>
> The name of datafile associated with this letter will be shown.

4 Write your letter. Below the greeting line type in:
I am writing to all my customers in

5 You will find the Mail Merge toolbar immediately above your document. Move your mouse over the buttons to find *Insert Merge Fields*. Click on this button, then click on *City*, then click on *Insert* (see Fig 6.49).The fieldname will appear on the letter like this <<City>>. This shows that it is a fieldname not actual text.

6 Complete the sentence with the words to tell you some exciting news.

7 Go through *Step 5* and *Step 6* to see what the letter now looks like.

Fig 6.49: Adding a fieldname to the document

Inserting text files, graphics and tables

You may want to combine a number of word processed documents into one large document. For example, perhaps you have been working on a project with a group of people, and each of you has written about a part of the project. You will then want to combine all the documents into one report. The steps below will be used if you want to insert a complete file.

Inserting files

1 In your main document, click in the position where you want to add the contents of another document.

2 Go to *Insert* → *Files*.

3 Find the file that you want to include, click once on it and click on *Insert*.

You may want to add a graphic (image) to your document to illustrate a point or make the document more visually interesting. You can do this with your own images, like photos, or by using the ones included with the software package.

Inserting graphics

1 Click in the position where you want to add the graphic.

2 If you want to insert a photo or other image that you have already saved, go to *Insert* → *Picture* → *From File*, and find the file.

3 If you want to insert a clipart image provided with the software, go to *Insert* → *Picture* → *Clipart*.

Sometimes you just want to copy a part of one document into another. Usually you can do this simply by copying and pasting.

Inserting text and tables by copying and pasting

1 Open the document that you are copying from. Select the text or table that you want to copy.

2 Click on the Copy button in the Standard toolbar.

3 Open the document that you are copying to. Click at the position where you want to insert the text or table. Click on the Paste button in the Standard toolbar.

Keeping your documents safe

At some time in the past you have probably lost a document you are working on. This may have happened because the system froze, or the power went off when you were in the middle of writing. Sometimes we just are careless and delete files by mistake. Sometimes someone else gets access to our work and deletes it, either in error or maliciously.

There are several things you can do to make sure that you still have a copy of your work whatever disaster happens. But the most important thing to do is to save it regularly. Save each document with a meaningful name as soon as you start work on it.

Automatic save

You can also set the software to save your work into a special recovery file at regular intervals, this is called Autorecover. If the system does crash, you will then be able to recover the version that was last saved by this method.

Setting up Autorecover

1 Go to *Tools* → *Options*, then click on the *Save* tab.

2 Make sure that *Save Autorecover info* is ticked. To the right of this it should state how frequently the automatic save should happen; 10 or 15 minutes is normal.

It is a good idea to also tick *Allow Background Saves*. This makes sure that the automatic saves do not interrupt your work.

THINK ABOUT IT
Do you use either Autorecover or backup copies for your own work? If not, why not?

Backup copies

A backup file is a copy of a document that is created when you save the original document that you are working on. It is usually saved to the same folder as the original document. If you were to lose your document or accidentally delete it, you would have a copy to fall back on. It will be as up-to-date as the last time you saved your original.

Creating a backup copy

1 Go to *Tools* → *Options*, then click on the *Save* tab.

2 Make sure that *Always create backup copy* is ticked.

3 A backup is given the name 'Backup of ….wbk'. If you ever have to use it, open it as usual then save it straightaway as a normal Word document.

THINK ABOUT IT
Would you find it useful to password protect any of the documents you have created? Why would you want to do this?

Password protection

You may want to protect a confidential document with a password. It is essential that you remember what the password is, otherwise you will not be able to open it again.

Creating a password

1 Go to *Tools* → *Options*, then click on the *Security* tab.

2 Key in your password beside *Password to open:*.

3 You can use any combination of letters, numbers and punctuation. Be aware that the password is case sensitive, that is, lower and uppercase letters are treated as different characters.

Tracking changes

Some documents are written by more than one person. For example, you and a friend might want to work on a single document about a project that you have been doing together.

You start by writing the first version of the report, which is then passed on to your friend. Your friend may want to suggest some changes, which are then discussed with you. The report will be changed and maybe changed back again several times before you are both are happy with it.

There is a useful tool to keep track of the changes, called Track Changes. The original text is written with a black font. Once the tracking tool has been switched on the changes suggested by the second person are shown in another colour, usually red. The first writer can then decide whether to accept each of the changes or not.

Using Track Changes

Two people should try this out together; we'll call them A and B.

1 A: Create a new document and write some text in the usual way. Save the document.

2 A: Make sure the second person has access to the document. You may have to email it to them, or transfer it on a memory device.

3 B: Open the document. Go to *Tools → Track Changes*. The Reviewing toolbar will appear (see Fig 6.50).

4 B: Insert some extra text to the document. It will appear in red and underlined. A vertical black line is shown in the left margin to draw attention to the change.

5 B: Now delete some words from the original text. They will be shown in the margin labelled as deleted text.

6 B: Save the document and pass it back to person A.

7 A: You can now decide whether to accept each change. Click on one of the changes and then click on the *Accept Change* button in the Reviewing toolbar. To reject a change click on the *Reject Change* button.

8 A: When you are satisfied with all the changes, go to *Tools → Track Changes* to switch off the tracking. Or, if you like, you can make some further changes yourself and pass it back to person B for them to review.

Fig 6.50: The Reviewing toolbar

End-of-section questions

Multiple-choice questions

1 When Sylvia tries to insert a word between two words, the letters of the second word are being erased. This is because she has the text in:
   A Delete mode   B Insert mode
   C Overwrite mode   D Correcting mode

2 A word processing feature that allows the text to be moved automatically to the next line as it approaches the right margin is:
   A Justification   B Alignment
   C Word wrap   D Enter key

3 Which of the following is NOT a line spacing setting in Microsoft Word?
   A 1"   B 1 ½"
   C 2"   D 2 ½"

4 Which type of alignment makes the text fit between left and right margins so the edges of paper do not appear ragged?
   A Left   B Right
   C Justified   D Center

5 In order to display text that appears at the bottom margin of every page of a multiple-page document use:
   A Footer   B Footnote
   C Header   D Endnote

Structured questions

1 State the difference between the following:
   a Type-over mode and insert mode
   b Copying and cutting
   c Footers and footnotes

2 a You completed half of the first page of a document and now would like to start on the second page. List two ways in which you could do this.
   b For the methods you identified in your answer to 2a, state which one is better and why.

3 a What are the default left, right, top and bottom margins of a word document?
   b List the steps that you can use to change the margins to .75 all around.
   c List the steps that you can use to change the page layout to landscape.

4 a You have six paragraphs on a page of a document that needs to be displayed as three newspaper columns. List three steps required to carry out this task.
   b You would like to see the first two paragraphs in the first column 1, the 3rd and 4th paragraphs in the second column and the 5th and 6th paragraphs in third column. List the steps in completing this task.

5 a What are the three documents that are involved in mail-merging?
  b List the steps that for completing a mail-merge.
  c You would like to create a table to store the marks of students. List the steps in creating a table that has appropriate number of column and rows.

Practice SBA

The board members of the Caribbean Sports Club (CSC) have decided to use a word processing program to launch a club brochure. This will notify the club members about upcoming club activities and inform the general public about the club.

You are required to:

Task A

1 Create a word processing document informing the club members of the activities that the club will host for this year. This year the club intends to host a Christmas concert, Beach picnic, Fun day and May fair.

2 Also for the new members, you need to include a brief introduction about the club, including various rates for different types of memberships. The text in the brochure must be fully justified with 1.5" line spacing. Use either two or three columns to make a brochure that can be folded.

Task B

1 Create a letterhead for the club with the logo of the club (an appropriate graphic of appropriate size), the address, phone number, fax and email address of the club. The motto of the club should appear as the footer.

2 Using the letterhead, create a covering letter in preparation for mail-merge informing the executive members about the launch of the new club brochure and the activities planned for this year.

Task C

1 Create a data source with the details of three members:

Mr. Tom Jack	Mrs. Lorna Mansfield	Ms. Jamilla Griffith
Suncrest Drive	Divine Road	Old Road
Brintown	Kingstown	St George
Jamaica	Jamaica	Jamaica

2 Using mail-merge facilities, merge the covering letter with the data source.

3 Ensure that the documents have been formatted properly and spell-checked.

Objective

By the end of this section you will be able to:

- Explain what a presentation is and how presentation software can help you to make a presentation.
- Describe and use wizards and templates to design a slide show for a presentation.
- Create your own slide show using slide layouts and design templates.
- Format the text and background on a slide.
- Insert various types of graphics into a slide.
- Use animation techniques in a slide show.
- Create your own design for a slide show by using the slide master.
- Create slide footers and headers.
- Create and use speaker notes.
- Use slide show tools, such as pointers, while making a presentation.
- Make a presentation to an audience, using a slide show and speaker notes.

Although you will probably have used word processing software before, presentation software may be new to you. Once you have learned how to use it – and it is not difficult – you will realise just how useful it can be.

Presentation software allows you to create a slide show, which is a series of pages of information. A slide show can be projected onto a large screen, or simply shown on a computer, to accompany a talk or lesson. You can add images, sounds and movies to the slide show and you can use some clever effects to make the presentation more eye-catching.

All the step-by-step instructions and screenshots in this section refer to Microsoft PowerPoint. However, it is possible to produce presentations using other packages, and you should check to see what facilities they offer.

Making a presentation

A talk can be much easier to follow with images and text shown on a large screen. This is known as a **presentation**.

Presentations are used for all sorts of purposes. Here are some of them:

THINK ABOUT IT

Have you seen a presentation that included a slide show? If so, what was its purpose? Was it successful?

- Teachers and trainers may use a presentation to deliver a lesson or lecture.
- A speaker at a conference or large meeting will use a presentation to give information and to illustrate a talk.
- Someone in an organisation will make a presentation to work colleagues to get support for an important proposal, or to report on a project.

The material that will be presented can be prepared on a computer and then projected onto a screen using a multi-media projector. The material is arranged into individual 'pages' called **slides**. All the slides taken together are referred to as a **slide show**.

WHAT DOES IT MEAN?

slide
A slide is a single 'page' that can be shown on a screen to an audience.

slide show
A slide show is a sequence of slides that can be used in a presentation.

presentation
A presentation is a talk to an audience that is supported by a slide show.

Using presentation software

Presentation software, such as Microsoft PowerPoint, makes it easy for you to create the slides that will make up a slide show and to prepare notes that you can use when speaking to an audience.

On the slides you can include a summary of what you want to say to your audience. There should only be a few lines on each slide, so you can hold their attention and talk about the points before moving on to the next slide.

You can include all kinds of images on presentation slides – photographs, charts, graphs, cartoons, maps etc. You can also add sound effects or short movies.

Getting started with PowerPoint

Microsoft PowerPoint is a commercial software package that is used to produce a slide show and notes for a presentation.

When you launch PowerPoint the window looks something like this:

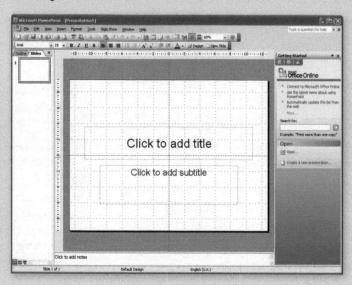

Fig 6.51: The PowerPoint window

As you can see, the formatting toolbar is very similar to the one in Word, but there are a few differences. Note:

1 The *New Slide* button. This allows you to add a slide to the presentation.
2 The task pane. This panel down the right-hand side of the screen allows you to choose tasks relevant to what you are currently doing. You will have used the task pane in Word when you used mail-merge, but in PowerPoint you will use it most of the time.
3 The outline pane. This panel on the left has two tabs labelled *Outline* and *Slides*. These give you an overall view of your slide show as it develops.

CHECK YOUR PROGRESS

What is the difference between a presentation and a slide show?

The AutoContent wizard

You may be familiar with **wizards** – those clever features that take you step-by-step through a process. Most wizards ask you to make some choices then create a ready-made document or presentation for you. These are often a very useful way to get started with a new application, but you will soon want to create your own from scratch.

Using the AutoContent wizard

1 Launch PowerPoint. In the Getting Started task pane click on *Create a new presentation*. If you have already been using PowerPoint then go to *File* → *New*.

2 In the New Presentation task pane, select *From AutoContent wizard*.

3 Click on *Next*, and then click on *All*. You will see a list of standard presentation topics, such as *Business Plan* and *Company Meeting*. You can check them all out, but start with *Selling a Product or Service* and then click on *Next* (see Fig 6.52).

4 On the next screen select *On-screen presentation*.

5 Next, choose a title for your presentation (e.g. 'Our new range of cosmetics') and make sure that your name is inserted in the footer. Click on *Next*.

6 Click on *Finish* on the last slide. When the wizard has finished a complete slide show will be displayed.

7 In the outline pane on the left, the Outline tab shows the structure of the complete presentation, with all the text that each slide contains (see Fig 6.53).

Fig 6.52: The AutoContent Wizard

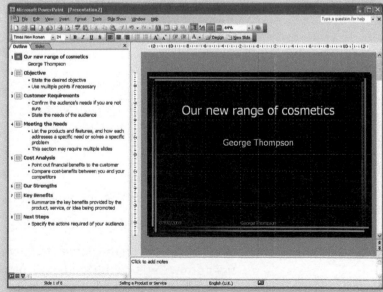

Fig 6.53: A slide show created with the wizard

8 Click on the Slide tab in the outline pane to see **thumbnails** of the slides (see Fig 6.54).

9 To view another slide, click on one of the thumbnails in the Slide tab.

10 Save the slide show if you want to keep it.

Fig 6.54: Thumbnails of the slides in the Slides tab

Views of slides

In the View menu, you can switch between four different 'views' of the slides (see Fig 6.55).

1 **Normal view** displays three panes – the outline pane on the left, the task pane on the right and the notes pane under the slide pane, as seen in Fig 6.51. The text in the notes pane will be printed in the speaker notes.

2 **Slide Sorter** shows thumbnails of all the slides. If you want to change their order you can drag and drop a slide to a new position.

3 **Slide Show** displays the slides full screen as they will be seen in the presentation.

4 **Notes page** displays a document with the slide at the top and the notes from the notes pane underneath. These can be printed as the speaker notes.

Fig 6.55: The four views in the Views menu

You will want to view the slide show as it will appear in a presentation so that you can see how it will look to your audience.

Viewing a slide show

1 Go to *View* → *Slide Show*, or press the F5 key.

2 The slide show will fill the entire screen.

3 Click anywhere on the screen to move to the next slide. You can also use the left and right arrow keys on the keyboard, or the Enter and Backspace keys if you do not have a mouse.

4 Use the Escape (Esc) key on your keyboard to jump out of the slide show at any point.

Customising the slide show

Once you have set up a slide show using the wizard, you will want to put in your own words. You may also want to delete some of the slides.

The first slide is the **title slide**. This usually has a different layout from the other slides.

Many of the slides have **bullet points**. The information is presented in a list. Each item in the list is marked with a dot, known as a bullet, at the beginning of the line. Other small icons can be used instead of a dot. The items are usually called bullet points.

If you look at any slide in the main window you will see that each block of text or image is held in a **placeholder**. In Normal view, you can usually see a faint dotted line around each placeholder, but they are invisible when you run a full-screen slide show. When you click inside a placeholder, its border changes to a thicker hatched border. You will also be able to see tiny dots, known as handles, at the corners and in the middle of each edge. (See Fig 6.56.)

THINK ABOUT IT

You will soon be creating some slide shows of your own. Can you think of any topics that could be presented in this way?

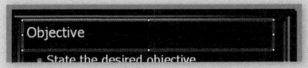

Fig 6.56: A placeholder with its handles

Customising slides

1 In the outline pane click on the *Slide* tab.

2 In the outline pane click on the first slide after the title slide.

3 In the main part of the window, click on the title of the slide. You will see that the title text is held in a placeholder. Delete the text and add your own.

4 Now click on the text in the main body of the slide. This placeholder has been set up with bullet points. Add your own text. Press Enter to create a new bullet point.

5 If you want to delete a slide, click on it in the outline pane. Then go to *Edit* → *Delete Slide*.

Slide shows without wizards

The AutoContent wizard has shown you some of the possibilities for slide shows, but it only produces slide shows for a limited range of standard business uses.

It is usually better to create your own slide show, so you can produce exactly what you need. With your own slide show you can:

- include photos and other images from your own collection of graphics.
- decide which slides should be included and how they will fit into the whole slide show.
- lay out the slides to suit the information.
- use a design template.

Creating your own slide show

1 Click on the *New* button in the Standard toolbar. The window should look like Fig 6.51.

2 Click on the *Save As* button to save your slide show before you start.

3 The first slide is a title slide that introduces the slide show. Click inside the title placeholder on the words *Click to add title*. The text disappears and you can now key in the title of your presentation (see Fig 6.57).

4 Click inside the second placeholder and type in some additional information about your presentation as a sub title. You could put your name here.

5 In the Formatting toolbar, click on *New Slide*.

6 The next slide is a normal slide, and here you can start giving your audience some information. Click in the title placeholder to create a title for that particular slide.

7 Click in the main placeholder to start adding information.

8 Add a couple more slides to the presentation. Don't forget to save it at regular intervals.

9 In the outline pane you can see thumbnails of all your slides. To view a slide click on its thumbnail.

You probably think that the slides look very plain, but don't try to format them yet. PowerPoint offers some very exciting options, which you will meet in a moment.

Fig 6.57: Creating your own slide show

Slide layouts

So far you have used the default layouts for the title and other slides. You can, in fact, choose from a variety of slide layouts, some using only text and others using graphics, or a combination of both. You can even design your own layout.

Adding text

1 Click on *New Slide* in the Formatting toolbar.

2 In the task pane you will see a number of layouts as in Fig 6.57. Click on one of the *Text Layouts*.

3 A text layout has one or more placeholders that can take text. Enter text into the placeholders.

Graphics and movies

Many types of graphics can be added to a slide, including photographs, clip art, diagrams and movies.

Graphics can be used in a slide show for three different purposes:

- To give information directly – a photograph or movie may show what a product or a place looks like, and a diagram may explain a complicated idea more easily than using words.
- To illustrate the information given in the text – a photo or clip art image may show something that is referred to in the text.
- To decorate the slide – you will be learning how to work with design templates very soon.

Adding Clip art

1 Click on *New Slide* in the formatting toolbar.

2 In the task pane, move the mouse over the *Content Layouts* to find the layout labelled *Content*. Click on it.

3 In the middle of the placeholder you will see a box containing six icons. Move your mouse over them to find the one labelled *Insert Clip Art* (see Fig 6.58), and click on it.

4 You will see a selection of clip art images. Find a suitable image and click *OK*.

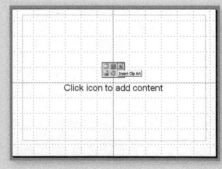

Fig 6.58: The Content layout

Adding photos

If you have already stored a photograph you can add it to a slide.

1 Click on *New Slide* in the Formatting toolbar.

2 Click on the *Content Layout* labelled *Content*.

3 Move your mouse over the icons to find the one labelled *Insert Picture*, and click on it.

4 Find your stored photo and click *OK*.

Size of a graphic

When you use a content layout to insert clip art or a photograph, it will automatically reduce any large images to fit inside the placeholder. This is very helpful if you want to use a full-size photo that may be too large to fit on the slide.

You may still want to make an image larger or smaller.

Changing the size of a graphic

1 To change the size of an image, click on it. You will see the handles at each corner and in the middle of each edge of the image (see Fig 6.59).

Fig 6.59: The handles around an image

2 Drag on one of the handles to resize the image. If you drag on an edge handle the image will be stretched. If you drag on a corner handle, the image will grow or shrink horizontally and vertically, keeping its true proportions.

You can easily make any image smaller. However, you can get into difficulties if you try to enlarge a photo, as it may appear fuzzy when enlarged. Check the effect by viewing the full-screen slide show.

Adding diagrams

Content layouts also let you add diagrams to a slide.

1 Click on *New Slide* in the Formatting toolbar.

2 As before, click on the *Content* layout.

3 In the middle of the slide, click on the icon labelled *Insert Diagram*.

4 Select the type of diagram you want, and click *OK*.

5 Edit the text on the diagram.

Adding movies

You can place a movie on a slide if you have one stored on your computer.

1 Click on *New Slide* in the Formatting toolbar.

2 As before, click on the *Content* layout.

3 In the middle of the slide, click on the icon labelled *Insert Media Clip*.

4 Find the stored movie, and click *OK*.

5 You will be asked *How do you want the movie to start in the slide show?*. You can choose to start the movie as soon as you reach the slide in the presentation, or you can choose to wait until the movie itself is clicked.

Choosing a layout to suit the information

You can choose from the remaining *Content Layouts*, which allow you to place up to three placeholders on the slide, with or without a heading. You can also try the *Text and Content Layouts*, which combine bullet point text with other content, such as graphs.

It is tempting to show off the skills you have acquired when creating a slide show. However, the important thing is to make a presentation that conveys exactly the right information to your audience.

You should ask yourself these questions:

- What am I trying to achieve with my presentation?
- Do I need to give a lot of information?
- Would it be better to give the information as text, images or diagrams?

Each slide should convey just one idea or piece of information. If you look again at the presentations created by the wizard you will see that each slide contains a very limited amount of information.

If you place a lot of text on a slide it can be difficult to read. It is better to spread it over several slides, so that your audience can take it in bit by bit. Remember that a presentation consists of a slide show and a talk, so the speaker can take time to provide extra information. State the key points very simply on the slide, then the speaker can fill in the details.

The same applies to diagrams and other images. One simple diagram on a slide will have far greater impact than several diagrams plus text. Occasionally you may need a little text alongside a photo, in which case you can use one of the Text and Content Layouts.

CHECK YOUR PROGRESS

What are the advantages of using a wizard to create a slide show over creating one yourself? What are the disadvantages?

Design templates

When you create a slide show you need to think about its design as well as the content. These are the elements you should consider in the design:

- background colour
- font styles, colours and sizes
- extra images used to make the slide look interesting

The simplest way to achieve these is to use one of the many design **templates** in PowerPoint. You can select your design before you start work on a presentation, or you can change it while you are working.

The slide show you created earlier was rather experimental, so it would be a good idea to create a new one in order to learn about design templates.

Creating a simple slide show

1 Decide on the topic for your slide show. Check whether you have any suitable photos or other graphics.

2 Click on the *New* button in the Standard toolbar.

3 Click on the *Save As* button to save your slide show before you start.

4 On the title slide add text to the title and subtitle placeholders.

5 In the Formatting toolbar, click on *New Slide*.

6 Choose a slide layout for your first slide. Add text or graphics.

7 Add two more slides to the presentation, using different slide layouts.

8 Save the slide show.

Choosing a design template

1 Using the slide show you have just created, click on *Slide Design* in the Formatting toolbar.

2 Design templates will appear in the task pane. Click on one to see its effect on your pages.

3 In the outline pane, click on the title slide. Most design templates use a slightly different design for the title slide.

4 You can change the colour scheme for any of the designs. Click on *Color Schemes* at the top of the task pane, and select a combination of colours that you like.

5 When you are happy that you have chosen a suitable design, save the slide show.

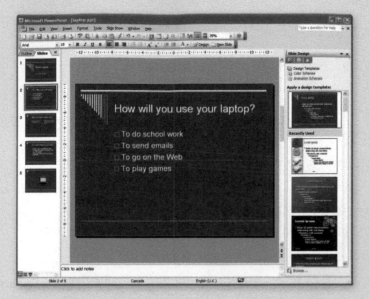

Fig 6.60: A design template has been applied to a slide show

A design template will ensure that the overall look of the slide show is consistent. However, you can make some further changes to the design you have chosen.

Changing the background colour or pattern

1 Go to *Format* ➔ *Background*.

2 The background colour is shown in a selection box near the bottom of the dialogue box. Click on the small arrow to see further options. You can now change the colour of the background to another colour in the same colour scheme.

3 Alternatively, you can click on *More Colors* or *Fill Effects* to choose from a wide range of colours and patterns.

4 Click on *Apply to All* to use the new background on all the slides. Click on *Apply* to use the new background colour only on the slide you can see.

Be careful about your use of strong backgrounds, as they can sometimes distract from the main content of a slide. Try to avoid clashing or garish colours The colour schemes in PowerPoint offer combinations of colours that work well together.

Changing the font formatting

Sometimes you may want to make changes to the fonts on an individual slide, for example, you may want to change the size of the text.

1 Choose the slide you want to change.

2 Select some text. The Formatting toolbar is very similar to the one you used for word processing in Section 6A. Use the buttons in the Formatting toolbar to change the font type, size, colour or style.

Slide headers and footers

You can create special headers and footers that will appear on every slide.

Creating headers and footers

1 Open a slide show that you have already created.

2 Go to *View* → *Header and Footer*.

3 Under *Include on Slide*, tick *Date and Time*. You can now click on *Update Automatically* to display the date when the slide show is viewed. Alternatively, you can click on *Fixed* to enter a date, for example, the date on which you created the slides.

4 Next tick *Slide Number*. This will number the slides for you.

5 Then tick on *Footer* and enter some text in the box. This could be your name, or the topic of the slide show.

6 Finally, tick the box labelled *Don't show on title slide* (see Fig 6.61).

THINK ABOUT IT

Think about the design of any slide shows you have seen. What sort of designs did they use for backgrounds and fonts? Did they work? If you cannot remember a slide show, then you might like to think about websites you have visited, where the same design issues apply.

Fig 6.61: The Header and Footer dialogue

Fig 6.62: Three footers at the bottom of a slide

Click on *Apply to All*. The date, footer text and page number appear at the bottom of each slide (see Fig 6.62).

7 Check through the slides. You can change any of your choices by going to *View* → *Header and Footer* again.

Sometimes the items you have added at the bottom of the screen get in the way of the graphics in a design template. You will learn how to move them to a new position in the next subsection.

Slide masters

You can create a slide show that looks completely original by choosing all the design features yourself.

You will probably want to use the same background and fonts on most of the slides. You could do that by setting up the background, font styles, etc on each individual slide, but PowerPoint offers a much simpler method, using a **slide master**.

Creating your own design with a slide master

1 Create and save a new presentation with three or four slides, using a different layout for each slide. Do not use a design template, and do not add any formatting.

2 Go to *View → Header and Footer* and click on all the options. Don't forget to add text for the footer.

3 Go to *View → Master → Slide Master*. You will now see a single thumbnail in the outline pane. This holds the design that will be used for all the slides in the slide show (see Fig 6.63).

4 Click on the text in the title placeholder. Use the buttons in the Formatting toolbar to choose the font type, style, size and colour of the text that will appear on each slide.

5 Click on the text in the main placeholder, and format the text.

6 Go to *Format → Background* and choose the colour of the background, plus any fill effects if you wish. Click on *Apply*.

7 Go to *View → Normal* to see the effect of your changes on the slides.

8 Go to *View → Slide Show* to see how your design works in the slide show.

You will probably want to have a different design for the title slide. You need to add a title master to the normal slide master.

Fig 6.63: The slide master

Adding a title master

1 Go to *View* → *Master* → *Slide Master*.

2 Go to *Insert* → *New Title Master*. A new slide master appears, linked to the main slide master.

3 Format the text on the title master. This will affect the title slide only.

4 Go to *Format* → *Background* and choose the colour of the background, plus any fill effects if you wish. If you click on the Picture tab you can use a photograph as a background.

5 Click on *Apply* (not *Apply to All*) so that the background applies only to the title master.

6 Go to *View* → *Normal* to see the effect of your changes on the slides.

7 Go to *View* → *Slide Show* to see how your design works in the slide show.

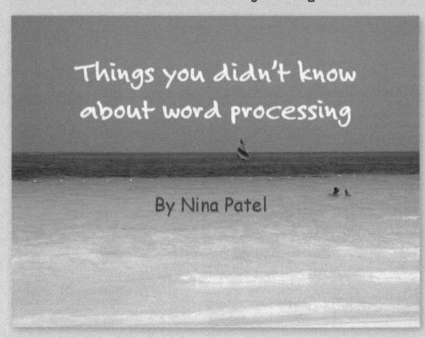

Fig 6.64: A title slide design created with the title master

Position of items on a slide master

There are five placeholders on the main slide master, which will include the title and main placeholders, as well as the ones you set up using the Header and Footer options. You may decide that you would like to rearrange any of these on the slide master. Any changes you make to the slide master will affect all the slides except the title slide.

Rearranging the items on a slide master

1 On the slide master, click on a placeholder that you want to move. Drag and drop the placeholder to a new position.

2 On the slide master, click on a placeholder that you want to remove completely. Go to *Edit* → *Clear* to remove the item.

3 On the slide master, click on a placeholder that you want to resize. Drag on a handle to make it larger or smaller.

4 Check your changes by viewing the slide show.

5 Make sure you save your slide show.

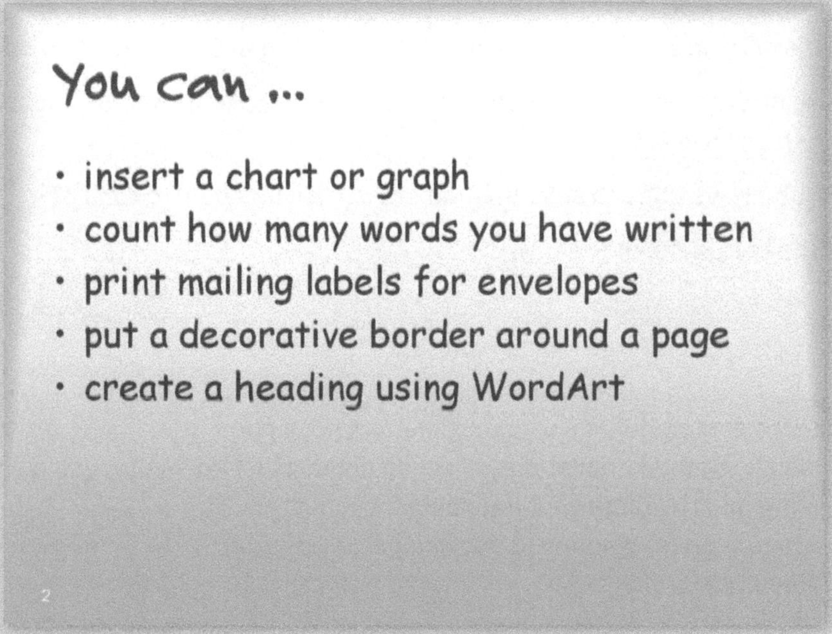

You can ...

• insert a chart or graph
• count how many words you have written
• print mailing labels for envelopes
• put a decorative border around a page
• create a heading using WordArt

Fig 6.65: A slide design created with the slide master

CHECK YOUR PROGRESS

What aspects of a design that you can achieve with a slide master that would be more difficult with the Autocontent wizard or with a template?

Animation effects with slides

When you present a slide show to an audience, you move from one slide to another by clicking with the mouse or using the left and right arrow keys. Once you switch to a new slide all the items on that slide appear at the same time. However, you may like to make the switch from one slide to another more interesting. You can also arrange for the items on each slide to appear in different ways, for example, by making the individual bullet points appear one at a time.

You can achieve these effects by using animation techniques. Once again, you have to use these effects very carefully so that they do not distract the audience.

Using an animation scheme

1 If you are looking at the slide masters, go to *View* ➜ *Normal*.

2 In the Formatting toolbar click on *Slide Design*.

3 In the task pane click on *Animation schemes* (see Fig 6.66).

4 Tick *Auto-Preview* at the bottom of the task pane so you can see each effect as you try it.

5 You are offered a choice of subtle, moderate and exciting effects. Select one of them and watch the preview.

6 When you have chosen an animation effect click on *Apply to All Slides*.

7 View the complete slide show.

You can add an animation to just one slide. It is not a good idea to use a variety of animations in a slide show, as it can be confusing and distracting for your audience, but you may have a reason for wanting to use one particular effect for one slide only.

Using an animation scheme on one slide only

1 Click on the slide you want to animate.

2 Select the effect you want in the task bar. Do not click on *Apply to All Slides*.

Fig 6.66: Animation schemes in the task pane

Removing animation schemes

1 In the Formatting toolbar click on *Slide Design*, and select *Animation Schemes*.

2 Select *No Animation*, then click on *Apply to All Slides*.

Custom animation

Animation schemes are very useful, but you can have more control over the effects by using custom animation. There is a huge range of effects you can try. You can also have more than one effect on a slide. But be careful not to make your viewer dizzy by using too many.

Using custom animation

1 Remove all existing animation schemes before using custom animation.

2 Go to *Slide Show* → *Custom animation*.

3 In the task pane, make sure that *AutoPreview* is ticked.

4 Select the title slide. Click anywhere inside the title placeholder.

5 In the task pane, click on *Add Effect*.

6 Go to *Entrance* → *Fly in*. You will immediately see what this does. To view the effect again, click on *Play* at the bottom of the pane.

Note that a small number has appeared to the left of the placeholder, and that this corresponds to the effect listed in the task pane (see Fig 6.67).

7 Change the effect by clicking on it in the task pane. Click on *Change* in the task pane.

8 Although the *Play* button does give you an idea about what an effect does, you really do need to view the slide in a slide show to see how it will look to your audience. Click on *Slide Show* at the bottom of the task pane.

9 In the slide show you have to click the mouse to make the effect happen.

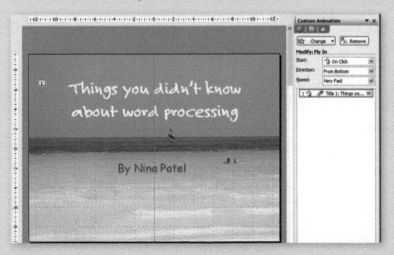

Fig 6.67: Custom animation applied to the title slide

Using custom animation for bullet points

1 Select a slide that has a text placeholder with bullet points.

2 Click anywhere inside the placeholder and choose an effect from the *Entrance* list.

3 The effect is applied to each bullet point in the placeholder, so a small number appears on the slide alongside each bullet.

4 Click on the *Slide Show* at the bottom of the task pane. Each bullet point appears as you click the mouse.

Removing an effect

1 When the slide show is finished, you can remove an effect by clicking on the effect in the task pane. Click on *Remove*.

Modifying custom animations

You can customise any of the effects you have chosen even further.

1 In the task pane, click on an effect that you want to modify.

2 You will see three selection boxes above the list of effects.

3 The *Start* option lets you choose between clicking to see an effect or making the effect happen automatically. Try out the options.

4 You can also try out the *Direction* and *Speed* options.

You can also add sound and timing effects to your animations.

Adding sound effects

1 Click on the down arrow next to an effect in the task pane list (see Fig 6.68). Select *Effect Options*.

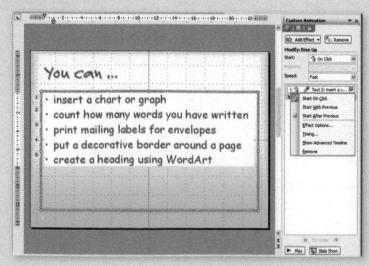

Fig 6.68: Advanced animation options

2 In the *Effect* tab select a sound from the drop-down list. You can hear what each sound is like by clicking on the speaker icon.

3 When you have selected a sound, click *OK*.

Adding timing effects

1 Click on the down arrow next to an effect and this time select *Timing*.

2 Make a choice in the Delay box to start an effect after a short interval.

3 Select from the Repeat box to repeat an effect a fixed number of times.

The slide sorter

As you saw earlier, the View menu in PowerPoint offers four views of the slides. You have so far used *Normal* view and *Slide Show* views. Now you will learn how to move and delete slides by using the slide sorter.

Using the slide sorter

1 Go to *View* → *Slide Sorter*.

2 You can now see thumbnails of the entire slide show (see Fig 6.69).

3 To change the order of the slides, click on one slide and drag and drop it to its new position.

4 To delete a slide, click on it in the slide sorter, then go to *Edit* → *Delete Slide*.

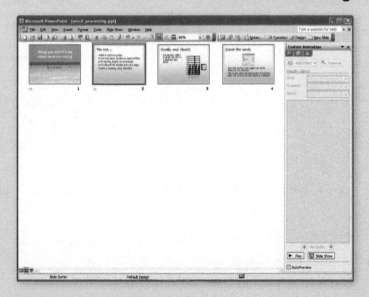

Fig 6.69: The slide sorter view

Making a presentation

Once your slide show is finished, you can get ready to present it to your audience.

Speaker notes

You will find it useful to have some printed notes to guide what you will say about each slide.

Creating speaker notes

1 The notes pane is at the bottom of the screen in Normal View. Type in some notes about the slide. You can drag the top margin of the notes pane to make it larger (see Fig 6.70).

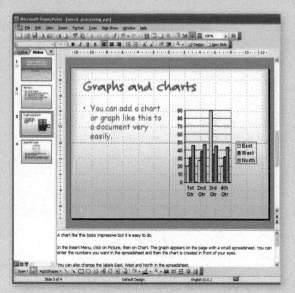

Fig 6.70: Entering speaker notes in the Notes pane

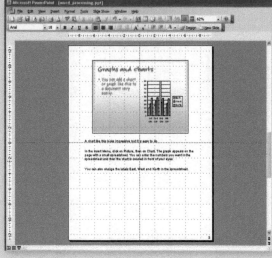

Fig 6.71: Viewing speakers notes in the Notes View

2 Go to *View* ➔ *Notes page*. You will see an image of the slide with the notes beneath it. This is how the page will appear when printed. You can make changes to your notes in this view.

3 Go to *View* ➔ *Normal*. Add notes to other pages.

4 To print out all the notes pages, go to *File* ➔ *Print*.

5 Under *Print What* select *Notes Pages*. Under *Print Range* you can either print notes pages for all the slides, or you can click on *Slides* and enter the numbers of the slides you want to be printed.

Fig 6.72: Printing speaker notes

CHECK YOUR PROGRESS

Why is it useful to print speaker notes?

Slide show tools

There are a few tools you can use while you are running a slide show. These will make your presentation look professional and impress your audience. You can use the slide navigator, you can use a pointer on the screen and you can even draw on the slides during a presentation. You can also make the screen go blank.

Using the slide navigator

1 Go to *View* → *Slide Show*, or press F5.

2 Right click anywhere on the screen and you will see a small menu. (All the instructions that follow refer to the options on this menu.)

3 Click on *Next* or *Previous* to move between slides.

4 Click on *Go To Slide* to jump to any of the slides in the slide show.

5 Click on *End Show* to return to the main screen.

Using the pointer

1 Go to *View* → *Slide Show*, or press F5.

2 Right click anywhere on the screen. Select *Pointer Options* → *Arrow Options*. This is normally set to *Automatic*. That means that the pointer arrow is only visible on screen for a few seconds after switching to a new slide. Click on *Visible*.

THINK ABOUT IT

Have you had a chance to make a presentation to an audience? If so, how did it go? Would you do things differently another time?

3 Move the pointer around the screen and you will see that it does not disappear. This is very useful if you want to point to things on the screen while talking to your audience.

4 Go to *Pointer Options* and click on one of the pens. You can now draw on the slide. This is useful for highlighting information on a slide for your audience.

5 To go back to a normal pointer, go to *Pointer Options* → *Arrow*. When you have finished with the pen you will be asked *Do you want to keep your ink annotations?*.

Fig 6.73: The menu you can use during a presentation

Using screen attributes

Sometimes you want to blank out the screen so that your audience can concentrate on what you are saying.

1 Go to *View* → *Slide Show*, or press F5.

2 On the keyboard press *B* to turn the screen black. Press *B* again to return to the slide show.

3 Press *W* to turn the screen white.

Speaking to an audience

Here are some tips for when you come to give your presentation:

1 Always practice your presentation first.

2 You should run through the complete show at the speed you expect to give it.

3 Read any speaker notes out loud at the right points. Speak more slowly than you normally do, and emphasise important words.

4 You may have been given a fixed amount of time for your presentation. If so, time your practice run and cut out some slides or text if it is too long.

5 When you make the presentation to your audience, be confident. Remember that you are the person who knows the information and that your audience wants to learn it.

End-of-section questions

Multiple-choice questions

1 Which of the following is an example of presentation software:
   A MS Excel   B MS Access
   C MS PowerPoint   D MS Word

2 A set of pre-designed formats of text or colour scheme in PowerPoint is called:
   A Slide   B Presentation scheme
   C Schema   D Template

3 All of the following are views present in PowerPoint except:
   A Normal view   B Slide sorter view
   C Slide show view   D Slide view

4 Which of the following are uses of presentation software:
   I   To enhance public speaking
   II   To deliver customised lectures
   III To present project reports
   IV   To present sales or marketing ideas
   A I, II and III only   B I, II and IV only
   C I, III and IV only   D I, II, III and IV

5 Flying, drive-in and camera effects are types of what type of slide effects?
   A Action   B Transition
   C Animation   D Colour scheme

Structured questions

1 a What is meant by slide layout?
  b List three types of slide layouts in PowerPoint.

2 a Name the basic elements of a slide.
  b Briefly describe each of the elements you identified in your answer to 2a.

3 In a well designed slide, speaker notes will be present.
  a What are speaker notes?
  b List the steps for inserting speaker notes in a slide.

4 a List four ways in which a new presentation can be created.
  b List four views of a slide.

5 Briefly describe the following terms as they relate to PowerPoint:
  a Slide
  b Template
  c Wizard

Web page design

Objectives

By the end of this section you will be able to:

- Plan a website to meet the needs of your intended audience.
- Plan the number and layout of pages within a website.
- Create a simple website with two pages.
- Choose a design for your website.
- Use text and images on web pages.
- Create hyperlinks between pages on your website.
- Create hyperlinks to pages on other websites, to email addresses and to downloadable files.
- Test your website.
- Publish your website to the World Wide Web.

There are a number of web design packages that you could use to gain experience of creating your own website. These include Microsoft FrontPage and its successor Microsoft Expression Web, Adobe Dreamweaver, and CoffeeCup Visual Site Designer.

In this section the illustrations have all been created using Microsoft FrontPage 2002. This was the last version of FrontPage to be included with Microsoft Office. Most of the functions can also be carried out in other web design packages.

It is also possible to create a simple web page using other software such as Microsoft Word or Publish, however, you will not be able to do everything listed in this section. Software that has been developed for word processing and desktop publishing produce complicated web pages that are not easy to modify.

You should study Section 4A before you start work on this section. In Section 4A the following terms were introduced and it would be sensible to read them again:

- web page
- website
- web browser
- URL
- file transfer protocol (FTP)
- web server
- HTML

WHAT IS MY WEBSITE ABOUT?
WHAT IS THE REASON FOR MY WEBSITE?
WHO ARE MY INTENDED AUDIENCE?
WHAT TEXT WILL I USE
ON EACH PAGE?
WHAT SORT OF A TITLE DO I WANT?
WHICH IMAGES WILL I USE?
WHAT LAYOUT WOULD BE BEST ON EACH PAGE?
WHERE WILL I LOCATE THE NAVIGATION LINKS?
WHAT COLOURS WOULD BE BEST FOR TEXT AND BACKGROUND?

Planning a website

A web designer has to design many things when working on a new website, including:

- The content of the website, that is, the text and images.
- The layout of the pages in the website.
- The artistic design of the whole website.

But, before getting down to work, the web designer has to ask a number of questions, such as:

- What is the purpose of the website? Why was it set up in the first place?
- Who is the intended audience? Who is going to look at it?

The answers to these questions will have a real effect on the content, layout and design of the website. A website that may be just right for one audience may be totally unsuitable for another. For example, a website for a fan club will look very different from a website for an online bookseller, but both could be just right for their purpose and intended audience.

You can ask the same questions about any website you visit. You can then judge whether the designer has made sensible decisions about the content, layout and artistic design of a site.

Fig 6.74: A website

Reasons for a website

Websites can be set up for many different reasons, such as:

- To inform – all websites provide some information, which is one reason why the Internet became known as the 'Information Superhighway'.

- To sell or promote – websites can be used to promote products and services to visitors.
- To create an online community – websites can allow visitors to interact with each other through comments, personal pages, discussion forums, chat rooms etc.

The website in Fig 6.74 was created for the second reason, that is, to sell flight tickets to customers. It also gives information, for example, about the places the airline flies to, but that information is provided to support its main purpose.

THINK ●
ABOUT IT
Look at one or two websites that you know well. Why was it created? What is its main purpose? Who is the intended audience?

Intended audience

A web designer needs to know whether the website should be aimed at the world in general or at a specific section of the population, e.g. young people, car owners, parents, cricket supporters, women, members of a particular religion, or people who live in a particular town. Most websites are built with a typical visitor in mind.

Here are some questions that you can ask about a website to help you judge whether it is right for its intended audience.

- Does the first page you reach give you a good idea of what the site contains?
- Are the pages informative and interesting for the intended audience?
- Does the site provide the expected information?
- Is there too much information or too little? – The right amount will depend on the purpose of the site. For example, a website aimed at children should give small amounts of information and be written at a language level that they can understand.
- If the website is about an organisation, does it provide basic information about the organisation, who it includes and what it does?
- Does the site say how to contact the owners of the site? Does the site allow a visitor to contact the owners directly? – This may be offered through an online form, or an email address may be given
- Is the site kept up to date? – sites should be maintained as frequently as appropriate; for example, a news site will be updated every day, while a site that gives advice on buying a kitchen freezer needs only to be updated when new freezers come on to the market.

Size and structure of a website

Pages in a website

A website can have just one page, thousands of pages, or anything in between. A website for a newspaper or television channel will often have a great many pages, some of them carrying news items that go back several years. They do not delete the old pages because visitors often want to research the background to an issue by looking at old items. On the other hand, the website for a hotel may have around six pages covering the main information that might be needed.

Many web pages are quite short, and fit easily on the screen without scrolling down. This should be considered when deciding how many pages to place on a website. It may be better to have more pages, each of which is short and easy to read, rather than fewer pages that are much longer.

Sites for organisations almost always have two important pages:

- About – This will tell the visitor about the organisation, what it does and probably the names of some of the people who work for it

- Contact – This will tell the visitor how to get in touch with the organisation. It may give a postal address, or a phone number, or may provide an on-line form that can be filled in to send a message.

A responsible website will always tell you something about the organisation or individuals who have created it. You should be wary of any site that is anonymous.

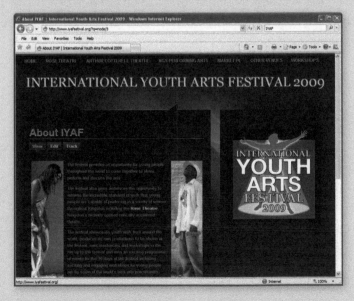

Fig 6.75: An About page on a website

Hyperlinks and navigation

One very special feature of a website is the way that one page can provide links to other pages. These **hyperlinks** can take the visitor to another page in the same site, or to another website altogether.

Websites always have one page that is labelled as the **home page**. This has hyperlinks to other pages, which in turn may link to further pages. The important thing is that every page on the website should be reachable from the home page, even if it takes a several steps to get there. Whatever page you visit you should always be able to get back to the home page easily.

It can sometimes be quite difficult to find your way around a website. That is why the web designer has to give some thought to the hyperlinks that are given on each page that will help the visitor find what they want.

The main links are usually given as a list across the top of the home page or down the side. These are known as **navigation** links and are often repeated on all the other pages as well. Sometimes when you follow one of the navigation links you find that the new page has a secondary set of links as well as the main navigation links. These could be links to pages that contain information directly related to the page you are on.

For example, in Fig 6.74 the main navigation links are the four large buttons at the top of the page. They appear on every page of the website. The secondary links are on the orange bar beneath the main navigation. Secondary links vary from page to page.

WHAT DOES IT MEAN?

hyperlink (or link)
A hyperlink is an image or section of text that a visitor can click on. The hyperlink then transfers the visitor to another web page or to another point in the same web page. Hyperlinks can also link to email addresses and downloadable files.

home page
The home page of a website is the main page and is often the first page that visitors will see when they go to a website for the first time.

navigation
Navigation is the method by which a visitor finds their way around a website, using hyperlinks.

Index page

The home page may not always be the first page that a visitor goes to. Sometimes a website has an introductory page, and you have to click through to get to the home page. The first page that a visitor downloads from a website is known as the **index page**.

The index page is always called index.htm or index.html. When you enter a domain name such as www.example.com in a browser it always downloads www.example.com/index.htm or www.example.com/index.html.

WHAT DOES IT MEAN?

index page
The index page is the first page that is downloaded when a visitor goes to a website. The index page may or may not be the home page.

Designing pages for a website

Page layout

A computer screen has landscape orientation. In comparison, most printed documents have portrait orientation, which makes them much easier to read. You may have seen a web page where the text has stretched from one side of the screen to the other and noticed how difficult it was to read. The web designer may get round this problem by arranging the page into columns or boxes (see Fig 6.74).

Web designers may choose to have a banner right across the top of a page that contains the name of the website and possibly a logo as well. There will often be a similar, but plainer area at the bottom of the page. These provide a kind of frame for the text and images between.

The web designer also has to decide where the main navigation links should be placed. They should be easy to find, and should be in the same position on every page. The navigation links should always include a link to the home page.

Combining text and images

Most web pages contain a mixture of text and images. Visitors can be put off by long articles on a web page, so it is best to keep the text short and crisp.

Images are often added to the text to provide further information. For example, a photo of people at an event, or a chart, can help the visitor to better understand the text they are reading. Images can also break up the text and make it visually more interesting.

Images on websites

Images used on a website are usually in one of these three formats:

- **jpg (jpeg)** – mainly for photos, with a large number of colours
- **png** – mainly for photos and often of higher quality than other formats
- **gif** – most other images, including clip art, with a smaller range of colours

The filename extensions tell you which format has been used, for example, flower.jpg, snake.gif or beach.png.

All these formats compress the size of the image, but they use different methods to do so. The gif format usually takes up far less memory than the jpg or png formats.

The dimensions of an image

The dimensions of an image, that is, its width and height, are measured in pixels. Most images on web pages are less than 800 pixels wide. You will find it helpful to check the dimensions of an image on a website that you visit, as it will give you some idea of what you need for your own web page.

Fig 6.76: An image

The size of image files

When you download a web page from the Internet, the browser first downloads the actual page file. It then downloads all the image files that are used on the page. If there are a lot of images this can take some time, especially on a slow connection.

Most of the image files that you use in word processed documents or presentation slides take a great deal of memory. The size of the image file can vary from a few Kilobytes up to several Megabytes. For example, photos taken with a digital camera are often 2 MB or 4 MB in size. If you put one of these on a website, then tried to download them, they would take many minutes on a slow connection. It is important that you are aware of the file size of any image that you use on a website.

You can reduce the size of an image file by making the whole image smaller onscreen or by compressing the image. When an image is compressed, some of the detail is lost. This means that compressed images are not suitable for very large detailed prints, but look fine as small images on the screen.

Checking the properties of an image on a web page

1 In a browser, go to a web page that has images.

2 Right click on an image. Go to *Properties*.

3 In the Properties window you will see:

- the format of the image, e.g. jpg
- the size of the image file in bytes
- the dimensions of the image in pixels, given as width x height

In Fig 6.77 you can see that the beach photo is in jpg format, that it is 27742 bytes (about 27 Kbytes) in size, and that its dimensions are 300 x 256 pixels.

Fig 6.77: Picture properties

Planning and designing your own website

In this section, you will be creating a two-page website, but first you need to plan it.

You should answer these questions before you start to create your website.

- What is my website about?
- What is the reason for my website?
- Who are my intended audience?
- What text will I use on each page?
- Which images will I use? (You should choose these in advance.)
- What layout would be best on each page?
- Where will I locate the navigation links?
- What colours would be best for text and background?

You should make notes on all these questions, and draw sketches of layouts on each page, showing where you will locate the images, text, navigation, etc.

When you create your website you may find that you are not able to do things exactly as you would like because you do not yet have the right skills. It is still important to plan your ideal site and to create something as close to it as you can.

CHECK YOUR PROGRESS

Describe some of the differences you might find between websites where the intended audience is:
a aged 7–12
b aged 15–18
c aged 60+

Web design software

You will have visited many websites yourself, and you may have experimented with designing web pages before. You are now going to use the notes you made when planning and designing your own website in order to create a web page using Microsoft FrontPage.

Web pages are written in a code called Hypertext MarkUp Language (HTML). Professional web designers create pages using this language. You will be pleased to know that when you use FrontPage, or any other web design package, you do not have to learn HTML. Instead, you create a page onscreen in much the same way as you would create a document in a word processing package. FrontPage then generates the HTML code for what you have done. You can look at the HTML code but do not attempt to alter it unless you really do understand it.

In FrontPage you design and create web pages and you save them on your own computer or network. FrontPage creates a folder called My Webs in My Documents on your computer. You should normally store all your web pages in that folder.

When you are happy with a web page you upload it to the web server. It then becomes a part of the World Wide Web and anyone in the world can see it.

Getting started with FrontPage

When you launch FrontPage the window looks something like Fig 6.78.

The Standard toolbar and Formatting toolbar are almost the same as the ones in Word. Pass your mouse over the buttons to see what each one does.

At the bottom of the page you will see three tabs:

- Normal – this is the page editor that you will usually use.
- HTML – this is the HTML editor where you can see the code that FrontPage has generated.
- Preview – this lets you check what the page will look like in a browser.

You can also check the final appearance of a page in a normal browser, such as Internet Explorer.

Fig 6.78: The FrontPage window

Web pages

A website consists of several pages that are linked together. You are going to create a single web page, and later add a second page. You should also gain enough knowledge to go on to build more website pages if you want to.

The page on the screen in Fig 6.78 has been given the default filename new_page_1.htm. FrontPage will name any new pages that you create as new_page_2.htm etc. You can change the first part of the filename when you save it. The filename for all the web pages you create will end with .htm or .html. Either can be used, but you need to realise that mypage.htm and mypage.html will be treated as two different pages.

Starting a new web page

1 If your screen looks like Fig 6.78 then you are ready to go.

If you cannot see a new page, then in the Standard toolbar click on the button at the far left, which is labelled 'Create a new normal page'.

2 Key in some text on the page.

3 Try out the text formatting and text alignment buttons on the Formatting toolbar. Do not underline text because on a web page hyperlinks are often underlined. You will learn how to create hyperlinks later.

4 Save the page with the filename index.htm.

Styles on a web page

Web pages work best when they use styles. You can find the list of styles available in the box at the left end of the formatting toolbar.

Using styles for headings

1 Select the text that will be the heading for the page.

2 On the Formatting toolbar, find the Style box that displays Normal. Click on the small arrow beside the box, then click on *Heading1*.

3 On the web page enter some text that can be used as a subheading. Select this text.

4 In the Style box click on *Heading2*.

Using styles for lists

1 On the web page, enter several lines of text that you want to present as a list.

2 Select all the lines in the list. In the Style box, select either *Bulleted list* or *Numbered list*.

You may think that you could have achieved the same results another way, but there is a very good reason for doing it like this: next you will be learning how to use a theme on a web page. Themes are based on the styles you have chosen in the style list and are not effective if you do not use styles.

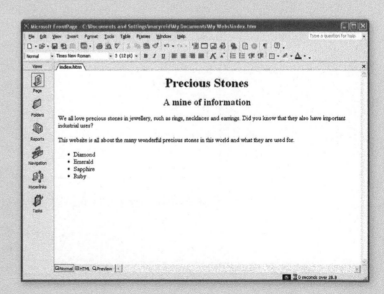

Fig 6.79: A web page using heading and bullet styles

Themes and templates

Themes

Design templates in FrontPage are known as themes. To get the best out of themes you have to use styles on your web page.

Using a theme

1 Select *Format* ➜ *Theme*.

2 Choose one of the themes from the list.

3 You have some choices below the list.

- Vivid colours – see what effect this has on your choice of theme.
- Active graphics – this option is not relevant at this stage
- Background Picture – if the design has a background picture or pattern you can see what it looks like with or without the picture.
- Apply using CSS – again, this option is not relevant at this stage, so do **not** tick this.

4 Click *OK*, and you will see an immediate improvement to your page.

5 Save the page. You will be prompted to Save Embedded Files. Click *OK*. This ensures that the images used in your theme are saved with your web page.

In the example in Fig 6.80, we have used the Ice theme.

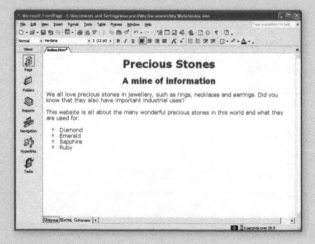

Fig 6.80: The web page with a theme

Page templates

Most web pages are laid out in columns or blocks. You can easily create a page with one of these layouts. This will be the second page of your website.

Using a page template

1 Go to *File* → *New* → *Page or Web*.

2 In the New Page or Web taskbar on the right, click on *Page Templates*.

3 The Page Templates dialogue window will offer you a number of templates. Click on one of the two-column or three-column templates. You will see a thumbnail (small image) of the layout under *Preview* (see Fig 6.81).

4 Click *OK* when you have found a page template that you like. You will notice the dotted lines around the columns. These are just for your reference while designing the page and will not be visible on the web page.

5 Delete the nonsense text and type in your own.

6 When you add a heading use a heading style from the style list.

7 Choose a theme for the page as before.

8 Save your page with a new name. In Fig 6.82 we have named it 'diamonds.htm'.

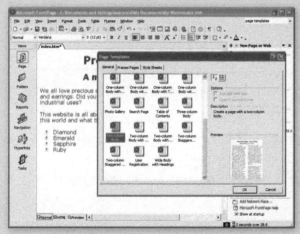

Fig 6.81: Choosing a page template

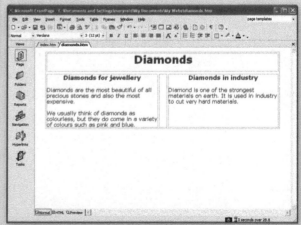

Fig 6.82: A page with two columns

Previewing your page

You can check what your web page will look like on the Web in three ways.

- Using the Preview tab – this enables you to make a quick check, but not all the functions work properly in Preview mode.
- Viewing it in a browser on your computer – this gives you a better idea of how the page will appear on the Web.
- Uploading it to the Web and then viewing it in a browser – later in this section you will learn how to do the final testing of your website in this way.

Using Preview

1 At the bottom of the page click on the *Preview* tab to see the page as it will appear to the visitor.

2 You will not be able to make any changes to the web page in Preview mode, so click on *Normal* to continue editing the page.

Viewing a page in a browser

1 In FrontPage open the page you want to view.

2 Go to *File* → *Preview in Browser*.

3 The Preview in Browser dialogue window may appear and ask you to select a browser from a list. If so select one of them.

4 The browser window opens with your page displayed.

CHECK YOUR PROGRESS

1 Why is it a good idea to use styles from the style list when creating a web page in Front Page?
2 List THREE ways of checking what a page will look like on the Web.

Images on a web page

Using clip art

You can insert clip art on a web page just as you can with word processing or presentation software. Most clip art will already be in jpg or gif format.

Inserting a clip art image

1 Click on the page where you want the clipart to appear.

2 Select *Insert* → *Picture* → *Clip art*, then choose the clip art image that you want. It will be inserted on the page.

3 The dimensions of the clip art image will probably have to be changed before it is right for your page. See below for instructions on how to do this.

Changing the dimensions of an image

Sometimes an image is too big for the page you are designing. You can reduce the dimensions of an image in the following way.

Resizing an image to make the dimensions smaller

1 Click on an image that you want to resize.

2 Drag one of the corner handles in order to make it smaller while keeping the correct proportions. If you drag on one of the handles along a side of the image you will squash it in one direction only.

When you make the dimensions of an image smaller on the page it does not change the size of the image file. This means that the image file uses more Kilobytes of memory than it needs to.

FrontPage has a useful function, called resampling, that actually reduces the size of an image file after you have resized it.

Resampling an image in FrontPage

1 Click on the image. You should now see the Pictures toolbar. This may be located as a floating toolbar. Pass your mouse over the buttons in the Pictures toolbar to identify the buttons.

2 Click on the Resample button in the Pictures toolbar. This reduces the size of the image file but it should also improve the appearance of the image.

3 Save the page. You will be prompted to Save Embedded Files. Click *OK*.

Note: Many of the other software packages you might use will allow you to reduce the dimensions of the image on the screen, but in most cases they do not allow you to change the size of the image file. In that case, you will need to use a separate graphics package to reduce the image before you insert it on the web page.

It is also possible to enlarge an image in this way, but the resampled file will be larger than the original. Often enlarged images suffer from the 'jaggies', which is the nickname for the jagged edges that you sometimes see on graphics.

Using photos

Photos are very effective on websites. You can insert any photo that you already have in a digital format. Most of them will already be stored in jpg format.

You are now going to insert some photos into your web page, so make sure you have saved some that are ready to use before moving onto the next step.

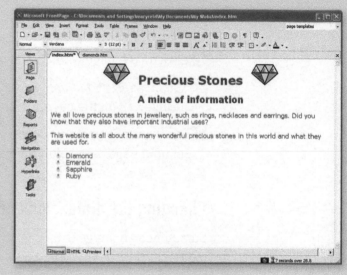

Fig 6.83: Clip art inserted on a page

Inserting a photo

1 Click on the page where you want the photo to appear.

2 Select *Insert* → *Picture* → *From File*, then choose the photo that you want. It will be inserted on the page.

3 Resample the photo.

Fig 6.84: A case of jaggies in an image that has been enlarged

Thumbnails

A thumbnail is a small version of an image that is also available in a full-size version. On a web page a thumbnail of an image can act as a hyperlink to another page that displays the full image.

Thumbnails are useful if the original image is quite large and would not fit easily on the main page. An example might be on a shop's website; small images of several products can be shown on one page, and the visitor would have the option of clicking on one to see an enlarged version.

FrontPage simplifies the process of creating thumbnails. If you are learning to create a web page in another software package then you may not be able to achieve this so easily.

You need a photo that is not too large to fit on the screen. A width of 800 pixels is probably the maximum you should consider.

Creating a thumbnail

1 Go to *Insert* → *Picture* → *From File*. Browse to find the photo you want to use.

The full size photo will eventually be replaced by a thumbnail, and the original photo will be displayed on a separate page. For the moment the full size photo appears in the position where the thumbnail will appear, so it may look at little odd.

2 Save the page and the photo before you go on to the next step.

3 Click on the photo, then click on the *Auto Thumbnail* button in the Pictures toolbar. The full size photo will be replaced by a thumbnail version.

4 Save the page. You will be prompted to save the thumbnail image.

5 You will have to check that this works in a browser, not in the Preview tab. Go to *File* → *Preview in Browser* (see Fig 6.85).

6 Click on the thumbnail, and the full size image should appear (see Fig 6.86).

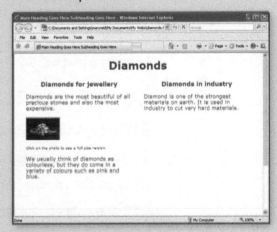

Fig 6.85: A thumbnail

Fig 6.86: When you click on the thumbnail the full size image is shown

Other image formats

Many of the images that you want to use on a web page will not be in one of the web formats (jpg, png or gif). However, you can still place them on a web page in FrontPage, and the software will convert them automatically for you into one of the acceptable formats.

Most of the other software that you might be using to create a web page will not convert the format for you. In that case, you will have to load the image into a graphics package and save it in one of the three formats yourself.

Text wrap

You will often want to place text alongside an image, as well as above and below it. This is known as text wrap.

Wrapping text around an image

1 Click on the page to the left of the text that you want to wrap around an image.

2 Insert an image as before. Resize and resample if necessary.

3 Right click on the image and select *Picture Properties*.

4 In the Appearance tab, under Wrapping Style, select either *Left* or *Right*. Click *OK*.

5 The image will now sit neatly to one side or other of the text, as in the right-hand column in Fig 6.87

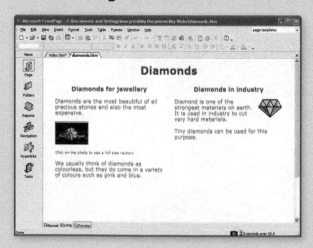

Fig 6.87: Text wrap

CHECK YOUR PROGRESS

What is a thumbnail? Give ONE example where a thumbnail could be used effectively on a website.

Hyperlinks

Any section of text or any image can be used as a hyperlink to another web page. But how does the visitor recognise that text or an image is a link? Originally text hyperlinks were all identified by underlining. Blue was the traditional colour for a link, with a link that had already been visited changing to magenta.

Text can be used as a hyperlink without underlining, and in any colour. But this can only be done if it is clear to the visitor that it is a hyperlink. Usually a different colour from the main text is used for the link.

Images can also be used as hyperlinks. Buttons are image-based links that look like the kind of buttons that you might press in the real world. But any image can be used as a link.

Creating hyperlinks to another web page

Linking to a page on the same website

You can set up a link from one page to another page on your website.

Creating a link to a page on your website

1 Open the index page. Somewhere near the top of the page, key in some text that will be used to link to the second page.

2 Select this text. Then go to *Insert* ➜ *Hyperlink* or click on the Hyperlink button in the Standard toolbar.

3 The Create Hyperlink dialogue window appears. Click on the page that you want to link to. Its filename appears in the Address box. Click *OK*. The hyperlinked text is now underlined (see Fig 6.88).

4 Save the page, and then go to *File* ➜ *Preview in Browser* to check that the link works.

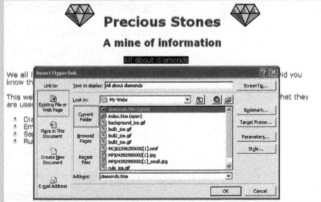

Fig 6.88: Creating a hyperlink

5 Repeat this process on the second page to create a link back to the index page.

Linking to a page on another website

You can also set up a link to any web page anywhere in the world.

Creating a link to another website

1 Write some suitable text, highlight it as before, and click on the Hyperlink button.

2 Enter the full URL of the website in the URL box, e.g. http://www.example.com
Do not forget to write http:// before the domain name.

3 Save the page.

4 Go to *File → Preview in Browser*. Click on the link you have created. If your computer is connected to the Internet it should find the new website.

Bookmarks

In a browser a hyperlink can let the visitor go to an invisible **bookmark** placed elsewhere on the same page. This is useful if a page contains a lot of information, and the visitor may only want to read a portion of it.

In our example, the page lists a number of frequently asked questions, then provides the answers further down the page. A visitor can click on a question and the browser will take the visitor directly to the information they need.

WHAT DOES IT MEAN?

bookmark
A bookmark is an invisible location on a page that a user can go to directly.

Creating a bookmark

1 On your web page add plenty of information so that the visitor has to scroll down to read it all.

2 Write a subheading for some of the information. Use the style heading2 or heading3 for the subheading. This subheading is going to become the bookmark.

3 Select the subheading. Go to *Insert → Bookmark*.

4 The subheading will now be underlined with a dotted line, which will not be visible in a browser. See the second line from the bottom of the window in Fig 6.89.

5 Repeat the process to add more bookmarks to the page if you like.

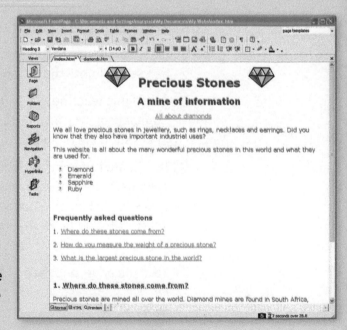

Fig 6.89: Using bookmarks

Creating a link to a bookmark

1 Near the top of the page write some text that will invite the visitor to jump to the information. In our example this is the first of the frequently asked questions.

2 Select the text that will act as the hyperlink. Go to *Insert* → *Hyperlink*.

3 In the Hyperlink dialogue window, click on *Bookmark …* A list of the bookmarks on the page is given. Select the bookmark you want. Click *OK*, then click *OK* in the Hyperlink window.

4 Save the page.

5 Go to *File* → *Preview in Browser* to check that the link works.

Email links

An email link enables the visitor to send an email directly to the owners of the website. When the visitor clicks on the link, a *New Message* is opened in the visitor's email client software, such as Outlook. The recipient will be displayed in the To box.

Creating an email link

1 On the web page key in some suitable words, e.g. 'Email me'.

2 Select this text. Go to *Insert* → *Hyperlink*.

3 Under *Link To:*, select *Email address*.

4 In the *Email address* box type in your email address. Click *OK*.

5 Go to *File* → *Preview in Browser* to check that the link works.

Files for downloading

You will probably have downloaded a file at sometime from the Web. This could be music, software or a document.

If you have a file that you would like to share with others from your website, you should first make sure that you are legally allowed to do so. There are copyright restrictions on music files, for example. However, there is no problem if the file is a document that you have created yourself. We refer to this as a user-created file.

To carry out the next steps you need to prepare a word processed document that you want to share.

Creating a link to a file you created

1 Copy the word processed document to the My Webs folder where your web pages are.

2 On the web page key in some words that will act as the link to the document, e.g. 'Download my report on the meeting'.

3 Select the link text, then go to *Insert* → *Hyperlink*.

4 Under *Link To:*, select *Existing page or file*.

5 Select the document that you want to link to. Click *OK*.

6 Save the page, then check that it works properly in a browser.

CHECK YOUR PROGRESS

List FOUR things that a hyperlink can link to.

Testing a website

You should always test a website, both before and after uploading it to the Web. Some things, such as document downloads, can only be tested when the site is on-line.

Testing a website in a browser

As you have experienced earlier in this section, FrontPage offers you a Preview tab at the bottom of the page. This is useful to quickly check the look of your page, but is not as reliable as testing in a browser.

Testing a website in a browser

1 Open the home page of your site.

2 Note in writing each of the links on the page.

3 Go to *File → Preview in Browser*.

4 Test each link in turn, and note the outcome in your notes.

5 If you find that any links do not work as expected then make the corrections and test again.

Testing a website with an audience

When you planned your website you made a note of the answers to these questions.

- What is my website about?
- What is the reason for my website?
- Who are my intended audience?

- What text will I use on each page?
- Which images will I use?
- What layout would be best on each page?
- Where will I locate the navigation links?
- What colours would be best for text and background?

You now need to test whether your website really does meet its purpose and suit your intended audience.

You should find one or two people who would fit into your intended audience. Ask them to have a look at the site, and to give you their honest opinions on it. Do not explain anything to them about what you were planning until after they have given you some feedback.

You may want to make some further changes after listening to your test audience.

Publishing and maintaining a website

Domain names

The **domain name** of a website is the core of its URL. It should be a sensible name for the organisation or individual who registered it.

Look at this URL: http://www.example.com. The domain name is example.com.

This has to be registered with one of the official domain name registries. There is a charge for registering a domain name.

Domain names can end with any of these:

- .com – for a commercial business
- .org – for a non-commercial organisation
- .info – for a site that provides information
- .com.jm – for a site registered in Jamaica
- .co.tt – for a site registered in Trinidad and Tobago
- .bb – for a site registered in Barbados
- .au – for a site registered in Australia

… and many more.

WHAT DOES IT MEAN?

domain name
The domain name is the main part of a URL. For example, in the URL http://www.example.com, the domain name is example.com.

Web hosts

A website has to be uploaded to a webserver in order to appear on the World Wide Web. The webserver will be owned by a web hosting company. If you want to put your website on the Web you will need to be in contact with a web hosting company who will be able to provide you with web space on the server. You will, of course, be charged for the service. The web host can also register a domain name for you and make sure that it is linked to your website.

Your school or college may already have an arrangement with a web host, so you may be able to upload your website to the Web at no cost to yourself.

It is important that websites are secure, that is, that only the right person is able to upload pages or change the website in any way. The web host will assign usernames and passwords to achieve this.

WHAT DOES IT MEAN?

web host
The company who provides space on a web server is called the web host.

Publishing a website

When you upload a website to the Web this is often described as publishing the website. This is done by using File Transfer Protocol (FTP) software, which is easily obtainable, to upload the files to the webserver. To get access to the webserver you will need to have three pieces of data:

1 The domain name   **2** Your username   **3** Your password

You must upload all of the following:

- The pages that you have created.
- The images that are included on the pages. These will usually be stored in a folder on the web server called 'images'.
- Any files that can be downloaded by a visitor from the site

Maintaining a website

Most websites need to be updated from time to time. Sometimes the contents will have to be changed because you want to give new information to visitors. Often new pages will be added and new links created.

Normally there will always be two copies of your website. One will be the working version on your computer and the other will be on the webserver. It is important that these two copies are identical. FrontPage checks for any differences between the two and uploads the latest version of pages. It will notice if files have been deleted or moved and will try match the server version with the working version.

You can get into a muddle if you try to keep further copies of the website. This could happen if you want to work on your website from home as well as from your school.

End-of-section questions

Multiple-choice questions

1 When you are creating a new website, which of the following needs to be considered?
   I   The intended audience
   II Layout of the web pages
   III Content of each page
   IV The number of web pages needed
   A I and II only   B I, II and III only
   C I, II and IV only   D I, II, III and IV

2 The first page that is displayed when a website is accessed is called:
   A Hyper link   B Home page
   C Thumbnail   D Search engine

3 What connects a website to another website?
   A Modem   B Hyperlink
   C Hypertext   D Connection

4 A company that rents web space is known as:
   A A webserver   B A web page
   C A web host   D A web browser

5 Which of the following is NOT a web browser:
   A Internet Explorer   B Mozilla Firefox
   C Google Chrome   D Yahoo

Structured questions

1 List four things that need to be considered when you are planning to create a website.

2 As it relates to a website, define the following:
   a Web browser
   b Hyperlink
   c Domain name
   d Home page

3 List four types of hyperlinks that can be created in a website.

4 a State the difference between a webserver and a web host.
   b Give the meaning of the following domain name extensions:
      i   com
      ii   edu
      iii org
      iv   net
      v   gov

5 List the steps in publishing a website.

Spreadsheets

Objectives

By the end of this section, you will be able to:

- Explain the purpose of a spreadsheet.
- Use the appropriate terminology associated with spreadsheets.
- Use functions to perform calculations.
- Create advanced arithmetic formulae.
- Explain the use of common features of spreadsheet software.
- Copy formulae.
- Manipulate data in a spreadsheet.
- Manipulate rows and columns, including locking.
- Format a spreadsheet.
- Sort and filter the data in a spreadsheet.
- Perform charting operations.
- Manipulate multiple spreadsheets.
- Import files.

Many organisations need to store data, analyse it and present it in a meaningful way. For example your school may need to prepare a table showing the number of male and female students who have sat the CSEC Information Technology examination over the past five years.

Spreadsheet software enables you to store your data in a table, manipulate that data and display it graphically. Spreadsheet programs are used for a variety of tasks including preparing budgets, creating charts and presenting data in an organised manner. This section will provide you with the knowledge and hands-on skills to use spreadsheet software to develop computer applications.

Many types of spreadsheet software are available and used by many people, but for this section we will focus on the spreadsheet program called Microsoft Excel. As such, all diagrams and step-by-step instructions provided are for Microsoft Excel 2003. Alternatively, you could use any available spreadsheet package, but you would need to check the buttons in the toolbars and the options in the menus to find the equivalent functions.

ADDING
=B5+C10

SUBTRACTING
=D7-F3

MULTIPLYING
=H5*H2

DIVIDING
=G10/D5

POWERING
=E10^2

=AVERAGE(B2:B5)
=SUM(B2:B5)
=DATE(2009,04,15
=MIN(B2:B5)
=COUNT(B2:B5)
=MAX(B2:B5)

Spreadsheet software

When we start the Excel program, the picture displayed in Fig 7.1 appears on the screen.

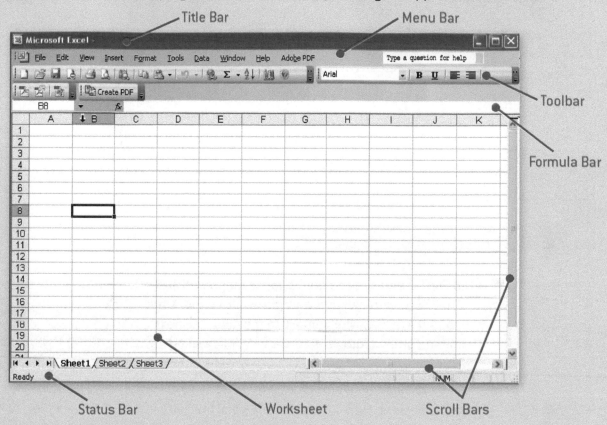

Fig 7.1: The Excel window

The Excel window shown in Fig. 7.1 indicates the different elements of the spreadsheet program.

The workbook and worksheet

A **workbook** is another name for a spreadsheet. It is the file in which you enter and store data. A **worksheet** is a collection of cells where you enter your data and charts. Each workbook contains many worksheets. As you can see in Fig 7.1, the current worksheet is Sheet1 and it is located in Book1. Each workbook can have up to 255 worksheets labeled as Sheet1, Sheet2, .., Sheet 255, and these can be named to suit your task. For example, we could have a workbook, named 'Year' with 12 worksheets, where each worksheet contains data about each month, so are named January, February, etc.

In this section we will refer to a workbook as a spreadsheet.

WHAT DOES IT MEAN?

workbook

A workbook is a spreadsheet file. It contains at least one worksheet, and may contain several worksheets.

worksheet

A worksheet is a single page in a spreadsheet file.

Rows, columns and cells

Fig 7.2: Rows and columns in a spreadsheet

In Fig 7.2 you can see that rows are numbered 1, 2, 3,..., 65536 vertically downwards, while columns are labeled A, B, C, ... horizontally to the right. The next column after column Z is column AA, followed by AB, AC, AD etc.

A **cell** is the intersection of a column and a row. Each cell is given a **cell address**. For example, the cell address A1 is given to the cell at the intersection of column A and row 1. In the same way, cell G10 is the intersection of column G and row 10.

Range

Often we will want to work with a group or block of cells that form a rectangle in the worksheet. This block of cells is called a **range**. A range is referenced by indicating the upper left cell and the lower right cell, placing a colon (:) between the two cells. For example, the range C2:D4, includes the following cells:

	C	D
2	C2	D2
3	C3	D3
4	C4	D4

Fig 7.3: A range of cells

WHAT DOES IT MEAN?

cell
A cell is an individual location in a spreadsheet. It is referred to by its column letter and row number.

cell address
A cell address identifies a single cell in a worksheet. It is given in the format B23, where the letter indicates the column and the number indicates the row.

WHAT DOES IT MEAN?

range
A range identifies a rectangular block of cells on a worksheet.

Types of data in a cell

A cell can contain three basic types of data:

1 Labels: Labels are non-numeric data that will not be used in calculations, e.g. a person's name.

2 Values: Values are data used for calculations, e.g. an employee's salary. Values can also include dates and times such as 10-Feb-2009 and 5:20 pm. There may be cases where you would want to enter a value in a cell but treat it as a text. For example, you may want to enter the year 2009 but treat it as a label. In this case, you use an apostrophe, e.g. '2009.

3 Formulae: Formulae can be entered in a cell to perform calculations on values in other cells. A formula always begins with =. For example, we could enter the formula, =B1+B2 in cell B4 so that cell B4 will contain the sum of the values in cell B1 and cell B2.

You will also be learning about functions. These are shortcuts that you use in place of entering lengthy and complicated formulae. We could enter the function =max(B1:B2) in cell B5 so that cell B5 will contain the higher of the values in cell B1 and B2.

WHAT DOES IT MEAN?

label
In a spreadsheet, a label is text entered into a cell that explains the contents of other cells.

value
The data entered into a cell in a spreadsheet is referred to as a value.

formula
A formula carries out calculations, using the values held in one or more cells on a worksheet, and displays the result in another cell.

function
A function is used within a formula to carry out complex calculations.

Entering values, formulae, functions and labels

1 Launch Excel.

2 In cell B1, key in the number 23. Then key in 45 in cell B2. You can use the Enter key to move to the next cell below. Notice that when you click on a cell each number also appears in the formula bar.

3 In cell B4, key in the following formula =B1+B2. When you press return, cell B4 should now display 68, which is the sum of the values.

4 In cell B5, key in the following formula =max(B1:B2). When you press return cell B5 should display 45, which is the higher of the two values. Max is a function. It is applied to the range of cells B1:B2.

5 It is a good idea to add labels so you can remember what the numbers represent. In cell A4 key in 'Total'. (Do not type the quote marks.) In cell A5 key in 'Maximum value'. (Do not type the quote marks.)

6 You will need to make the column wider so you can see the second label. Move the cursor so it lies on the boundary line dividing the headings A and B. Click and drag the boundary to the right until it is the right size.

	A	B	C
1		23	
2		45	
3			
4	Total	68	
5	Maximim value	45	
6			
7			

Fig 7.4: Entering values, formulae, functions and labels

CHECK YOUR PROGRESS

1 Explain the difference between a spreadsheet and a worksheet.
2 List the cells in the range A2:B3.
3 In which row and which column does the cell P64 lie?
4 What character must always used when a formula is entered into a cell?
5 Suppose that you want to enter the value 2010 as a label in a cell. How would you do this to avoid it being used in a calculation?

Arithmetic formulae

In Section 2 you met the arithmetic operators that can be used in algorithms, and in Section 3 you learned how to use arithmetic operators in Pascal.

In a spreadsheet, formulae can be used to perform arithmetic calculations on values. Table 7.1 below shows the different operators that can be used in formulae:

Operator	Meaning	Example
+	Adding	=B5+C10
-	Subtracting	=D3-H2
*	Multiplying	=H5*H2
/	Dividing	=G10/D5
^	Powering	=G10^2 = G5^0.5

Table 7.1: Formula operators

When using operators, you should remember the standard rules regarding order that you have met before:

1 Brackets are done first.
2 Powers is done second, e.g. 10^2.
3 Division and multiplication are done third.
4 Addition and subtraction are done last.

When two operators at the same level are in the same formula, then the operators are executed from left to right. For example, in the formula =A2+A8-A10, because the operators + and - have the same level, then they are executed from left to right.

CHECK YOUR PROGRESS

Consider the following worksheet that is used to compute the monthly payroll of an organisation.

1 Indicate the cell and the formula to compute the Gross Pay for Khemraj.
2 Write the formulae that you are going to need to compute the tax paid by Lawrence. (Hint, there will be a formula in D2 for Gross Pay. The formula for Tax in F2 will use the result in D2.)
3 Write the formula to compute the Medical paid by Seeram.
4 Indicate the cell and the formulae required in order to compute the Net Pay for Karen.
5 Write the formula to compute the total tax paid by all the employees.
6 Create the worksheet in Excel and enter all the fo rmulae in this exercise.

	A	B	C	D	E	F	G
1	Employee	Salary	Allowance	Gross Pay	Medical	Tax	Net Pay
2	Lawrence	980000	40000				
3	Karen	45000	9000				
4	Seeram	750000	35000				
5	Khemraj	40000	8000				
6	Mohan	54000	8000				

Fig 7.5: Note: **a** Gross Pay = Salary + Allowance
              b Medical is 5% of Salary
              c Tax is 33% of (Gross Pay – 35000)
              d Net Pay = Gross Pay – (Medical + Tax)

Templates

A template is a worksheet that is already prepared with the appropriate formulae programmed in, and formatting and layout already completed. In using a template, all you have to do is to enter the relevant data and the spreadsheet program performs the necessary calculation, charts and presentation. For example, you could have a personal budget template in which you enter your income and expenditure for each month and the spreadsheet program makes the necessary computation. Templates are great time savers.

Some templates may be available to you on your school network or on the PC that you are using. You can usually access them by selecting *File* → *New* in Excel.

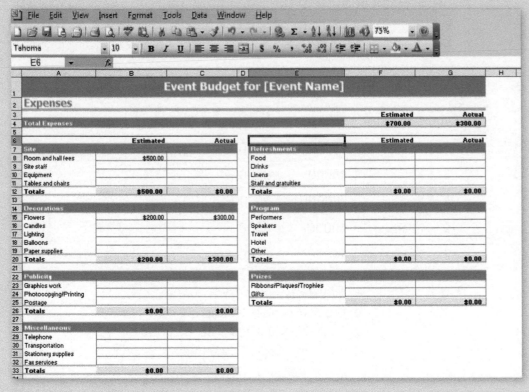

Fig 7.6: An example of a template in Excel

Functions

Excel has many predefined functions that are used within formulae to perform common calculations on values in a worksheet. Functions are always structured like this:

functionname(argument1, argument2, argument3 …)

The arguments are usually cell addresses, which tell the function where to find the values it must use. A range of cell addresses can be used instead of a single cell address. Some functions do not have any arguments, while others have only one.

The SUM function

The SUM function can be used to add the values in a range of cells. For example, =SUM(A1:F1) can be entered in a cell to sum the values in the range, A1:F1.

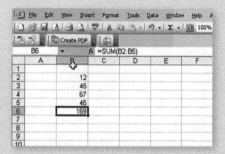

Fig 7.7: Use of the SUM function

In the example in Fig 7.7, the formula =SUM(B2:B5) has been entered in cell B6 to give the sum of the range B2:B5.

The same result could be achieved by using the formula =B2+B3+B4+B5. The SUM function is very useful when you want to add a lot of numbers.

Using the SUM function

1 Open a new worksheet and enter only the values as shown in cells B1 to B5 in Fig 7.7.

2 Click in cell B6, and key in =SUM(B2:B5). Make sure you do not place a space between SUM and the opening bracket.

3 Press return and the number 169 should appear in cell B6.

4 Note that the formula is also displayed in the formula bar.

Selecting a range of cells

You can also select a range of cells using a neat shortcut.

1 Delete the formula in B6.

2 This time, key in the first part of the formula =SUM(

3 Now click on the first cell in the range (B2), and hold the mouse button down as you click on the last cell in the range (B5). Release the mouse button and the formula should read =SUM(B2:B5. You must now key in the closing bracket) to finish the formula.

The AVERAGE function

The AVERAGE function is used to find the average or arithmetic mean for a range of cells. For example, =AVERAGE(A1:F1) can be entered into a cell to find the average value for the range A1:F1.

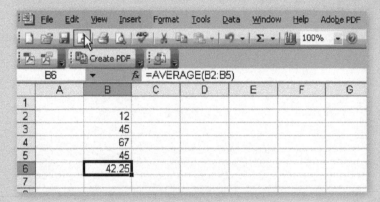

Fig. 7.8: Use of the AVERAGE function

In Fig 7.8, the function =AVERAGE (B2:B5) has been inserted in cell B6 to give the average of the range B2:B5.

Using the AVERAGE function

1 In the worksheet you were using just now, delete the sum formula in B6.

2 Key in the formula, =AVERAGE(B2:B5). You can either type in B2:B5 or you can select a range as explained in the last set of instructions.

From now on, try out all the functions as shown in the examples below, following the same methods as given for the sum and average functions.

The NOW and TODAY functions

The NOW and TODAY functions are use to display the date and time in your worksheet. The NOW function provides the current date and time according to your computer system clock. The TODAY function provides the current date only. Neither of these functions requires any arguments, you just enter =NOW() or =TODAY() into the cell.

In Fig 7.9, the function =TODAY() has been inserted in cell E6 to display the computer system date. The function has no arguments.

In Fig 7.10, the function =NOW() has been inserted in cell D6 to display the current system date and time.

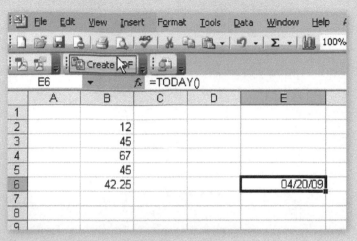

Fig 7.9: Use of the TODAY function

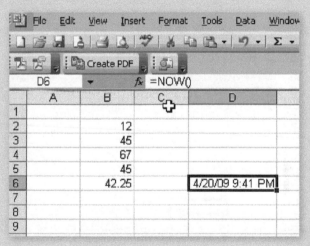

Fig 7.10: Use of the NOW function

The DATE function

The DATE function is also used to enter a date in the worksheet, giving the year, month and day. For example =DATE(year,month,day) can be entered in a cell to provide the system date. You must put in the appropriate numbers in place of year, etc.

In Fig 7.11, the DATE function =DATE(2009,04,15) has been inserted in cell D6 to display the date in cell D6.

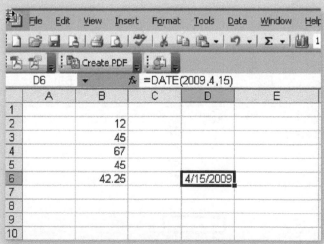

Fig 7.11: Use of the DATE function

The MIN and MAX functions

The MIN and MAX functions can be used to determine the minimum (lowest) and maximum (highest) values in a range of cells.

In Fig 7.12 the function, =MIN(B2:B5) has been entered in cell B8 to display the minimum value in the range B2:B5.

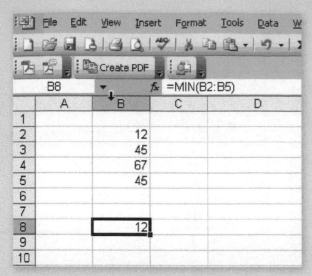

Fig 7.12: Use of the MIN function

In Fig 7.13 the function, =MAX(B2:B5) has been inserted in cell B8 to display the maximum value in the range B2:B5.

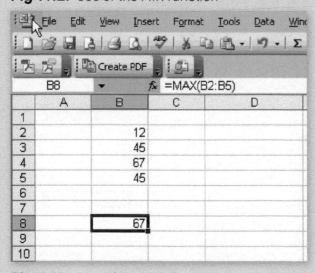

Fig 7.13: Use of the MAX function

The COUNT function

The COUNT function is used to count the number of cells in a range that contains numeric or date values. The function ignores cells containing text labels.

In Fig 7.13 the function, =COUNT (B2:B5) has been inserted in cell B8 to display the number of cells with values.

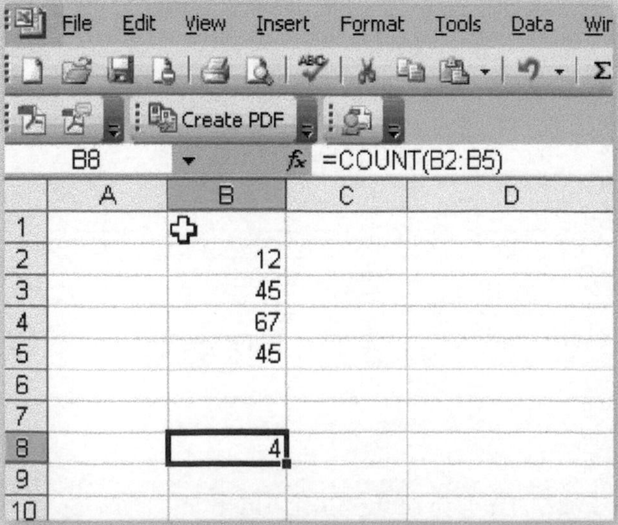

Fig 7.14: Use of the COUNT function

The IF function

In Section 2 you met IF statements used in algorithms, and in Section 3 you learned how they were implemented in Pascal. IF statements can also be implemented in spreadsheet programs.

The IF function in a spreadsheet program is used for making decisions. This function tests for a condition and then depending on the result of the test, it performs one of two calculations. The following comparison operators can be used in an IF function:

- Equal (=)
- Not equal (<>)
- Less than (<)
- Less than or equal to (<=)
- Greater than (>)
- Greater than or equal to (>=)

The format of the IF function is =IF(condition, true, false). This is the equivalent of an if-then-else statement in Pascal.

In Fig 7.15 the IF function, =IF(B4>50,"pass","fail") has been entered in D4 to display the result of the test (B4>50). The word 'pass' is displayed because the value in B4 is greater than 50.

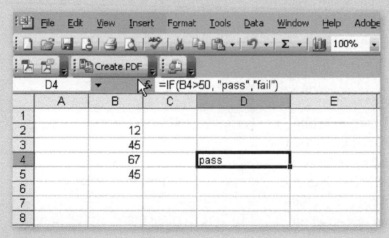

Fig 7.15: Use of the IF function

The VLOOKUP function

The cells holding data are often arranged in more than one column. We normally refer to this as a table. Often the values in one column will be related to the values in another column. For example, in a table showing the growth pattern of a plant, one column could hold the number of days that have passed since measurements began, and another column could hold the height of the plant.

The VLOOKUP function is a useful function that allows us to search the first column of a table and match it with the corresponding value in another column. In the example, we could find day 23 and check the height of the plant on that day.

So VLOOKUP is used to search for a value in the first column of a table and return the value in the same row from another column you specify. Note the table must be sorted in ascending order (using the first column) for the function to work.

The format of the command is =VLOOKUP(lookup_value, table_array, col_index_no), where:

- lookup_value is the value you are searching for in column 1.
- table_array is the range of the data in the table, e.g. A3:D11.
- col_index_no is the number of the column that will contain the value you want.

In Fig 7.16, in cell B11, the function, =VLOOKUP(10, A3:B7, 2) has been entered. In this case the lookup value is 10, the table data is all to be found in the range A3:B7. The data that is displayed (25) is in column 2, on the same row as where the value 10 lies.

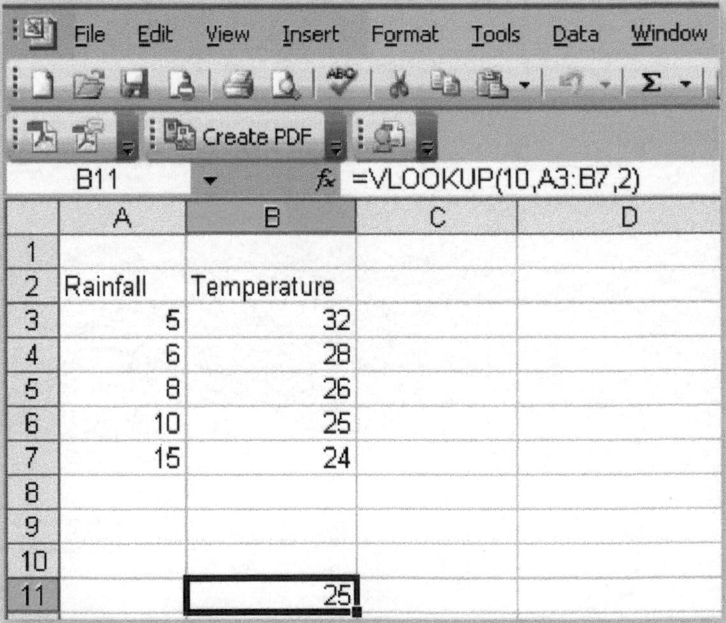

	A	B	C	D
1				
2	Rainfall	Temperature		
3	5	32		
4	6	28		
5	8	26		
6	10	25		
7	15	24		
8				
9				
10				
11		25		

Fig 7.16: Use of the VLOOKUP function

The RANK function

The RANK function returns the rank of a number in a list of numbers. The rank of a number is its position in a list that has been sorted. For example, the top mark achieved in an exam will have the rank 1.

You can use RANK on a list of numbers that have not been sorted, but it will still work out the correct rank as if they had been sorted.

If you were to sort the list, the rank of the number would be its position. The format of the command is =RANK(number, range, order), where:

- number is the value whose rank you want to know.
- range is the range of cells containing the list.
- order identifies whether you want the number to be considered in ascending (1) or descending (0) order.

The formula =RANK(C5,C2:C7,1) has been entered in cell C10 to display the rank of the value 11 in the range C2:C7, arranged in ascending order.

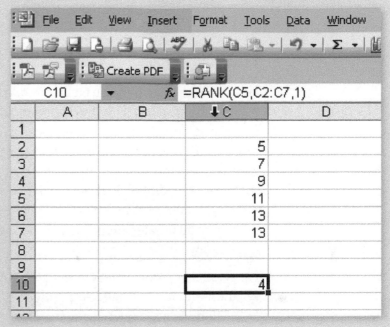

Fig 7.17: Use of the RANK function

CHECK YOUR PROGRESS

Consider the following worksheet:

	A	B	C
1	Student	Mark	Status
2	Mohan	65	
3	Khemraj	72	
4	Triko	45	
5	Adrial	35	
6	Jones	40	

1 Write the function to find the maximum marks obtain by a student.
2 A student is given a status 'PASS' if his mark is over 60; else he is awarded a status of 'FAIL'. Write the function you would insert in cell C2 to display the status.
3 Write the function to find the average marks for the class.
4 The function =TODAY() is entered into cell C10. What will be displayed in C10?

Manipulating data on a worksheet

Relative addressing

Most of the time, when you create a worksheet with numeric data, you will have to use formulae to perform calculations. To make it easier, you can create one formula and copy it to other cells to perform similar calculations. In doing so, you want to ensure that when the formula is copied to the new location then it is adjusted automatically to reference the cells relative to its new location. This is called **relative addressing**.

WHAT DOES IT MEAN?

relative address
A relative address is used in a formula, and is adjusted automatically if the formula is copied to another cell.

For example, if we have the formula =A1+A2 in cell A3 and if we copy this formula to cell C3, then with relative cell addressing, the formula in C3 will be =C1+C2. Note that the cells in the formula are adjusted automatically to suit the new location of the formula.

Copying a formula

To demonstrate how relative addressing works when we copy a formula, we will look at this example showing the number of graduates from a university in the various programs.

The years 2001, 2002 and 2003 are labels. On page 329 you learned that to avoid them being treated as numbers you should start each year with an apostrophe, like this: '2001. The apostrophe is not visible in the cell.

	A	B	C	D	E
1	Program	2001	2002	2003	Total
2	Certificate	15	21	18	
3	Diploma	500	600	700	
4	Degree	1200	1100	900	
5	Post-grad	10	15	12	

Fig 7.18

Using relative addressing

1 Create the worksheet shown in Fig 7.18 containing the number of graduates from a university in the various programs.

2 In cell E2, enter the formula, =SUM(B2:D2). This adds the contents of cells B2, C2 and D2, so should give the result 54.

3 Click on cell E2, right click and select *Copy*. The formula will be copied, not the result. Paste it in E3. Note that the formula changes to =SUM(B3:D3).

4 Copy the formula into E4 and E5, noting the results.

5 Change the value in Cell B2 to 25. What happens to the value in E2?

Note: Save your file as 'University.xls' as you will need it later in the section.

How to delete a formula

If we delete a cell with a formula, the formula and the results of the formula disappear. You should note that if we delete values in cells referenced in a formula, the formula is automatically recalculated.

Deleting a formula

1 Click on E2, right click and select *Clear Contents*. This deletes the formula. You will see that this does not affect the formulae in E3, E4 and E5.

How to move a formula

When we move a cell with a formula, then the results of the formula and the formula itself are placed in another location. The cells in the formula remain unchanged. This is like moving the location where you want the result of the calculations to be.

The only way to move a formula from one cell to another is to cut it from the first cell and paste it into the second.

Moving a formula

1 Click on cell E5, right click and select *Cut*.

2 Click on another cell, well away from the table, and paste.

3 Look at the formula and the result in this new cell. It should be identical to what was previously in E5.

Absolute addressing

Absolute cell referencing is used when we do NOT want a cell in a formula to be changed relative to its new position when a formula is copied. To do this, we use a dollar sign ($) before the column or row reference (or both) that we do not want to change.

For example, if we do not want cell A5 to change in a formula when we copied or moved it, then we use A5 in the formula. In this case both the row and column reference will not change when the formula is copied. However, if we want the row reference to change but the column reference to be fixed, we use $A5 and similarly with A$5 the row reference is fixed but the column reference will change.

Using absolute addressing

In the following example, a manufacturer of candy bars has decided to reduce the weight of each bar by 15 grams.

	A	B	C	D	E
1	Original weight	Net weight			
2	100			Reduction	15
3	150				
4	200				
5	250				

Fig 7.19

1 Set up a worksheet as shown in Fig 7.19.

2 In B2 enter the formula =A2-E2. You should get the result 85.

3 Copy this formula and paste it into B3, B4 and B5.

4 The formula in B3 will become =A3-E2. Notice that the absolute address E2 has not changed, whereas the relative address, A2, has changed to A3.

CHECK YOUR PROGRESS

1 In a new worksheet, cell E3 has the formula = SUM (B3:D3). If this formula is copied to cell E10, what formula would appear in cell E10?

2 Cell E5 has the formula, = C5+D5. If this formula is copied to cell E10, what formula would be displayed in E10?

Rows and columns

Deleting rows and columns

You can easily delete a row or column of a worksheet. To delete a row or column we do the following:

Deleting a column

	A	B	C	D	E
1	Program	2001	2002	2003	Total
2	Certificate	15	21	18	54
3	Diploma	500	600	700	1800
4	Degree	1200	1100	900	3200
5	Post-grad	10	15	12	37

Fig 7.20

1 Open the spreadsheet 'University.xls' you have already created, as in Fig 7.20 above.

2 Select column E by clicking on the letter E at the top of the column

3 Go to *Edit → Delete*.

Deleting a row

1 Select row 2 (Certificate) by clicking on the number 2 to the left of the column.

2 Go to *Edit → Delete*.

3 Save your document for later use.

Observe that when a row is deleted the other rows move up and when a column is deleted, the other columns move to the left.

Inserting rows and columns

Often you will create a worksheet and realise later that you need to insert additional data within it. This can be done by inserting new rows or columns into which you will enter the additional data.

Inserting a column

	A	B	C	D
1	Program	2001	2002	2003
2	Diploma	500	600	700
3	Degree	1200	1100	900
4	Post-grad	10	15	12

Fig 7.21

1 Open the spreadsheet 'University.xls' you have already created, as in Fig 7.21 above.

2 To add a column to the left of column B, click on the letter B at the top of the column.

3 Go to *Insert* ➞ *Column*.

4 Give the new column the heading '2000'.

5 Insert the following data in the new column:

750
1450
15

Observe that when you insert a new column, the existing columns are shifted one column to the right. If you want to insert more than one column, then in Step 2 you will have to select more than one column letters.

Inserting a row

1 Using the table from Fig 7.21, click on the number 2 to insert a row directly above.

2 Go to *Insert* ➞ *Column*.

3 In A2, enter the heading 'Special Program'.

4 Insert the following data in the new row:

12	44	22	15

Observe that when you insert a new row, the existing rows are shifted down. If you want to insert more than one row, then in Step 1 you will have to select more than one row numbers.

Your worksheet should now look like this:

	A	B	C	D	E
1	Program	2000	2001	2002	2003
2	Special program	12	44	22	15
3	Diploma	750	500	600	700
4	Degree	1450	1200	1100	900
5	Post-grad	15	10	15	12

Fig 7.22

Save it so that you can use it later.

Row and column titles

A title can be the heading of a row of data or a column of data. Titles are useful to navigate your way around the worksheet. You may want them to remain visible so that you always know what data you are looking at. But, if you have a very large worksheet, then as you scroll down, the headings of the columns will not be visible on the screen. This makes it difficult to know what the data represent. Similarly when you scroll across the worksheet, the headings of the rows will not be visible on the screen.

To make it easier to know what the data represent, the spreadsheet program has a feature that allows you to lock or freeze rows or columns, or both. This will ensure that the headings of columns or rows are always visible as you scroll down or across.

Locking a column title

1 Open 'University.xls' that you were working on before and add extra datas in columns F to J as shown in Fig 7.23.

	A	B	C	D	E	F	G	H	I	J
1	Program	2000	2001	2002	2003	2004	2005	2006	2007	2008
2	Special Programm	12	44	22	15	35	42	33	21	16
3	Diploma	750	500	600	700	800	750	450	390	300
4	Degree	1450	1200	1100	900	1200	1500	1700	2100	2000
5	Post-grad	15	10	15	12	18	16	14	22	18

Fig 7.23

2 Select column B, which is immediately to the right of the column you want to lock.

3 Go to *Windows* → *Freeze Panes*.

As you scroll across the worksheet, column A remains static while the other columns move. If you cannot see this effect, then add further columns for years 2009, 2010, etc. Alternatively, reduce the size of the spreadsheet window.

Unlocking a column

1 Go to *Windows* → *Unfreeze Panes*.

Locking a row title

1 Select row 2, which is the row below the row that you want to lock.

2 Go to *Windows* → *Freeze Panes*.

3 To unlock the row go to *Windows* → *Unfreeze Panes*.

Locking both a row title and a column title

1 Select B2, the cell beneath and to the right of the section to remain visible.

2 Go to *Windows* → *Freeze Panes*.

CHECK YOUR PROGRESS

1 You have scrolled down your worksheet and noticed that the headings of your columns have disappeared. What can you do to make the headings of your columns visible at all times?

2 Give a scenario where you would apply title locking on both a row and column.

How to format a worksheet

Now that you have completed your worksheet with the necessary data and formulae, it is time to make it presentable by applying a variety of formatting features, such as alignment, borders and fonts.

Using formatting features

1 Select the cells containing the data you want to format.

2 Go to *Format* → *Cells*

3 The Format Cells dialogue box shown in Fig. 7.24 will appear

4 Select the type of format and attributes you want to use.

Numeric data can be formatted to look more presentable by using a number of features including currency, accounting and percentages. In addition some features allow you to select the styles, including comma after thousand and decimal places.

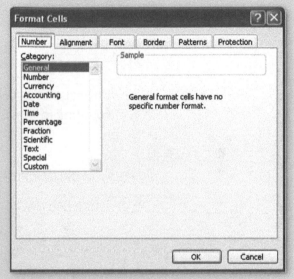

Fig 7.24: The Format Cells dialogue box

Using the comma format

The comma format is used to separate thousands with a comma. In addition you can also determine the number of decimal places to use.

Using the comma format with no decimal places on a set of numbers

1 Open 'University.xls'.

2 Select cells B4 to J4. You can do this by clicking on B4 and holding the mouse down as you move across to J4.

3 Go to *Format* → *Cells*. Select the Number tab, then under Category, select Number.

4 Check the *Use 1000 separator (,)* box.

5 Change the decimal places to 0 (default is 2).

6 Click *OK*.

Consider the following numbers:

2006.3	5426.271	978.05

When we apply the number format as indicated in the above steps, we get the following:

2,006	5,426	978

Observe that all the thousands have been separated with commas and there are no decimal places.

Currency and accounting formats

Both currency and accounting formats are used for monetary data. The difference is that the accounting format lines up the currency symbol and the decimal points in the column.

Using the currency format

1 On a new worksheet, enter the following data:

9
23
145

2 Select the cells containing the numbers you want to format.

3 Go to *Format* → *Cells*. Select the Number tab, then under Category, select Currency.

4 Select the currency symbol you want to use (default is $).

5 Select the number of decimal places (default is 2).

6 Click on *OK*.

When we apply the currency format in the default settings, we get the following:

$9.00
$23.00
$145.00

Using the accounting format

1 Select the same cells as before.

2 Go to *Format* → *Cells*. Select the Number tab, then under Category, select Accountancy.

3 Select the currency symbol to use (default is $).

4 Select the number of decimal places (default is 2).

5 Click on *OK*.

When we apply the accounting format in the default settings, we get

$	9.00
$	23.00
$	145.00

Observe the alignment of the currency symbol ($) and the decimal places.

Percentage format

The percentage format can be used to display data as a percentage.

Using the percentage format

1 On a new worksheet, enter the following data:

| 0.25 |
| 0.15 |
| 0.6 |

2 Select the cells that contain the numbers you want to format.

3 Go to *Format* → *Cells*. Select the Number tab, then under Category, select Percentage.

4 Select the number of decimal places.

5 Click on *OK*.

When we apply the percentage format with one decimal place, we get:

| 25.0% |
| 15.0% |
| 60.0% |

Date format

We can change the format of the date by the using the following steps.

Formatting dates

1 In a cell, enter a date in a standard format, such as 3/14/2009.

2 Select the cell and go to *Format* → *Cells*. Select the Number tab, then under Category, select Date.

3 Select the date format you want.

4 Click on *OK*.

For example, the date 3/14/2009 can be formatted as March 14 2009.

Formatting text in a worksheet

We can apply a variety of formatting features to text data by using the Formatting toolbar given in fig 7.25

Fig 7.25: The Formatting toolbar

For example, we can change the font type, size and colour. We can also embolden, italicise and underline the text.

Applying text formatting

1 Select the cells containing the text to format.

2 Select the relevant formatting icon in the toolbar menu above. For example, if you want the text to be bold, you would click on the bold icon **B**.

Data alignment

Data in a cell can be aligned as left align, right align, center, and merge and centre.

Aligning data

1 Select the cells.

2 Click on the relevant alignment icon in the Formatting toolbar. For example, click on the Center icon to center the cells ☰.

Note that by default, numbers are right aligned while text is left aligned.

The merge and centre feature is useful when you want to centre a title across the columns in the worksheet.

Using merge and centre

1 Select the range of cells across which you want the text to centre in the row that contains the title.

2 Click on the Merge and Center icon ▦.

Borders

Borders can be applied to one cell or a number of cells of the worksheet. Different border options are available such as giving all cells borders or just the outside border of a range of cells.

These are shown in Fig 7.26.

Fig 7.26: The types of border available

Adding borders

1 Select the cells to which you want to add a border.

2 Click on the down arrow of the border icon on the Formatting toolbar ⊞⁻.

3 Select the border type, in this case let's put borders around all cells. Select the *All Borders* icon ⊞ .

This gives you the following border to a range of cells:

12	13
13	56

Formatting a worksheet

Now let's use all that you've learned about formatting and apply it to a worksheet.

1 Set up a new worksheet as shown in Fig 7.27.

2 Align the headings of columns B, C and D to the right of the cell.

3 Apply the currency format to column B and the comma format to column C.

4 Format column D so that the date is given as year-month-day. For example, 2009-05-15.

5 Give the range A4:D9 'All borders'.

6 Centre the title 'Jagat Grocery Store' across columns A to D and change the font to Arial size 20.

	A	B	C	D	E
1	Jagat Grocery Store				
2	Items in stock				
3					
4	Items	Price	Qty	Expiry	
5	Fruit Juice	75	3300	15-May-09	
6	Butter	230	1500	12-Jan-10	
7	Milk	450	2000	21-Dec-09	
8	Salmon	600	900	30-Sep-09	
9	Sausage	240	300	11-Nov-09	
10					
11					

Fig 7.27

Fruit	Jan	Feb	Mar
Papaya	56	18	24
Mango	12	33	32
Pear	45	25	28
Banana	10	56	20

Fig 7.28

Fruit	Jan	Feb	Mar
Banana	10	56	20
Mango	12	33	32
Papaya	56	18	24
Pear	45	25	28

Fig 7.29

Employee	Gender	Salary
Mary	Female	3500
Joan	Female	3200
John	Male	4500
Allan	Male	1800

Fig 7.30

How to sort a worksheet

Data in the worksheet can be rearranged in ascending or descending order. Ascending order lists data from A to Z or 1 to 9, while descending order lists data from Z to A or 9 to 1. Data in a worksheet can be sorted on one or more rows or columns.

Sorting data

1. Set up a worksheet as shown in Fig 7.28.

2. Select all the cells in the table, including the titles.

3. Go to *Data* → *Sort*. A sort dialogue box will appear.

4. Select one or more row or column to sort by.

5. Select the order of sort (ascending or descending).

6. Click on *OK*.

In Fig 7.29, the data is sorted by the column with heading 'Fruit' in ascending order.

In the case where it is required to sort by more than one field, then the first sort field is called the primary sort field and the other fields are called the secondary sort fields.

In the Fig 7.30, the data is sorted on the primary field 'Gender' in ascending order and then by the secondary field 'Salary' in descending order.

Observe that females are placed before males, because Female comes before Male alphabetically. In each group, the salaries are then sorted by the Salary field in descending order. Note the secondary field only operates on each gender group. Sorting on more than one field will only be meaningful depending on the data to be sorted.

CHECK YOUR PROGRESS

Consider the worksheet in Fig 7.31.
1. What would happen if you sorted the worksheet with Status as the primary sort field in descending order and Salary as the secondary sort field in ascending order?
2. Set up the worksheet in Excel and see if your answers were correct.

Records

Sometimes the data arranged in a spreadsheet can be considered as a simple database. In worksheets, such databases are often referred to as lists. In the worksheet in Fig 7.31 the headings Staff, Status and Salary are referred to as field names. Each row holds data about one member of staff, and is known as a record. Records are rows of data where each cell, called a field, contains an item of data relating to the record.

WHAT DOES IT MEAN?

list
In a spreadsheet, a simple database is known as a list.

record
In a spreadsheet, a record is a row of data in a list.

field and field names
In a spreadsheet, a field is a cell in a record. Field names are labels at the top of the columns containing the field data.

Fig 7.31

Often we create a large worksheet with data and we want to find all the data matching some criterion. Rather than manually going through the worksheet and searching for the data matching the criterion, the spreadsheet software has a feature that allows us to filter the records.

Consider the worksheet in Fig 7.32.

	A	B	C
1	Employee	Sex	Salary
2	Allan	Male	5600
3	Mary	Female	3500
4	Peter	Male	2500
5	Triko	Female	6000
5	Mohan	Male	8000

Fig 7.32

If we want to find all employees whose salary is greater than 5000, then we have to create a filter that will display the data matching the given criterion.

Finding records that match a simple criterion

1 On a worksheet create the list shown in Fig 7.32.

2 Click on any of the cells in the list.

3 Go to *Window* → *Filter* → *AutoFilter*. Small arrows will appear beside each fieldname, as in Fig 7.33.

	A	B	C
1	Employee	Sex	Salary
2	Allan	Male	5600
3	Mary	Female	3500
4	Peter	Male	2500
5	Triko	Female	6000
6	Mohan	Male	8000
7			

Fig 7.33: AutoFilter

4 Click on the arrow beside the fieldname 'Sex'. A drop down list appears. Select 'Male'. You are now filtering the list using the criterion 'Male' and the list will only display the records of male employees.

5 Notice that the arrow has changed colour, to indicate that the data is filtered on this field.

6 To restore the full list, click on the arrow beside the fieldname again, and select (All).

If we want to find all employees whose salary is greater than 5000, then we can use a custom criterion.

Creating a custom filter

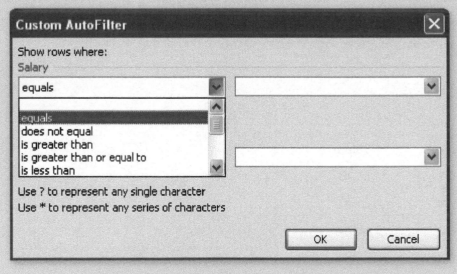

1 With AutoFilter on, click on the arrow beside the Salary field name.

2 Select (Custom…). The Custom AutoFilter dialogue box will appear.

3 Click on the arrow in the first box and select 'is greater than'.

4 Click in the box to the right and enter 5000. Click on *OK*.

5 The list will now display only those employees who earn more than 5000.

Fig 7.34: The Custom AutoFilter dialogue box

Finding records that match complex criteria

You can use two or more criteria to find matching records. Suppose you want to list all the male employees who earn more than 5000.

1 In the same list as in the previous set of instructions, first make sure that the AutoFilter is on, but that all the filters are set to (All).

2 In the Salary field, filter for employees whose salary is greater than 5000.

3 In the Sex field, filter for Male.

4 The list will now only display male employees whose salary is greater than 5000.

You can also use complex criteria on one field only. Suppose you want to find all the employees whose salaries lie in the range 3000 to 6000.

1 In the same list as above, make sure that the AutoFilter is on, but that all the filters are set to (All).

2 In the Salary field, select (Custom…).

3 In the first box, select 'is less than or equal to'. (You may have to scroll down the list to find this option.)

4 In the box to the right of this, enter 6000.

5 Below the box make sure that 'And' is selected.

6 In the bottom box, select 'is greater than or equal to'.

7 In the box to the right of this, enter 3000. Click on *OK*.

8 The list should now display those employees who earn from 3000 to 6000.

CHECK YOUR PROGRESS

	A	B	C	
	A	**B**	**C**	
1	Employee	Sex	Salary	Age
2	Allan	Male	5600	26
3	Mary	Female	3500	20
4	Peter	Male	2500	31
5	Triko	Female	6000	19
6	Mohan	Male	8000	28
7	Susan	Female	3500	22
8	Vick	Male	5400	28
9	Tota	Male	4500	32
10	Amrita	Female	6500	35

Fig 7.35

1 Add further data to your existing worksheet to match Fig 7.35.
2 Filter the data to find all male employees who are over 25 years and who earn more that 5000 in salary.
3 Find all employees who are Female or who earn less than 5000 in salary.

Advanced filtering

Sometimes after creating a large spreadsheet, we want to extract or filter and display the information that meets some criterion in a separate section. The Auto filter only allows you to display records in the same position by removing the rest of the data that does not meet the criterion. But the advanced filter allows you to display records in a separate section.

Before you learn about how to perform advanced filtering you need to understand some terms related to it:

List range: This is the table from which information will be extracted, including the column headings and rows containing data, but excluding title rows and total rows, if any.

Criteria range: This is where you set the criteria. The criteria range contains the column headings and the criteria under the correct column headings. This contains two or more rows based on the number of criteria you set.

Copy to range: This is where the records that meet the criteria will be displayed.

Consider the following spreadsheet:

	A	B	C	D	E
1	Sun & Sands				
2	Employee Salaries				
3	First Name	Last Name	Sex	Position	Salary
4	Allan	Isaac	Male	Manager	5600
5	Mary	Jane	Female	Asst. Manager	3500
6	Peter	Thomas	Male	Supervisor	2500
7	Triko	Matthew	Female	Asst. Manager	6000
8	Mohan	Walters	Male	Supervisor	8000
9	Total				25600
10					
11					
12					
13	First Name	Last Name	Sex	Position	Salary
14					>5000

Fig 7.36

Suppose you want to extract all *Male* employees whose salary is *more than 5000* in a separate section using advanced filtering from the spreadsheet above, you can use the following steps.

Using advanced filtering

1 Copy and paste the column headings to a blank area of the worksheet and set the criteria 'Male' under the Gender column and '>5000' under the salary column. Now your worksheet looks like this:

	A	B	C	D	E
1	Sun & Sands				
2	Employee Salaries				
3	First Name	Last Name	Sex	Position	Salary
4	Allan	Isaac	Male	Manager	5600
5	Mary	Jane	Female	Asst. Manager	3500
6	Peter	Thomas	Male	Supervisor	2500
7	Triko	Matthew	Female	Asst. Manager	6000
8	Mohan	Walters	Male	Supervisor	8000
9	Total				25600
10					
11					
12					
13	First Name	Last Name	Sex	Position	Salary
14					>5000

Fig 7.37

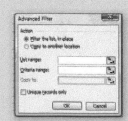

2 Select *Data* → *Filter* → *Advanced Filter* from the menu bar. You will get an advanced filter window that looks like this:

Fig 7.38

3 Select *Copy to another location* from the 'Action' section of the window that appears, as you want to display the records in another location. This will activate the third option *Copy to*.

Fig 7.39

4 Click inside the list range box and select the list range A3:E8 (remember that you need to exclude the title rows such as 'Sun & Sands', 'Employee Salaries', etc and total rows). The worksheet will look similar to Fig 7.40. Note the area being highlighted:

Fig 7.40

5 Now click inside the criteria range box and select the criteria range A13:E14 and the worksheet will look like this:

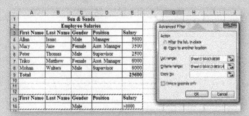

Fig 7.41

6 Click inside the 'Copy to' box and select a cell where you want to display the results of the filtering. In this example we have used A18. Now your worksheet looks like this:

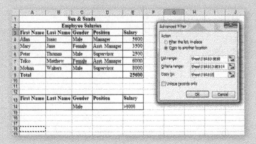

Fig 7.42

7 Click on *OK*. The rows that meet the criteria will be displayed and the spreadsheet will look like this:

Fig 7.43

Charts and graphs

Charts and graphs are used to present your data graphically. Charts can make your data easier to analyse than when it is in the spreadsheet format.

Many types of charts are available for presenting data in a spreadsheet. For this section, we will focus on three type of charts: line chart, bar or column chart, and pie chart

1 Line charts are used to plot trends or show changes over a period of time.

2 Bar or column charts are used to compare values at a given point in time. Like the line chart, it also shows variations over a period of time. The bar chart uses rectangular bars that run horizontally while the column chart uses rectangular bars that are vertical.

3 Pie charts are used to show the proportion of individual components that make up the total.

Fig 7.44: Illustration of a line chart

Fig. 7.45: Illustration of a bar chart and a column chart

Fig 7.46: Illustration of a pie chart

How to use charts in spreadsheets

	A	B	C	D
1	Program	2006	2007	2008
2	Certificate	256	365	289
3	Diploma	1280	1450	1190
4	Degree	590	860	380
5	Total	2126	2675	1859

Fig 7.47

Suppose we want to create charts to show the total graduates for each year, we can use a line chart or a column chart. To show what percentage of the total graduates for one year were accounted for by each program, we can use a pie chart.

Creating a pie chart

1 Set up the worksheet as shown in Fig 7.47. The years 2006, 2007 and 2008 are labels, not numbers, so you should enter them as '2006 etc.

2 Enter the numerical data for cells B2:D4. Use a formula to calculate the value in B5.

3 Copy this formula to C5 and D5. Check that all the totals match those shown.

4 Go to *Insert* → *Chart*, or click on the Chart Wizard button.

5 Under chart type, select *Pie*. Click *Next*.

6 You will see a box labelled 'Data Range'. This will contain the cells where the data and titles are held. On the worksheet itself, select cells A2:B4.

7 Under 'Chart Title' insert an appropriate title, e.g. 'Programs in 2006'. Click *Next*.

8 Indicate if you want to have the chart on a new sheet or as an object to the same sheet.

9 Click on *Finish*.

The pie chart will look like Fig 7.48.

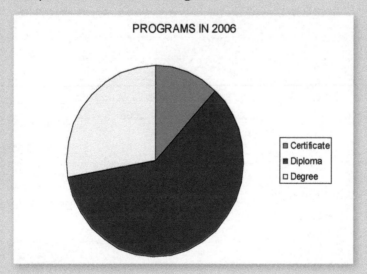

Fig 7.48: A pie chart

Creating a line chart

For this chart we will use the data in the range B5:D5, and the titles in the range B1:D1 from Fig 7.47.

1 Go to *Insert* → *Chart*, or click on the Chart Wizard button.

2 Under chart type, select *Line*. Click *Next*.

3 Click on the 'Series' tab.

4 Click on the 'Values' box, then select cells B5:D5 on the worksheet. This is the range with the total for each year.

5 Click in the 'Category (X) axis label' box, then select B1:D1 on the worksheet. This is the range with the year headings. Click *Next*.

6 Under 'Chart Title' insert an appropriate title e.g. GRADUATES PER YEAR.

7 Use appropriate labels to label the X-axis and the Y-axis, e.g. YEAR and GRADUATES. Click *Next*.

8 Indicate if you want to have the chart on a new sheet or as on object to the same sheet.

9 Click on *Finish*.

The line chart will look like Fig 7.49.

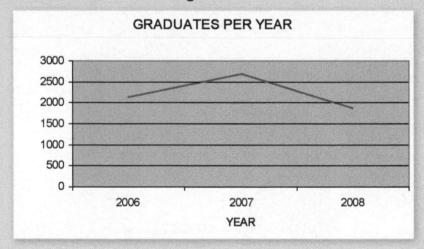

Fig 7.49: Line chart

Creating a bar or column chart is similar to creating a line chart. In Step 2, select *Bar* or *Column* instead of *Line*.

The column chart for the worksheet in Fig 7.47 will look like Fig 7.50 below.

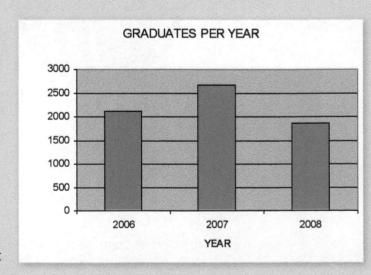

Fig 7.50: A column chart

Modifying a chart

1 Select the chart.

2 Go to *Insert* → *Chart*, or click on the Chart Wizard button.

3 You can now select a different chart type, change the range, or amend the labels and title.

4 Select *Finish*.

Moving a chart

1 Select the chart.

2 Drag it to its new location.

Deleting a chart

1 Right click on the chart.

2 Select *Clear* to delete the chart.

CHECK YOUR PROGRESS

The number of registered IPv6 addresses by country is given in the worksheet in Fig 7.51 below.

Country	Country Code	IPv6 addresses
Germany	DE	9500
Japan	JP	8300
Australia	AU	8210
United Kingdom	UK	1200
United States of America	US	1100

Fig 7.51

Although you do not have to understand IPv6 addresses in order follow this example, you might be interested to know that an IP address is a way of labeling a computer in a network, and that IPv6 is the latest protocol.

In a new worksheet, create a pie chart to show the number of IPv6 addresses registered by each country. The pie chart should have the title, 'IPv6 Addresses by Country'. Each slice of the pie chart should be properly labeled to indicate the country it represents or a legend should be provided. Each slice of the pie chart should indicate the percentage of total IPv6 addresses registered.

How to manipulate multiple worksheets

Often, you will create a worksheet and want to use data that is in another worksheet. The spreadsheet program allows you to link data in multiple worksheets.

As an example, let us make a spreadsheet consisting of three worksheets named Jan, Feb and Year as indicated in Fig. 7.52. The 'Jan' and 'Feb' worksheets will store the items exported and the value of the exports for each month, respectively. Now we want the 'Year' worksheet to store the total exports for each month. In this case, cells in the worksheet 'Year' will have to be linked with cells in the worksheets 'Jan' and 'Feb' as indicated in Fig 7.53.

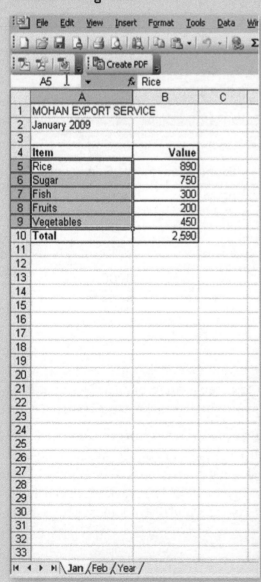

Fig 7.52: A spreadsheet with three worksheets

In the above example, we want to link the cells containing the total exports for the 'Jan' and 'Feb' worksheets to cells in the worksheet 'Year'. Observe that Cell B10 in the 'Jan' and 'Feb' worksheets have the total exports for each month.

Linking worksheets

1 Identify the cells in the 'Jan' and 'Feb' worksheets to be linked with worksheet 'Year'. In this exercise, Cell B10 in worksheet 'Jan' and Cell B10 in worksheet 'Feb' will be linked to worksheet 'Year'.

2 In the 'Year' worksheet identify the cells where the linked data will be placed. In this case, Cell B10 of the 'Jan' worksheet will be placed in cell B6 of the 'Year' worksheet and Cell B10 of the 'Feb' worksheet will be placed in cell B7 of the 'Year' worksheet.

3 In cell B6 of the 'Year' worksheet, enter the formula =Jan!B10, and in cell B7 of the 'Year' worksheet, enter the formula =Feb!B10.

Observe the format of the link formula =Jan!B10. The formula contains the name of the worksheet (Jan), followed by an exclamation mark (!) and followed by the cell in the 'Jan' worksheet (B10). Note also that if any value in the 'Jan' or 'Feb' worksheets is changed then the value of the cell with the link formula in the 'Year' worksheet will be updated automatically.

	A	B	C
1	MOHAN EXPORT SERVICE		
2	January 2009		
3			
4	Item	Value	
5	Rice	890	
6	Sugar	750	
7	Fish	300	
8	Fruits	200	
9	Vegetables	450	
10	Total	2,590	

Fig 7.53: The 'year' spreadsheet with cells linked to 'Jan' and 'Feb' worksheets

CHECK YOUR PROGRESS

Create a spreadsheet and name it 'College.xls'. This spreadsheet should have two worksheets named 'Student' and 'Fees'. The 'Student' worksheet is given in Fig 7.54 below.

Surname	First name	Sex	Department	Credits
Singh	Mohan	M	Computer Science	32
James	Allan	M	Mathematics	20
Monroe	Mary	F	History	28
Ally	Miriam	F	Sociology	24
White	Michael	M	Chemistry	30

Fig 7.54

The 'Fees' worksheet should have the same data as the 'Student' worksheet but without the 'Sex' and 'Department' columns. Use the link formula to copy the relevant data from the 'Student' worksheet. Add a column to the 'Fees' worksheet with the heading 'Tuition' and compute the tuition paid by each student. The tuition paid by each student is obtained by the formula, Tuition = credits * 4000.

In a blank area of the worksheet, enter the following data in different cells of the same column:
Total Tuition
Maximum Credits
Minimum Tuition
Enter the appropriate formulae in the cells to the right of the new text above to perform the computation.

How to import graphics and tables

Sometimes it may be necessary to insert graphics and tables into a worksheet from a source outside the spreadsheet program. For example, we may want to import a graphic file containing a logo, a database table or another worksheet.

Importing graphics

1 Go to *Insert* → *Picture* → *From file*.

2 Find and select the picture you want to insert.

3 Click on *Insert*.

4 Move the picture to the required location and resize it if necessary.

Tables created from other programs such as spreadsheet or database programs can be imported into an existing worksheet.

Importing tables

1 Select the cell in the worksheet where you want the imported data to be inserted.

2 Go to *Data* → *Import external data* → *Import data*.

3 Select the location of the file you want to import.

4 Select the file type and the file to be imported.

5 Click *Open*. If you are importing from a spreadsheet you will have to indicate which worksheet to open.

6 Click *OK*.

CHECK YOUR PROGRESS

1 Create the following spreadsheet, starting at cell A1 and save it as 'Course.xls'.

Semester 1	Semester 2	Summer
4	4	2

2 Create a new spreadsheet, starting at cell A1 with the following data and save it as 'Credit.xls'.

Semester 1	Semester 2	Summer
16	12	4

3 Open the spreadsheet 'Course.xls' and import the spreadsheet 'Credit.xls' to begin in cell A10.

End-of-section questions

Multiple choice questions

1 A group of adjacent cells in a spreadsheet is known as:
   A A worksheet   B A template
   C A range   D A record

2 All text entries into the spreadsheet are known as:
   A Values   B String
   C Labels   D Characters

3 By default, numerical entries into the spreadsheet are aligned:
   A Left   B Right
   C Centre   D Justified

4 If cell address contains B7, it is what type of a cell reference?
   A Mixed   B Relative
   C Absolute   D Combined

5 All of the following are formatting of numeric values in a spreadsheet except:
   A General   B Custom
   C Percentage   D Value

Structured questions

1 Give the meanings of the following terms as they relate to a spreadsheet:
   a Cell   b Formula
   c Range   d Cell address

2 a List five commonly used spreadsheet functions.
   b State the purpose of each of the functions you identified in your answer to 2a.

3 a State the difference between relative referencing and absolute referencing.
   b Give one example of a cell with relative referencing.
   c Give one example of a cell with absolute referencing.

4 a List five types of formatting that can be applied to numeric values.
   b State the purpose of each of the types of formatting you identified in your answer to 4a.

5 List the steps in creating a chart in a spreadsheet.

Practice SBA

The Treasurer of the Caribbean Sports Club (CSC) wants to use a spreadsheet package to create, manipulate and monitor the club's finances.

There are 25 members in the club. There are different categories of member and each category attracts a different rate of membership fee. The membership rates remained the same for the period 2003–2009. Based on the category of membership, members have different responsibilities and privileges. The categories of membership with current rates are given in Table SBA1.

Category	Code	Rate per month
Regular	R	$50
Special	S	$100
Gold	G	$150
Platinum	P	$200

Table SBA1

You are required to:
Create a spreadsheet with at least three worksheets that will enable the treasurer of the CSC to view the members' payment details and income and expenses. Your design must be easy to follow.

Task A

1 On a worksheet store the data given in the table above.

2 On a second worksheet, create information on each of the 25 members' payments for the last five years with at least five members in each category. The members should be sorted by last name then by first name. For each member, the club maintains a history of payments based on their category, by year. For example, member Jason Browne would have payment details from 2005 to 2009. These records will indicate how much money was paid for each of those years and how much is still outstanding.

3 In the Payments area of the spreadsheet, create a column called **Status**. Based on each member's payments it should display 'Outstanding' if they owe money for fees and 'Paid', if they paid their dues.

4 In 2010, it was decided that if a member has outstanding fees, he or she would be charged 25% of the outstanding amount as a fine. On a separate section of the spreadsheet, create a summary section with the following information.
  a The largest amount outstanding by any one member.
  b The number of people with an outstanding amount.
  c The total amount due for the five years, total amount paid, total amount outstanding, total fines owed by members.
  d The average amount outstanding.

5 Save your worksheet as Task(A).

Task B

1 Jason Browne is no longer a part of the club as he has migrated to Canada. Remove him from the spreadsheet. Save the spreadsheet as TaskB1.

2 The Club Treasurer has decided to change the fine rate for outstanding fees to 34.5%. Adjust this rate in your spreadsheet. Save the spreadsheet as TaskB2.

3 Sort the worksheets by the amount outstanding. Save the spreadsheet as TaskB3.

4 Create a complex criterion to select all information on members who have an outstanding status and are in the Special category. Save the spreadsheet as TaskB4.

5 Create a graph showing the total membership dues collected each year for the period 2005–2009. Save your spreadsheet as TaskB5.

6 Print all the formulae or functions used.

Objectives

By the end of this section, you will be able to:

- Explain the concept of a database and the terms used in files and databases.
- List the advantages and disadvantages of using databases over files.
- Identify MS Access as a database program.
- Create databases and modify the structure of tables.
- Add, delete and change field definitions.
- Sort a database on given field(s).
- Establish relationships for linking or joining tables.
- Use queries to search for information.
- Create queries with calculated fields and summary information.
- Create forms for entering data in a structured way.
- Create queries using tables to search for particular information.
- Create reports using tables or queries.

Early computers were mainly used to solve complicated scientific and mathematical problems. Now computers are used in almost every field to store and process data. Database management systems can be used to store data in databases and to search for and display the data as meaningful information.

Some databases are very simple, and can be represented by a single table. Database management systems allow us to create more complex databases, in which different types of data are linked together. These are known as relational databases.

All the step-by-step instructions in this section refer to Microsoft Access, and the diagrams were created in that package. However, you can gain the same skills by using any available database management system, such as Filemaker or Corel Paradox. Check the buttons in the toolbars and the options in the menus to find the equivalent functions.

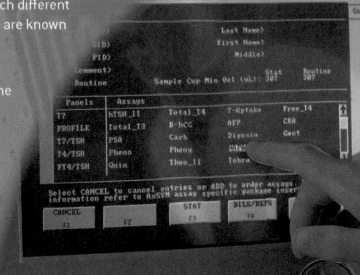

Database management systems

A **database** is a place where data can be stored and retrieved. Data can be stored manually, such as in a filing cabinet with many drawers at your school. Each drawer might contain different files of different things, like your marks, attendance and personal details. Other examples of manual databases include the phone book, patient information at a hospital, library catalogues, and national voter information.

The manual storage of information has the following disadvantages:

1 Data is often duplicated.

2 It is time-consuming to retrieve records.

3 Inconsistency of data.

4 Data cannot be shared easily.

So database programs or database management systems were developed to make the storage and retrieval of information faster and easier. In computerised databases, data can be stored in a structured and organised way so that data can be retrieved much faster. They also require less space than manual databases such as filing cabinets. Examples of popular database programs are Microsoft Access, Corel Project, Lotus Approach and Oracle.

Database management systems have some advantages and disadvantages. The advantages are:

- Information can be retrieved faster in ad hoc situations using queries.

- You can design and create your own queries with minimal knowledge of databases.

- There are reduced updating errors and increased consistency as data is in a standardised form.

- Data duplication is reduced.

- Data entry, storage and retrieval costs are reduced.

- Security of data is increased.

- You are able to present multiple views of data using report features.

The following are some disadvantages of database management systems:

- They are more time-consuming to design than a manual database.

- Initial training is required.

- Suitable hardware and software are needed to run the program.

- They can be expensive to buy and maintain.

Before you learn about the database programs in detail, it would be good to get a clear picture of certain database terms and concepts.

WHAT DOES IT MEAN?

database
A database is an organised collection of related information such as the accounting details of a company. It provides easy and fast storage and retrieval of information.

Fig 8.1: A filing cabinet – an example of a manual database

Basic terms/concepts used in a database

Databases contain data about things in the real world. An **entity** is a type of item about which data is stored in a database. Examples of entities can be a physical object such as a house or a car, an event such as a house sale or a car service, or a concept such as a customer transaction or order.

Each entity has **attributes**. These are the properties of an entity. For example, an entity 'house' could have the attributes 'address' and 'year built'. The combination of all the attributes of one entity is known as a **tuple**, such as all the data about one house.

The terms entity, attribute and tuple are rather abstract. Once we are working in a database program you will see that we use the terms record instead of tuple and field instead of attribute.

WHAT DOES IT MEAN?

entity
An entity is an item in the real world that is represented in a database.

attribute
The individual properties of an entity are called its attributes. An attribute is represented by a field in a database.

tuple
The details about a particular entity are called a tuple. A tuple is represented by a record in a database.

We usually group information about lots of similar entities together in a database. For example, we could store information about a number of houses that are for sale. We will be storing such information in a table.

Database management software

In this book we will use the program Microsoft Access 2003 to learn about database management systems. Access 2003 is a very flexible program that can be used for both simple and complex databases. It is also a **relational database**, which means the various components of the database can be linked together by setting relationships among them.

WHAT DOES IT MEAN?

relational database
A relational database is a database that contains more than one table with tables sharing data among them by having a link (relationship) between them.

Starting Microsoft Access 2003

You can launch Access 2003 in many ways. The following are two common methods:

Method 1: Click on *Start* ➜ *Microsoft Office* ➜ *Microsoft Access 2003*

Method 2: Double click on the *Microsoft Access 2003* icon on the desktop.

You will see the screen as in Fig 8.2 below.

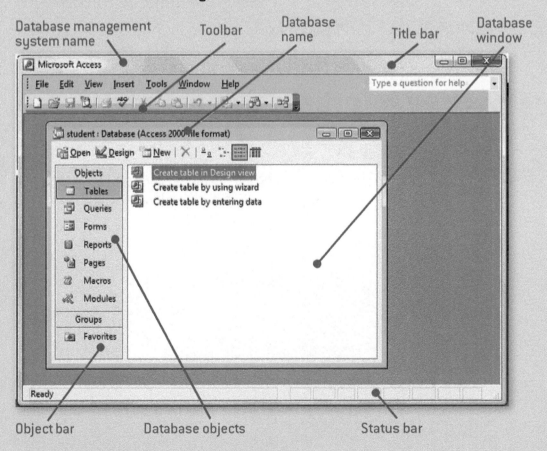

Fig 8.2: The database window in Microsoft Access

When you create an Access database, the window being displayed is called the database window, which shows the name of the database. This window has title bar, toolbar and status bar similar to Microsoft Excel and Word. It also has an object bar with objects like tables, queries, forms, reports, pages, macros and modules. In this book, we will concentrate only on tables, queries, forms and reports.

Toolbars in Access 2003

Toolbars are shortcut buttons of commonly used commands that help us to perform actions in a faster way. Fig 8.3 shows the main icons that are present in the toolbar of Access 2003.

new database file | save a file | print | cut | paste | office links – link with other applications like Word/Excel | relationships – used to link tables

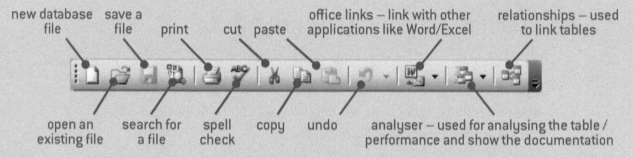

open an existing file | search for a file | spell check | copy | undo | analyser – used for analysing the table / performance and show the documentation

Fig 8.3: The Access toolbar

How to create a new database

Creating a new database

1 Launch Access 2003 using either of the methods identified on page 369. Now your screen will appear with a task pane at the right. It should look like Fig 8.4 below.

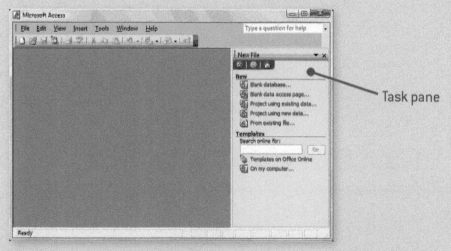

Task pane

Fig 8.4: The New File task pane

2 Choose *Blank database* from the task pane. Then a new window will appear where you have to provide the name for the database and the location where you want to store it, as shown in Fig 8.5.

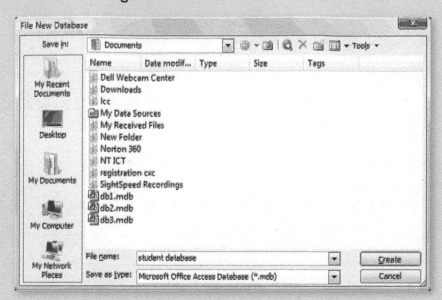

Fig 8.5: Creating a new database

3 Click on *Create* and a new database will be created in the location specified.

Tables and the information they contain

Now the database you have created acts as a filing cabinet for the storage of information about entities. You need to decide how many drawers (in the case of a filing cabinet) or files you need in which to place the information or records. The individual files that are created are called **tables**. Tables are used in word processing and in spreadsheets, but they have a much more precise meaning in databases. In relational databases, tables are also known as relations. You will learn how to create tables in just a moment.

Many tables can be found in a database, each storing a particular type of information – for example a student database may contain personal details, fees details and attendance details. In order to create a **record** of a student, you need to complete the details on a pre-designed form. The form would contain words or phrases (for example, First

WHAT DOES IT MEAN?

table

A table is a collection of records, made of a set of rows and columns. The information you enter into the database will be stored in a table. In relational databases, tables are also known as relations.

record

A record is a collection of related fields. It contains a single row and many columns. In relational databases, records are also known as tuples.

Name) with spaces after them to fill in. In Access, the individual words or phrases used in a table are called the **fields**. When the fields of a particular row are completed, it becomes a record.

The form requesting information would indicate what type of information it requires and in what format. For example, for a Date of Birth field you might indicate that the information should be given in the format mm/dd/yyyy. Similarly, in Access, it is important that you set the **field type** or **data type** for each field.

The main data types used in Access 2003 are text, number, currency, date/time, autonumber, memo, and yes/no. Table 8.1 shows the purpose of the different data types in Access.

Data Type	Purpose
Text	Used to store alphanumeric characters (letters or numbers) up to 255 characters. Examples include 'name', 'address', 'phone number' and 'country'.
Number	Used to store numbers with or without decimal places. Examples include 'age', 'quantity' and 'average'.
Currency	Used to store money values. Examples include 'salary', 'price' and 'discount'.
Date/Time	Used to store date/time type values. Examples include 'date of birth', 'purchase date' and 'date joined'.
Autonumber	Creates automatic numbers, such as an ID Number.
Memo	Used to store blocks of text like notes up to 65536 characters long. Examples include 'remarks' and 'project details'.
Yes/No	Used for storing a yes or no value. Examples include 'available' and 'passed'.

Table 8.1

Sometimes you need to explain what each field represents. For example, you might have a field named 'Fees' and you need the user of the database to be aware that they should enter the fee that has been paid for one term. To do this, you would use a **field description** that states 'Fee paid for one term'.

On a form you fill in by hand there are only an adequate number of spaces to fill in each field. For example, a field that will store a number representing a person's age does not need the same amount of characters as a field to store an address. Similarly, in Access, you can specify the space for certain fields such as text and number. This is known as its **field size**.

In Access, there are default field sizes and a maximum limit for each data type. The text and number data types can be altered, but other the types are pre-set. The default field size of the Text data type is 50 characters. But sometimes your field may not need so many characters. For example, the field 'First name' can be set to 20, as the maximum number of characters that first name would contain is unlikely to be more than 20 characters.

For the Number data type, the field size can be set to byte, integer, long integer, single, double or decimal. The default setting for Number is long integer. The most commonly used field sizes of Number data type are *Long integer* and *Double*.

- Byte – used to store integer values between 0 and 255 without decimal places.
- Integer – used to store integer values between -32,768 to 32,767 without decimal places.
- Long integer – used to store integer values between approximately -2 billion and +2 billion *without* any decimal places. If you enter any values with decimal values, it will be rounded off to next whole number.
- Decimal – stores numbers from $-9.999... \times 10^{27}$ to $+9.999... \times 10^{27}$ with decimal places.
- Single – stores numbers from -3.4×10^{38} to $+3.4 \times 10^{38}$ with decimal places.
- Double – stores numbers from -1.797×10^{308} to $+1.797 \times 10^{308}$ with decimal places.

CHECK YOUR PROGRESS

1 List six data types used in Microsoft Access.
2 Suggest an appropriate data type for the following fields:
   a Salary
   b Details of an accident
   c Date of visit
   d Absent
   e Location
3 What is the default field size of the Text type data?
4 What is the difference between long integer and double field sizes of Number?

Creating tables

Table structures

Before you create a table in your database, it would be wise for you to plan what you want it to contain. You need to think about the field names, field types and field sizes. Such a plan is called the **table structure**.

For example, if you want to create a table called 'Personal Details' that stores the name, address, date of birth, age, gender, average mark, passed and fees rate of students, you might create a table structure like Table 8.2.

Notice that you have to split the name into First name and Last name fields. That is because you want to sort the records on the last name only, which would not be possible if the whole name is stored on one held. As mentioned earlier, for fields like date of birth, passed, fees rate and currency, the field size is not needed as their field sizes are pre-set.

Field name	Field type	Field Size
First name	Text	20
Last name	Text	20
Date of birth	Date/Time	Pre-set field size
Age	Number	Long integer
Gender	Text	10
Average mark	Number	Long integer
Passed	Yes/No	Pre-set field size
Fees rate	Currency	Pre-set field size

Table 8.2

Creating tables in Access

Once you have completed the table structure, you can create your database table in Access.

If you click on *Tables* in the Objects pane, you will be given three options for creating tables:

1 Create table in Design view.

2 Create table by using wizard.

3 Create table by entering data.

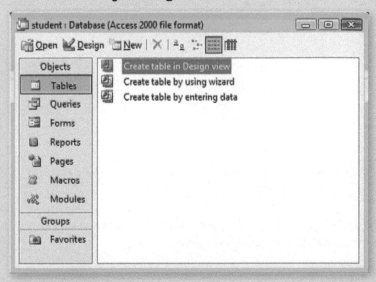

Fig 8.6: Options for creating tables

The first option, *Create table in Design view*, allows you to create the table with your choice of field names, descriptions and field sizes. The second option, *Create table by using wizard*, allows you to create a table by following the instructions provided by the table wizard dialogue boxes. The *Create table by entering data* option, allows you to enter data first and then do all the formatting needed.

Creating a table in Design view

1 Double click on the option *Create table in Design view* from the database window. A new window called a Table window will appear that will allow you to enter the field name, field type, description and size, as shown in Fig 8.7.

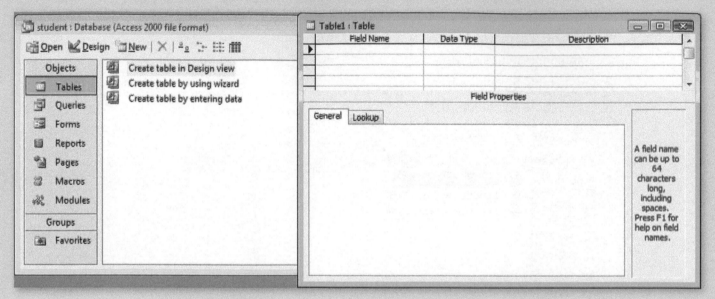

Fig 8.7: The Table window

2 Enter your field names and choose appropriate data types that can be chosen from a pulled down menu as shown in Fig 8.8 below.

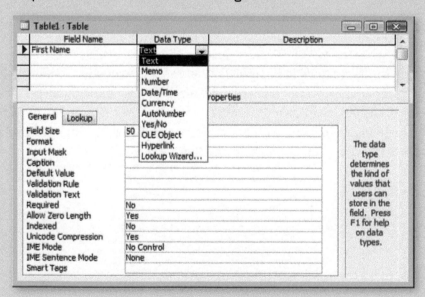

Fig 8.8: Data type options in the pull-down menu

3 Set the field size to the required amount of characters.

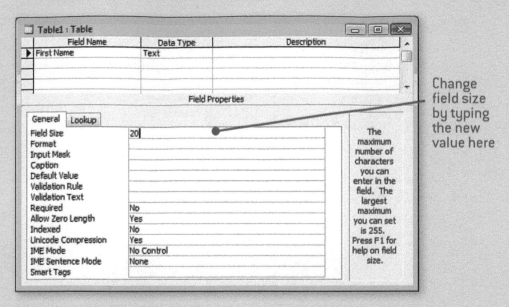

Fig 8.9: Setting the field size

4 Repeat steps 1–3 until you finish entering all the field names, data types and field sizes.

5 Once you have completed all the fields, close the window. A dialogue box will appear to ask you whether you want to save the table, as shown in Fig 8.10.

Fig 8.10: Saving the table

Choose *Yes* to save the table structure so that you can enter records into the table.

6 A new dialogue box will appear asking you to give a name for the table. Give it a name (in the example, it is called 'Personal Details') and choose *OK*.

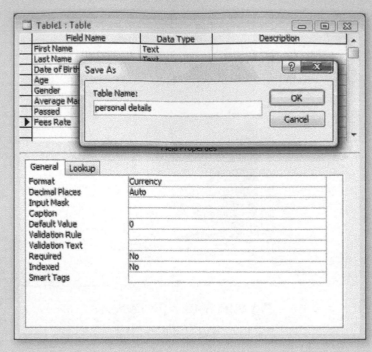

Fig 8.11: Naming the table

7 Now another dialogue box will appear asking whether you want Access to set a primary key, as in Fig 8.12 below.

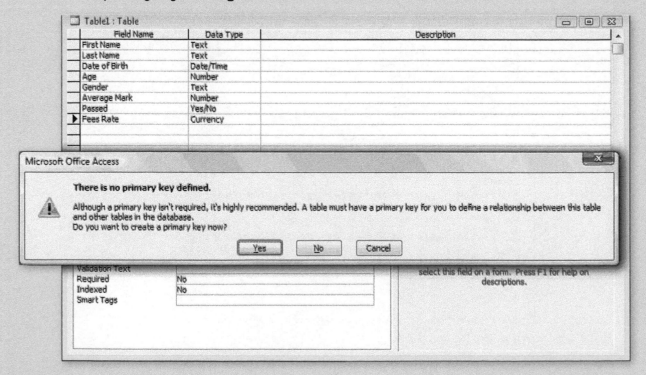

Fig 8.12: Dialogue about primary key

If you choose *Yes*, Access will set a primary key with the field name ID and the field type as Autonumber as in Fig 8.13.

Primary
key set
by Access

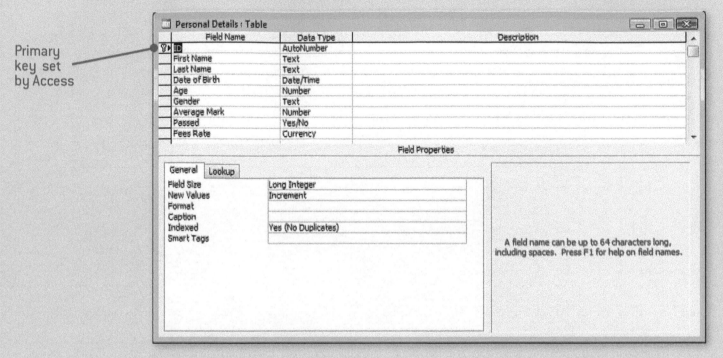

Fig 8.13: Setting the primary key

But you might want to create a primary key of your own, such as Student ID. So choose *No* so that you can create your own primary key later.

8 Now you have a table named 'Personal Details' in the database window as demonstrated in Fig 8.14 below:

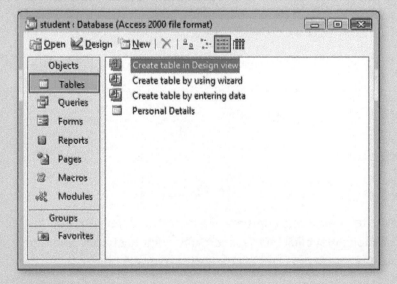

Fig 8.14: Personal details table

Entering data into a table

Entering data

1 Double click on the table that you have created. A window with a row for entering a record appears with the field names as the column headings, as shown in Fig 8.15. Enter your record by typing in each cell of the table and use the right arrow key or tab key to go to the next cell.

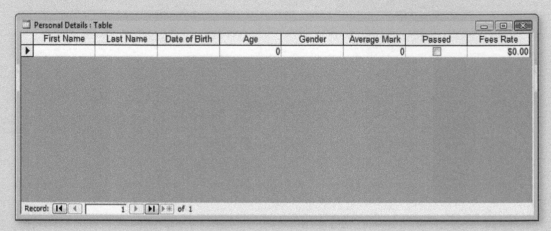

Fig 8.15: Viewing the data in a table

2 When you finish entering one record, a new row automatically appears for entering another record. Once you finish entering records, just close the window.

	First Name	Last Name	Date of Birth	Age	Gender	Average Mark	Passed	Fees Rate
	John	Browne	14/02/1995	15	Male	47	☐	$50.00
	Mary	Jane	03/12/1993	17	Female	71	☑	$75.00
✎	Tom	Jack	13/03/1994	16	Male	72	☑	$0.00
✳				0		0	☐	$0.00

Record: ◀◀ ◀   3 ▶ ▶▶ ▶✳ of 3

Fig 8.16: Entering a new record

Row for entering new record

Modifying records in a table

You may have to change the contents of a record, or delete a particular record. In order to modify your table, just click on the record you want to change and type in the new value. For example, suppose you want to change the average mark of Mary Jane to 75 in Fig 8.16, click on the cell containing her average mark and type in the new amount.

Deleting records from a table

Deleting records

1 Select the record by clicking on the row button on the left.

2 Choose the *Delete* key from the keyboard or right click and choose *Delete Record*.

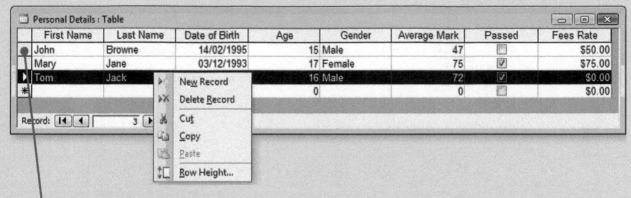

Row butons

Fig 8.17: Deleting a row

3 A dialogue box appears asking if you want to confirm the deletion (as seen in Fig 8.18), because you would not be able to undo the deleted operation. Choose *Yes* to delete the record or choose *No* if you accidentally selected to delete it.

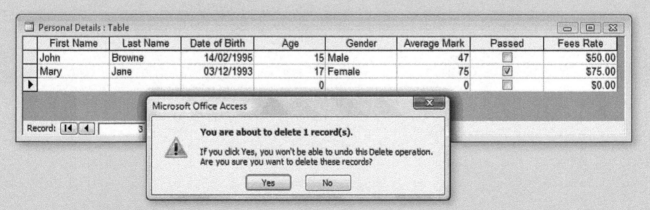

Fig 8.18: Confirming a deletion

4 Close the table to automatically save the changes.

CHECK YOUR PROGRESS

1 a In Access 2003, create a database named 'Storms' to store the storm details for the hurricane season 2008. In the database, create a table named 'Hurricanes' with the following structure.

Field name	Data type	Field size	Description
StormName	Text	20	Name of the storm
Origin	Text	20	Place of origin of storm
Date of origin	Date/Time		Date storm was formed
Category	Number	Long integer	Category of storm (1 to 5)
Major hurricane	Yes/No		Whether the storm became major hurricane or not

b Enter the following records into the table.

StormName	Origin	Date of origin	Category	Major hurricane
Bertha	Coast of Africa	03/07/08	3	Yes
Dolly	Caribbean Sea	20/07/08	2	No
Gustav	Windward Islands	25/08/08	4	Yes
Hanna	Leeward Islands	28/08/07	2	No
Kyle	Caribbean Sea	29/09/07	2	No

c Change the category of hurricane Kyle to 1 instead of 2.

How to modify the table structure

You might have to modify the structure of a table for various reasons, such as to:

- add a new field.
- delete a field.
- change the field type/size/description of an existing field.

Adding a new field or deleting a field

In order to add a new field or delete a field, you need to open the table in Design view. You can do this using either of the following methods.

Method 1: Right click on the table and select the *Design view* option, as shown in Fig 8.19.

Fig 8.19: How to open the table in Design view – Method 1

Method 2: Select the table and choose the *Design* icon that appears in the database window.

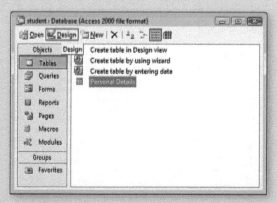

Fig 8.20: How to open the table in Design view – Method 2

Adding a new field

Once you open the table in Design view, you can add a field in a new row or in between the fields.

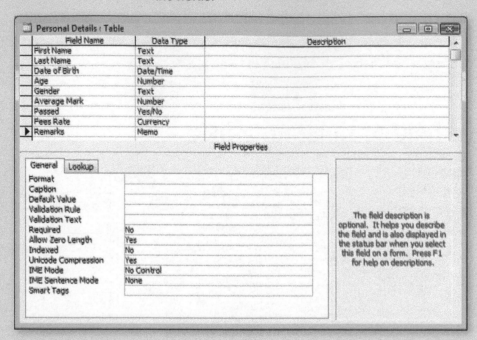

Fig 8.21: Adding a new field

1 Click on the new row after the last field to select it.

2 Type in the field name, data type, and field size as in Fig 8.21. As you can see, a new field called 'Remarks' with the data type 'Memo' was created in a new row.

3 Close the table and choose *Yes* to save the table with changes.

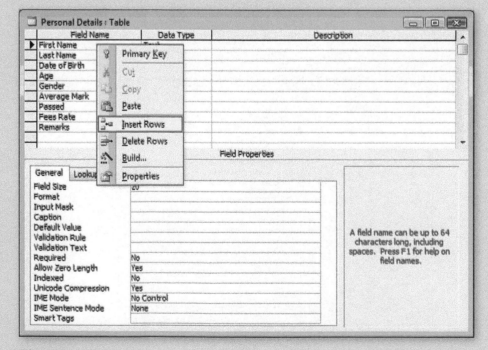

Fig 8.22: Inserting a new row in a table in Design view

Inserting a new field

Suppose you want to insert a new field called 'StudentID' at the first row to store the identification numbers of students. You can use the following steps:

1 Click on the row 'First Name' as you want your row to be inserted above it.

2 Right click on the row containing 'First Name' to get a pop-up window with options for inserting or deleting rows.

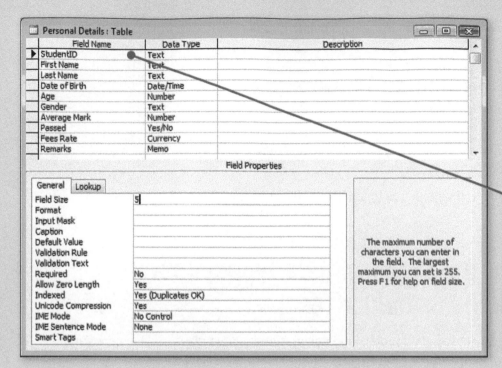

Fig 8.23: A new field is added

3 Choose the *Insert Rows* option, as shown in Fig 8.22.

You will get a blank row for you to type in the field name 'StudentID', as in Fig 8.23. You can also set the field name, data type and field size for the new field.

New row being created

4 Close the table and choose *Yes* for saving the table with changes.

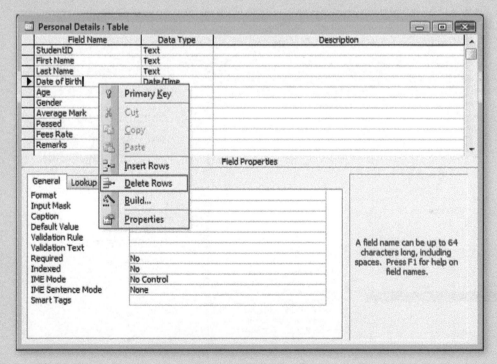

Fig 8.24: The pop-up menu to delete a row

Deleting fields

Suppose you want to delete the field 'Remarks'.

1 Select the 'Remarks' row and right click on it to get a pop-up window with options for inserting or deleting rows, as shown in Fig 8.24.

2 Choose the *Delete Rows* option.

3 A dialogue box will appear as in Fig 8.25 below. Choose *Yes* to confirm the deletion.

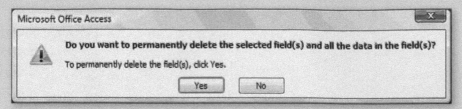

Fig 8.25: Confirming a deletion

4 Close the table and choose *Yes* to save the table with changes.

Changing field names, data types, field descriptions or field sizes

Changing the field names, data types, field descriptions or field sizes involves the same steps that you used in adding a new field.

Changing field size

Suppose you want to change the field size of the field 'Average mark' to double so that it can hold decimal places. You would use the following steps:

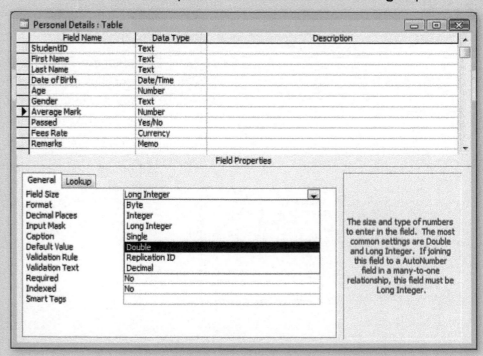

1 Open the table in Design view.

2 Choose the field 'Average mark' by clicking on the row containing it and select *Double* as shown in Fig 8.26.

3 Close the table and choose *Yes* to save the changes.

Fig 8.26: Changing the field size

CHECK YOUR PROGRESS

1 a Modify the structure of the database table 'Hurricane' that you created earlier to include a 'Fatality' with a Yes/No value as the last field.

b Enter the following data in the Fatality field.

StormName	Fatality
Bertha	No
Dolly	No
Gustav	Yes
Hanna	Yes
Kyle	No

c Modify the structure of the database again to include a field description for the field 'Fatality'. The field description should be *whether storm lead to deaths*.

Sorting a database table

Sorting means putting records together in a meaningful order such as ascending order, (A–Z or smallest to largest) or descending order (Z–A or largest to smallest) in alphabetical, numerical or date format. Sorting can be done in a table using one field or more than one field.

Sorting a table using one field

To sort a table on a single field, use the following steps:

1 Open the table by double clicking on it. Highlight the field you want to sort on by clicking on the column name at the top of the column.

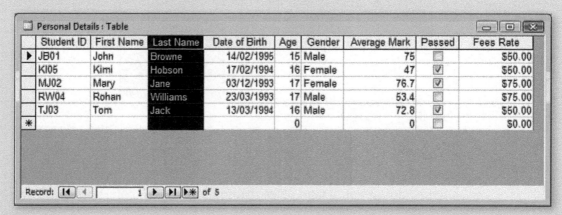

Fig 8.27: Highlighting a field

2 Right click on the highlighted area or choose the sort icon ⬇ for ascending order and ⬆ for descending order from the toolbar, as shown in Fig 8.28. The table will be sorted in the order you specified.

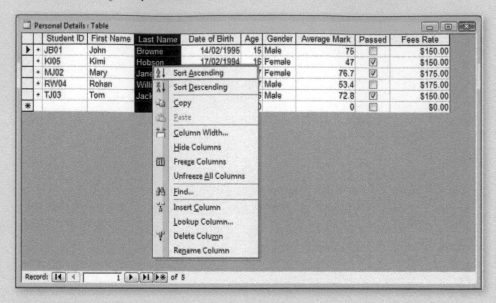

Fig 8.28: Sorting the table

Sorting a table in two or more fields

Suppose you want to sort the table by the 'Age' field and then by the 'Gender' field in ascending order. You can use the following steps:

1 Highlight both fields that you wish to sort by.

2 Choose the sort icon ⬇ from the toolbar for sorting in ascending order (if you want to sort in descending order choose icon ⬆ from the toolbar). The table will be sorted in ascending order of age first and then in ascending order of gender in alphabetical order as displayed in Fig 8.29.

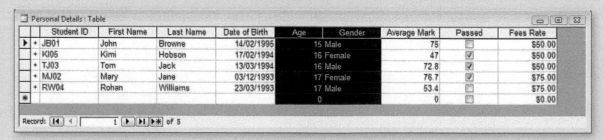

Fig 8.29: Sorting with two fields

Note: Ensure that the first sort key ('Age') is placed before the second sort key ('Gender') as the sorting would take place starting with the left column that is being highlighted.

Primary keys

A **primary key field** is a field that acts as a unique identifier for each record in a table. That means that the data in this field must only appear once in the whole table. For example, in a table containing details of bank accounts, the account number would uniquely identify each account. In other words, each account has its own account number, and the same account number is never used for more than one account.

In our example, in the table called 'Personal Details' the student ID number can be considered as a primary key because it uniquely identifies a student. (No other student should have the same student ID number.)

In many cases, codes and numbers are used for primary keys. If a table holds data about people you might think that you could use each person's name as the primary key, but this will not work because two people may have the same name.

WHAT DOES IT MEAN?

primary key field
A primary key field is a field that acts as a unique identifier for each record in a table.

Setting a primary key field

1 Open the 'Personal Details' table in Design view.

2 Right click on the 'StudentID' field and choose the *Primary Key* option or select the primary key icon 🔑 from the toolbar, as in Fig 8.30.

3 Close the database window and choose *OK* to save the changes.

Fig 8.30: Setting the primary key field

Candidate, secondary and composite keys

It is sometimes difficult to decide which field should act as the primary key field for a table. We need to look carefully at the fields and identify which could possibly act as a primary key, and then choose the best one for the job.

These terms are used to help us decide which field to use as the primary key:

- **Candidate key** – Candidate keys are the possible fields that can be used as a primary key field. In a table, there can be more than one field that can be chosen as a primary key. For example, in a table containing details of employees, you can have a choice of employee ID and employee registration number as the primary key. Each of these fields can be considered as a candidate key.

- **Secondary key or Alternative key** – A candidate key that is not being used as a primary key is called secondary key or alternate key. For example, if the employee ID and employee registration number are the candidate keys in a table called 'Employee' and you choose employee ID as the primary key, the employee registration number is a secondary key or alternate key.

- **Composite key** – Sometimes you need to use two or more fields together to form a primary key. For example, a table called 'Phone directory' has fields containing the phone numbers and telephone country codes of the phones used by people working for an international organisation. It is possible for two phones in different countries to have the same phone number, but the combination of country code and phone number will be unique for each phone, so could act as a composite key.

> ## WHAT DOES IT MEAN?
>
> **candidate key**
> A candidate key is a field that could possibly act as the primary key for the table.
>
> **secondary or alternate key**
> A secondary key (or alternate key) is a candidate key that has not been selected as the primary key.
>
> **composite key**
> A composite key is a primary key that consists of two or more fields together.

Linking tables

A relational database can handle more than one table at the same time.

Creating a second table

Suppose your student database contains another table called 'Fees Details' with the following fields: Student ID, Course name, Term 1 fees, Term 2 fees and Term 3 fees. The steps in creating this table would be:

1 Double click on the option *Create table in Design view* from the database window. A new window called a Table window will appear that will allow you to enter the field name, field type, description and field size.

2 Enter your field names and choose appropriate data types that can be chosen from a pull-down menu.

3 Set the field size to the required amount of characters.

4 Repeat steps 1–3 until you finish entering all the field names, data types and field sizes.

5 Once you have completed all the fields, close the window. A dialogue box will appear to ask you whether you want to save the table, Choose *Yes* to save the table structure so that you can enter records into the table.

6 A new dialogue box will appear asking you to give a name for the table. Give it the name 'Fees Details' and choose *OK*.

7 Now another dialogue box will appear asking whether you want Access to set a primary key. Choose *No*.

8 Now you have a table named 'Fees Details' in the database window as in Fig 8.31.

In this table there is no obvious primary key. Each record contains data about the fees paid by one student for one course. If a student takes more than one course, then their student ID appears in more than one record. In the same way, data is repeated – or could be repeated – in each of the other fields. A primary key cannot be repeated in a table, so none of the fields can act as a primary key field.

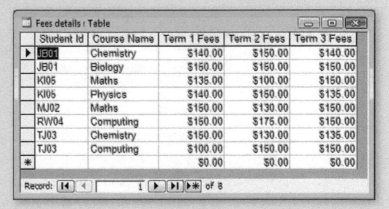

Fig 8.31: Creating a second table

Relationships

A database is known as a relational database when the tables and files are linked together. If you want to make a relational database, your tables and files must have **relationship**. By setting up relationships you will be able to join the tables to share records, thereby preventing the duplication or repetition of data.

When you are about to set up a relationship between two tables, you can follow the following rules:

1 Both tables must have at least one field containing common data. For example, in the tables in Fig 8.32 called 'Personal Details' and 'Fees Details', the Student ID column contains common information. So you will be able to link these tables.

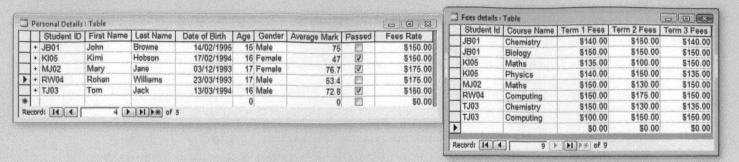

Fig 8.32: Comparing the two tables to find common information

2 The fields containing common information *must* be of the same data type. For example, if the data type of field 'Student ID' in the table 'Personal Details' is text, the data type of 'Student ID' field in the table 'Fees Details' also must be text.

3 At least one of these fields *must* be a primary key.

We set up the relationship between the two fields with common data. One of these will be the primary key in its table. The field that is used in the other table is known as the **foreign key**. We always make the link *from* the primary key *to* the foreign key.

Linking tables

The following steps can be used to link the two tables.

1 Open the Relationship icon from the toolbar or select *Tools* ➜ *Relationships* from the Menu bar to open the Relationship window with the Show Table dialogue box as shown in Fig 8.33.

2 Select the tables you want to link by clicking on them and clicking the *Add* button for each one. Then select *Close* in the Show Table dialogue box. In Fig 8.34, Fees Details and Personal Details have been chosen. This will give you a Relationship window with the following tables selected.

3 Select the primary key and drag it to the foreign key of the second table. (In the example here, the Personal Details table has Student ID as the primary key and the Fees Details table has Student ID as the foreign key.) Make sure you drag the primary key to the foreign key, and not the other way round.

WHAT DOES IT MEAN?

foreign key field

A foreign key field is a field in a table that has been linked with the primary key field of another table.

Fig 8.33: Selecting tables in a relationship

The Edit Relationships dialogue window will appear as in Fig 8.35

4 Select the *Create* button to create the relationship. It would be wise to select the *Enforce Referential Integrity* option too, as it will ensure that records of the related table correspond with each other, and it will not let you create the relationship if they do not correspond. Enforcing referential integrity also would make sure that there is a primary key in one of the tables.

5 Now the relationship is set between the two tables and you can retrieve information from both of them. Choose the *Close* button and select *Yes* to save your changes as shown in Fig 8.36.

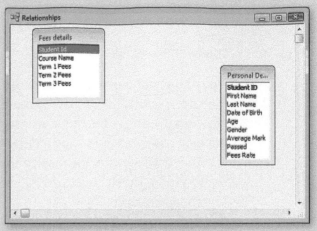

Fig 8.34: The Relationships window

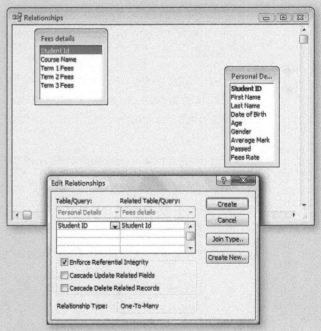

Fig 8.35: The Edit Relationships window

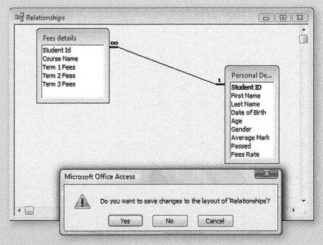

Fig 8.36: Saving changes to relationships

Queries

You know that the main purpose of creating a database is to retrieve the information quickly when you need it. To get the required information, you might have to ask questions to your database and the database will search and display the relevant information. These questions that are asked to the database are called queries.

In Access, queries are special views of data in the tables. The results of the queries are stored separately and can be viewed any time. For example, you can have a query based on the Personal Details table where you want to 'list all the students who passed the exam'. This can be done in Access using query options and is called 'querying the database'.

Queries can be used for selecting fields and displaying them with or without criteria (called select queries), or to get summary information such as sum and average about fields, or to create calculated fields (called action queries).

Creating a new query with criteria using one table

Suppose you want to use the table Personal Details to display the first name, last name and average marks of students who scored more than or equal to 70 marks. You can use the following steps:

1 In the database window choose the *Queries* tab from the object bar.

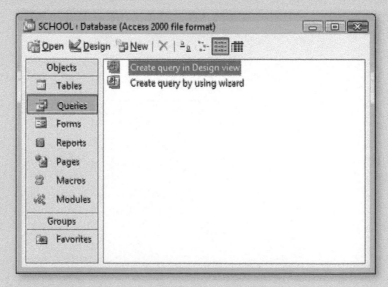

Fig 8.37: The Queries tab in the database window

2 You will be provided with two options *Create query in Design view* or *Create query using wizard* at the right pane of the database window. Select *Create query in Design* *view*, as it is helpful to know how to select the fields yourself. Once you choose this option by double clicking on it, you will get a window like Fig 8.38.

3 The Show Table dialogue box that appears along with the window (as shown in Fig 8.38) lists all the tables and queries that are available in the database. Select the Personal Details table by double clicking on it or choosing the *Add* button.

4 Click on the *Close* button. Now your query window would look like Fig 8.39 with the selected table being displayed in the design grid with many rows such

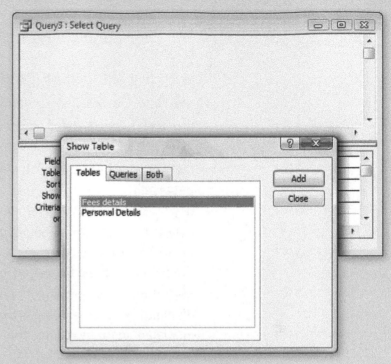

Fig 8.38: Selecting a table for a query

as Field, Table, etc. These rows will show the field names that will be displayed, the tables that are used, the sorted order and the criteria used.

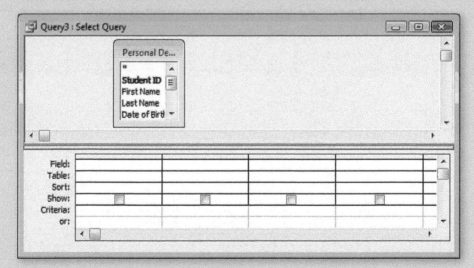

Fig 8.39: The query design grid

5 Select your required fields by using any one of the following methods.

1 Drag the field name from the selected table list and drop it in the field column of the grid.

2 Double click the field name from the selected table list and it will be automatically added to the field column of the grid.

3 Select the field name from the drop-down list displayed in the field column and click it.

Once the required fields are added into the query window,

- the 'Field' row will display all the selected fields.
- the 'Table' row will display the table or tables from which the fields are being selected. In the case of the example, it will display the table name 'Personal Details'.
- the 'Sort' row can be used to display the fields in sorted order (ascending or descending).
- the 'Show field' row will contain a check box. Using this you can either show or hide a particular field when the results of a query are being displayed. By default the check box is in the selected state. To deselect it, click on the check box again and the field will not be displayed in the output.
- the 'Criteria' row can be used to set the conditions for the values of the fields to be displayed when the query is executed. These conditions will filter the record and display only those records that satisfy all the conditions as set in the query. You can leave this row blank if you do not have any criteria.
- The 'Or' row can be used to check for any Or condition, for example, listing all students who passed OR have an average mark of above 60.

6 Select the three fields that you need and set the criteria using the relational operator (>=70), in the criteria row under the field 'average marks'. Your query window will now look like Fig 8.40.

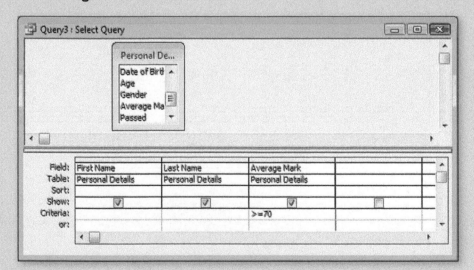

Fig 8.40: A query

7 Choose the run icon ▶ from the toolbar or select *Query* → *Run* from the menu bar to view the results of the query.

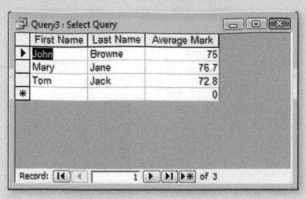

8 If your results are correct, i.e. if you get the first name, last name and average marks of students with average marks more than or equal to 70, select the *Close* button to save the query. If not, modify the criteria to ensure that the correct records are being displayed.

Fig 8.41: Running a query

9 Give the query an appropriate name when the Save dialogue box appears, as shown in Fig 8.42, and choose *Yes*.

10 Your saved query will appear in the right pane of the Queries tab of the object bar as in Fig 8.43. It can be opened and viewed at any time.

Fig 8.42: Naming a query

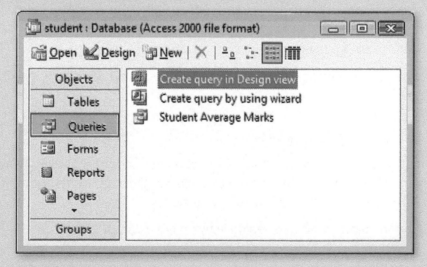

Fig 8.43: A saved query

Creating a new query with criteria using more than one table

Suppose you want to create a query using both the Personal Details and Fees Details tables to display the First Name, Last Name, Term 1 Fees, Term 2 Fees, Term 3 Fees and Average Marks of all *male* students who have average marks between 70 and 75.

For this query, use the same steps that are used for the last example and modify Steps 3 and 6 as follows:

3 Since you want fields from both tables in this query, you need to select both tables (i.e. Personal Details and Fees Details).

6 Now you select the fields that you need to display – First Name, Last Name, Term 1 Fees, Term 2 Fees, Term 3 Fees and Average Marks. Also you need to set the criteria under the Gender as 'male' and Average Mark criteria as 'average marks to more than 70 and less than 75'.

Since you need to set the criteria under the Gender field, you need to include it and do not display it by removing the tick (√) from the show row. Set the criteria >70 and <75 under the Average Marks field with logical and relational operators. Your query window will now look like Fig 8.44.

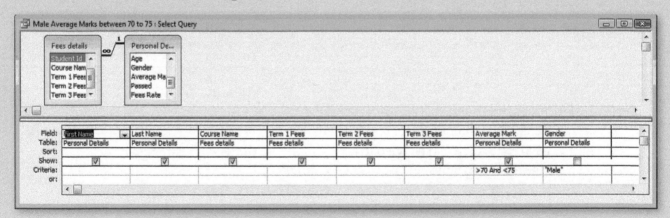

Fig 8.44: A query using two tables

If your results are correct, select the *Close* button to save the query, give it a name, and choose *OK* to save the query.

Creating a query that displays summary information

Queries can also be used to display summary information such as Sum, Average, Minimum, Maximum and Count. Suppose you want to get the average marks of students for Mark1. You would perform the following steps:

1 Select the option *Query in Design view* from the database window.

2 Select the table Fees Details from the Show Table dialogue box. Click on *Add*, then click on *Close*. Select the field for which you require the summary information. In Fig 8.45 we are using the field Term 1 Fees.

3 Choose the totals button Σ from the toolbar or select *View* → *Totals* from the menu bar. A new row called 'Total' with a pull-down menu option will appear after the Table row as in Fig 8.46.

4 Select the *Group By* drop-down menu option and select average (*Avg*), then select the Run icon ▶ from the toolbar to see the results.

5 If your results are correct (i.e. if the average value of Term 1 Fees is correct), select the *Close* button to save the query, give it a name, and choose *OK* to save the query as in Fig 8.47.

Note that you would perform the same steps for calculating Sum, Minimum (Min), Maximum (Max) and Count, but selecting the appropriate function from the drop-down menu in Step 4.

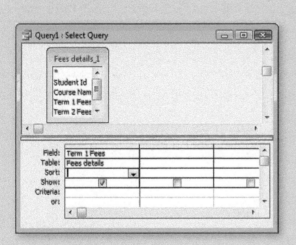

Fig 8.45: Setting up a query on one field

Fig 8.46: Selecting average from the Total menu

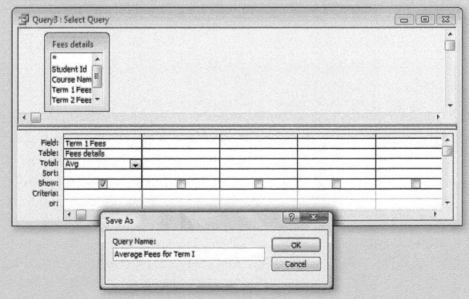

Fig 8.47: Saving the new query

Queries involving calculated fields

Queries can also be used for performing calculations on fields. Suppose you want to give 15% discount on the fee rate, you can create a calculated field called Discount using the Personal Details table. Discount is calculated by multiplying the fee amount by the discount rate, so the formula would be Discount = Fees Rate * 15%. Using this value you can also calculate the new fees rate using the formula New Fees Rate = Fees Rate – Discount.

Creating calculated fields

1 Select the option *Query in Design view* from the database window.

2 Select the table Personal Details from the Show Table dialogue box and choose *Add → Close*. Select the fields required from the Personal Details table (in this case we will include the fields First Name, Last Name and Fees Rate), and in the empty column next to the Fees Rate, type as follows:

Discount: [Fees rate] * .15

(Note: The equal sign (=) has been replaced with a colon (:); the field name 'Fees Rate' is enclosed in square brackets; 15% is converted into its decimal form (.15) as % is considered as a text value.)

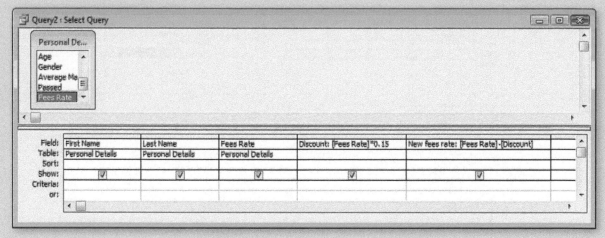

Fig 8.48: Creating a calculated field

Fig 8.49: Viewing the calculated field

3 In the next empty column create the new field 'New Fees Rate' as follows:

New Fees Rate: [Fees Rate] - [Discount]

(Note: Both field names are enclosed in squared brackets. Make sure the fields are typed in exactly as shown, for example 'Fees Rate' should not be typed as 'Feesrate').

4 Run the query by selecting the Run icon ▶ to see the results and save it for viewing or printing later. It will look like Fig 8.49.

Forms

Forms are similar to user interfaces, which allow database users to type data into a database using specially designed templates, rather than straight into a table. Using forms we can format and display data, change or delete data and create visual effects by adding colours, shades, lines and boxes to the fields.

In Access, we can create forms in two ways:

Method 1: Create Form in Design View

Method 2: Create Form by using Wizard

Creating forms using the Form Wizard

Access provides a built-in wizard to design forms and they take you through a step-by-step process towards designing and completing the form. At each stage you have to enter some information to proceed to the next step.

To create a form using the Form Wizard:

1 Select the *Forms* object in the database window and then double click *Create Form by using Wizard*. The Form Wizard window is displayed as shown in Fig 8.50, which will help you to select and include the fields from tables or queries that will appear in the form.

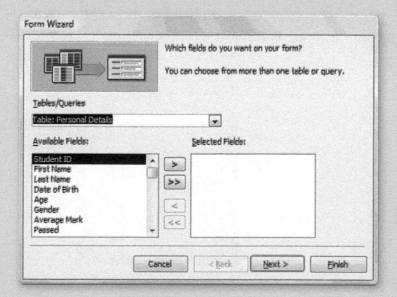

Fig 8.50: The Form Wizard

2 Select the table or queries you want from the drop-down list. The field names present in the table or query will appear in the Available Fields pane. Now click the *Add* button to add the field(s) to the Selected Fields pane. After selecting and including the required fields, select *Next*. The Form Wizard displays the next window as shown in Fig 8.51.

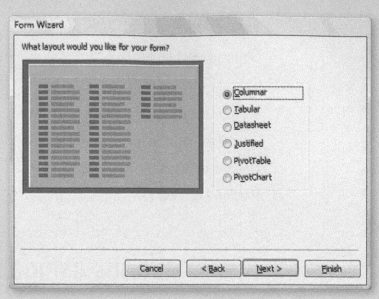

Fig 8.51: Choosing a form layout

3 From this window choose the layout of the form and select one of the layout options. Note that in this example, we will only be looking at the first four options:

- Columnar
- Tabular
- Datasheet
- Justified

We can preview each option by clicking it. After selecting the desired layout, select *Next*. The Form Wizard displays another window as shown in Fig 8.52.

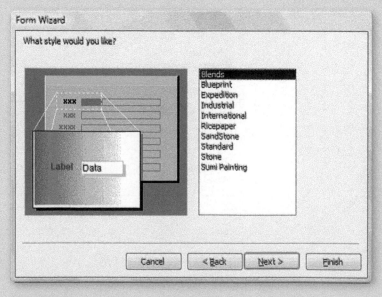

Fig 8.52: Choosing a style for a form

4 Fig 8.52 displays the various styles that can be applied to the form. We can preview each style by clicking at each style name. Select the style suitable to the form and select *Next*. Now the Form Wizard displays another window as shown in Fig 8.53, where you need to give a name to the form and select *Finish*.

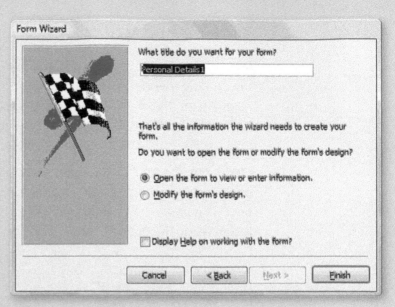

Fig 8.53: Naming a form

5 Your form will be displayed with the first record of the table or query being used for creating the form, as shown in Fig 8.54. You can move to the next record (or one of your choice) by clicking the button ⏭, or to go to the last record by choosing the button ⏮. The ▶* button creates a new record.

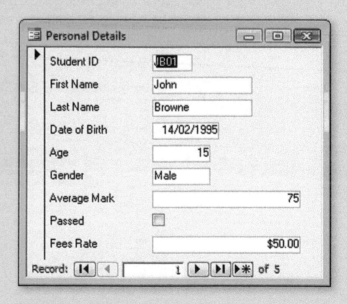

Fig 8.54: The new form

Reports

Reports are used to present the information retrieved from the tables of a database in a presentable manner so that it is useful and appealing to the user. Reports can be created based on queries or tables. You can group, sort and have summary features incorporated in a report. To attract the attention of the users, each report may also contain a variety of design elements like fonts, borders, lines, colours and graphics.

As with queries and forms, reports can be created in Design view or by using a wizard. Since you have queries and tables already created using Design view from which your report is going to be created, you can create your reports using the wizard and modify the design using the option *Create reports in Design view*.

Reports using the Report Wizard

Access provides a built-in wizard to assist in creating reports. We can create a report based on the options and styles provided by the wizard. To create a report using the Report Wizard use the following steps:

Using wizard to create reports

1 In the database window, click on the *Reports* tab from the object bar.

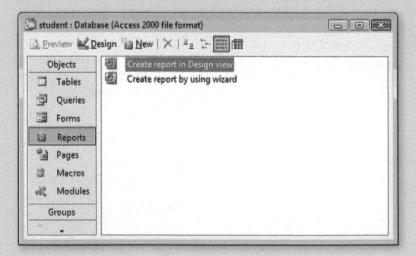

Fig 8.55: The Reports tab

2 Double click on the *Create report by using wizard* option. The Report Wizard window will be displayed as in Fig 8.56.

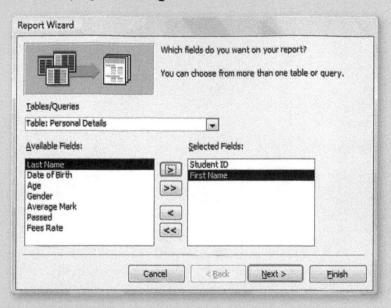

Fig 8.56: The Report Wizard

3 In this window you need to choose the fields from the tables or queries from the drop-down list. This process is similar to what you have done in selecting fields for a form. After selecting and including the required fields, select *Next*.

4 A new window will appear that allows you to group the records by specified fields. Grouping will group together the records with the same value for a field. Using the button ▷ select your field(s) on which you want the grouping to be. For example, in Fig 8.57 the records are grouped on Gender.

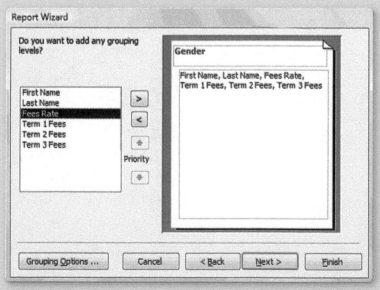

Fig 8.57: Grouping the records in a report

5 Select *Next* to get the new window as in Fig 8.58.

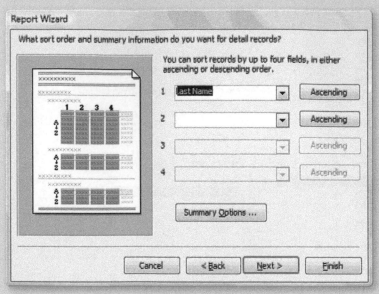

Fig 8.58: Sorting the records in a report

As shown in Fig 8.58, you can sort records by up to four fields, in either ascending or descending order. If you have included grouping and the report contains fields with numeric values, a *Summary Options* button will be present (as shown) for you to include some summary features such as sum, average and count. If you want to include summary features, just click on the *Summary Options* button and a new window will appear for you to select your choice of summary features, as shown in Fig 8.59.

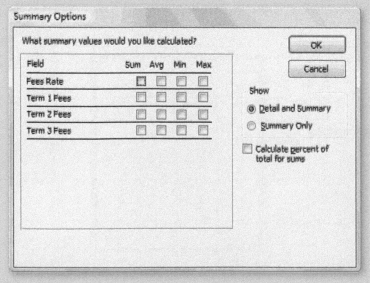

Fig 8.59: Summary options

Choose *OK* when you are finished making your selection, and select *Next* to move to the next window.

6 The new window that appears allows you to choose the layout and paper orientation as shown in Fig 8.60.

As you can see there are six layouts – stepped, block, outline1, outline2, align left1, and align left2. Clicking any of the layout options displays a preview of the report in that particular format. The orientation can be in portrait or landscape. Choose your layout and orientation and select *Next* to go to the next window.

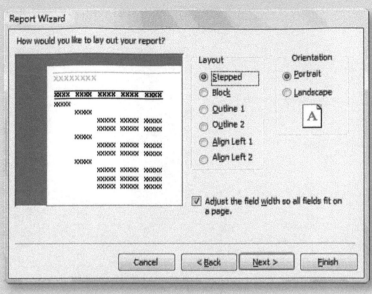

Fig 8.60: Choosing the layout for a report

7 The next window, Fig 8.61, allows you to choose a style for the report.

You can select the style you would like for the report from the following choices: Bold, Causal, Compact, Corporate, Formal or Soft Grey. Clicking on a style displays it in a preview. Select the preferred style and click *Next*.

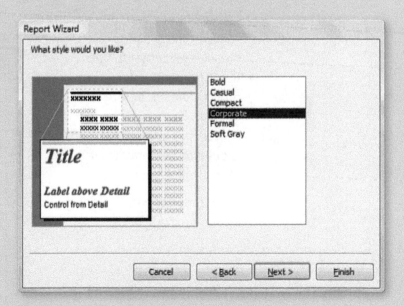

Fig 8.61: Choosing the style for a report

8 Fig 8.62 is the last window of the report wizard and it allows you to give a title for the report, which you type in the box provided.

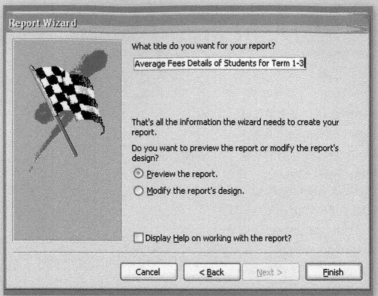

Fig 8.62: Choosing the title

This window also provides the choice of whether to preview the report or to modify the report's design before saving it as final. By default the first choice, previewing the report, is selected. To preview the report, click *Finish*.

The created report is displayed as shown in Fig 8.63.

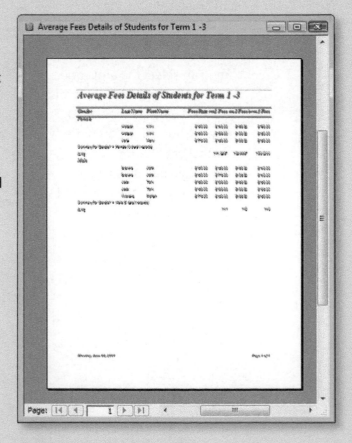

Fig 8.63 The finished report

How to modify your report using the Design view

Sometimes you have to modify the report design. For example, you may want the title to appear on two separate lines, or to add a picture or a header or footer. You would then have to open the report you have already created in Design view so that modifications can be made. To do this, you would use the following steps:

Modifying your report

1 Select the report you want to open by single clicking on it.

2 Right click on the report selected and choose the *Design view* option or choose the ▦ button from the database window.

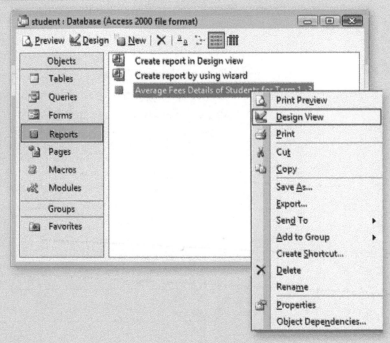

3 The report will be displayed in Design view as in Fig 8.65. Here you can make any required modifications.

Fig 8.64: Selecting a report in Design view

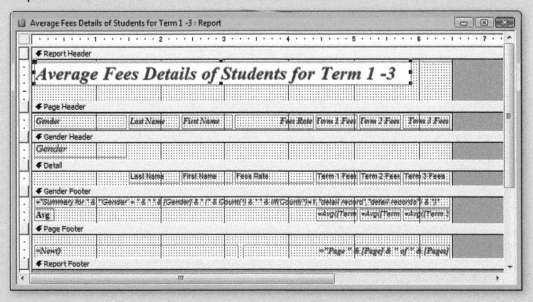

Fig 8.65: Design view for a report

4 Suppose you want to have a subtitle after the first title. Click on the tool box button  from the toolbar. Now a new toolbar will appear as shown in Fig 8.66.

Label option

Fig 8.66: The Report toolbar

Choose the Label option from the new toolbar and draw a box to type in the new title. You can also go to the end of the first title and press the *Shift* and *Enter* keys together to get a new line to create a second title.

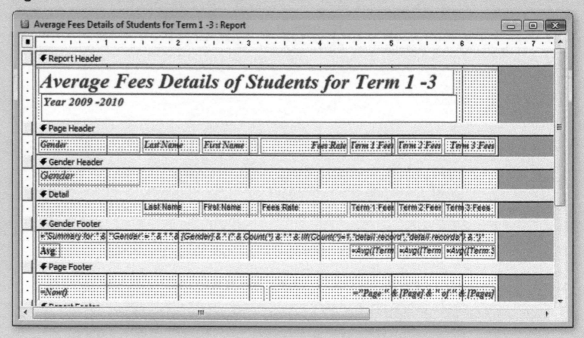

Fig 8.67: Creating a label

End-of-section questions

Multiple-choice questions

1   A collection of related fields in a database is known as:
    A Record   B Database
    C Table   D Entity

2   A unique identifier of a record is called:
    A A foreign key   B A candidate key
    C A primary key   D An alternate key

3   All of the following are data types present in MS Access except:
    A Number   B Text
    C Character   D Yes/No

4   A column of data in a table is known as a:
    A Tuple   B Field
    C Key   D Row

5   A field that can be used as a primary key is called:
    A A composite key   B A candidate key
    C A secondary key   D An alternate key

Structured questions

1   Give appropriate database terms for the following:
    a The details about a particular entity
    b linking of tables or files to share records
    c type of data that a field can store
    d amount of information that a field can store
    e a plan that shows the names, data types and the field sizes of fields in a table.

2   State the difference between:
    a A primary key and a foreign key
    b A secondary key and a composite key
    c A candidate key and an alternate key

3 The following questions are based on the table given below:

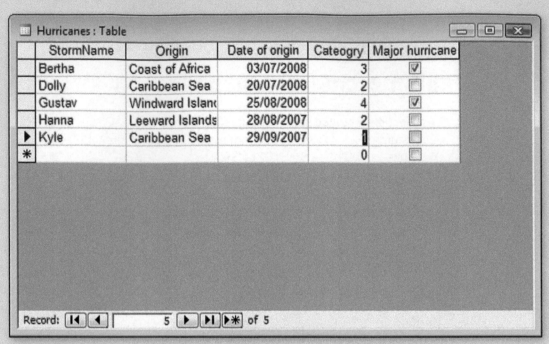

a How many fields are there in the table above?
b How many records are there in the table above?
c You want to list the StormName, origin and date of origin of all the storms that grown up to category 2 only. Prepare a query using the following query design template.
d What would be the output of this query? (you can use a table to show the results)

Field				
Table				
Sort				
Show				
Criteria				
Or				

e International Aid Fund committee has decided to provide aid to all islands who got hit by these hurricanes. They have decided to give aid at the rate of US$100 000 based on the category of hurricane. Create a query design with a calculated field called Aid which will calculate the aid by using the formula: Category × 100 000. List the StormName, category and Aid fields. Use the following for the query design table.

Field				
Table				
Sort				
Show				
Criteria				
Or				

f Show the results of the query using a table.

4 Victory College decided to store the personal details of students in a database table named STUDENT. Create a table structure for the table that can store the following details of the students: ID, First Name, Last Name, Gender, Age, Date of Birth, Passed (yes/no), and Fees Rate. The structure should show the field name, data type and field size.

5 Name the database features that allow you to do the following:
 a Display records from a table that meet a particular criterion.
 b Present the information retrieved from tables of a database in a presentable manner.
 c Type data into a database using specially designed templates, rather than straight into a table.

Practice SBA

Club member details for the Caribbean Sports Club (CSC) and the club fund raising activities over the years have to be stored for reference and retrieval. There are FOUR levels of club membership. They are **Regular**, **Special**, **Gold** and **Platinum**. The corresponding category codes are: **R, S, G** and **P**, respectively. The dues payable by each member will be dependent on his or her category of membership.

Use the following tables, names and descriptions to assist you in populating the tables.

Table: Personal Details

This table stores the personal details of the club members.

The fields needed are:

Title, First name, Last name, Category code, Address, Phone number, Date of birth, Gender, Date of joining the club, ID (created by using the initials of the member's name and two digits, e.g. James Kennedy would be JK00)

Table: Activity details

Each club member is attached to the four activities that the club hosts. For the last few years the activities were Christmas Concert (CC), Bake Sale(BS), Tennis Tournament (TT) and May Fair (MF). For the club activities, each member is responsible for selling tickets and collecting monies from selling these tickets.

The fields needed are:

ID, Tickets sold for CC, Tickets sold for BS, Tickets sold for TT, Tickets sold for MF and Total number of tickets sold.

Table: Rate

This table stores the four categories, their codes and the rates per month for each category.

The fields needed are:

Category code, Category name and Monthly rate (R – $50, S –$100, G –$150, P – $200) for each of the four categories.

You are required to:

Task A

Set up a database with tables/files as specified above with appropriate field names, data types and field sizes, containing information for the twenty-five club members with at least five members in EACH category.

Perform the following queries:

1 List ID, Title, First name, Last name, Category name and Monthly rate of all Gold OR Platinum members. Save the query as 'Category'.

2 List ID, Title, First name, Last name, Address and Date of joining of ALL Gold members who joined in 2003 or 2004. Save the list as 'Life'.

3 List ID, Title, First name, Last name, Address and Phone number of all members who sold more than 200 tickets. Sort the members in descending order of their last name. Save the query as 'Tickets'.

4 The ticket for each club activity costs $20. Create a calculated field called 'Total monies collected' to store the total monies collected by each member. List the ID, Title, First name, Last name and Total monies collected fields. Save the query as 'Money'.

5 Using query summary features calculate:
   a The maximum number of tickets sold. Save it as 'Maxqry'.
   b The total amount collected from selling tickets. Save it as 'Totqry'.

6 Prepare a report containing the members grouped by Category and sorted by Last name in ascending order. The fields to be displayed are Title, First name, Last name, Date of joining, Category name and Phone number. It should have the following title.

Caribbean Sports Club

List of Members 2005–2009

7 Produce another report that displays ID, Title, First name, Last name, Category name, Total tickets sold and Total monies collected. The report should be grouped by Category and should display the overall total tickets sold, the total monies collected for each category and a grand total. The report should have the following title.

Caribbean Sports Club

Activity Details

9 ⟩ Guidelines for the School-Based Assessment

Objectives

By the end of this section, you will be able to:

- Understand the kinds of tasks required in a School-Based Assessment project.
- Understand how your project will be marked.
- Know how to present your School-Based Assessment project.

The School-Based Assessment is a practical project that accounts for 30% of the marks in the CXC CSEC Information Technology examination.

In this section you will find:

- Guidelines for students
- Guidelines for teachers
- A sample assignment

The School-Based Assessment project assignment

Your teacher will set you a project assignment that you will carry out at school. The assignment will describe a set of real-world problems that require IT-based solutions.

The assignment will be split into five tasks. These will test your skills in:

- Word processing (see Section 6A)
- Spreadsheets (see Section 7)
- Database management (see Section 8)
- Problem-solving (see Section 2)
- Program implementation (see Section 3)

Your teacher may choose to set each task as you complete the section that relates to it. Alternatively, you may be given time later on in your course to complete all five tasks together. In either case, your teacher will encourage you to plan your work using a project management chart.

When you are working on the School-Based Assessment assignment, your teacher can only offer you limited help. The examination syllabus states:

'The role of the teacher is to guide the candidate through the SBA by helping to clarify the problem or by discussing possible approaches to solving the problem. Teachers, while giving guidance, should guard against providing a complete solution to the problem for the candidate or prescribing a specifi c format that should be followed.'

Sample tasks

This book contains some sample tasks to give you some practice.

End-of-section SBA practice questions

At the end of Sections 2, 3, 6A, 7 and 8 you will find a sample task modelled on the School-Based Assessment. You can use these for practice.

Warning to students and teachers: the sample tasks given in Sections 2, 3, 6A, 7 and 8 should not be included in an assignment that is set for the School-Based Assessment. The examiners are aware that solutions have been provided for these tasks, so any attempt to use them would count as cheating.

Sample assignment

In this section you will find a complete sample assignment. You can read this to see how all the tasks in an assignment fit together.

No solutions are given for the sample assignment. Your teacher may set it for you as practice, or may choose to base your School-Based Assessment assignment on this one.

SBA Guidelines for Students

- Make sure that you clear all your doubts on the SBA with your teacher before you attempt it.
- Perform **all** sections of the SBA given to you by your teacher.
- The printed sheets of SBA must be stapled or bound together, because a loose leaf format is not acceptable by CXC. If folders are used, please ensure that the papers are stapled together and placed inside the folder.
- Make sure that you print all the files that you are being asked to print and make sure that they are in the order. Use of separator sheets to indicate the different parts of each section such as queries, tables etc would be a good idea.
- Try to meet the deadlines for drafts set by the teacher and make sure to correct the mistakes if any are pointed out by your teacher before you submit the final SBA.
- Remember that SBA carries 30% of the final exam grade. So having a good percentage in SBA means that you can score a high grade in the exam.
- There must be a cover page present for **each** of the four sections of the SBA with the following details:
  - Your name
  - CXC registration number
  - School code/name
  - Your teacher's name
  - Territory
  - Section of the SBA – e.g. Word processing

For **each** of the four sections of the SBA you must have the following:

Word processing

Cover page

Table of contents

The printout of documents of various tasks done.

For mail merging, make sure you print the primary document, data source and merged document. (If there are many merged documents, you can ask the teacher if you can print just the first, middle and last documents.)

Spreadsheets

Cover page

Table of contents

The spreadsheet printouts showing the various tasks completed.

If there are changes, make sure to print the spreadsheet before and after the change.

For graphs/charts you must have an appropriate title. For bar or column graphs make sure that you have axis labels and legends. For pie charts you must make sure that you have percentages and legends.

Formula sheets showing all functions and formulas used.

Database

Cover page

Table of contents

The printed sheets showing the skills being tested – tables, queries and reports.

For tables, you must print the table structure with correct field names, field types and field sizes.

For queries, list only the fields needed and the fields listed must be in the order given.

In reports, all field names must be visible – use the correct layout so that it is well presented.

Problem-solving and programming

Cover page with candidate details

Table of contents

Problem definition and algorithm

Implemented program (program listing)

Tests on program (trace tables)

SBA Guidelines for Teachers

Conducting the SBA

- Guide the students through all the sections of the SBA.
- You can let the students start the SBA at any time of the course of study once you have completed all the relevant topics.
- The SBA must NOT be treated as exams/tests. Students should be given opportunities to make draft copies of the SBA so that corrections can be made in order to improve their grade. Setting earlier deadlines would give you and the students more time to make corrections.
- Inform the students what skills will be tested in each section of the SBA before the start of the SBA.

Submission of samples for moderation

- Submit only printed copies of the SBA for moderation.
- After the selection of five sets of samples, make sure that they have the following in the CXC envelope:
  a. Five samples for **each** of the FOUR sections of the SBA required by the CXC's Registration program.
  b. The SBA question.
- Moderation sheets – Make sure that the marks awarded for SBA samples are the same as the marks present in the moderation sheet. If you don't have access to a moderation sheet you can download it from the CXC website www.cxc.org.
- SBA sample sheet from Registration program – ensure that the samples submitted are the ones that are present in the sample sheet.
- Make sure that **each** sample is bound or stapled together by the students. Encourage students to have separator sheets in each section of the SBA to group different parts – tables together, queries together, reports together, etc in database, for example.
- Each sample must have a mark scheme showing the allocation of marks for the skills tested for **each** section of the SBA. Make sure the there is student's work to substantiate the marks awarded.
- Ensure that you stick to the mark scheme provided CXC in pages 24–29 of the syllabus and choose appropriate skills on which you would like to test the students and allocate marks for those skills. Do not award fractions of marks.
- It would be good to set the deadlines for each section of the SBA rather than setting a deadline for the whole SBA. Encourage students to meet the deadlines set. Even though the CXC's official deadline for submission of SBA is April 30 of the year of examination, the local registrars of CXC would rather have an earlier deadline. So finish your SBA before the deadline set by the local registrar.

Sample school-based assessment

Description of the project

The Caribbean Fashion Store (CFS) is a prominent clothes store in the district of Sands in the island of Sheeba. The store has been using the manual method of operations in all areas of their business. This year the company's management team has decided to computerise its operations for the efficient running of the business. The computer system they purchased came with general purpose software that has word processor, spreadsheet and database management components.

As a test, the owner of the store would like to use the software to carry out the following tasks for the month of October:

1 Generation of a club brochure that informs the public about the clothes store and details of the Christmas Sale.

2 Analysis of the salary details of the employees for the month.

3 Storage of personal information of employees and their sales details.

4 Preparation of letters for the outstanding employees who achieved their sales target to inform them about their commission amounts.

You are in charge of setting up the word processing, spreadsheet and database templates that will permit all employees of the store to efficiently carry out these activities.

Your assumptions or modifications have to be stated clearly along with your printouts. You can attempt the sections in any order.

SECTION A – SPREADSHEETS

The spreadsheet package will be used to create a model that will allow the owner of the store to manipulate and monitor the monthly salary details of the employees.

Currently, there are 25 employees in the club. There are FOUR categories of employees and EACH category attracts a different basic monthly salary. There are six Supervisors, 17 Sales people, one Manager and one Assistant Manager at the store. The categories of membership with current rates are given in the table below. This table should be on a separate worksheet.

Category	Code	Basic Monthly Salary
Manager	M	$8000
Assistant Manager	AM	$7000
Supervisor	S	$5000
Sales Staff	SS	$3000

There are allowances and deductions in the employees' salaries. The allowances are Daily Allowance, Travel Allowance and Entertainment Allowance and the deductions are Social Security, Levy and Insurance. These are calculated based on their basic salary. The Travel Allowance and Entertainment Allowance are available to the Manager and the Assistant Manager ONLY. The rate of payments of these allowances and deductions also need to be kept on the worksheet with the basic salary rate.

Allowance	Code	Rate (%)
Daily Allowance	DA	11%
Travel Allowance	TA	6%
Entertainment Allowance	EA	3.5%
Sales Staff	SS	$3000

Deductions	Code	Rate (%)
Social Security	SS	6%
Environmental Levy	EL	1%
Insurance	INS	2%

You are required to:

Create one or more worksheets that will enable the owner of the store to easily analyse, modify and monitor the salary details of his staff. The following is a sample section of the worksheet. If you have already attempted the database task you can copy the information from the database to form the worksheets.

First Name	Last Name	Category Code	Basic Salary	Allowances			Deductions			Total Allowances	Total Deductions
				DA	TA	EA	SS	EL	Ins		
John	Browne	SS	$3000	$330	0	0	$180	$30	$60	$330	$270

Task A

1. Create the information for the 25 employees' salary details for the month of October 2009. They should be sorted by last name then by first name. The allowances and deductions must be calculated using cell references only as there may be changes in their rates.

2. Add extra columns to include the Gross income and Net income. Gross income is calculated by the following formula: Basic Salary + Allowances

   Net income is calculated by the following formula: Gross Income – Deductions.

3. Include a row to calculate the totals of each of the numeric columns.

4. Save your worksheet as Task A.

Task B

1. John Browne got a new job and he resigned from his post at CFS. Remove him from the spreadsheet. Save the spreadsheet as TaskB1.

2. The management team decided to change the Daily Allowance (DA) rate to12.5%. Adjust this rate. Save the spreadsheet as TaskB2.

3. Sort the worksheet of TaskB2 by employee category first and then by last names. Save as TaskB3.

4. Create a complex criterion to select all information on all employees whose last name begins with 'B' and are in the Sales Staff or Assistant Manager category. Save the spreadsheet as TaskB4.

5. Create a pie chart to compare the total allowances (DA, TA and EA) and total deductions (SS, EL and INS) paid by the store for the month of October 2009.

6. Print all formulae or functions used.

SECTION B – DATABASE MANAGEMENT

The database management component of the software that CFS purchased will be used to store personal details of the employees, their sales details (used to determine their promotions, commissions and further employment) and their basic salary rates.

Currently, there are 25 employees in the club. There are FOUR categories of employees and EACH category attracts a different basic monthly salary. There are six Supervisors, 17 Sales people, one Manager and one Assistant Manager at the store. The categories of membership with current rates are given in the table below. This table must be stored in a separate table called Basic Salary Rates.

Category	Code	Basic Monthly Salary
Manager	M	$8000
Assistant Manager	AM	$7000
Supervisor	S	$5000
Sales Staff	SS	$3000

The Personal Details table stores the Employee ID (ID), First Name (Fname), Last Name (Lname), Gender, Date joined, Category code, Address and Contact number. Employee ID is created by using the employee's initials and three decimal digits, e.g. the employee John Browne would have the Employee ID JB100.

The Sales Details table stores the details of individual Sales Staff ONLY. It should contain Employee ID, Week1sales($), Week2sales($), Week3sales($), Week4sales($) and TotalSales($).

You are required to:

1 Set up a database with THREE tables with appropriate field names, data types and field sizes, containing information on the employees' details. If you have already attempted the spreadsheet task, you can copy some of the information from the spreadsheet to form the database tables.

2 Test your database by performing the following queries:

a List ID, Fname, Lname, Address and Date joined of ALL Sales Staff who joined the store after 2005. Save it as 2005qry.

b List ID, Fname, Lname, Address and Contact number of all Sales Staff who created more than $15000 in the total sales($). Sort the members in descending order of their last name. Save the query as Salesqry.

c The store has decided to give a commission to all sales staff at a rate of 3% of their total sales. Create a calculated field called Commission. List Fname, Lname, Basic salary and Commission fields. Save the query as Commqry.

   d Using query summary features calculate:

      i The largest (maximum) TotalSales($) amount achieved by an employee. Save it as Maxqry.

      ii The total commission earned by all the Sales Staff. Save it as Totqry.

      ii The number of employees who are not entitled to commission. Save it as Countqry.

   e Prepare a report containing the employees grouped by category and sorted by Lname in ascending order. The fields to be displayed are ID, Fname, Lname, Gender, Date joined, Category, Contact number and Basic salary. It should have the following title:

   Caribbean Fashion Store
   Staff List 2009

   e Produce another report that displays ID, Fname, Lname, Gender, Basic salary and Commission of all the Sales Staff. The report should be grouped by gender and should display the commission earned by each employee and the grand total of commission paid out by the company. The report should have the following title in ALL pages:

   Caribbean Fashion Store
   Commission Details of Sales Staff

SECTION C – WORD PROCESSING

The owner of Caribbean Fashion Stores plans to launch a brochure to notify the customers about the variety of clothes that are sold at the store and also about the Christmas Sale.

The President of the club also would like to get a report of the salary and sales details of the activities of the store for the month of October 2009.

You are required to:

1 Create a brochure to inform the public about the variety of clothes available at the store and also about the Christmas Sale. The text in the brochure must be fully justified with 1.5 line spacing. Use columns to create a leaflet that can be folded. Use appropriate margins and layouts so that folding of the brochure can be easily done. Be creative!!

2 Prepare a letterhead with the name, address and logo of the store. The logo can be a suitable graphic. Using mail merge facilities, prepare a letter on the letterhead for the staff members who will be provided with a commission to commend the staff about their hard work and dedication.

3 Prepare a brief report addressed to Mr. Dave Phillip, Caribbean Fashion Store, Mayor Street, Sands, Sheeba, including the following elements:

   a A list of members who will be given a commission.

   b A graph showing the total allowances and deductions.

4 Ensure that the documents have been formatted properly and spell checked.

SECTION D – PROBLEM-SOLVING AND PROGRAM DESIGN

Problem-solving

You are required to:

1 Develop an algorithm in narrative and pseudocode or flowchart that will accept the names of all sales staff members and their total sales for the month. The algorithm must calculate the commission at 3% of their total sales amount. It should also display the name, total sales and commission of the member with the highest commission and the number of persons without commission.

2 Design and execute a trace table with the column headings 'Name', 'Total sales' and 'Commission'. Using the trace table, display the highest commission and the number of persons without commission.

Program implementation

You are required to:

1. Write a program to implement the algorithm in Task 1 of Problem-solving, using the programming language Pascal.

MARK SCHEME – SPREADSHEETS

No.	Criteria	Marks
1	**Use of predefined formulae/functions**	
	a awareness of existence of appropriate formulae or function	1
	b use of appropriate formulae/function to solve numeric problems	2
	c replicate formulae/functions	2
	d use of range names, relative and absolute addressing	2
2	**Manipulate spreadsheet**	
	a copy data	
	b move data	
	c formatting to increase clarity	2
	d insert page breaks appropriately	
	e delete/insert rows such that formulae remain unaffected	

3	Sorting	
	a correct sorting using primary and secondary fields	1
4	Graphs	
	a creating appropriate charts with relevant data	3
	b correct axis labels/percentages and legends	1
	c correct graph titles	1
5	Effective spreadsheet design	
	a solution easy to follow	1
	b appropriate column and row labels	1
	c design allows easy additions and deletions	1
	d use constants in cells, instead of placing values directly in formula	1
	e extracting data to allow summary information	1
	Total Marks	**20**

MARK SCHEME – DATABASE MANAGEMENT

No.	Criteria	Marks
1	**Efficient use of formatting features**	
	Formatting for presentation	
	a justification, line spacing, paragraph style	
	b set margins, page orientation, paper size, text orientation	4
	Formatting for emphasis	
	a bold, italics, borders/shading, font/font size	2
	Other features	
	a use of spell checker, find and replace	1
	b headers/footers/footnotes	1
	c tables with correct number of rows/columns	2
2	**Flyers or brochures**	
	a appropriate use of columns and their features	2
	b use of graphics	1
	c information presented in a logical manner	1
	d block operations (cut/copy/paste)	1
3	Mail merge	
	a create primary document with correct field names in correct places	2
	b create secondary document	1
	c correct merge	2
	Total Marks	**20**

MARK SCHEME – WORD PROCESSING

No.	Criteria	Marks
1	**Algorithm development**	
	a clearly defined problem statement	1
	b start and end of the solution	1
	c identification of all variables	1
	d initialisation of relevant variables	1
	e request for data from user	1
	f storing data	2
	g correct use of appropriate control structures	2
	h outputs	1
	Total Marks	**10**
2	**Trace Table**	
	Construct trace tables with:	
	a all variables present and correctly used	1
	b appropriate test data	1
	c data set for all areas	2
	d change in values correctly demonstrated	1
	Total Marks	**5**
3	**Program working to specification using Pascal**	
	a program compiles without errors	1
	b output correct for all values in data set	2
	c correct data types for all variables	2
	d appropriate initialisation of variables	1
	e appropriate use of sequence construct	1
	f appropriate use of selection construct	2
	g appropriate use of iteration construct	2
	h use of meaningful variable names	1
	i readability (indentation and comments)	1
	j user friendliness	1
	Total Marks	**15**
	Overall Total Marks	**30**

Guidelines for Private Candidates

As a private candidate you can register for January exams or May/June exams.

- If you are registering for January exams, you are allowed to do a Paper 3, which is an alternative to SBA along with the other two papers. So students who wish not to do the SBA should opt for this.
- It is strongly recommended that you practice the SBA even if you are opting to write the alternative to SBA paper as all the questions tested will be based around the skills that are tested in a typical SBA.
- For January exams, you can opt to self-study or study with guidance from a teacher.
- For May/June exams, there is no alternative paper so you should be under the guidance of a teacher who will mark your SBA and submit it to CXC for moderation similar to regular school students.
- The alternative paper consists of four sections testing skills in Wordprocessing, Spreadsheets, Database Management, and Program Design/Program Implementation.

Index

Hachette UK's policy is to use papers that are natural, renewable and recyclable products and made from wood grown in well-managed forests and other controlled sources. The logging and manufacturing processes are expected to conform to the environmental regulations of the country of origin.

Orders: please contact Hachette UK Distribution, Hely Hutchinson Centre, Milton Road, Didcot, Oxfordshire, OX11 7HH. Telephone: +44 (0)1235 827827. Email education@hachette.co.uk. Lines are open from 9 a.m. to 5 p.m., Monday to Friday. You can also order through our website: www.hoddereducation.com

Text © Hodder & Stoughton Limited 2009
First published 2009 by Pearson Education Limited.
Published from 2015 by Hodder Education,
An Hachette UK Company, Carmelite House,
50 Victoria Embankment, London EC4Y 0DZ.
www.hoddereducation.com

2024
IMP 10
ISBN 978 1 4082 2932 3

Designed and typeset by Clare Webber
Original illustrations © Hodder & Stoughton Limited 2009
Indexed by Indexing Specialist (UK) Ltd
Illustrated by Simon Clare and Tech Type
Picture Research by Kevin Brown
Printed in India by Replika Press Pvt. Ltd.

Acknowledgements

The publisher would like to thank the following for their kind permission to reproduce their photographs:

(Key: b-bottom; c-centre; l-left; r-right; t-top]

Alamy Images: Adam van Bunnens 18tl; adiseshan shankar 217b; Antonia Iva 166tr; Blend Images 70br, 167c; Bruno SINNAH 2; Compix 27b; D. Hurst 23b, 227cr; DIOMEDIA 31t; Henry George Beeker 18tr; imagebroker 218tr; Jeff Morgan technology 33bl, 37tl; MBI 420b; Mikael Karlsson 213tr; Mouse in the House 3b; Oleksiy Maksymenko 22cr, 160bl; Red Cover 25b; STOCK FOLIO 13tr; Ted Foxx 23t; vario images GmbH & Co. KG 224b; **Art Directors and TRIP photo Library:** 31b; Helene Rogers 13b, 14b, 17bl, 17cr, 17tl, 24br, 44b; **DK Images:** 371r; Tom Ridley 11bl; **Fotolia:** 30br; **Getty Images:** Dennis O'Clair 220r; **Ronald Grant Archive:** Disney Enterprises Inc & Walden Media 213br; **Inclusive Technology Ltd:** Image courtesy of **Inclusive Technology** 44c; Intel: 5b, 26cr; **iStockphoto:** 161, 16r,17tr, 18bl, 19t, 20br, 20tl, 30cr, 213cr, 244br; Mary Read: 294c, 297b; **Microsoft Corporation:** 32br, 33tl, 35tr; **Pearson Education Ltd:** Photodisc 24tl; **Photolibrary.com: Corbis** 44t, 370br; **Image Source** 191b; **POD-Pearson Online Database:** Pearson Education/Trevor Clifford 61; Photodisc/Kim Steele 229r; PunchStock: Tetra Images 19b; **Rex Features:** Geoff Robinson 45tr; ISOPRESS 30tr; WestEnd61 14t; Science Photo Library Ltd: Andrew Brookes, National Physical Laboratory 185br; Gerry Mason 193b; Peter Aprahamian 25t; Philippe Psaila 208tr

Cover Images: Front: Corbis: Hill Street Studios/Blend Images/Corbis br; iStockphoto: (background); Jupiterimages: Mike Kemp/ Rubberball tr; **POD - Pearson Online Database:** Digital Stock tr (background); Digital Vision/Rob van Petten bl; Photodisc bl (background), br (background)

All other images © Hodder & Stoughton Limited

Every effort has been made to trace the copyright holders and we apologise in advance for any unintentional omissions. We would be pleased to insert the appropriate acknowledgement in any subsequent edition of this publication.